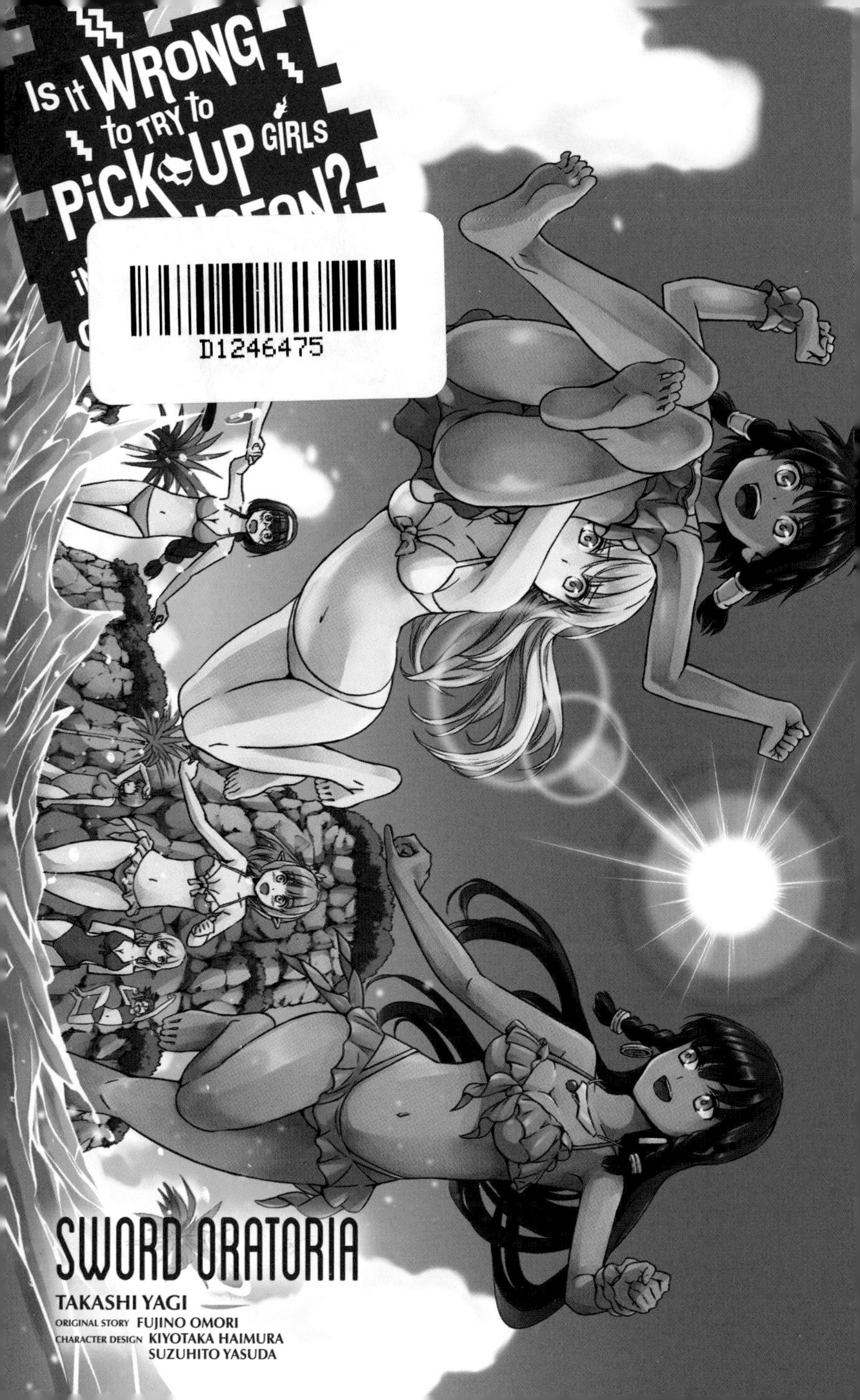

Is it WRONG to TRY to PiCK UP GIRLS

SWORD ORATORIA

TAKASHI YAGI
ORIGINAL STORY FUJINO OMORI
CHARACTER DESIGN KIYOTAKA HAIMURA
SUZUHITO YASUDA

CONTENTS

quest 46.
The Two Lost Children 003

quest 47.
Cooperation 043

quest 48.
Signs 081

quest 49.
Travel Trouble 117

quest 50.
Inquiry 155

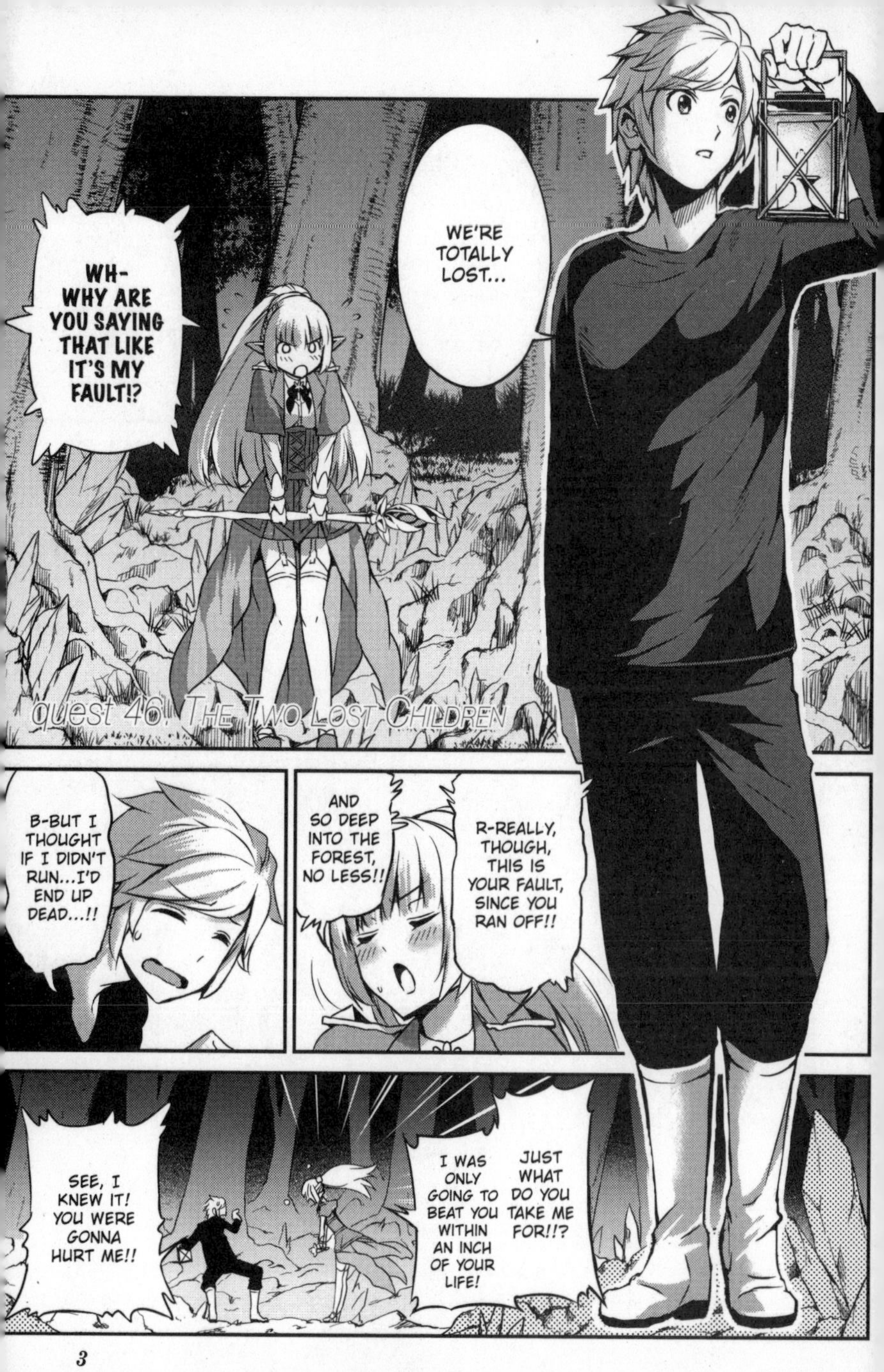
WE'RE TOTALLY LOST...
WH- WHY ARE YOU SAYING THAT LIKE IT'S MY FAULT!?
quest 46. The Two Lost Children
R-REALLY, THOUGH, THIS IS YOUR FAULT, SINCE YOU RAN OFF!!
AND SO DEEP INTO THE FOREST, NO LESS!!
B-BUT I THOUGHT IF I DIDN'T RUN...I'D END UP DEAD...!!
JUST WHAT DO YOU TAKE ME FOR!!?
I WAS ONLY GOING TO BEAT YOU WITHIN AN INCH OF YOUR LIFE!
SEE, I KNEW IT! YOU WERE GONNA HURT ME!!

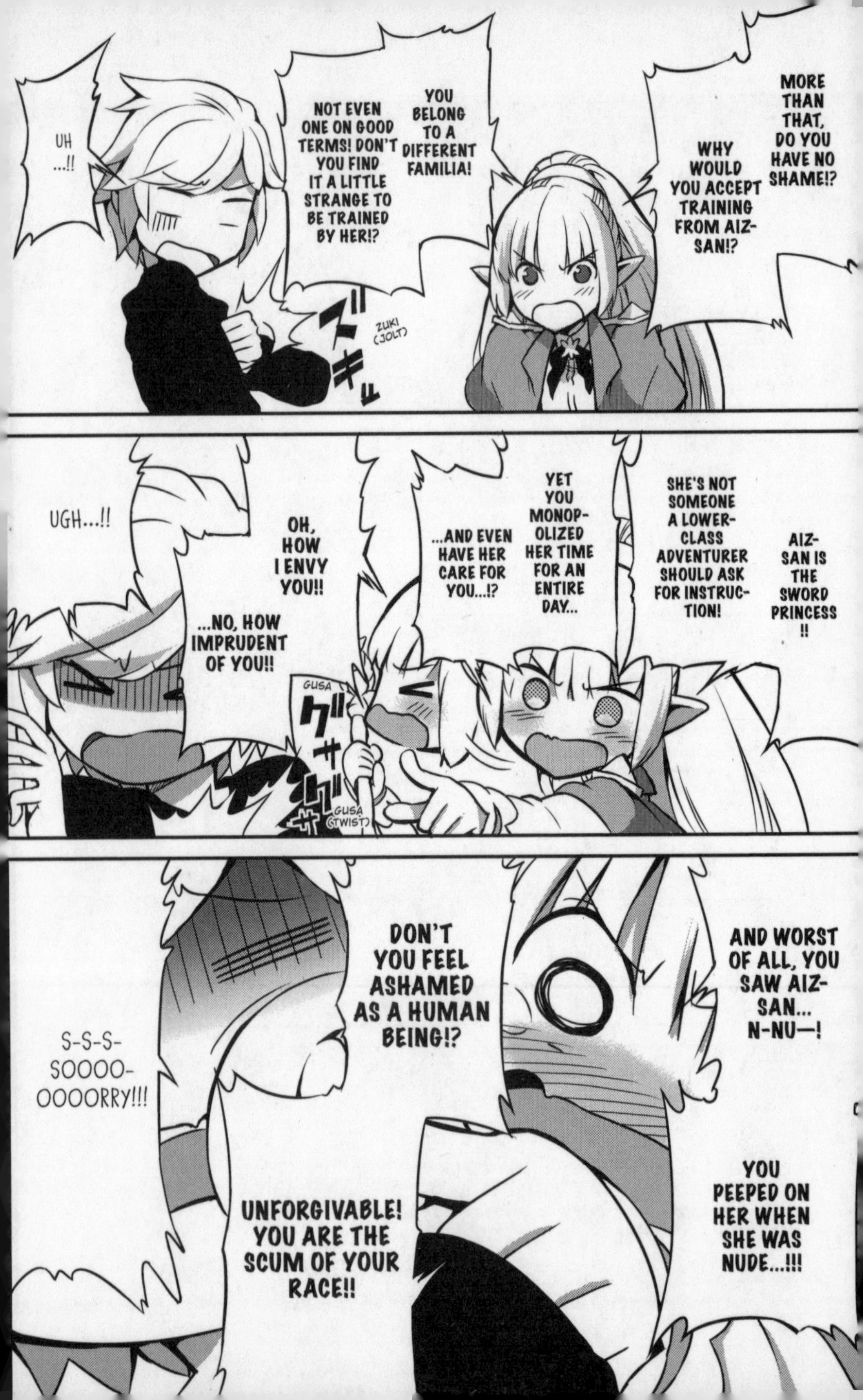
MORE THAN THAT, DO YOU HAVE NO SHAME!?
WHY WOULD YOU ACCEPT TRAINING FROM AIZ-SAN!?
YOU BELONG TO A DIFFERENT FAMILIA!
NOT EVEN ONE ON GOOD TERMS! DON'T YOU FIND IT A LITTLE STRANGE TO BE TRAINED BY HER!?
ZUKI (JOLT)
UH ...!!
AIZ-SAN IS THE SWORD PRINCESS !!
SHE'S NOT SOMEONE A LOWER-CLASS ADVENTURER SHOULD ASK FOR INSTRUCTION!
YET YOU MONOPOLIZED HER TIME FOR AN ENTIRE DAY...
...AND EVEN HAVE HER CARE FOR YOU...!?
OH, HOW I ENVY YOU!!
...NO, HOW IMPRUDENT OF YOU!!
GUSA
GUSA (TWIST)
UGH...!!
AND WORST OF ALL, YOU SAW AIZ-SAN... N-NU—!
YOU PEEPED ON HER WHEN SHE WAS NUDE...!!!
DON'T YOU FEEL ASHAMED AS A HUMAN BEING!?
UNFORGIVABLE! YOU ARE THE SCUM OF YOUR RACE!!
S-S-S-SOOOO-OOOORRY!!!

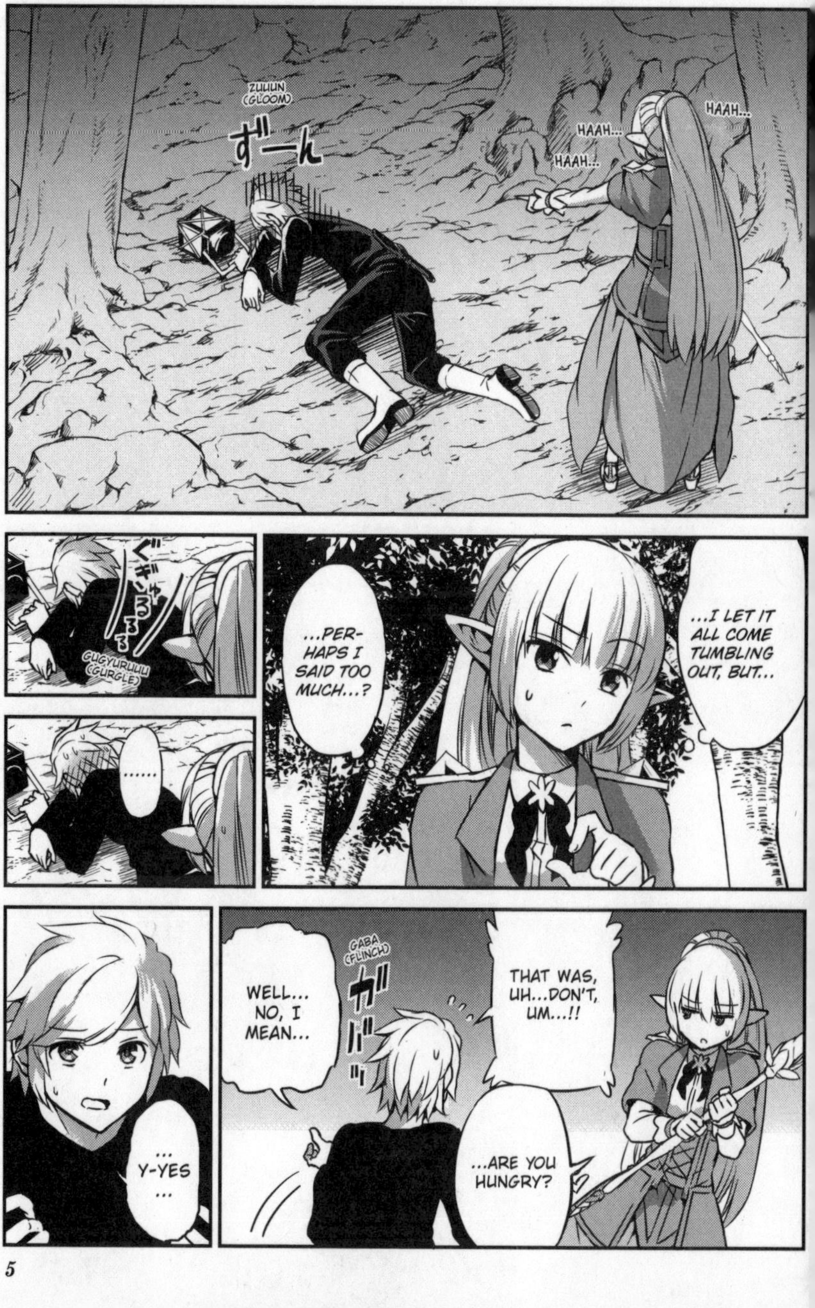
ZUUUN (GLOOM)
ずーん
HAAH...
HAAH...
HAAH...
...I LET IT ALL COME TUMBLING OUT, BUT...
...PER-HAPS I SAID TOO MUCH...?
ぐぎゅるるる
GUGYURUUU (GURGLE)
......
THAT WAS, UH...DON'T, UM...!!
GABA (FLINCH)
ガバッ
WELL... NO, I MEAN...
...ARE YOU HUNGRY?
... Y-YES ...

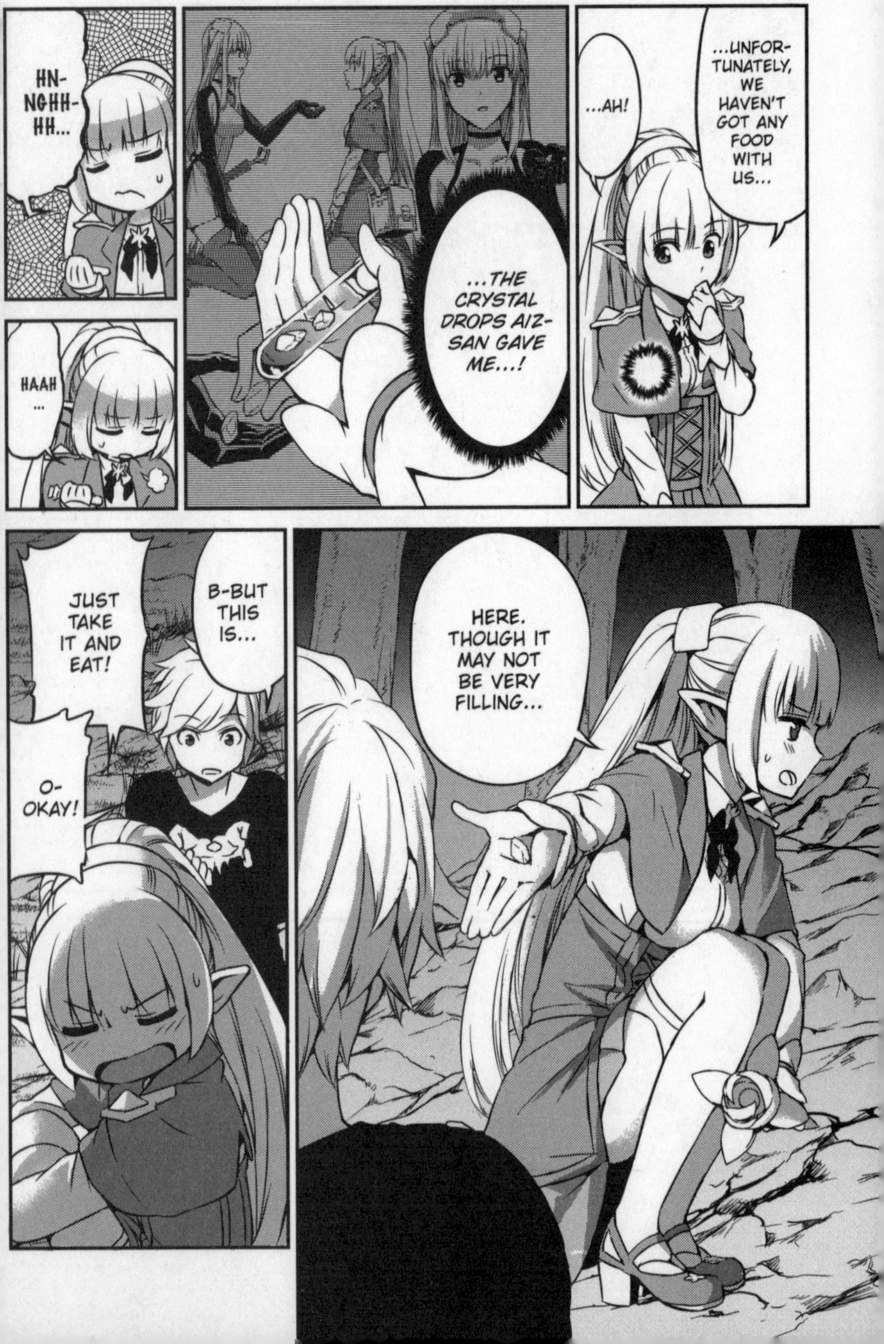
...UNFORTUNATELY, WE HAVEN'T GOT ANY FOOD WITH US...
...AH!
...THE CRYSTAL DROPS AIZ-SAN GAVE ME...!
HN-NGHHHH...
HAAH...
HERE. THOUGH IT MAY NOT BE VERY FILLING...
B-BUT THIS IS...
JUST TAKE IT AND EAT!
O-OKAY!

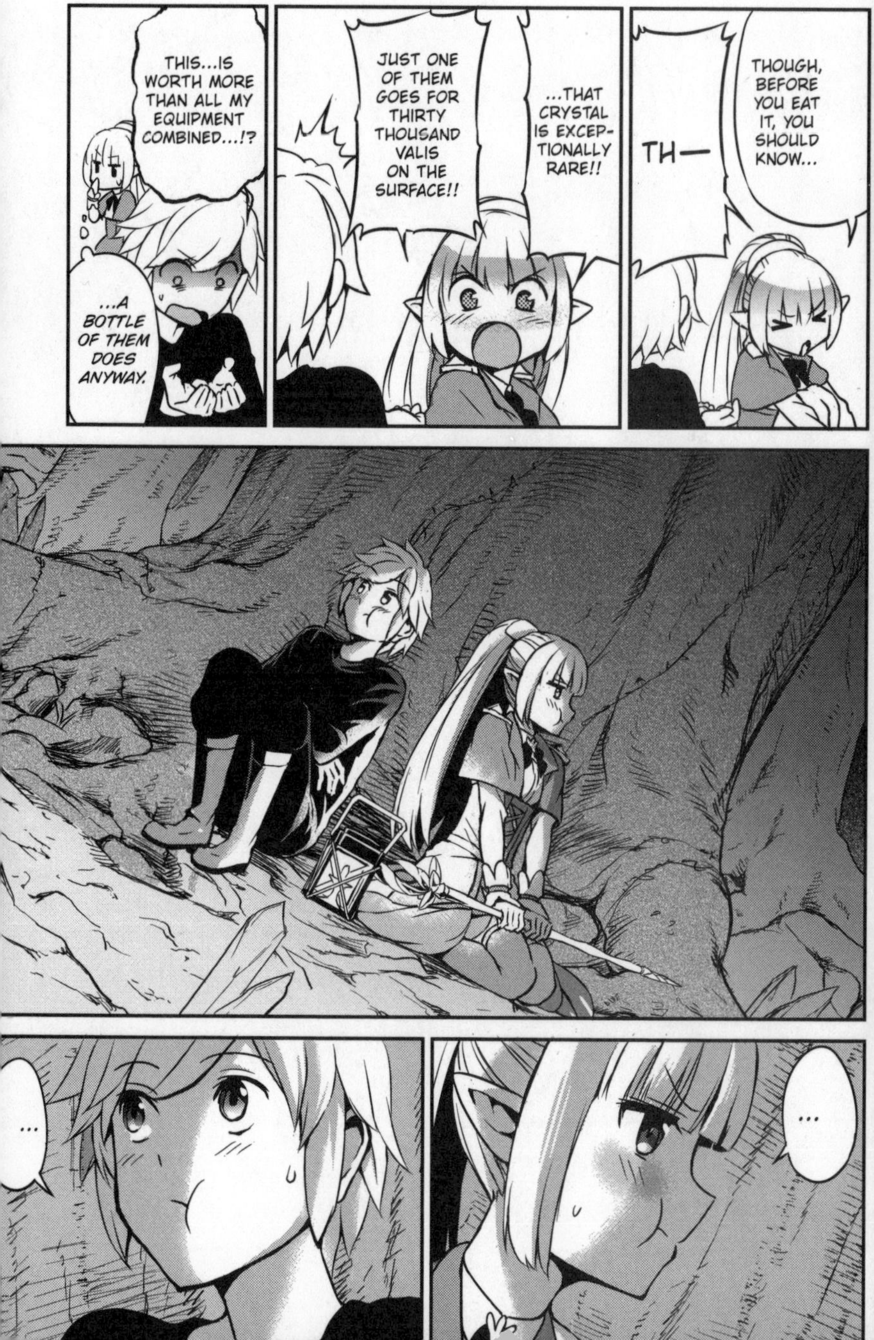
THOUGH, BEFORE YOU EAT IT, YOU SHOULD KNOW...
TH—
...THAT CRYSTAL IS EXCEPTIONALLY RARE!!
JUST ONE OF THEM GOES FOR THIRTY THOUSAND VALIS ON THE SURFACE!!
THIS...IS WORTH MORE THAN ALL MY EQUIPMENT COMBINED...!?
...A BOTTLE OF THEM DOES ANYWAY.
...
...

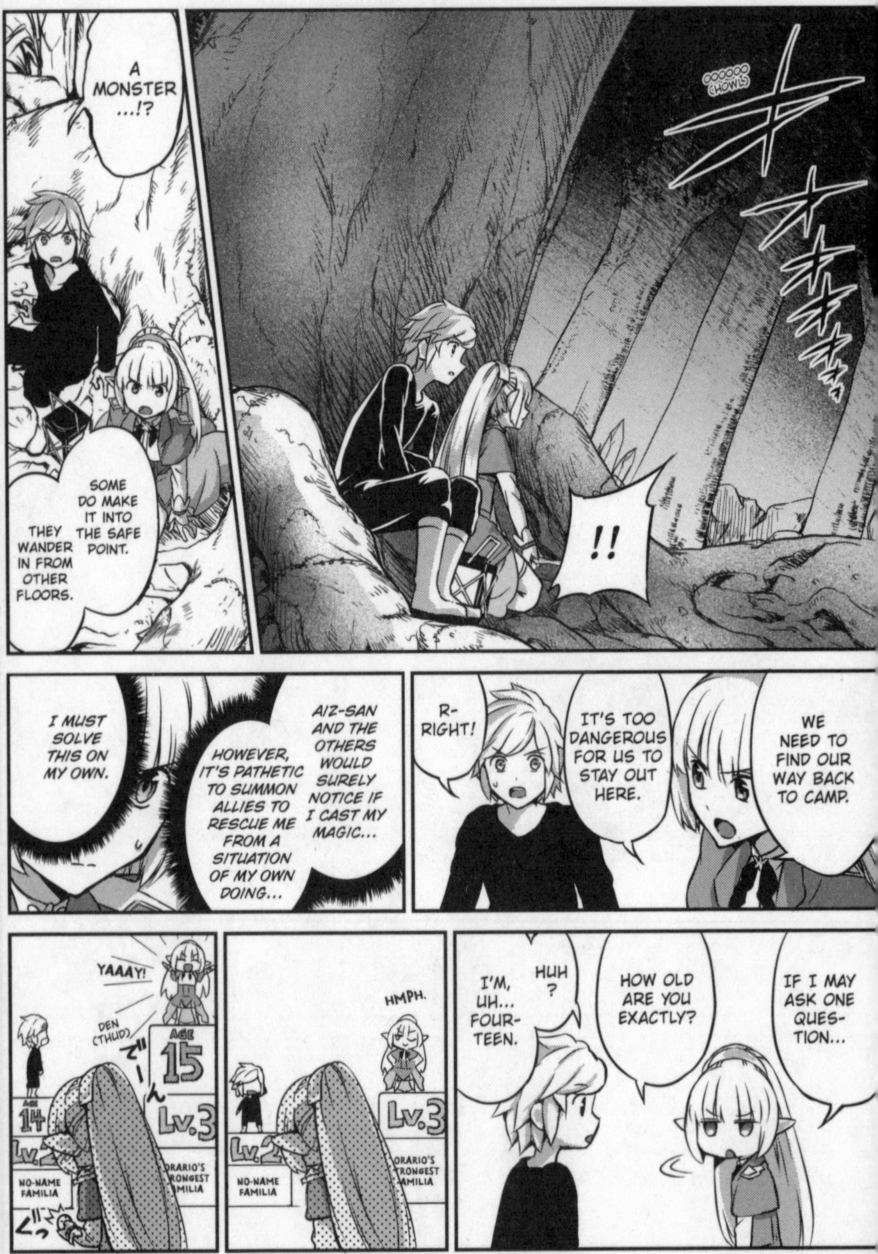
OOOOOO (HOWL)
!!
A MONSTER ...!?
SOME DO MAKE IT INTO THE SAFE POINT.
THEY WANDER IN FROM OTHER FLOORS.
WE NEED TO FIND OUR WAY BACK TO CAMP.
IT'S TOO DANGEROUS FOR US TO STAY OUT HERE.
R-RIGHT!
AIZ-SAN AND THE OTHERS WOULD SURELY NOTICE IF I CAST MY MAGIC...
HOWEVER, IT'S PATHETIC TO SUMMON ALLIES TO RESCUE ME FROM A SITUATION OF MY OWN DOING...
I MUST SOLVE THIS ON MY OWN.
IF I MAY ASK ONE QUES-TION...
HOW OLD ARE YOU EXACTLY?
HUH?
I'M, UH... FOUR-TEEN.
HMPH.
Lv.3
ORARIO'S TRONGEST AMILIA
Lv.2
NO-NAME FAMILIA
YAAAY!
DEN (THUD)
AGE 15
Lv.3
ORARIO'S RONGEST AMILIA
AGE 14
NO-NAME FAMILIA

SFX: GU (CLENCH)

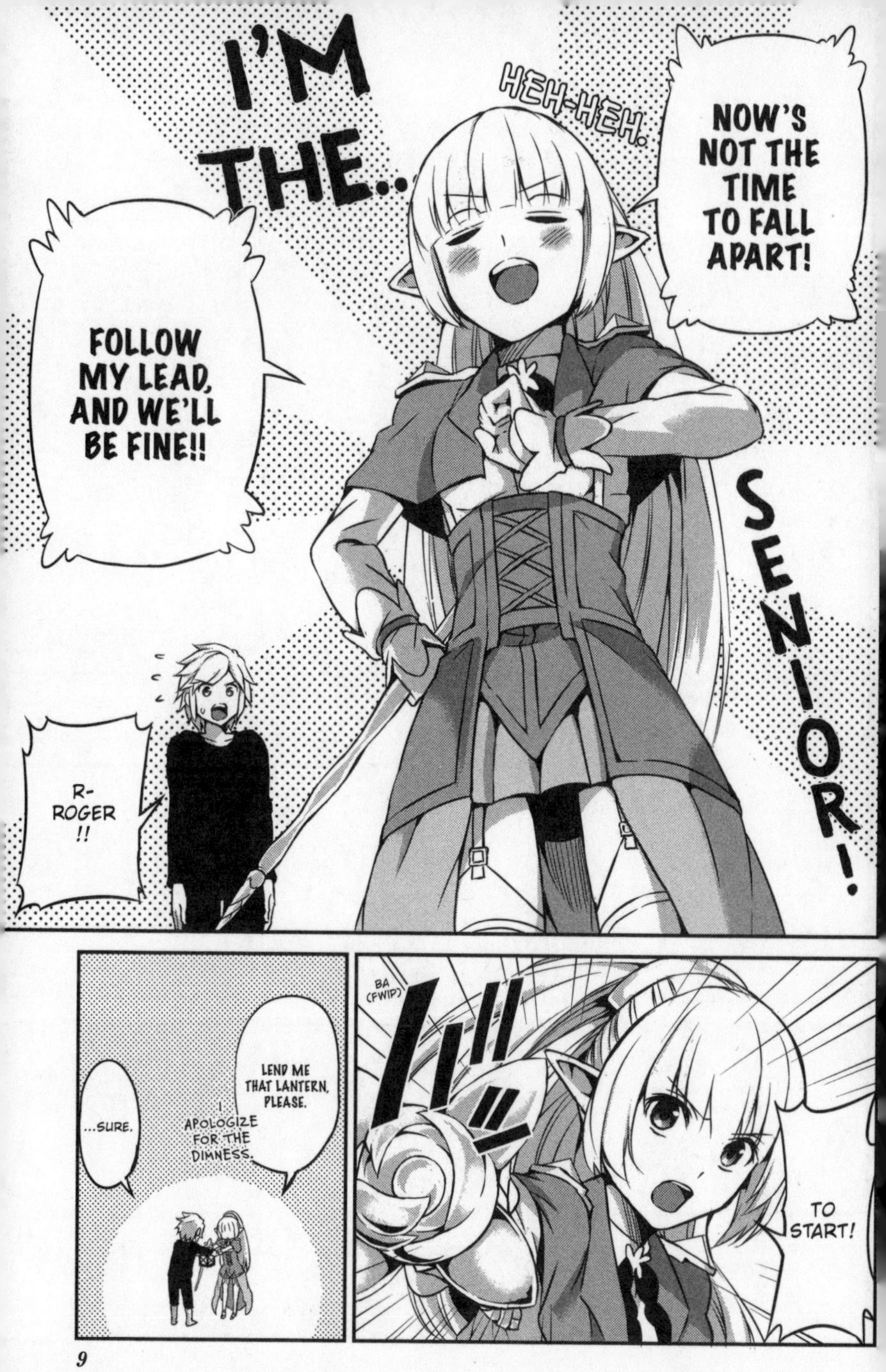
HEH-HEH.
NOW'S NOT THE TIME TO FALL APART!
I'M THE...
SENIOR!
FOLLOW MY LEAD, AND WE'LL BE FINE!!
R-ROGER!!
BA (FWIP)
TO START!
LEND ME THAT LANTERN, PLEASE.
I APOLOGIZE FOR THE DIMNESS.
...SURE.

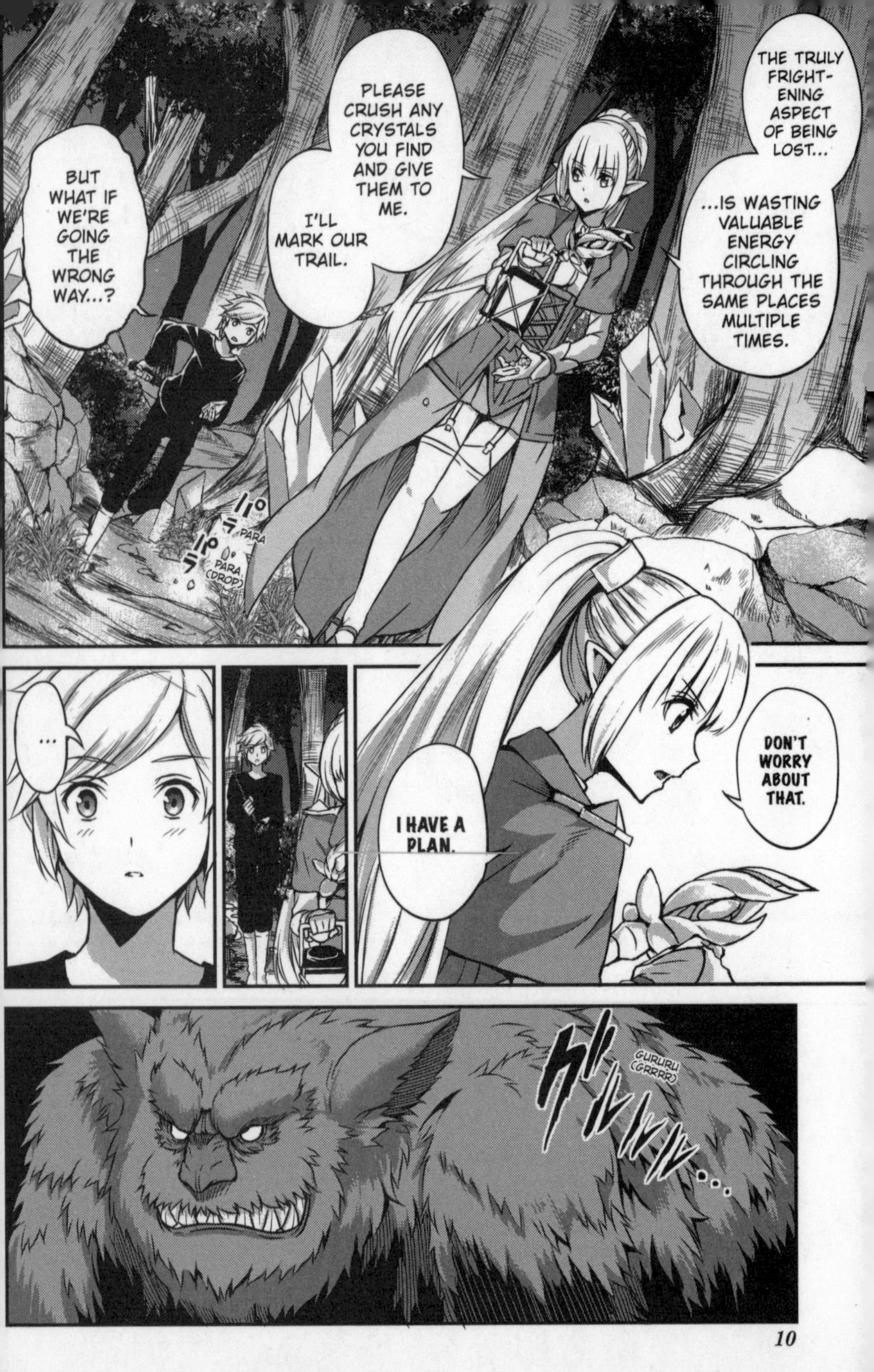
THE TRULY FRIGHT-ENING ASPECT OF BEING LOST...
...IS WASTING VALUABLE ENERGY CIRCLING THROUGH THE SAME PLACES MULTIPLE TIMES.
PLEASE CRUSH ANY CRYSTALS YOU FIND AND GIVE THEM TO ME.
I'LL MARK OUR TRAIL.
BUT WHAT IF WE'RE GOING THE WRONG WAY...?
PARA
PARA (DROP)
DON'T WORRY ABOUT THAT.
I HAVE A PLAN.
...
GURURU (GRRRR)

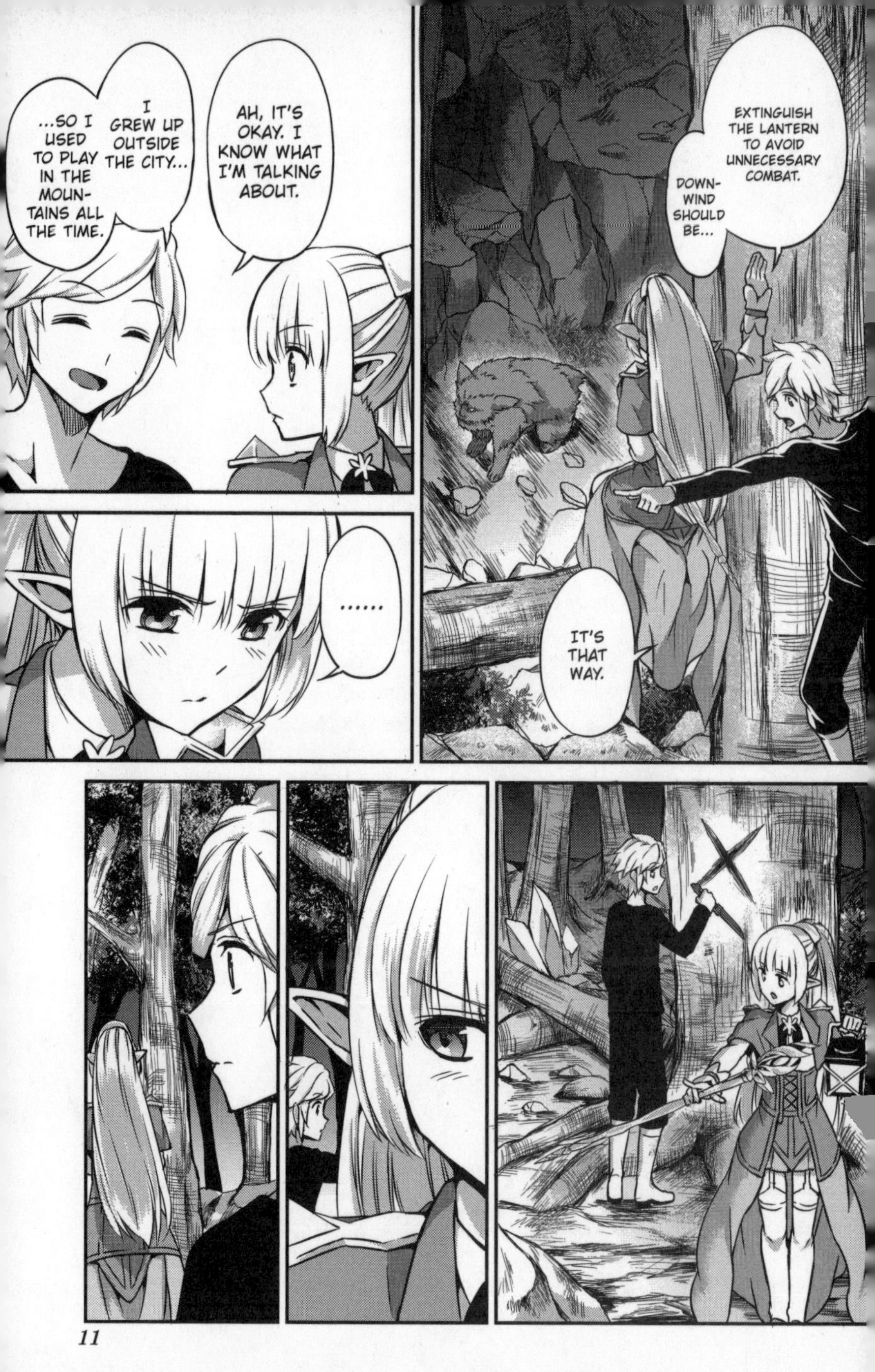
EXTINGUISH THE LANTERN TO AVOID UNNECESSARY COMBAT.
DOWN-WIND SHOULD BE...
IT'S THAT WAY.
AH, IT'S OKAY. I KNOW WHAT I'M TALKING ABOUT.
I GREW UP OUTSIDE THE CITY...
...SO I USED TO PLAY IN THE MOUN-TAINS ALL THE TIME.
......

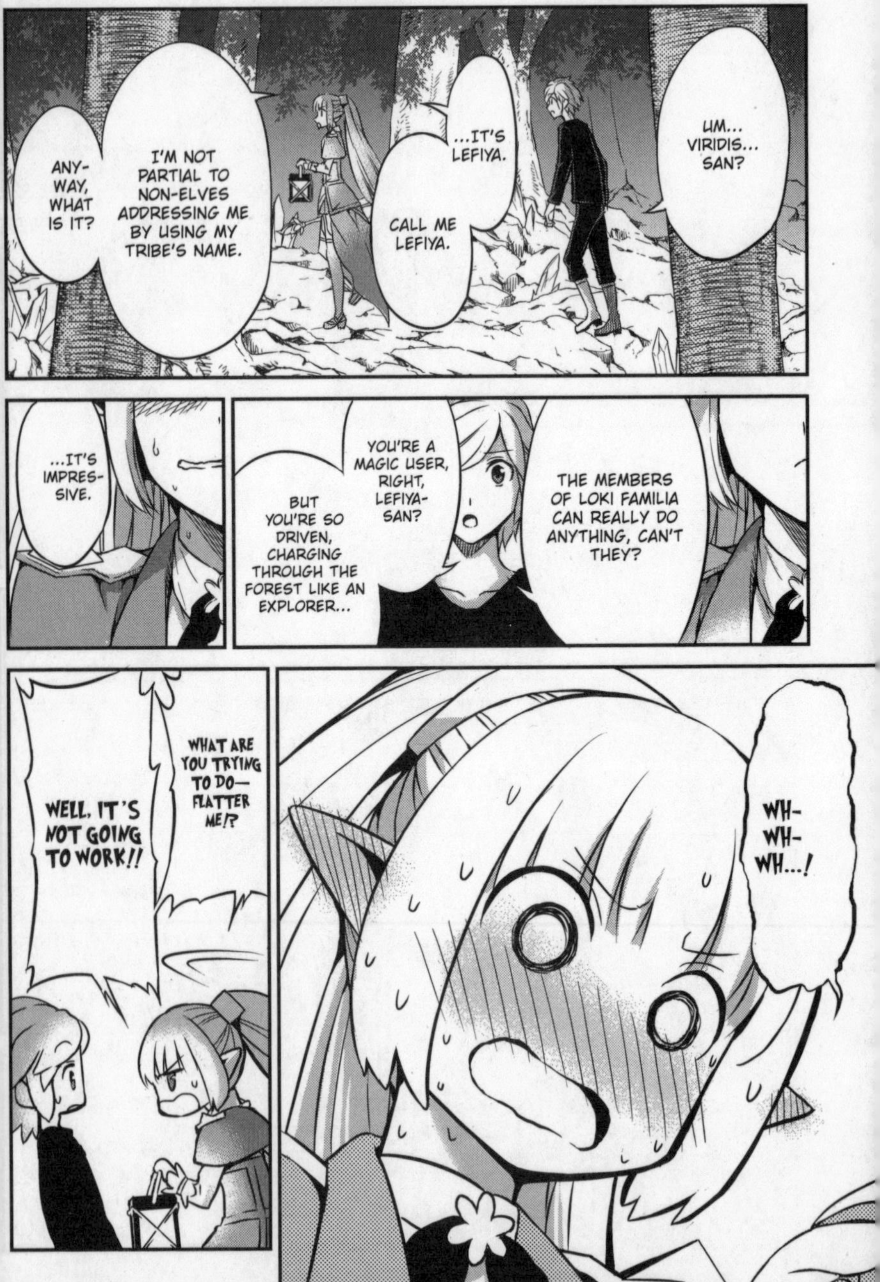
UM... VIRIDIS... SAN?
...IT'S LEFIYA.
CALL ME LEFIYA.
I'M NOT PARTIAL TO NON-ELVES ADDRESSING ME BY USING MY TRIBE'S NAME.
ANY-WAY, WHAT IS IT?
THE MEMBERS OF LOKI FAMILIA CAN REALLY DO ANYTHING, CAN'T THEY?
YOU'RE A MAGIC USER, RIGHT, LEFIYA-SAN?
BUT YOU'RE SO DRIVEN, CHARGING THROUGH THE FOREST LIKE AN EXPLORER...
...IT'S IMPRES-SIVE.
WH-WH-WH...!
WHAT ARE YOU TRYING TO DO—FLATTER ME!?
WELL, IT'S NOT GOING TO WORK!!

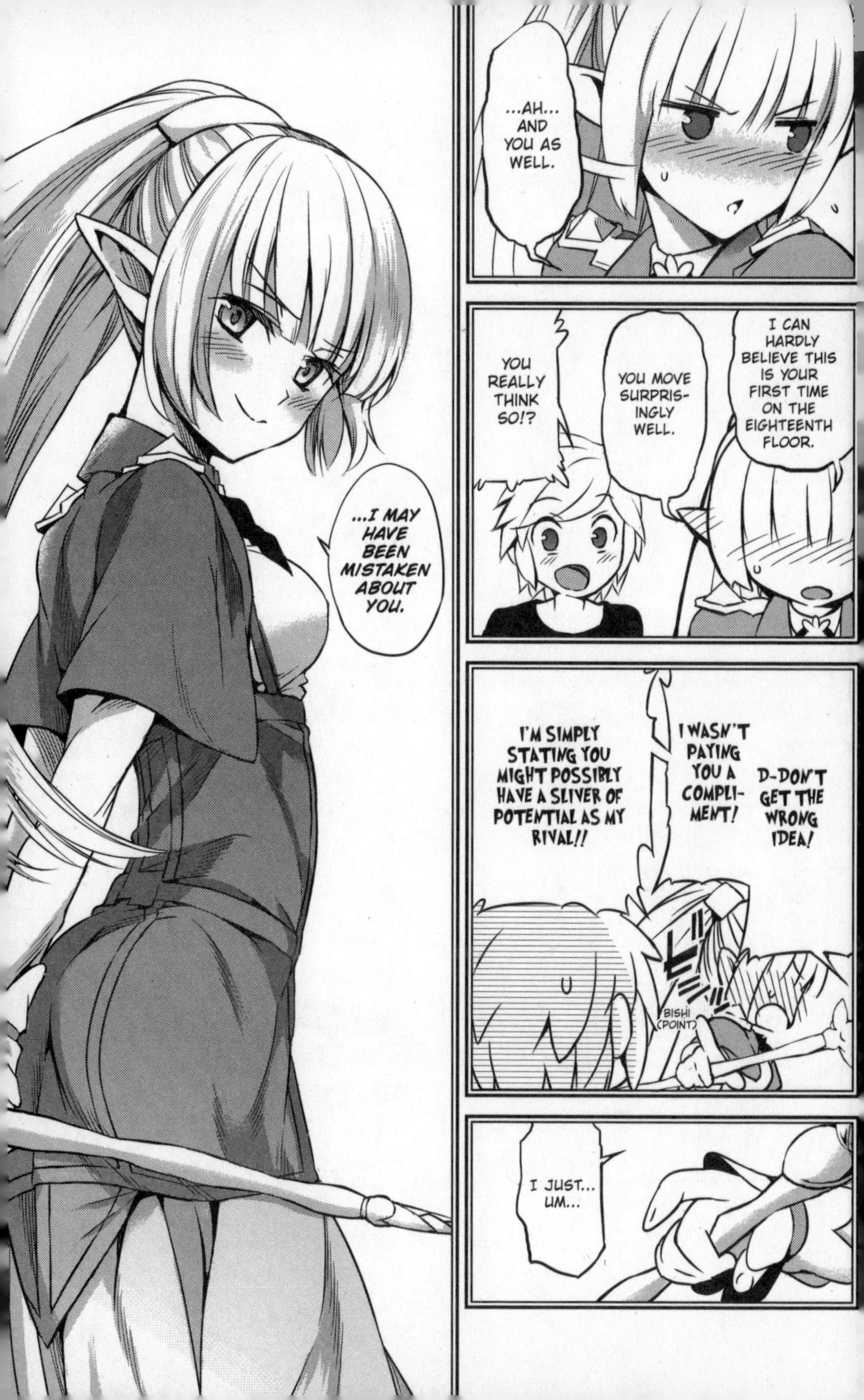
...AH... AND YOU AS WELL.
I CAN HARDLY BELIEVE THIS IS YOUR FIRST TIME ON THE EIGHTEENTH FLOOR.
YOU MOVE SURPRIS-INGLY WELL.
YOU REALLY THINK SO!?
D-DON'T GET THE WRONG IDEA!
I WASN'T PAYING YOU A COMPLI-MENT!
I'M SIMPLY STATING YOU MIGHT POSSIBLY HAVE A SLIVER OF POTENTIAL AS MY RIVAL!!
BISHI (POINT)
I JUST... UM...
...I MAY HAVE BEEN MISTAKEN ABOUT YOU.

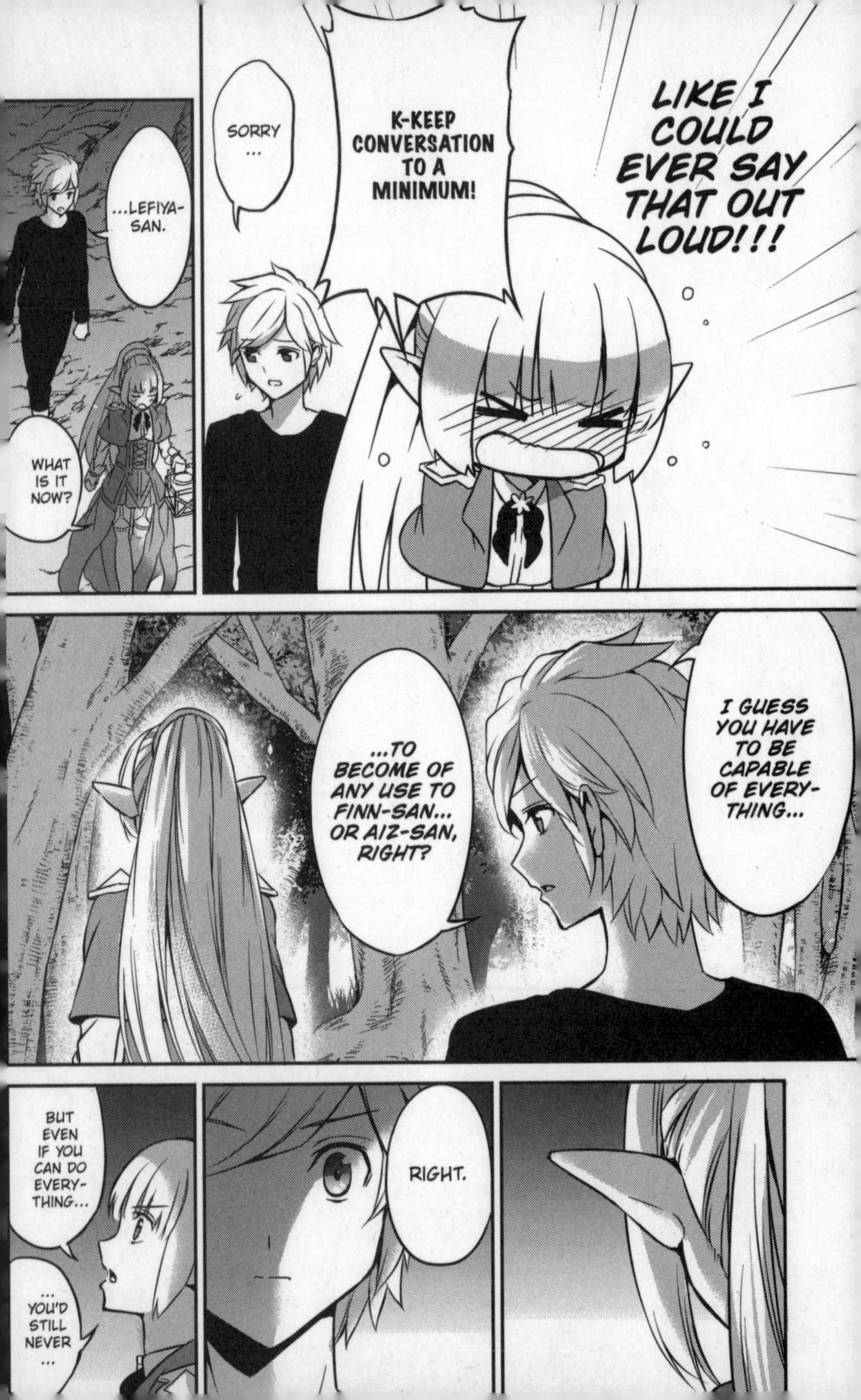
LIKE I COULD EVER SAY THAT OUT LOUD!!!
K-KEEP CONVERSATION TO A MINIMUM!
SORRY...
...LEFIYA-SAN.
WHAT IS IT NOW?
I GUESS YOU HAVE TO BE CAPABLE OF EVERY-THING...
...TO BECOME OF ANY USE TO FINN-SAN... OR AIZ-SAN, RIGHT?
RIGHT.
BUT EVEN IF YOU CAN DO EVERY-THING...
...YOU'D STILL NEVER...

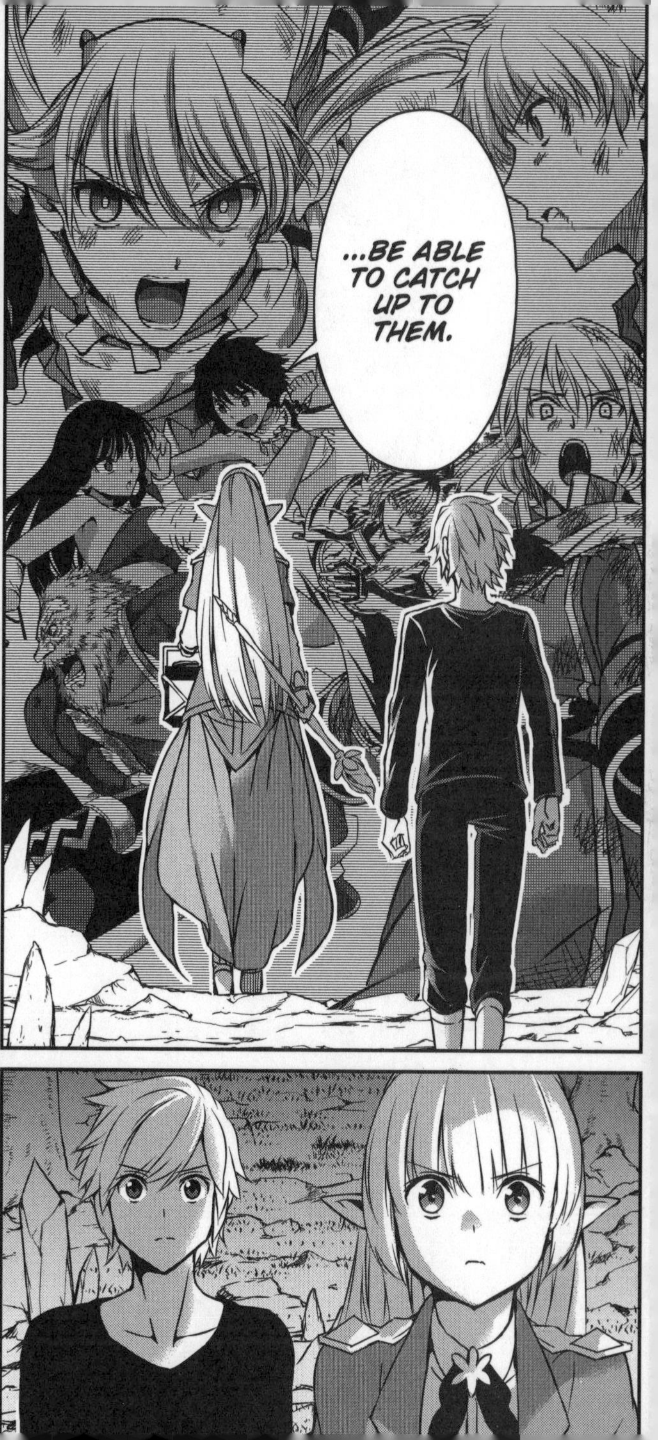
...BE ABLE TO CATCH UP TO THEM.
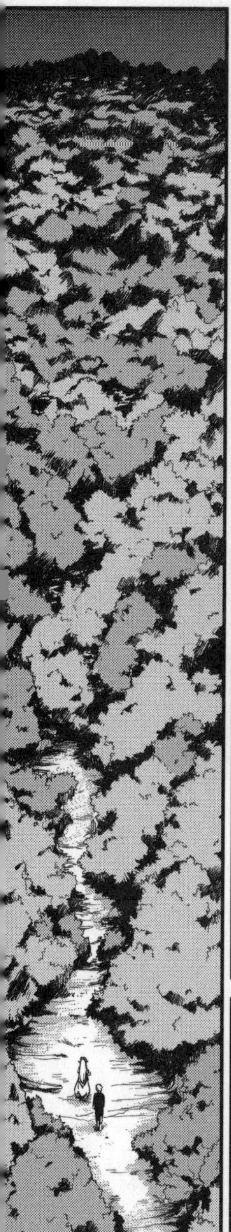

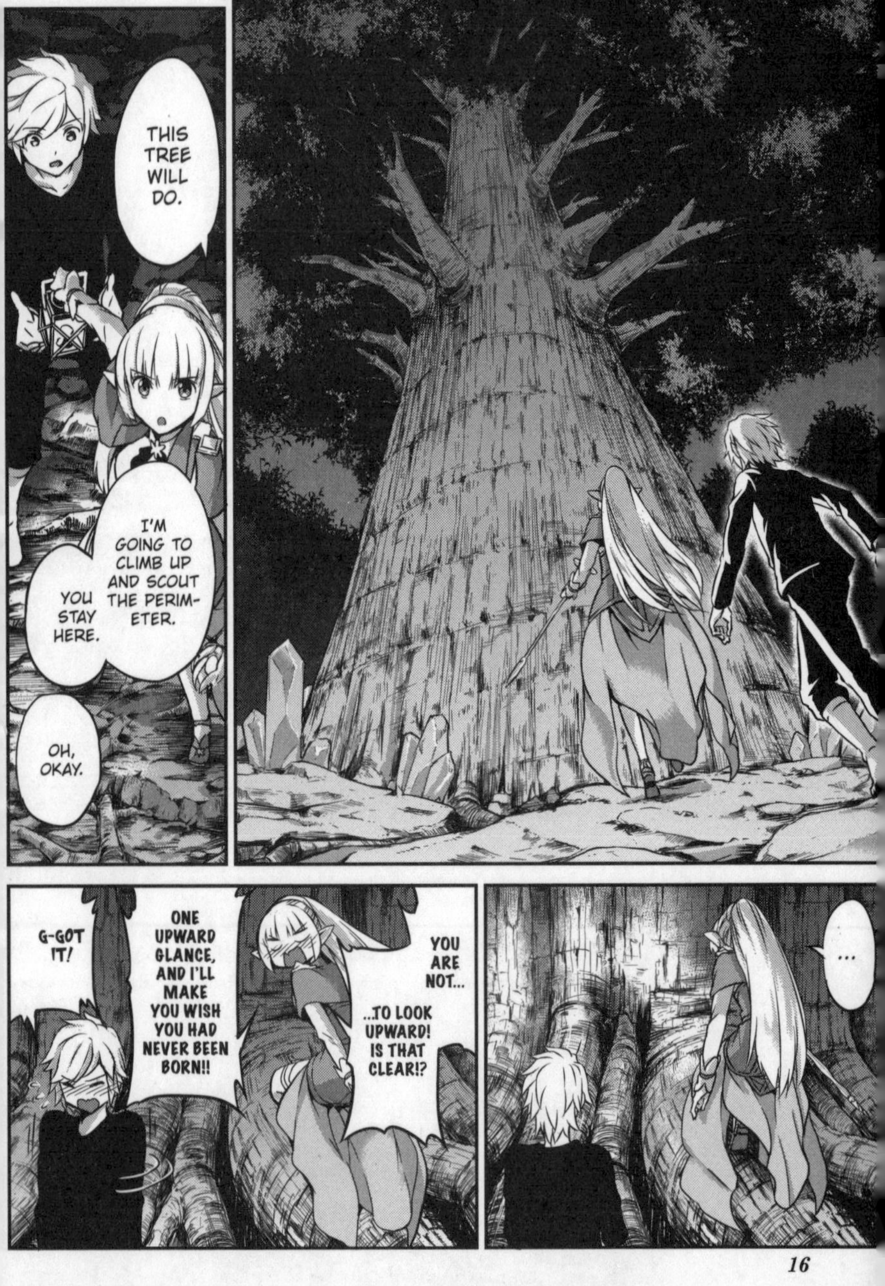
THIS TREE WILL DO.
I'M GOING TO CLIMB UP AND SCOUT THE PERIMETER.
YOU STAY HERE.
OH, OKAY.
...
YOU ARE NOT...
...TO LOOK UPWARD! IS THAT CLEAR!?
ONE UPWARD GLANCE, AND I'LL MAKE YOU WISH YOU HAD NEVER BEEN BORN!!
G-GOT IT!

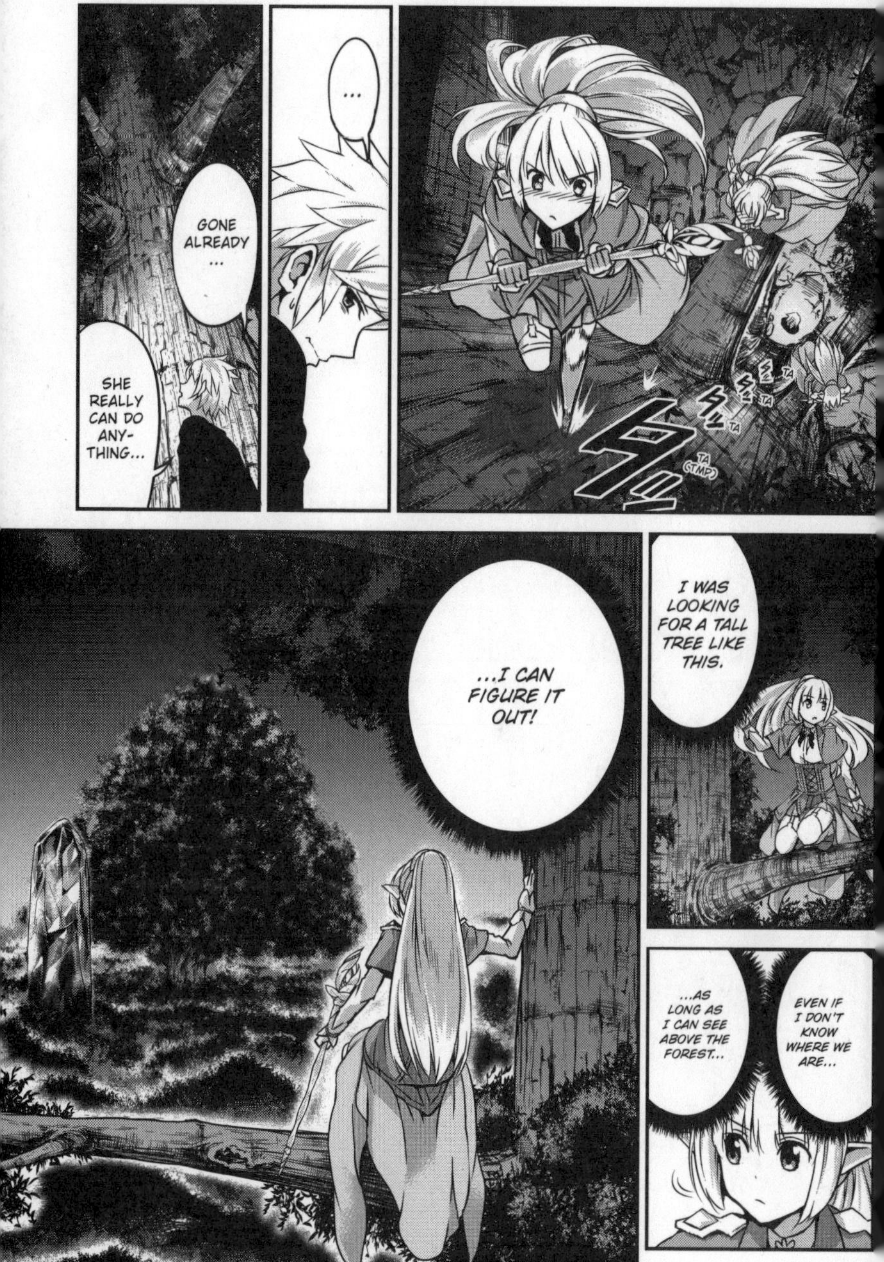
TA
TA
TA
TA (TMP)
...
GONE ALREADY ...
SHE REALLY CAN DO ANY-THING...
I WAS LOOKING FOR A TALL TREE LIKE THIS.
EVEN IF I DON'T KNOW WHERE WE ARE...
...AS LONG AS I CAN SEE ABOVE THE FOREST...
...I CAN FIGURE IT OUT!

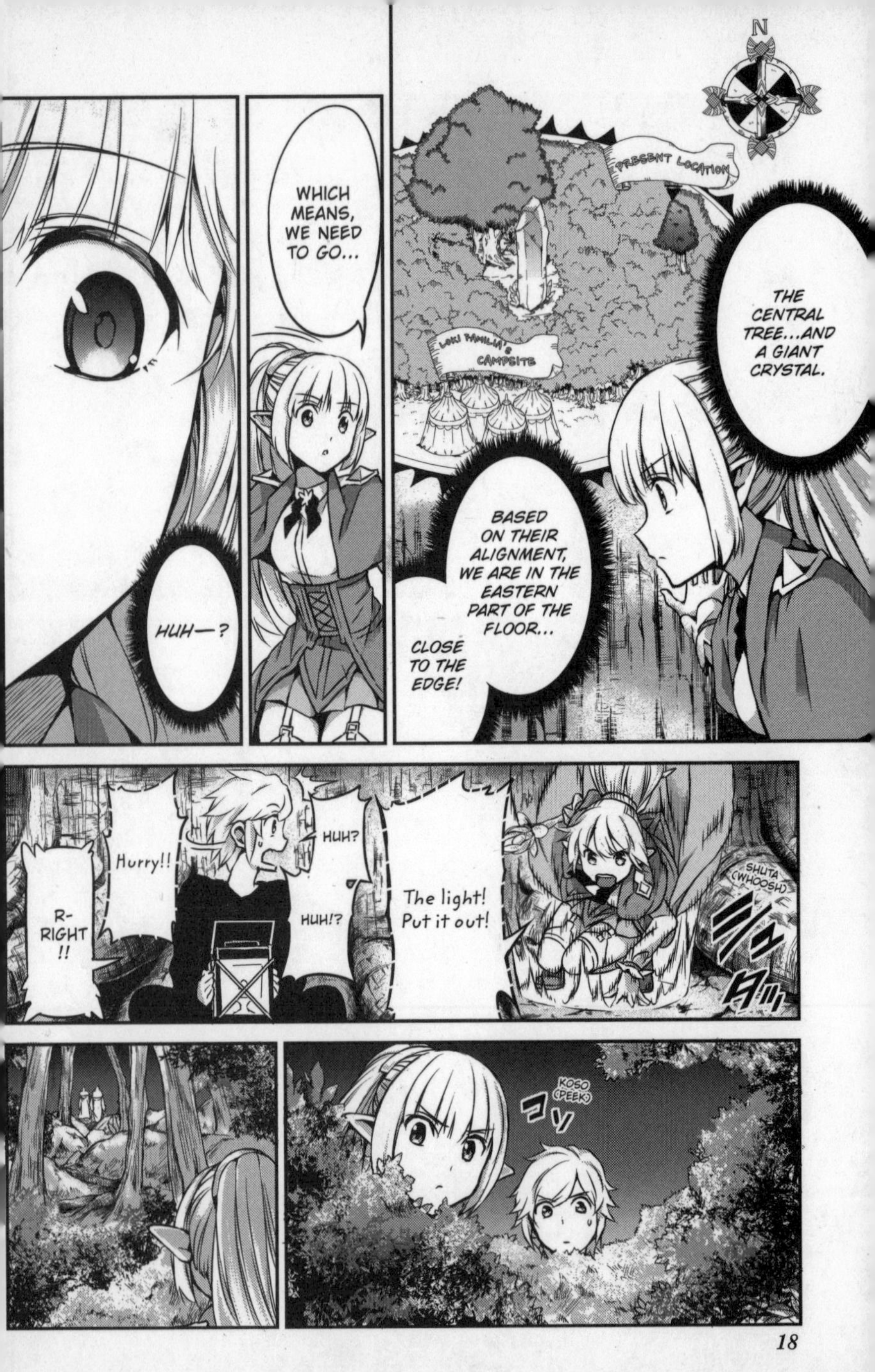
N
PRESENT LOCATION
THE CENTRAL TREE...AND A GIANT CRYSTAL.
LOKI FAMILIA'S CAMPSITE
BASED ON THEIR ALIGNMENT, WE ARE IN THE EASTERN PART OF THE FLOOR...
CLOSE TO THE EDGE!
WHICH MEANS, WE NEED TO GO...
HUH—?
SHUTA (WHOOSH)
The light! Put it out!
HUH?
HUH!?
Hurry!!
R-RIGHT!!
KOSO (PEEK)

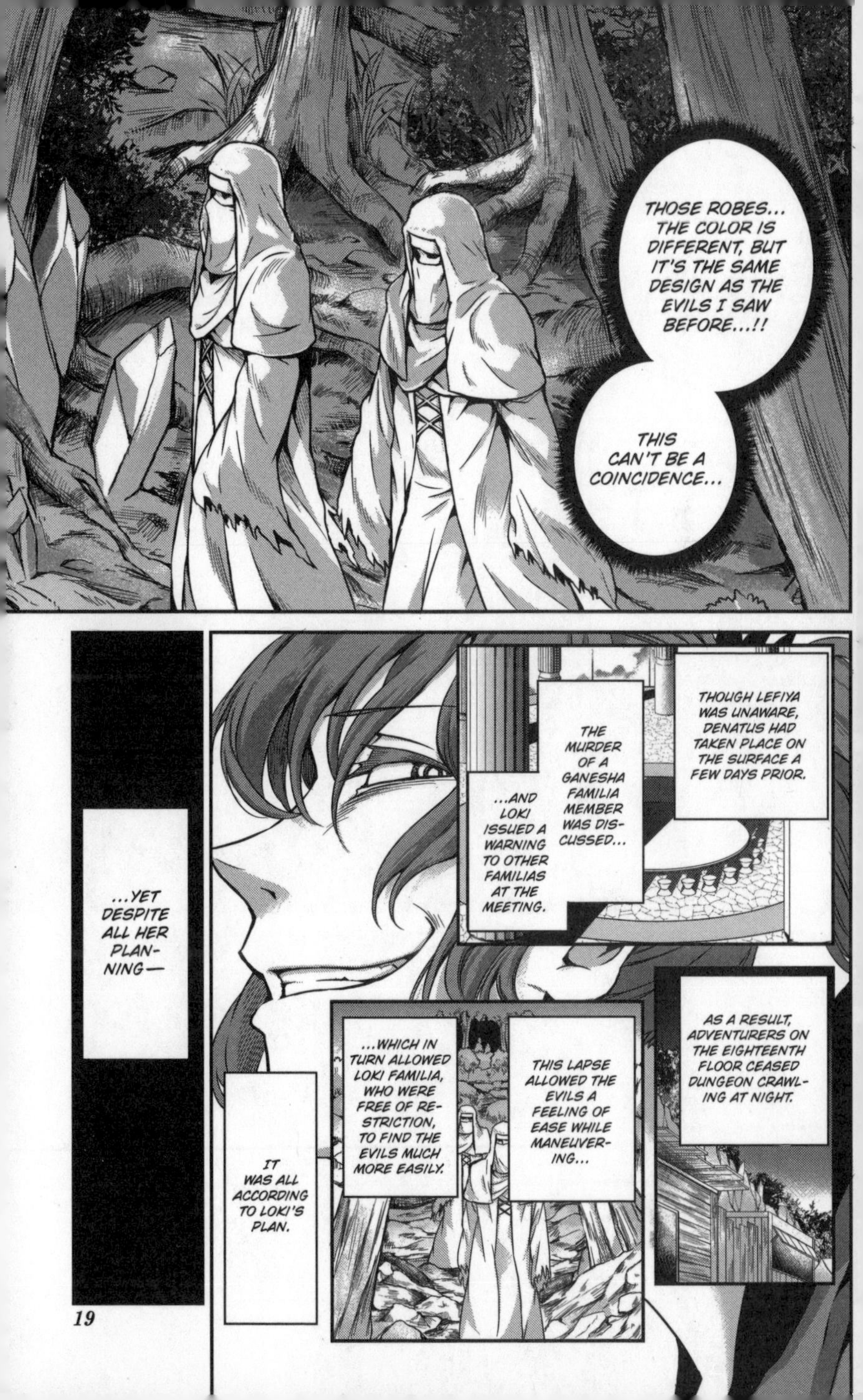
THOSE ROBES... THE COLOR IS DIFFERENT, BUT IT'S THE SAME DESIGN AS THE EVILS I SAW BEFORE...!!
THIS CAN'T BE A COINCIDENCE...
THOUGH LEFIYA WAS UNAWARE, DENATUS HAD TAKEN PLACE ON THE SURFACE A FEW DAYS PRIOR.
THE MURDER OF A GANESHA FAMILIA MEMBER WAS DIS-CUSSED...
...AND LOKI ISSUED A WARNING TO OTHER FAMILIAS AT THE MEETING.
AS A RESULT, ADVENTURERS ON THE EIGHTEENTH FLOOR CEASED DUNGEON CRAWL-ING AT NIGHT.
THIS LAPSE ALLOWED THE EVILS A FEELING OF EASE WHILE MANEUVER-ING...
...WHICH IN TURN ALLOWED LOKI FAMILIA, WHO WERE FREE OF RE-STRICTION, TO FIND THE EVILS MUCH MORE EASILY.
IT WAS ALL ACCORDING TO LOKI'S PLAN.
...YET DESPITE ALL HER PLAN-NING—

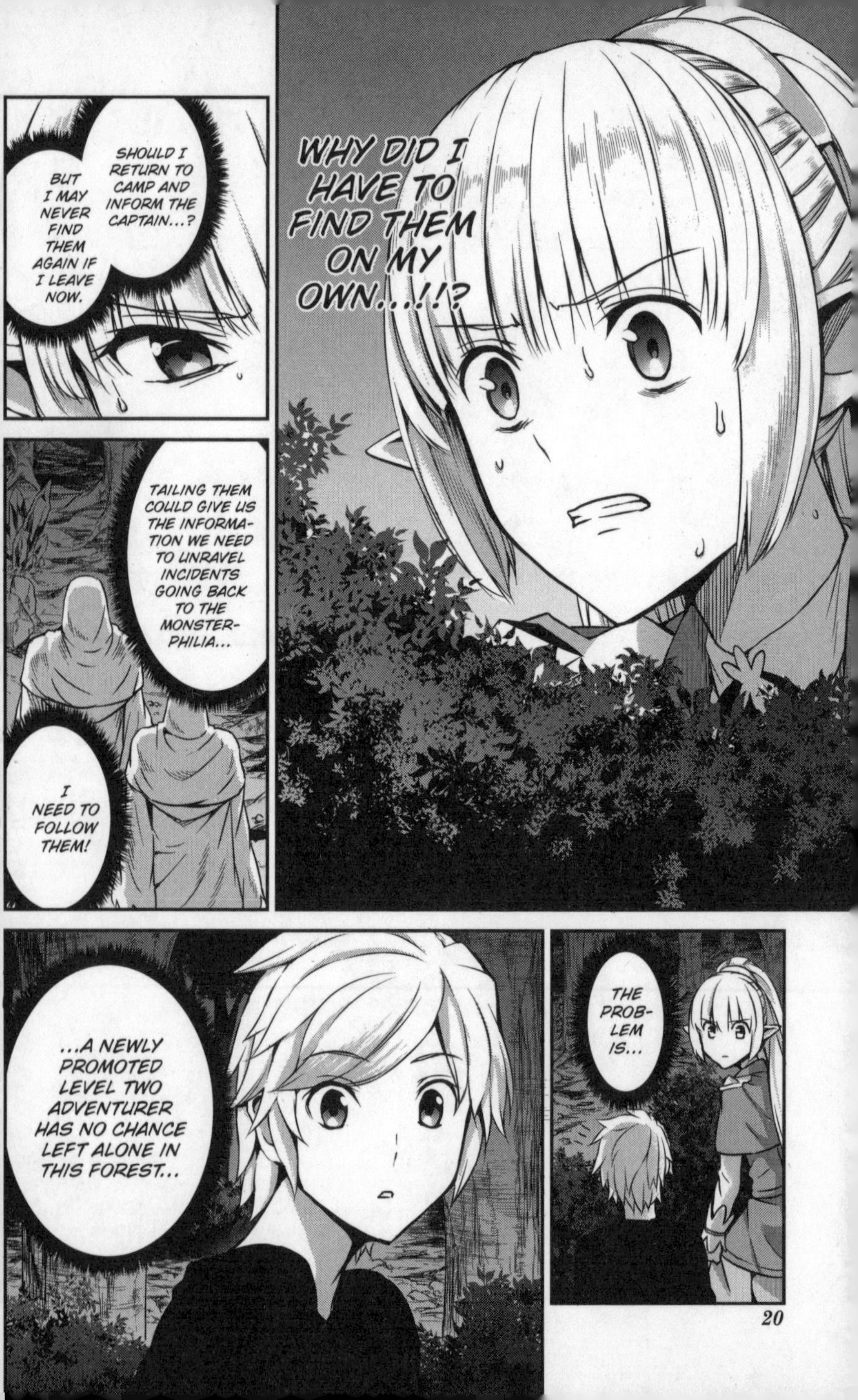
WHY DID I HAVE TO FIND THEM ON MY OWN...!!?
SHOULD I RETURN TO CAMP AND INFORM THE CAPTAIN...?
BUT I MAY NEVER FIND THEM AGAIN IF I LEAVE NOW.
TAILING THEM COULD GIVE US THE INFORMATION WE NEED TO UNRAVEL INCIDENTS GOING BACK TO THE MONSTERPHILIA...
I NEED TO FOLLOW THEM!
THE PROBLEM IS...
...A NEWLY PROMOTED LEVEL TWO ADVENTURER HAS NO CHANCE LEFT ALONE IN THIS FOREST...

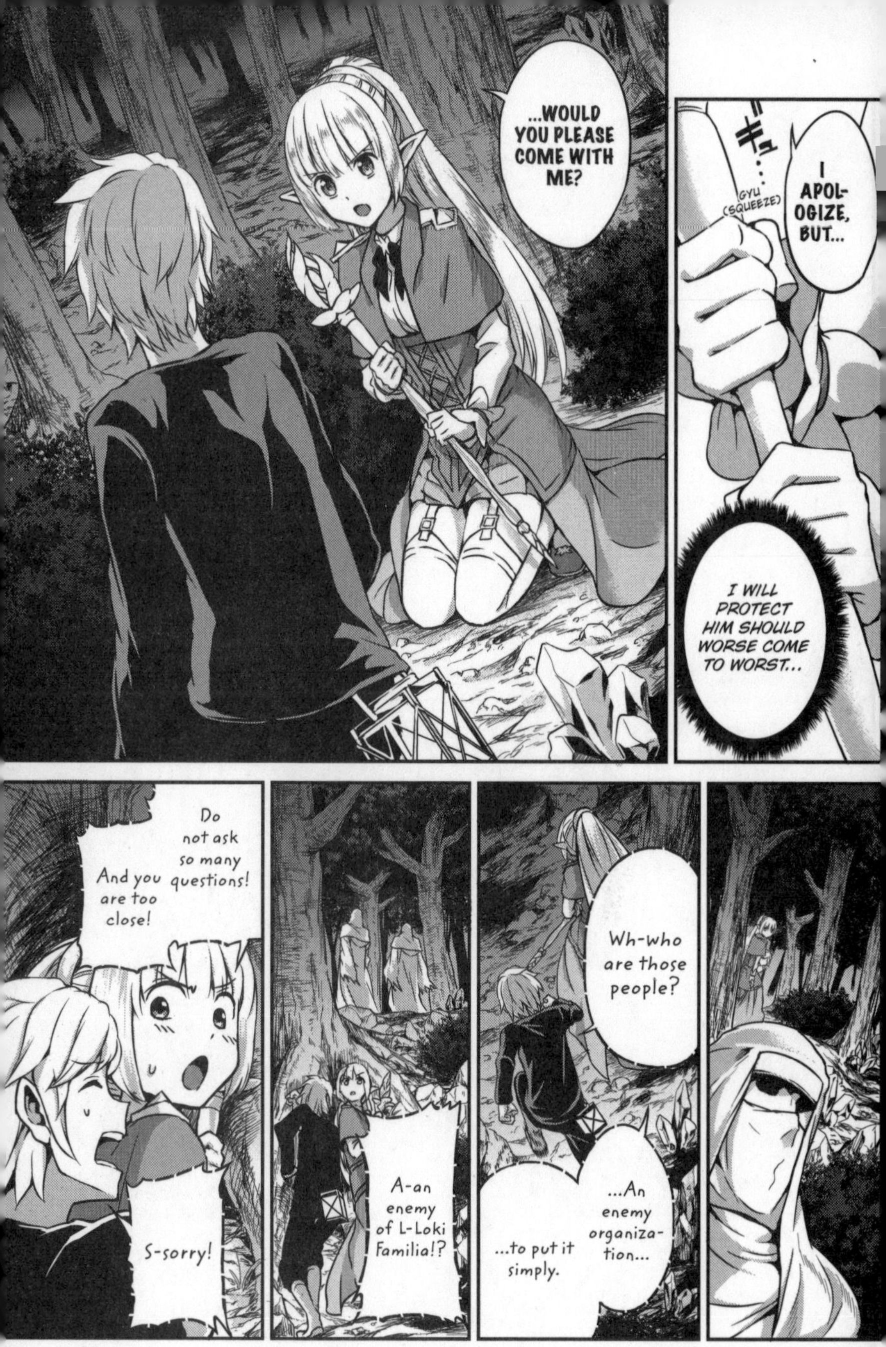
I APOLOGIZE, BUT...
GYU (SQUEEZE)
I WILL PROTECT HIM SHOULD WORSE COME TO WORST...
...WOULD YOU PLEASE COME WITH ME?
Wh-who are those people?
...An enemy organization...
...to put it simply.
A-an enemy of L-Loki Familia!?
Do not ask so many questions!
And you are too close!
S-sorry!

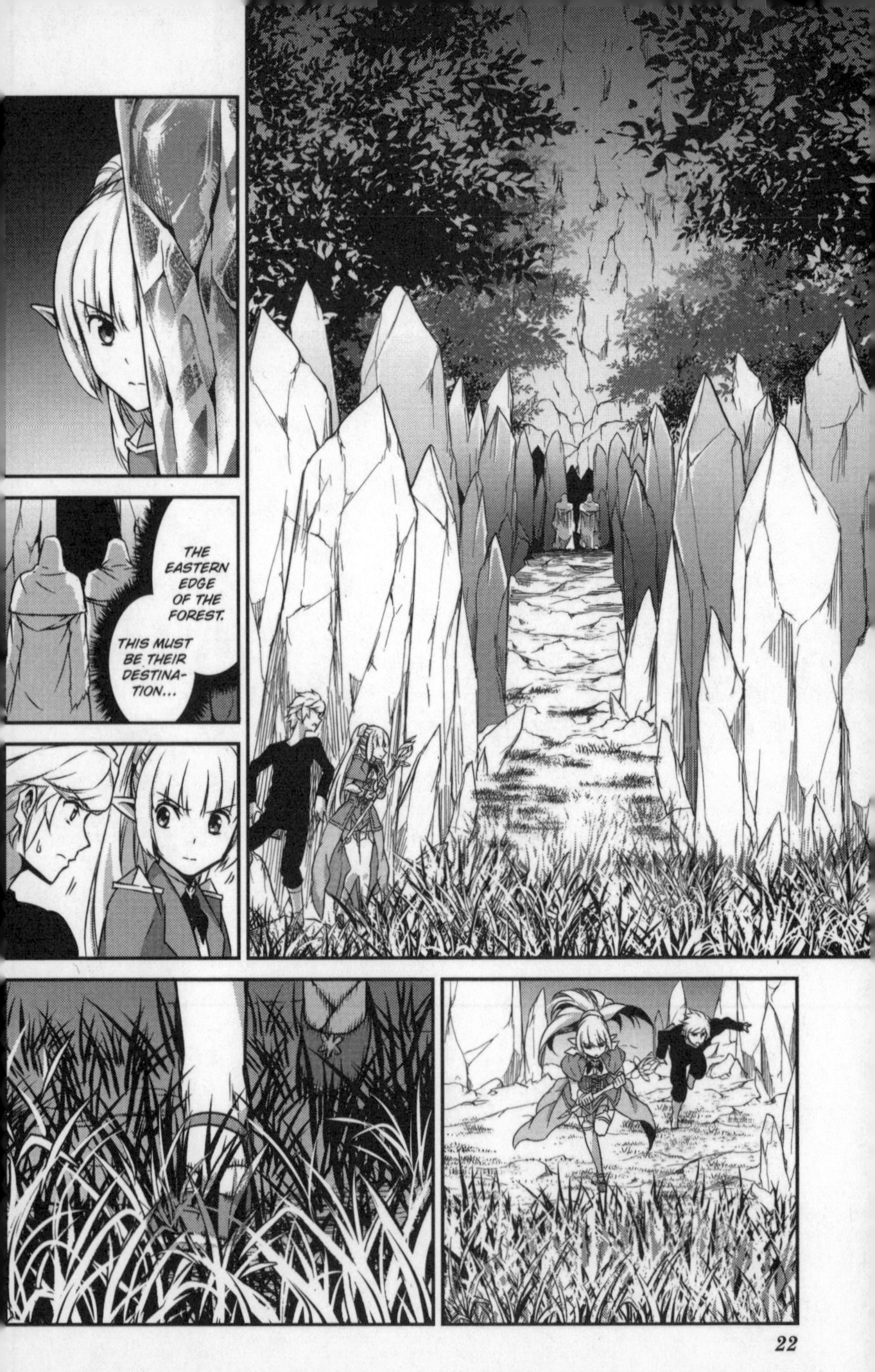
THE EASTERN EDGE OF THE FOREST.
THIS MUST BE THEIR DESTINA-TION...

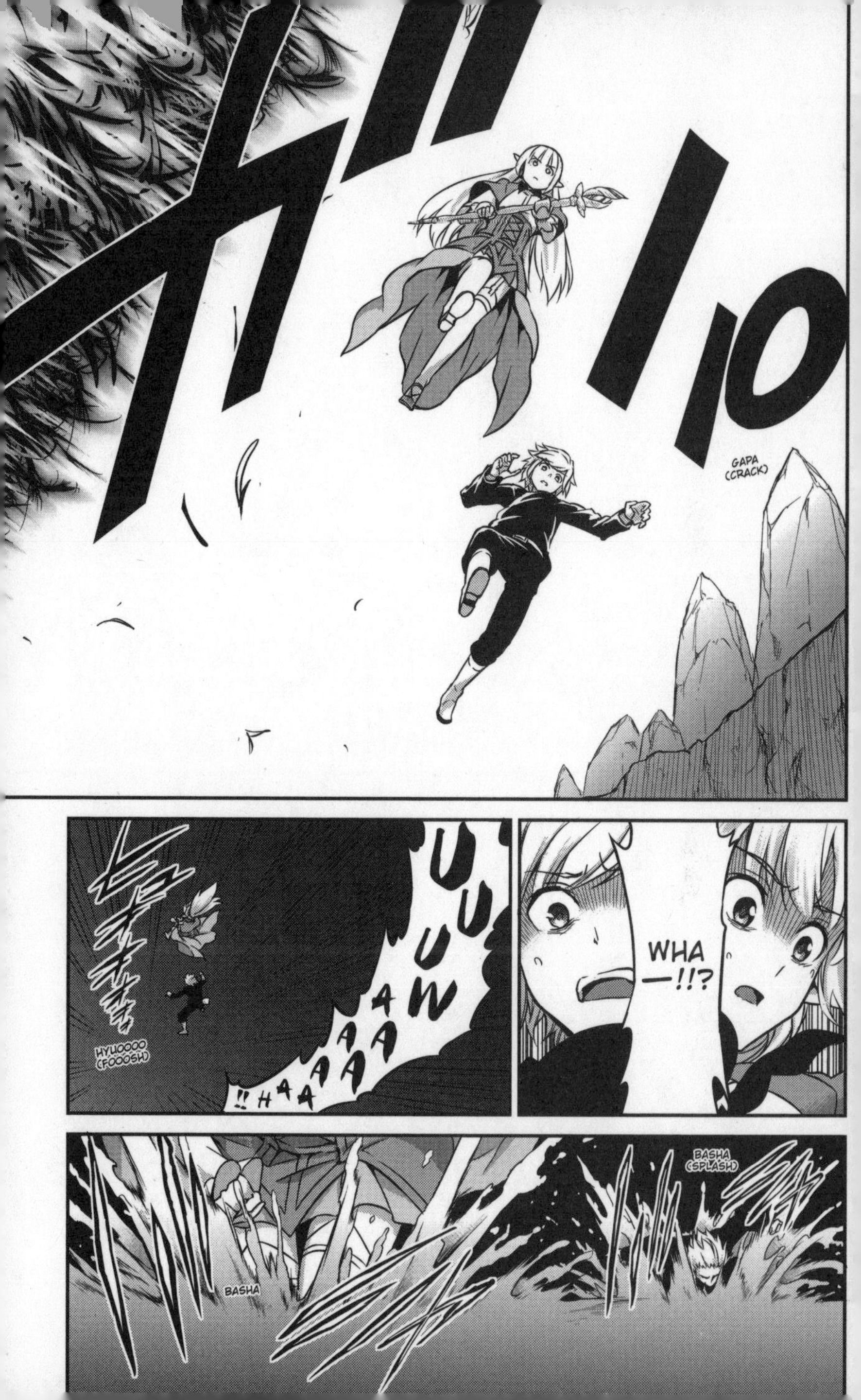
GAPA
(CRACK)
WHA—!!?
UUUUWAAAAAAAHH!!
HYUOOOO
(FOOOSH)
BASHA
(SPLASH)
BASHA

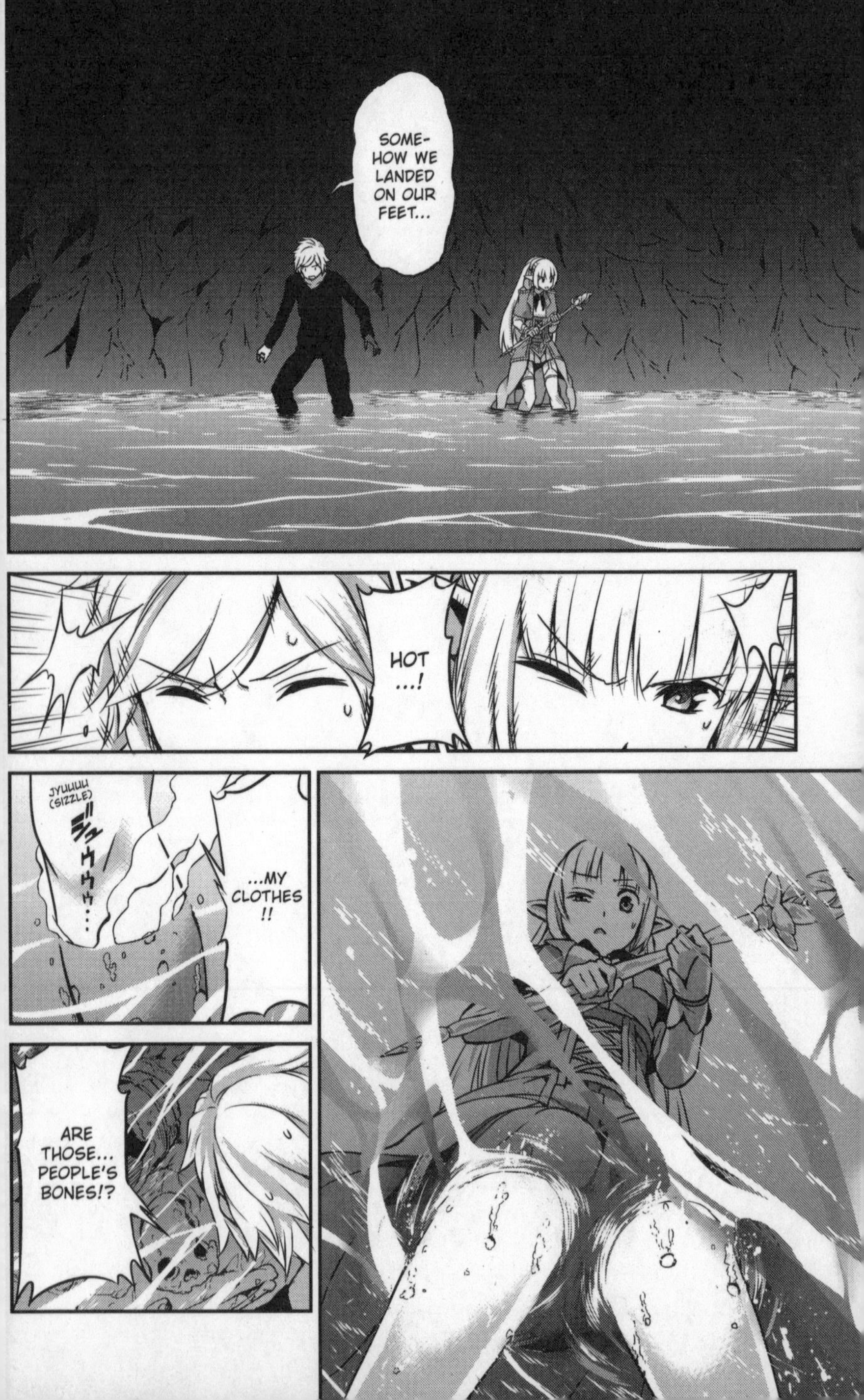
SOME-HOW WE LANDED ON OUR FEET...
HOT ...!
JYUUUU (SIZZLE)
ジュウウウ…
...MY CLOTHES !!
ARE THOSE... PEOPLE'S BONES!?

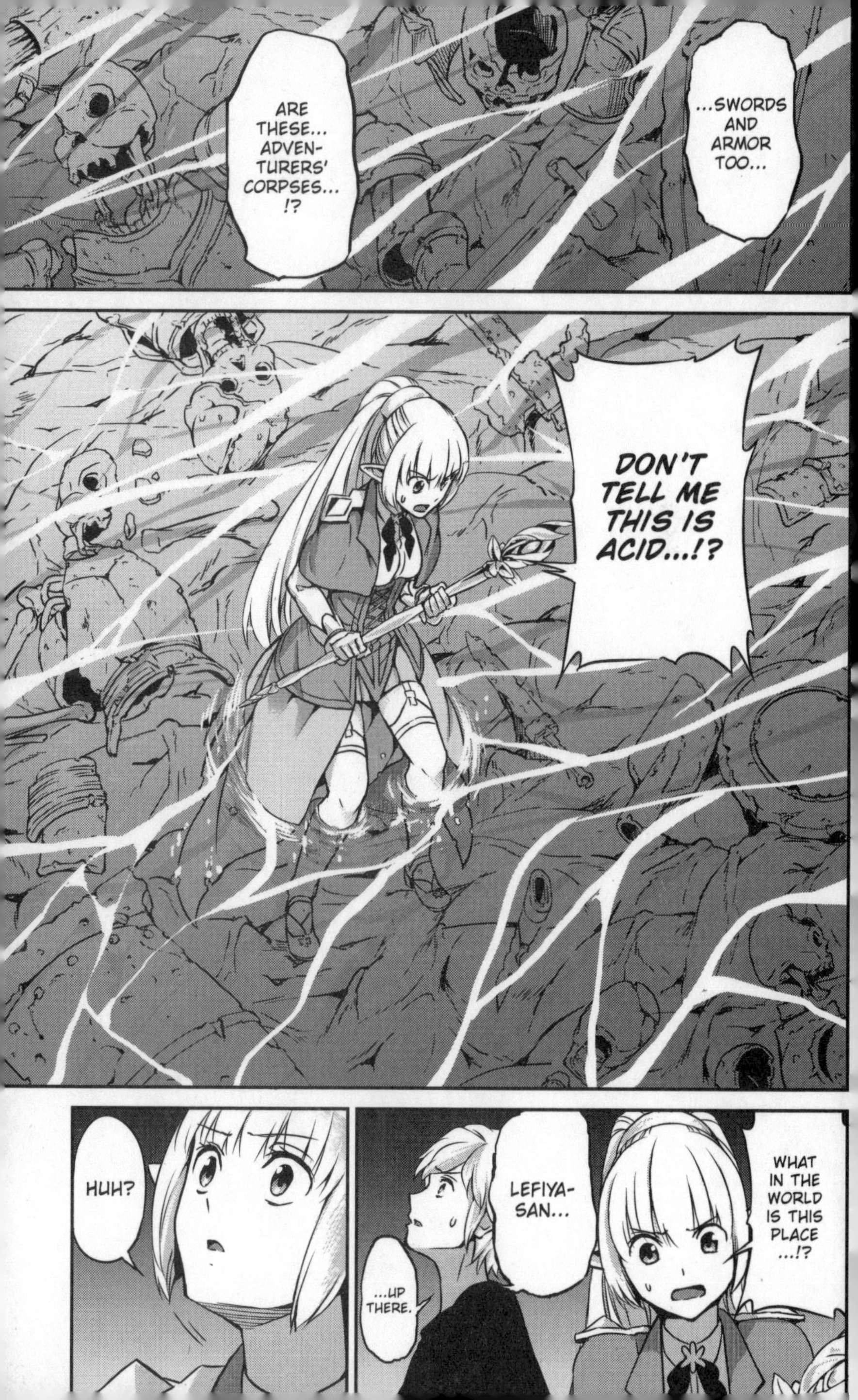
...SWORDS AND ARMOR TOO...
ARE THESE... ADVENTURERS' CORPSES...!?
DON'T TELL ME THIS IS ACID...!?
WHAT IN THE WORLD IS THIS PLACE...!?
LEFIYA-SAN...
...UP THERE.
HUH?

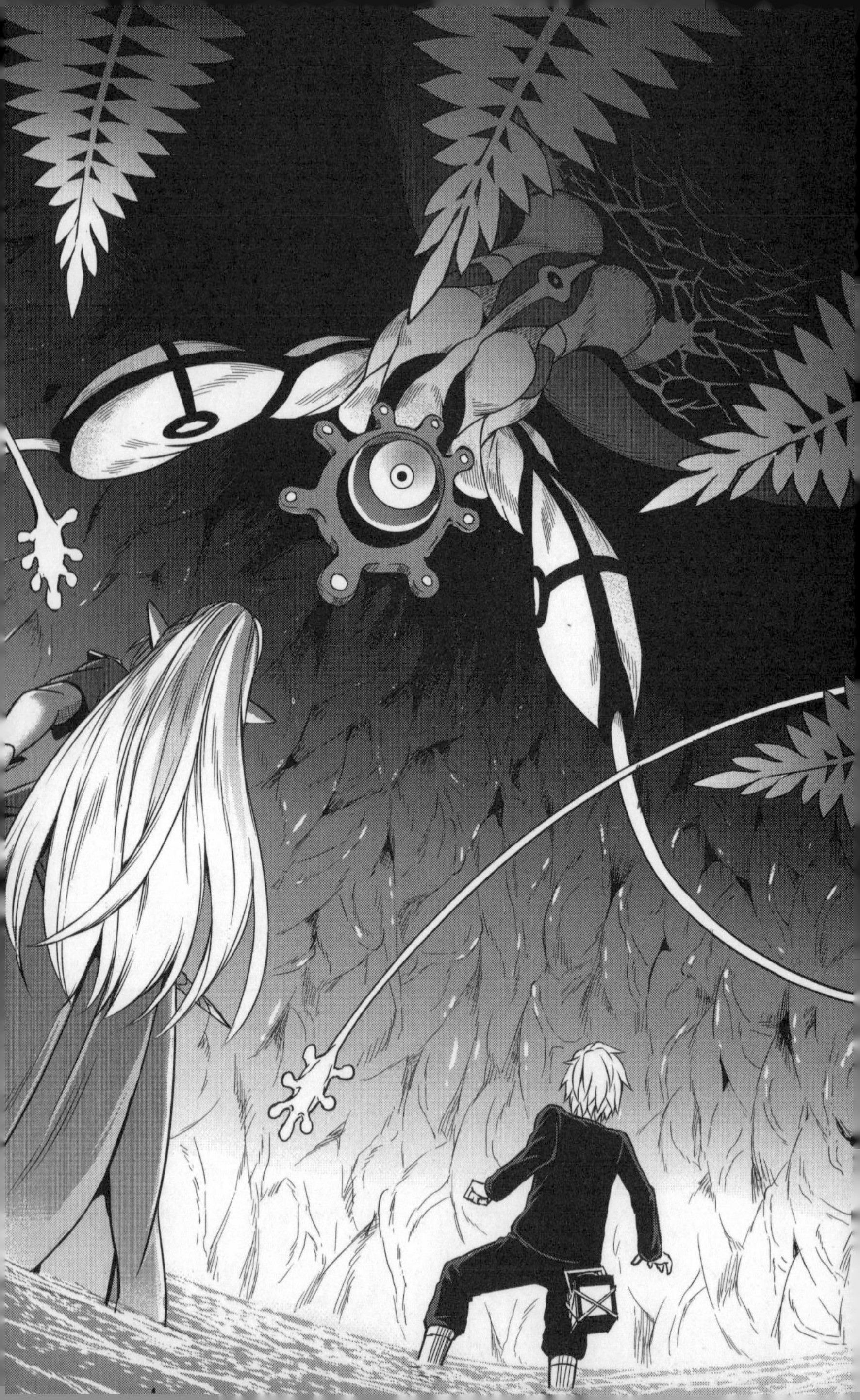

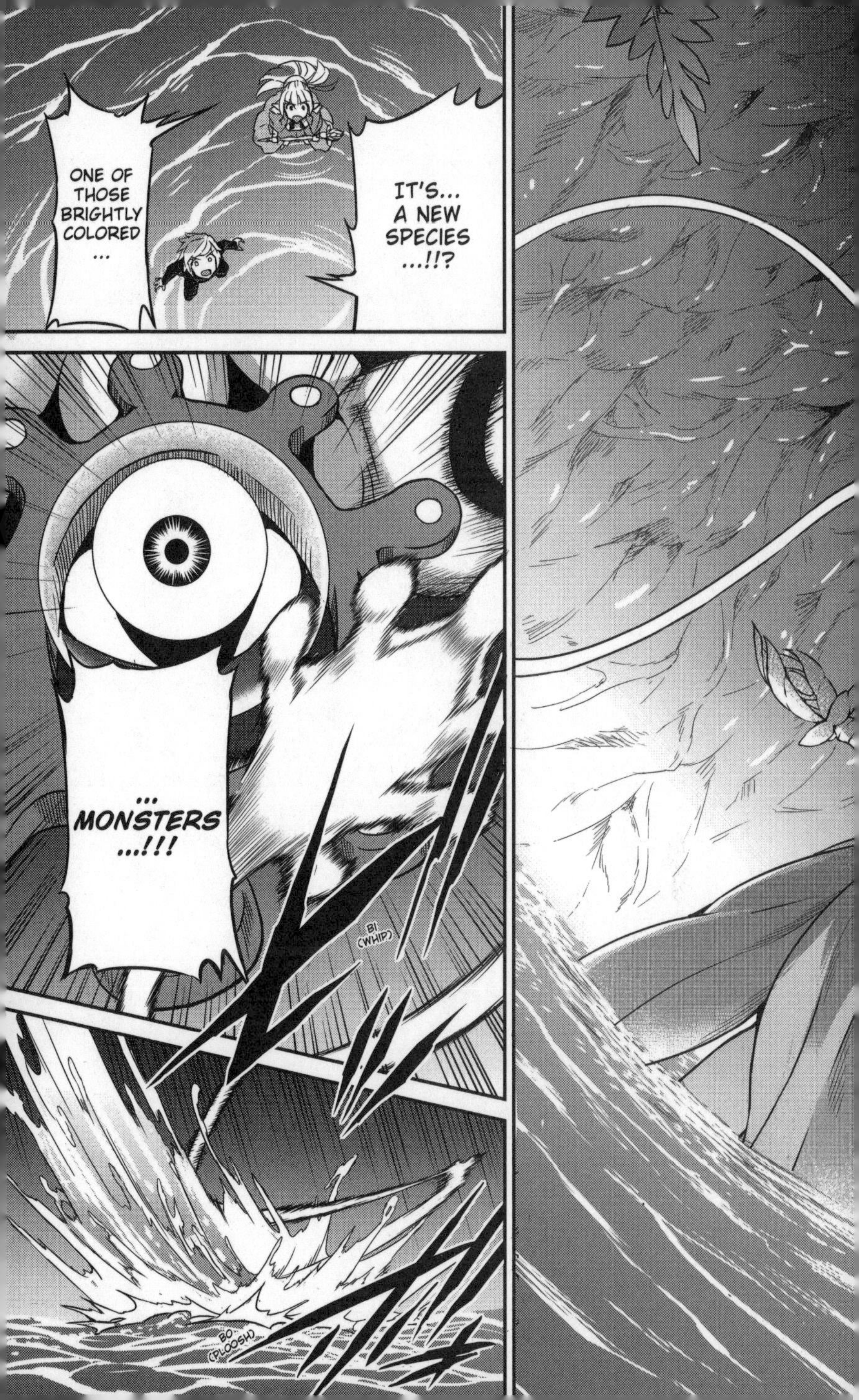
IT'S... A NEW SPECIES ...!!?
ONE OF THOSE BRIGHTLY COLORED ...
... MONSTERS ...!!!
BI (WHIP)
BO (PLOOSH)

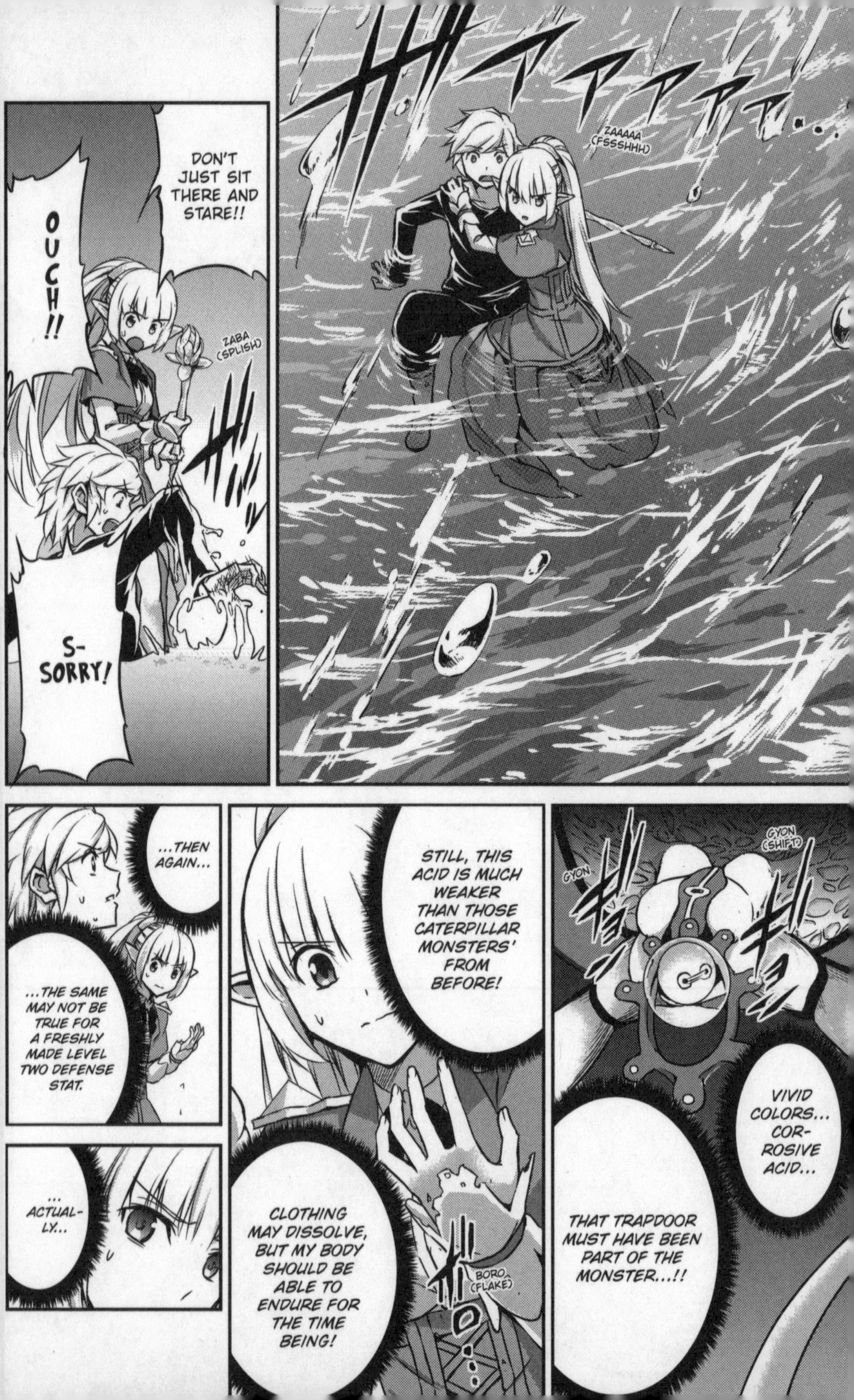
ZAAAAA (FSSSHHH)
DON'T JUST SIT THERE AND STARE!!
OUCH!!
ZABA (SPLISH)
S-SORRY!
GYON (SHIFT)
GYON
VIVID COLORS... COR-ROSIVE ACID...
THAT TRAPDOOR MUST HAVE BEEN PART OF THE MONSTER...!!
STILL, THIS ACID IS MUCH WEAKER THAN THOSE CATERPILLAR MONSTERS' FROM BEFORE!
CLOTHING MAY DISSOLVE, BUT MY BODY SHOULD BE ABLE TO ENDURE FOR THE TIME BEING!
BORO (FLAKE)
...THEN AGAIN...
...THE SAME MAY NOT BE TRUE FOR A FRESHLY MADE LEVEL TWO DEFENSE STAT.
... ACTUAL-LY...

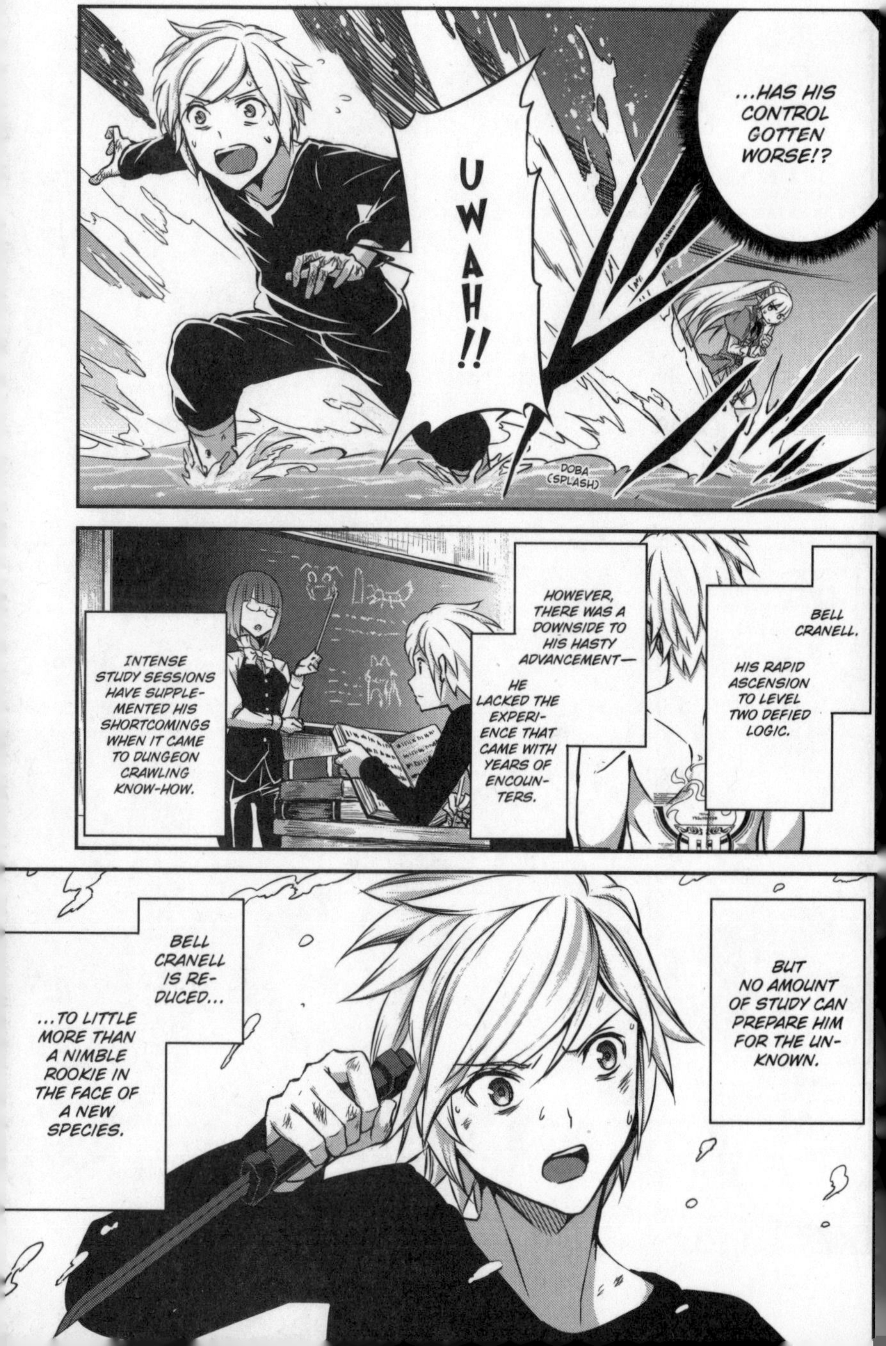
...HAS HIS CONTROL GOTTEN WORSE!?
UWAH!!
DOBA (SPLASH)
BELL CRANELL.
HIS RAPID ASCENSION TO LEVEL TWO DEFIED LOGIC.
HOWEVER, THERE WAS A DOWNSIDE TO HIS HASTY ADVANCEMENT—
HE LACKED THE EXPERIENCE THAT CAME WITH YEARS OF ENCOUNTERS.
INTENSE STUDY SESSIONS HAVE SUPPLEMENTED HIS SHORTCOMINGS WHEN IT CAME TO DUNGEON CRAWLING KNOW-HOW.
BUT NO AMOUNT OF STUDY CAN PREPARE HIM FOR THE UNKNOWN.
BELL CRANELL IS REDUCED...
...TO LITTLE MORE THAN A NIMBLE ROOKIE IN THE FACE OF A NEW SPECIES.

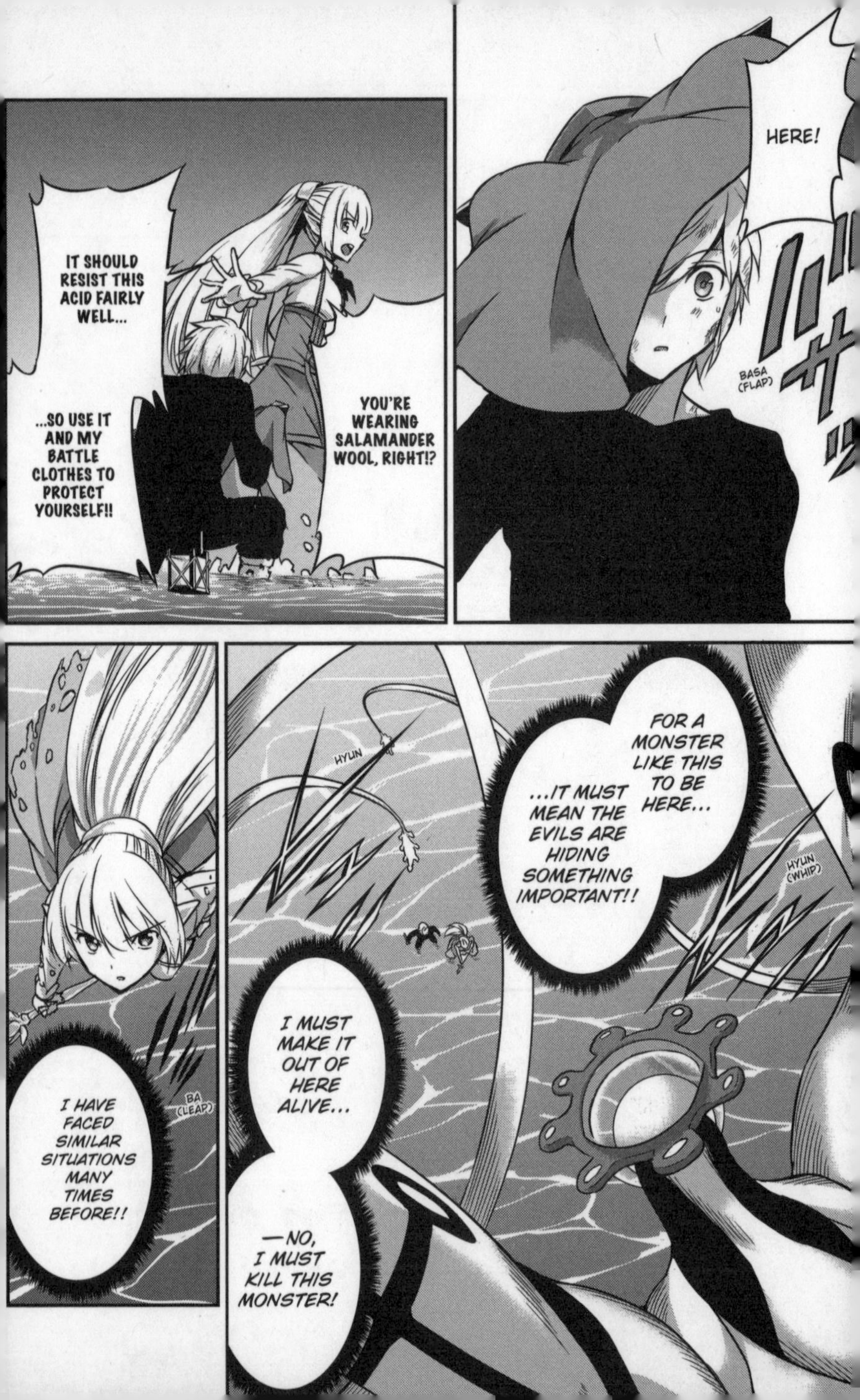
HERE!
BASA (FLAP)
YOU'RE WEARING SALAMANDER WOOL, RIGHT!?
IT SHOULD RESIST THIS ACID FAIRLY WELL...
...SO USE IT AND MY BATTLE CLOTHES TO PROTECT YOURSELF!!
FOR A MONSTER LIKE THIS TO BE HERE...
...IT MUST MEAN THE EVILS ARE HIDING SOMETHING IMPORTANT!!
HYUN (WHIP)
HYUN
I MUST MAKE IT OUT OF HERE ALIVE...
—NO, I MUST KILL THIS MONSTER!
BA (LEAP)
I HAVE FACED SIMILAR SITUATIONS MANY TIMES BEFORE!!

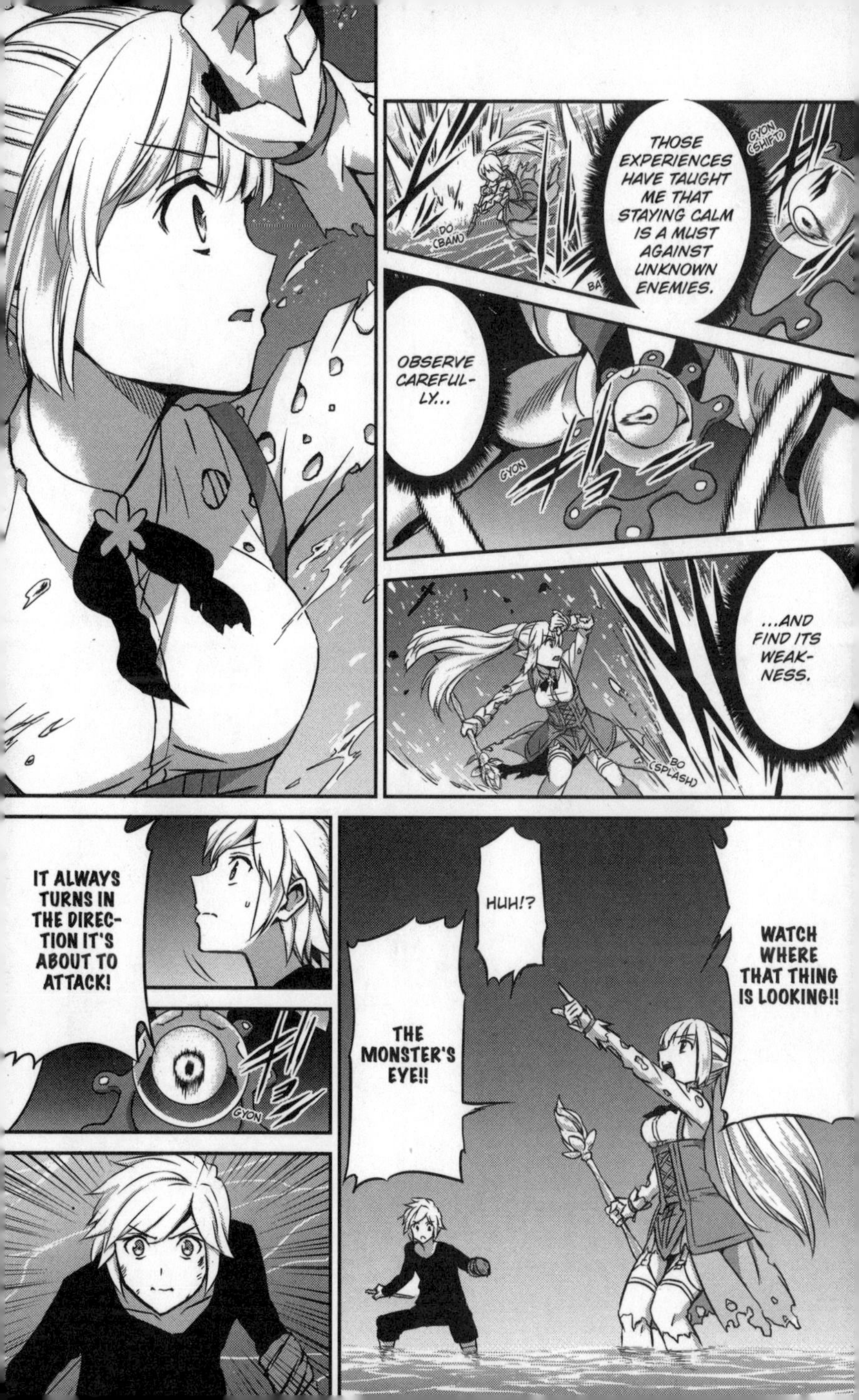
THOSE EXPERIENCES HAVE TAUGHT ME THAT STAYING CALM IS A MUST AGAINST UNKNOWN ENEMIES.
GYON (SHIFT)
DO (BAM)
BA
OBSERVE CAREFUL-LY...
GYON
...AND FIND ITS WEAK-NESS.
BO (SPLASH)
WATCH WHERE THAT THING IS LOOKING!!
HUH!?
THE MONSTER'S EYE!!
IT ALWAYS TURNS IN THE DIREC-TION IT'S ABOUT TO ATTACK!
GYON

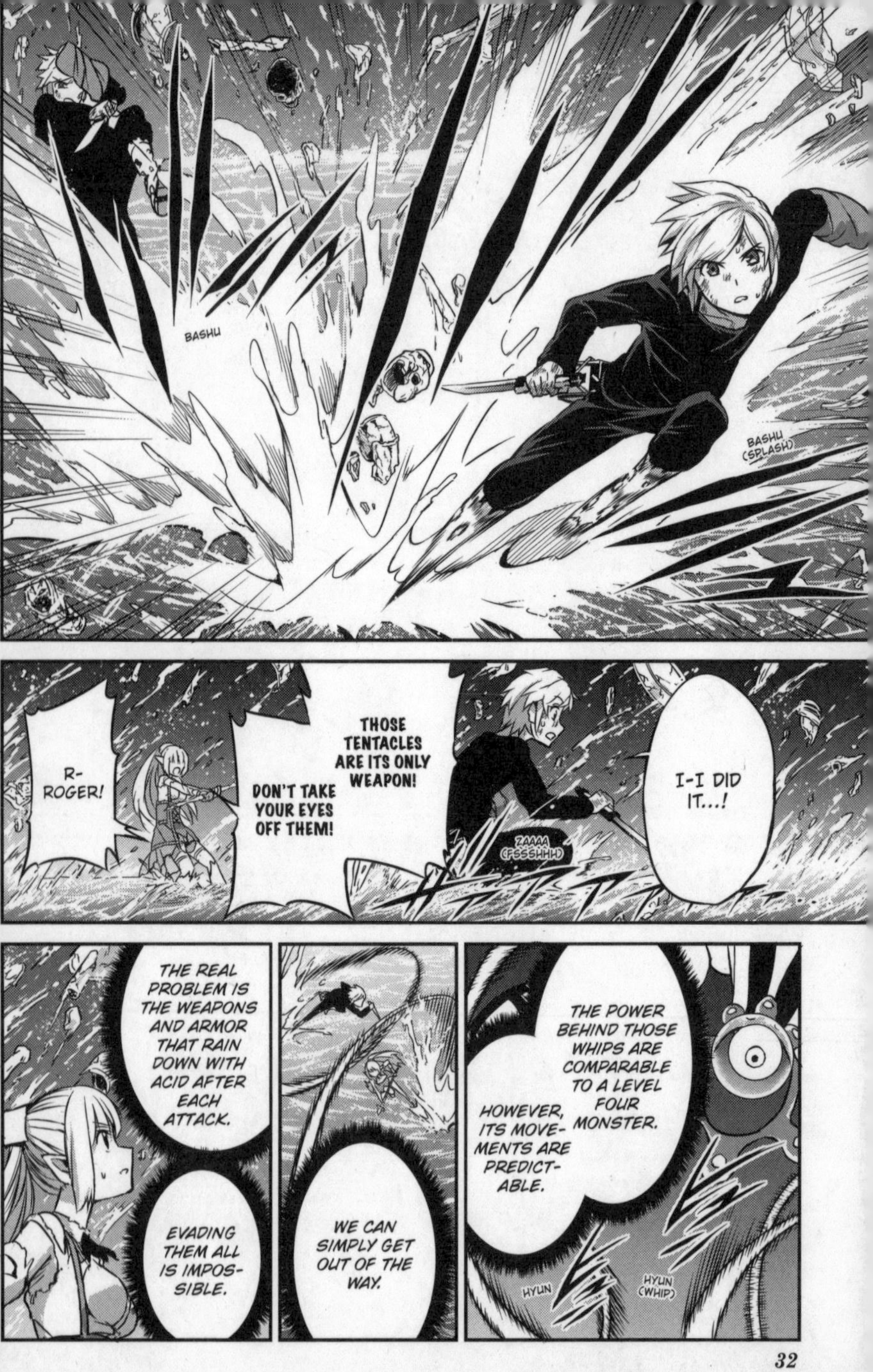
BASHU (SPLASH)
BASHU
I-I DID IT...!
ZAAAA (FSSSHHH)
THOSE TENTACLES ARE ITS ONLY WEAPON!
DON'T TAKE YOUR EYES OFF THEM!
R-ROGER!
THE POWER BEHIND THOSE WHIPS ARE COMPARABLE TO A LEVEL FOUR MONSTER.
HOWEVER, ITS MOVEMENTS ARE PREDICTABLE.
HYUN (WHIP)
HYUN
WE CAN SIMPLY GET OUT OF THE WAY.
THE REAL PROBLEM IS THE WEAPONS AND ARMOR THAT RAIN DOWN WITH ACID AFTER EACH ATTACK.
EVADING THEM ALL IS IMPOSSIBLE.

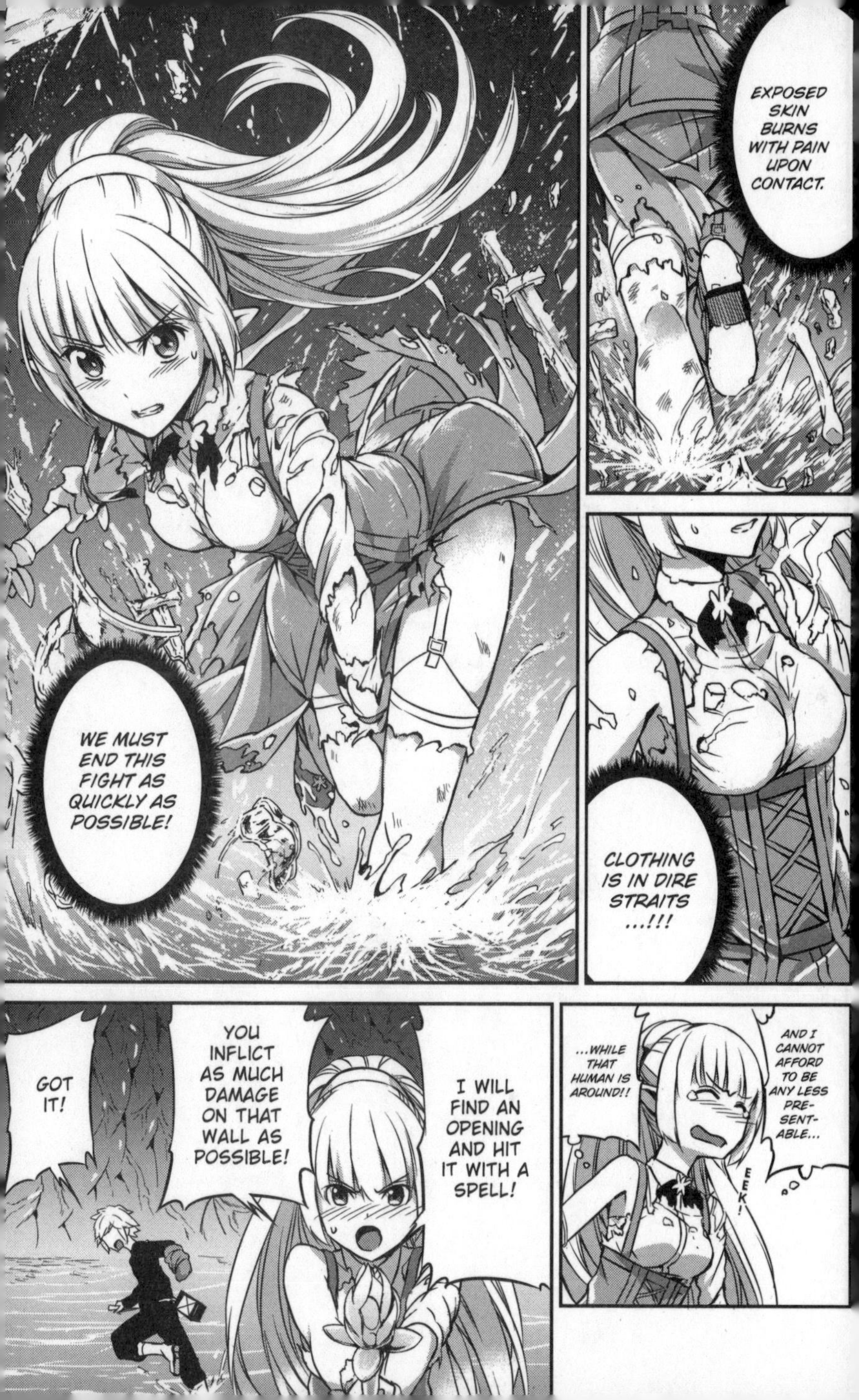
EXPOSED SKIN BURNS WITH PAIN UPON CONTACT.
CLOTHING IS IN DIRE STRAITS ...!!!
WE MUST END THIS FIGHT AS QUICKLY AS POSSIBLE!
AND I CANNOT AFFORD TO BE ANY LESS PRE-SENT-ABLE...
...WHILE THAT HUMAN IS AROUND!!
EEEK!
YOU INFLICT AS MUCH DAMAGE ON THAT WALL AS POSSIBLE!
I WILL FIND AN OPENING AND HIT IT WITH A SPELL!
GOT IT!

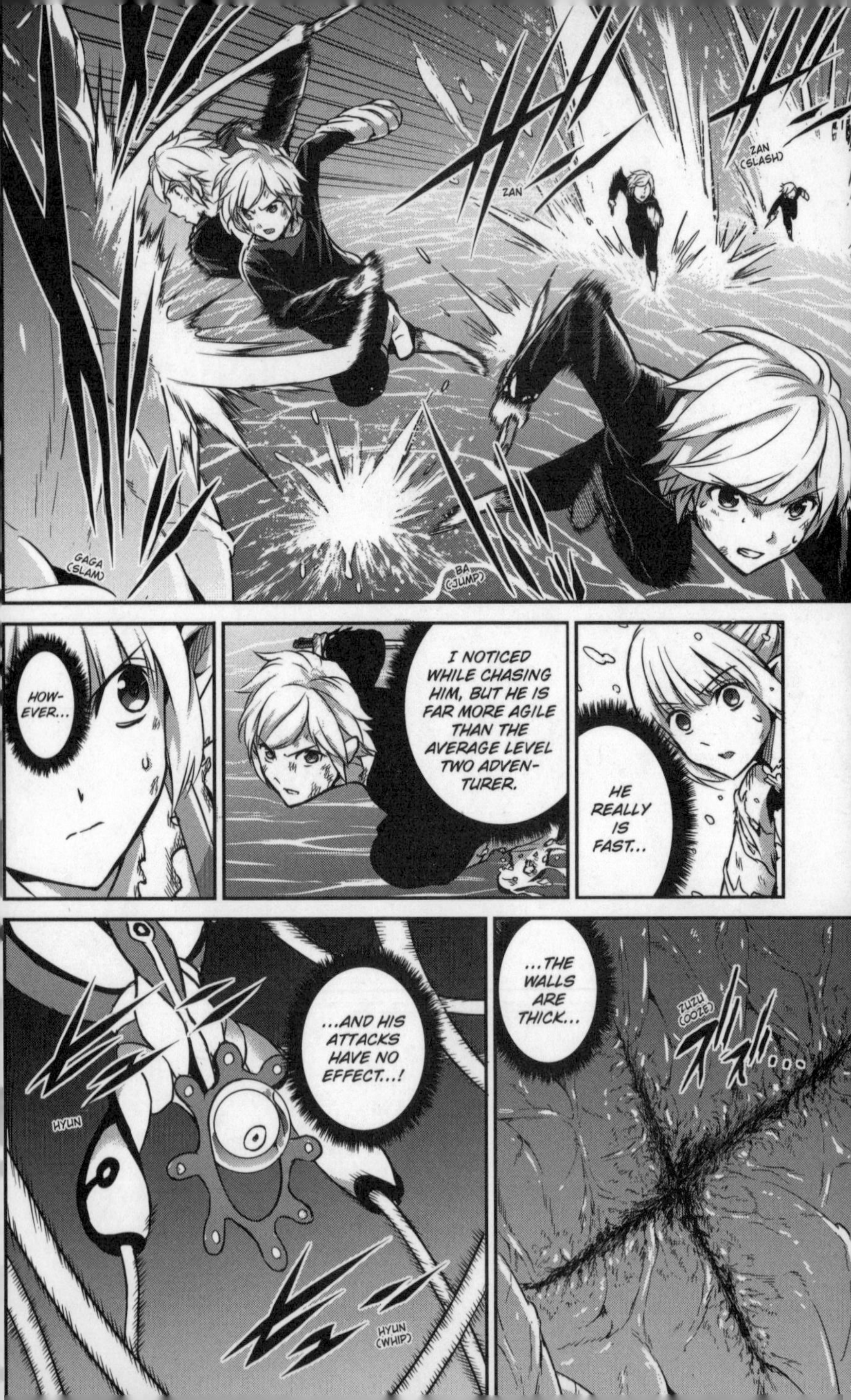
ZAN (SLASH)
ZAN
BA (JUMP)
GAGA (SLAM)
HE REALLY IS FAST...
I NOTICED WHILE CHASING HIM, BUT HE IS FAR MORE AGILE THAN THE AVERAGE LEVEL TWO ADVEN-TURER.
HOW-EVER...
...THE WALLS ARE THICK...
ZUZU (OOZE)
...AND HIS ATTACKS HAVE NO EFFECT...!
HYUN
HYUN (WHIP)

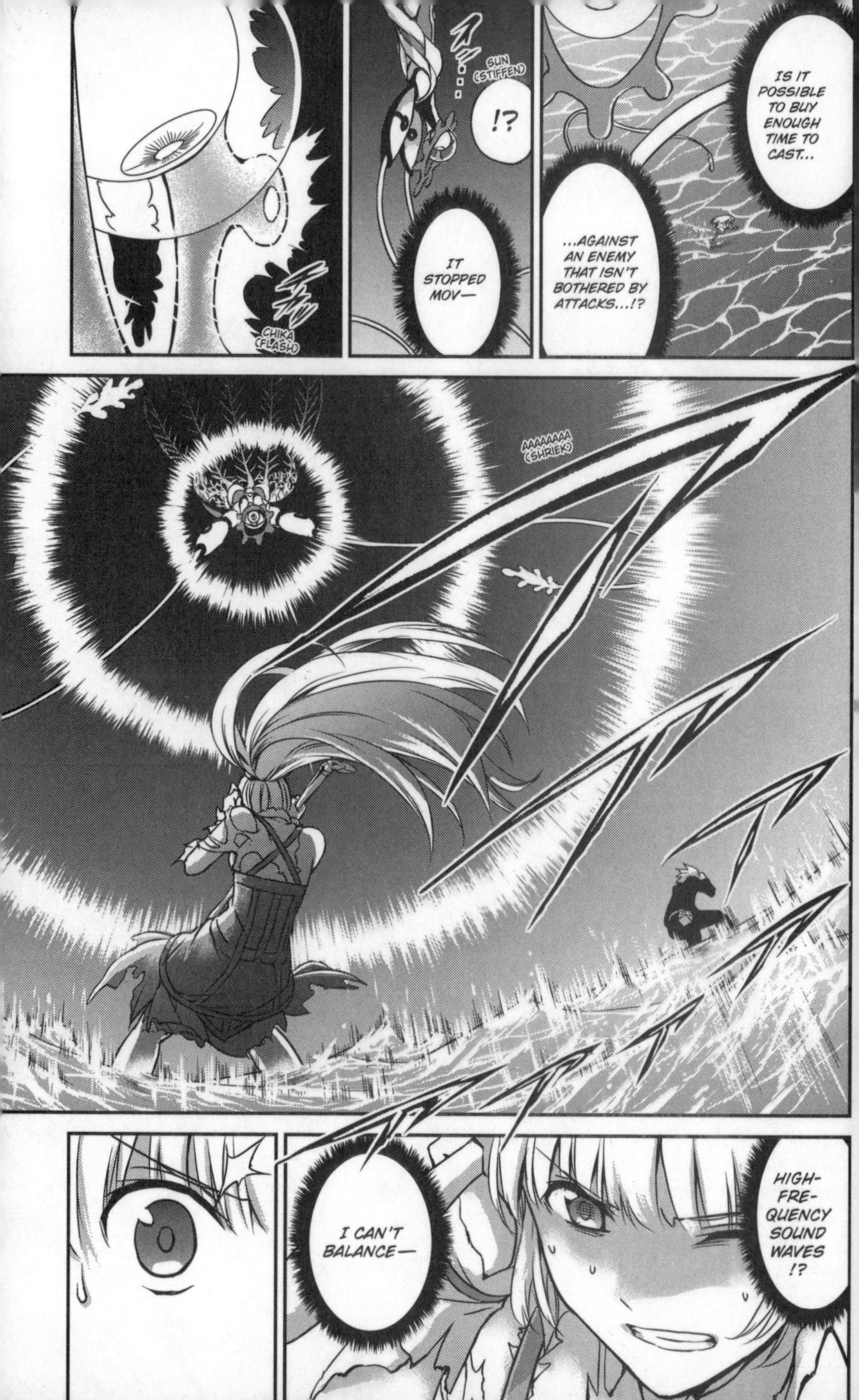
IS IT POSSIBLE TO BUY ENOUGH TIME TO CAST...
...AGAINST AN ENEMY THAT ISN'T BOTHERED BY ATTACKS...!?
SUN (STIFFEN)
!?
IT STOPPED MOV—
CHIKA (FLASH)
AAAAAAAA (SHRIEK)
HIGH-FRE-QUENCY SOUND WAVES !?
I CAN'T BALANCE—

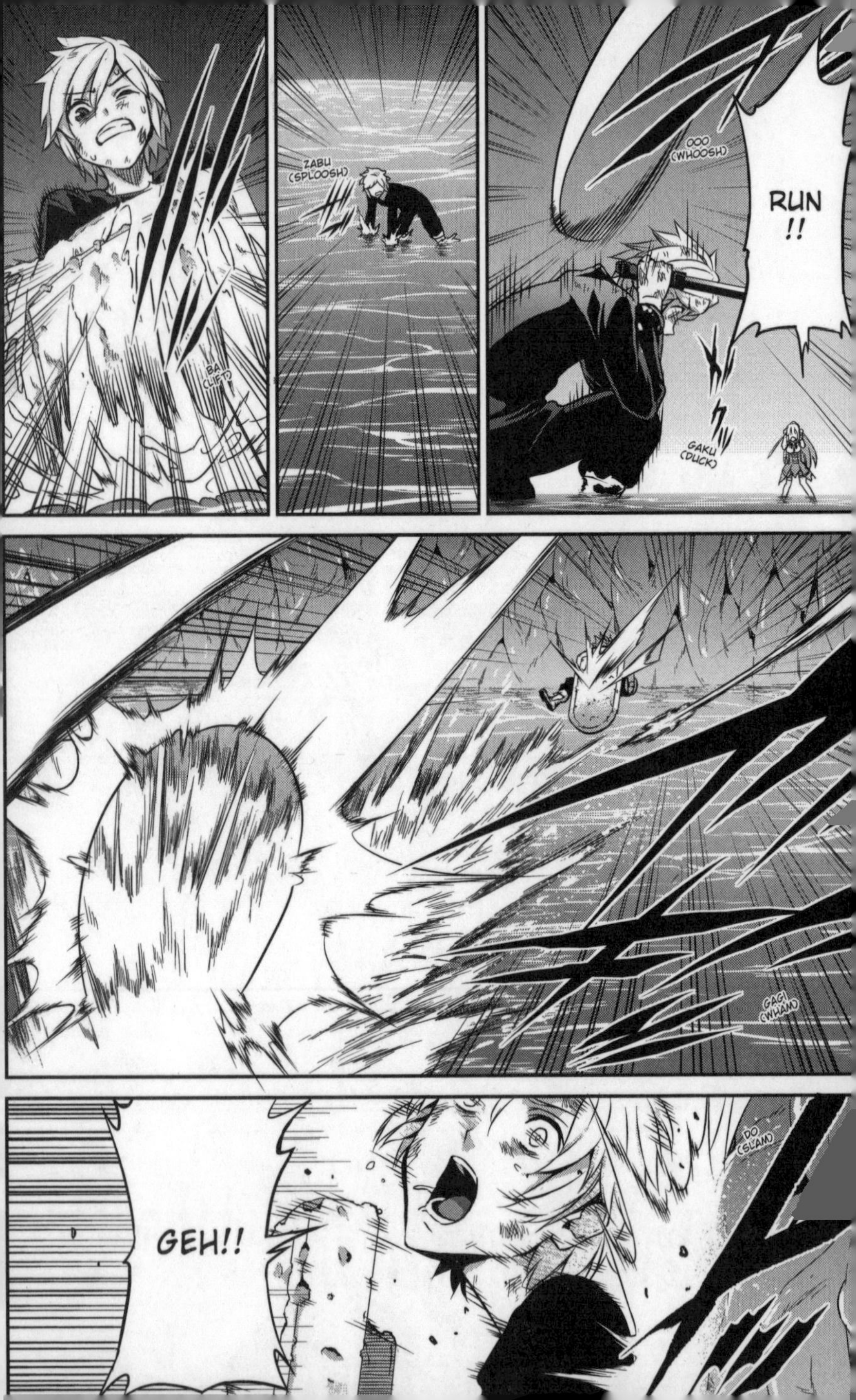
RUN!!
OOO (WHOOSH)
GAKU (DUCK)
ZABU (SPLOOSH)
BA (LIFT)
GAGI (WHAM)
DO (SLAM)
GEH!!

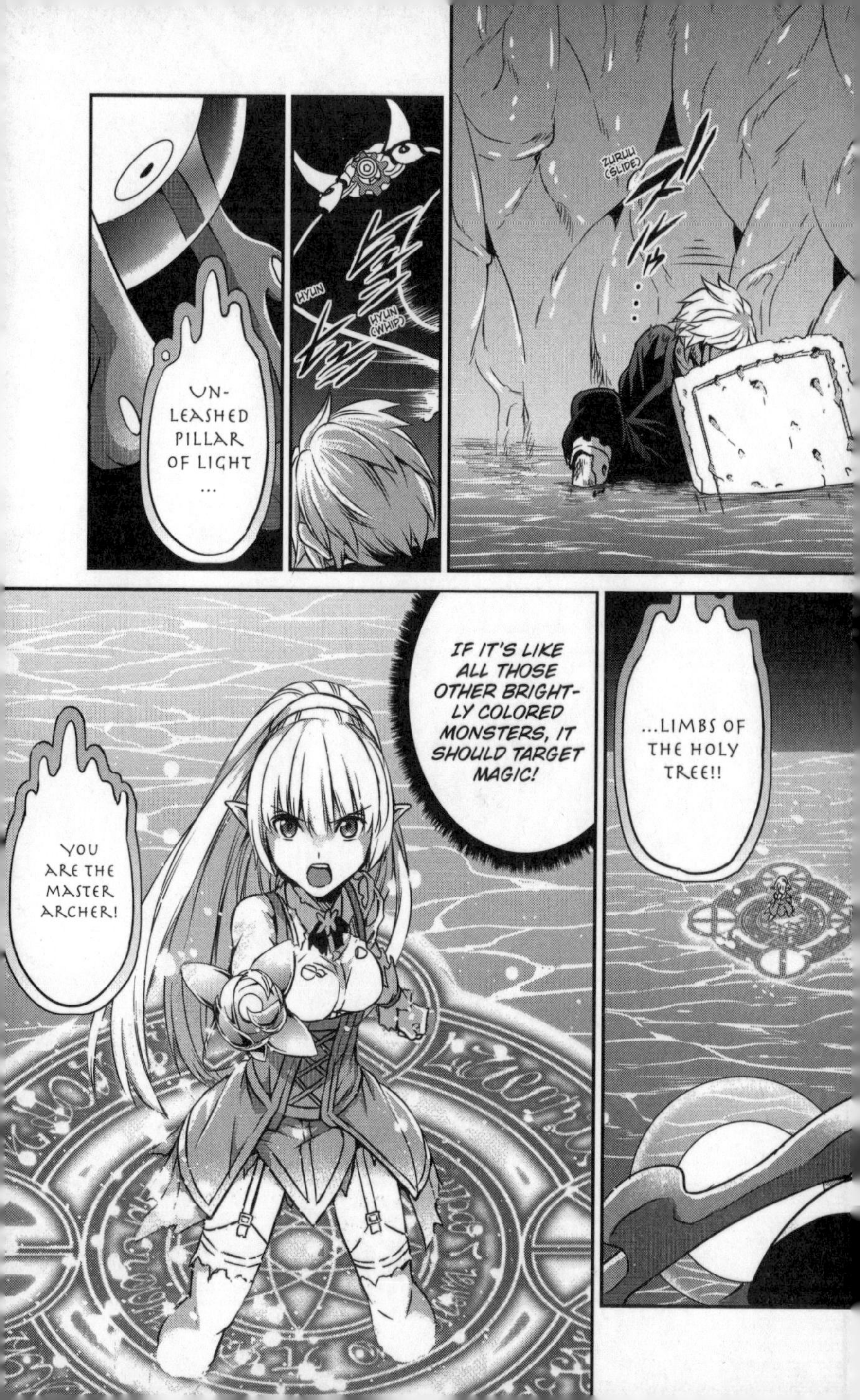
ZURUU (SLIDE)
HYUN (WHIP)
HYUN
UN-LEASHED PILLAR OF LIGHT...
...LIMBS OF THE HOLY TREE!!
IF IT'S LIKE ALL THOSE OTHER BRIGHTLY COLORED MONSTERS, IT SHOULD TARGET MAGIC!
YOU ARE THE MASTER ARCHER!

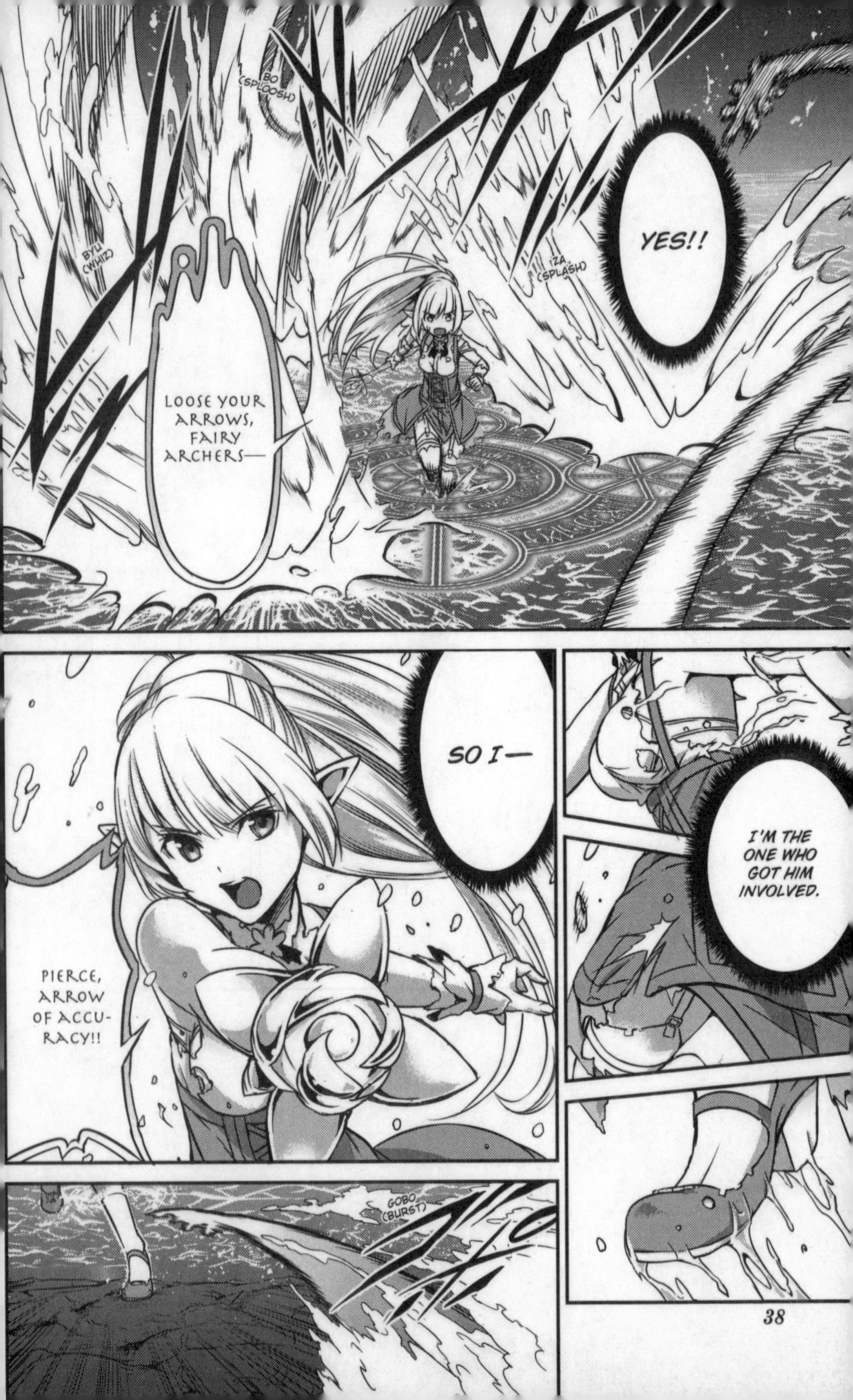
YES!!
BO (SPLOOSH)
IZA (SPLASH)
LOOSE YOUR ARROWS, FAIRY ARCHERS—
BYU (WHIZ)
I'M THE ONE WHO GOT HIM INVOLVED.
SO I—
PIERCE, ARROW OF ACCU-RACY!!
GOBO (BURST)

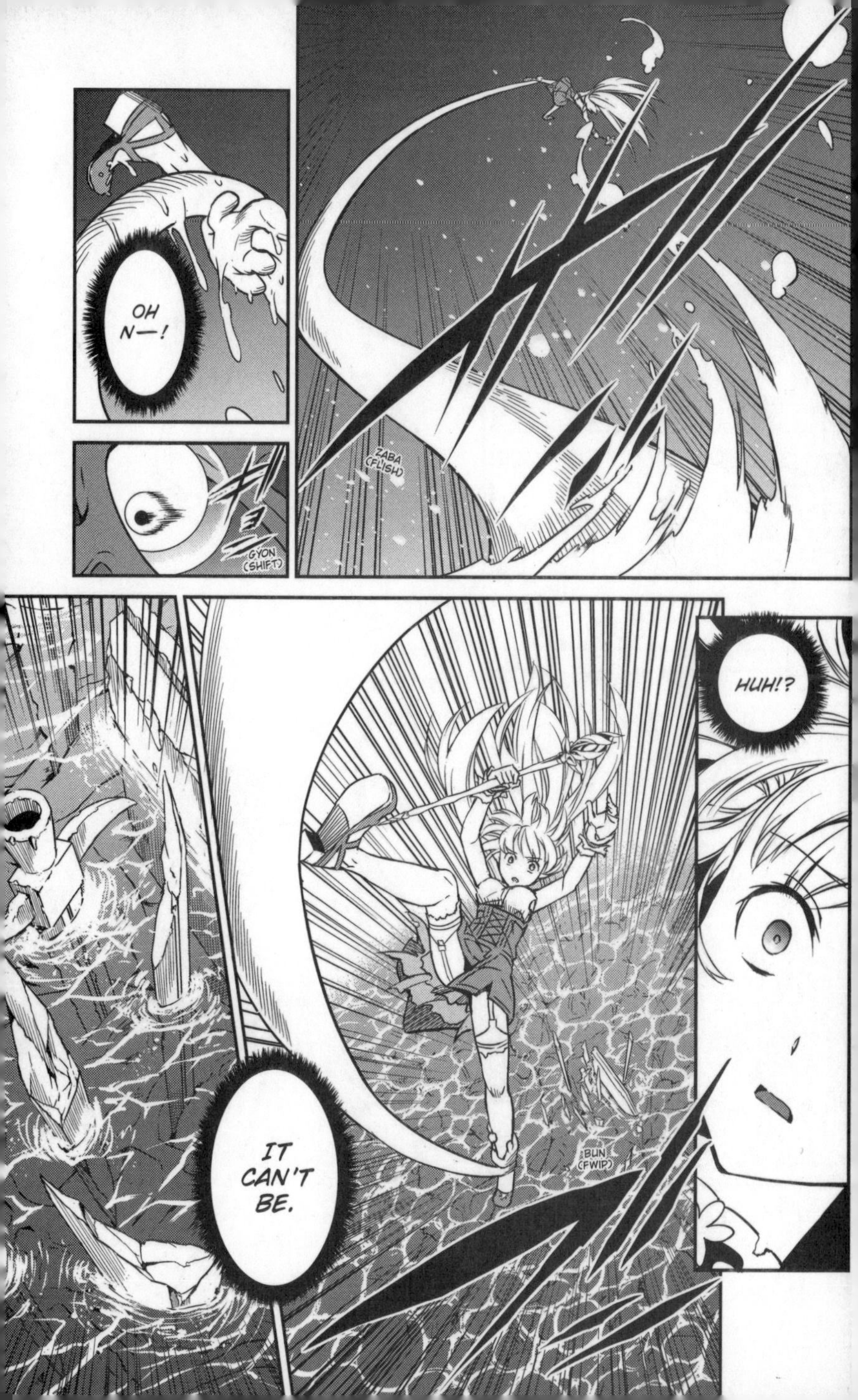
ZABA (FLISH)
OH N—!
GYON (SHIFT)
HUH!?
BUN (FWIP)
IT CAN'T BE.

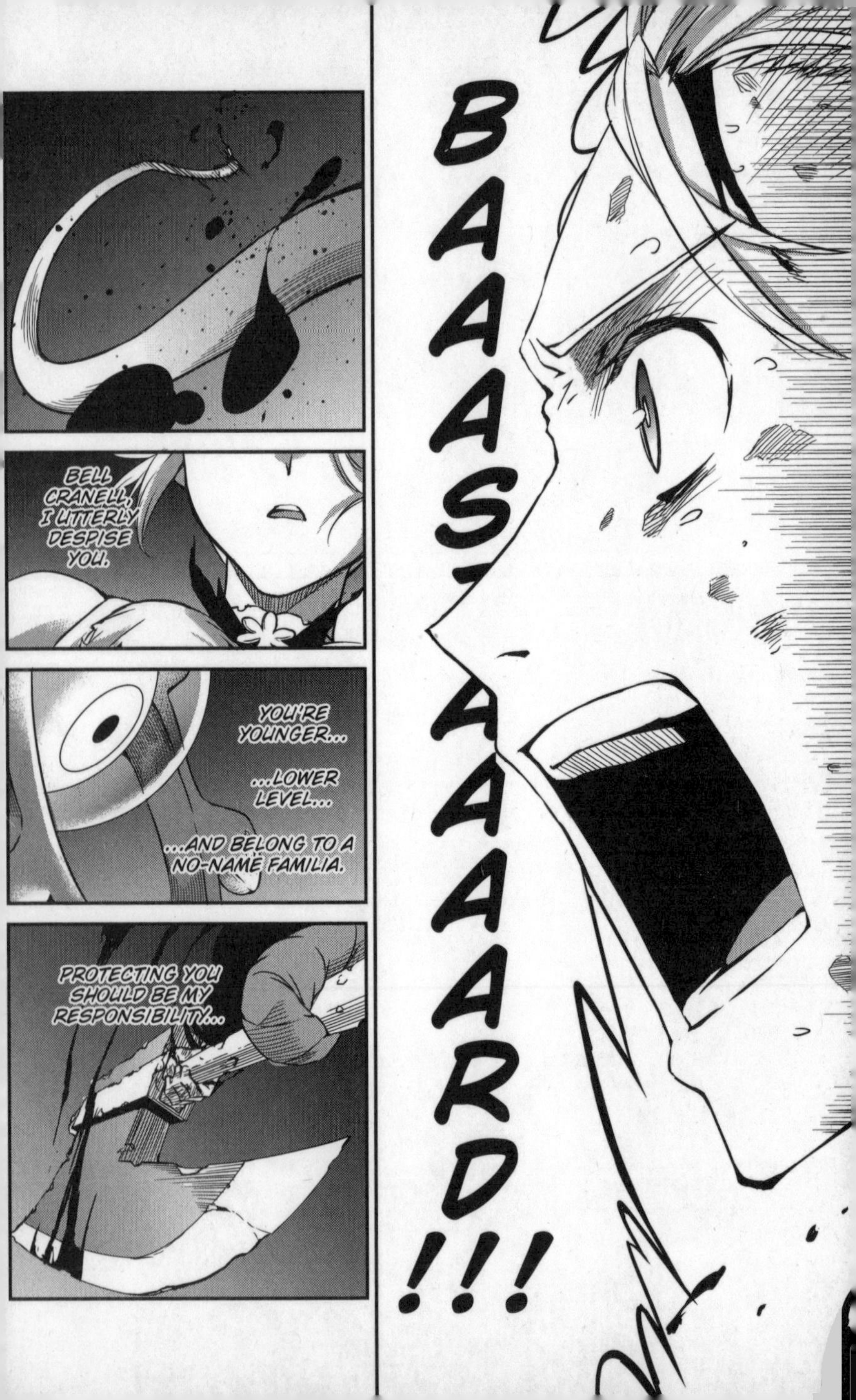
BAAASTAAAARD!!!
BELL CRANELL, I UTTERLY DESPISE YOU.
YOU'RE YOUNGER...
...LOWER LEVEL...
...AND BELONG TO A NO-NAME FAMILIA.
PROTECTING YOU SHOULD BE MY RESPONSIBILITY...

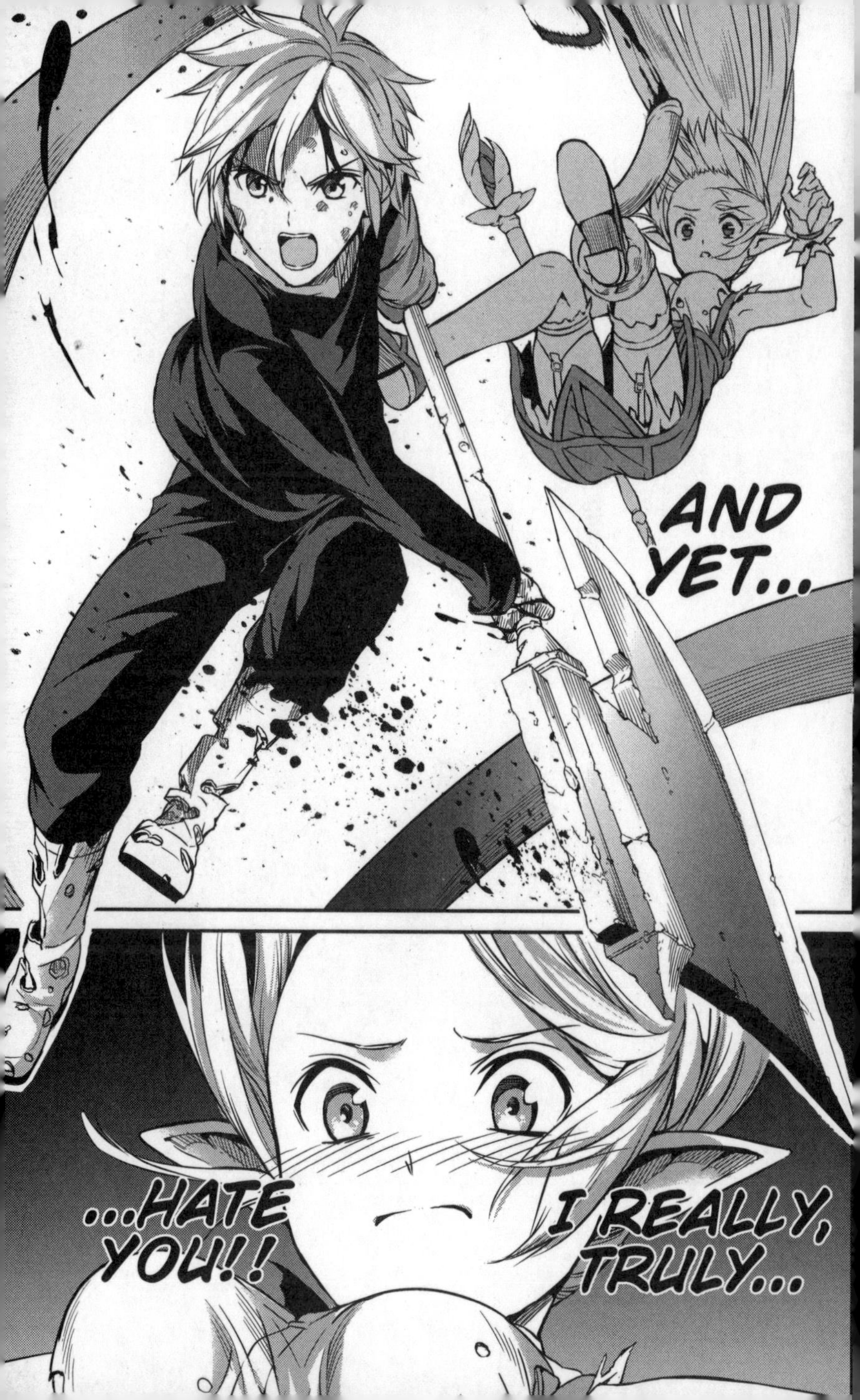
AND YET...
I REALLY, TRULY...
...HATE YOU!!

IS IT WRONG TO TRY TO PICK UP GIRLS IN A DUNGEON? ON THE SIDE

Sword Oratoria

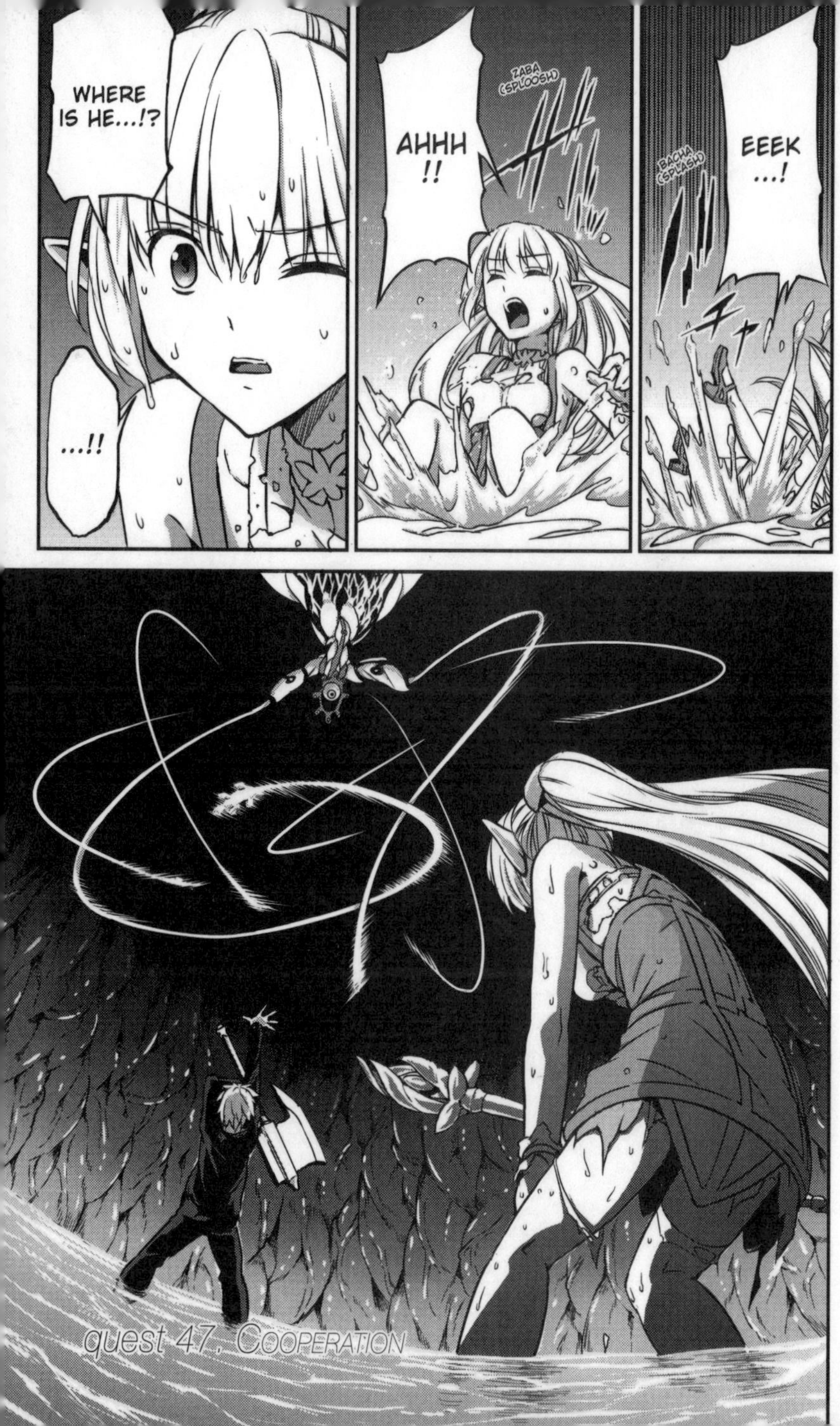
BACHA (SPLASH)
EEEK ...!
ZABA (SPLOOSH)
AHHH !!
WHERE IS HE...!?
...!!
quest 47. Cooperation

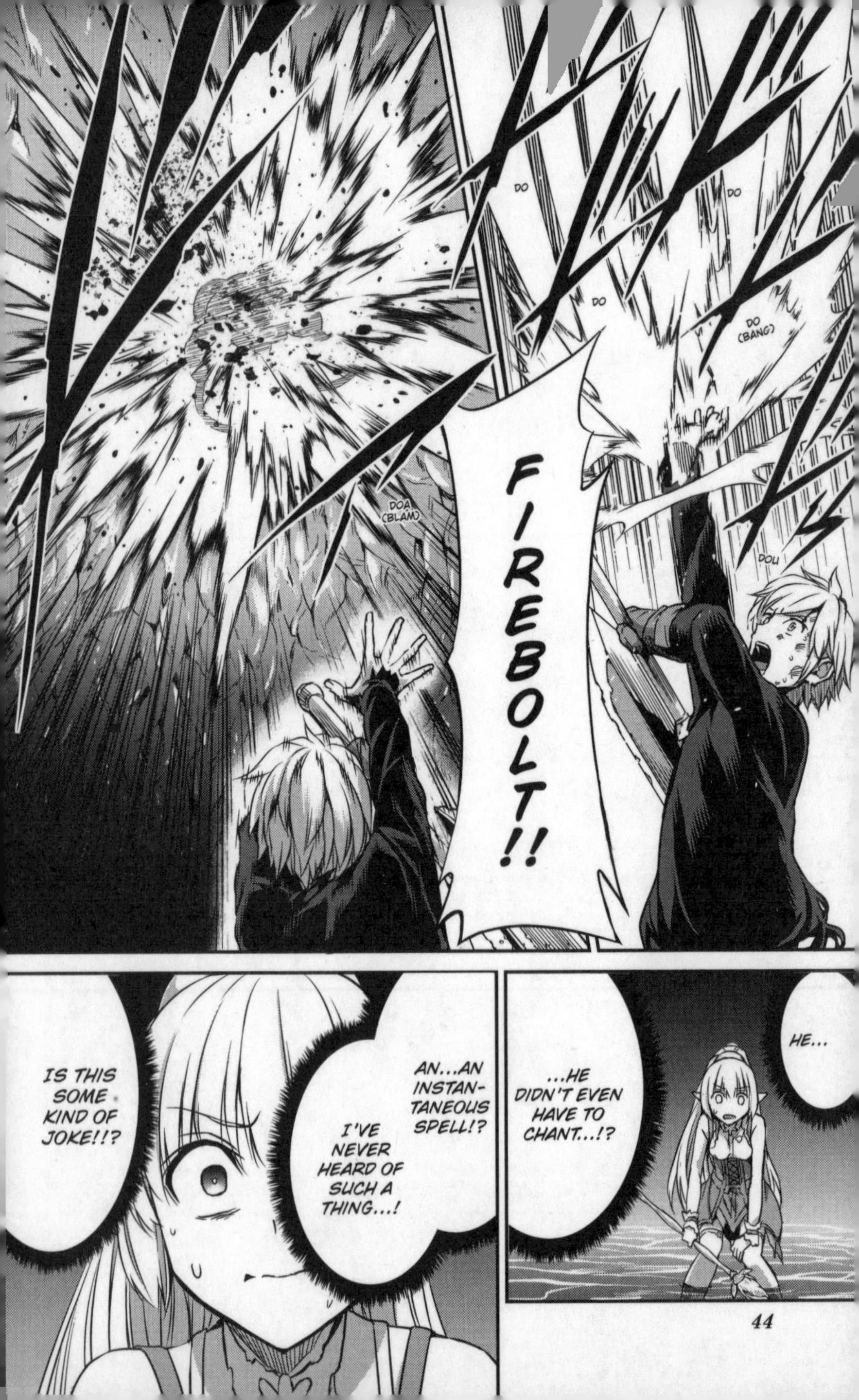
DO
DO
DO (BANG)
DO
FIREBOLT!!
DOU
DOA (BLAM)
HE...
...HE DIDN'T EVEN HAVE TO CHANT...!?
AN...AN INSTAN-TANEOUS SPELL!?
I'VE NEVER HEARD OF SUCH A THING...!
IS THIS SOME KIND OF JOKE!!?

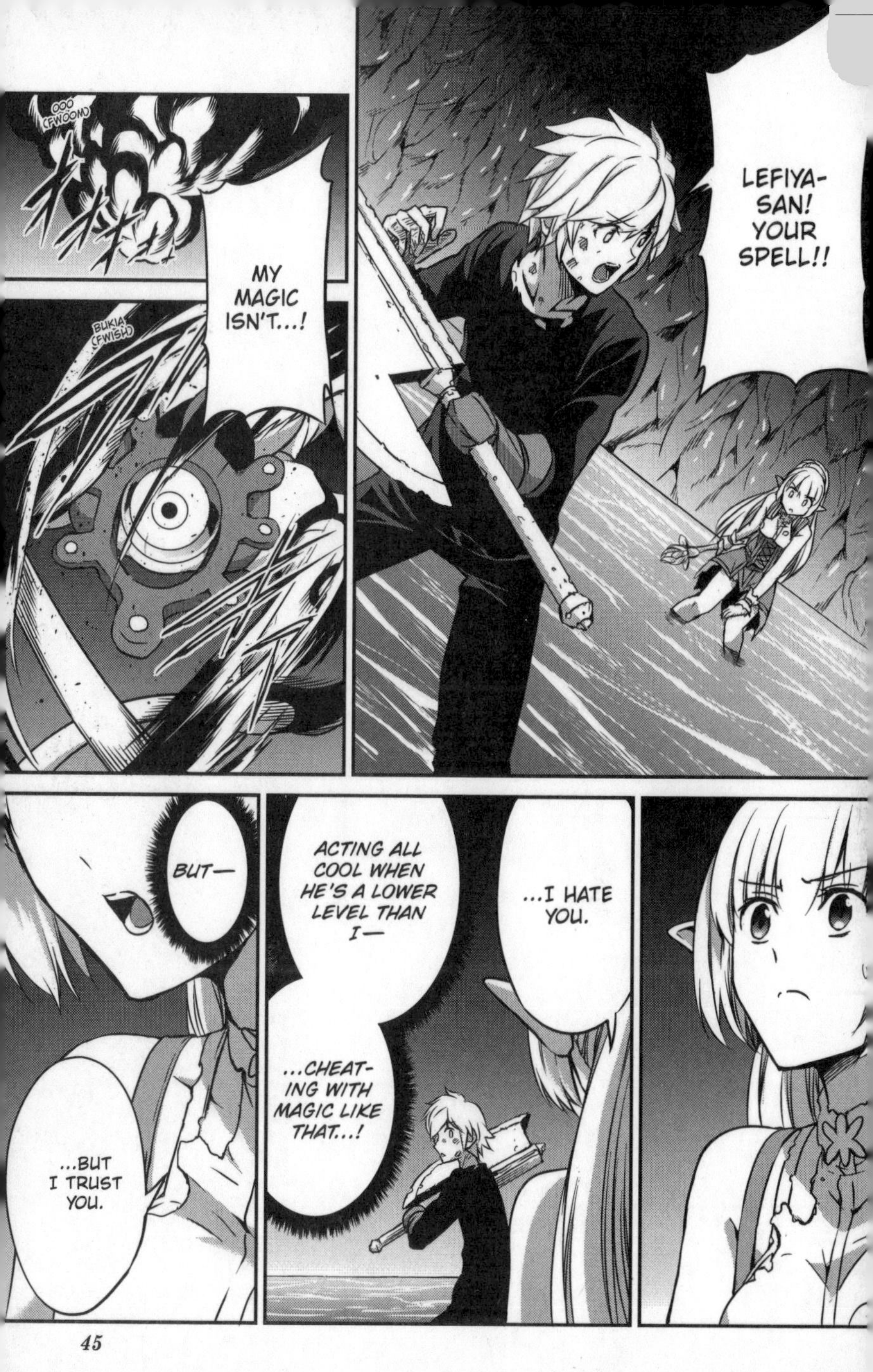
LEFIYA-SAN! YOUR SPELL!!
OOO (FWOOM)
MY MAGIC ISN'T...!
BUKIA (FWISH)
...I HATE YOU.
ACTING ALL COOL WHEN HE'S A LOWER LEVEL THAN I—
...CHEATING WITH MAGIC LIKE THAT...!
BUT—
...BUT I TRUST YOU.

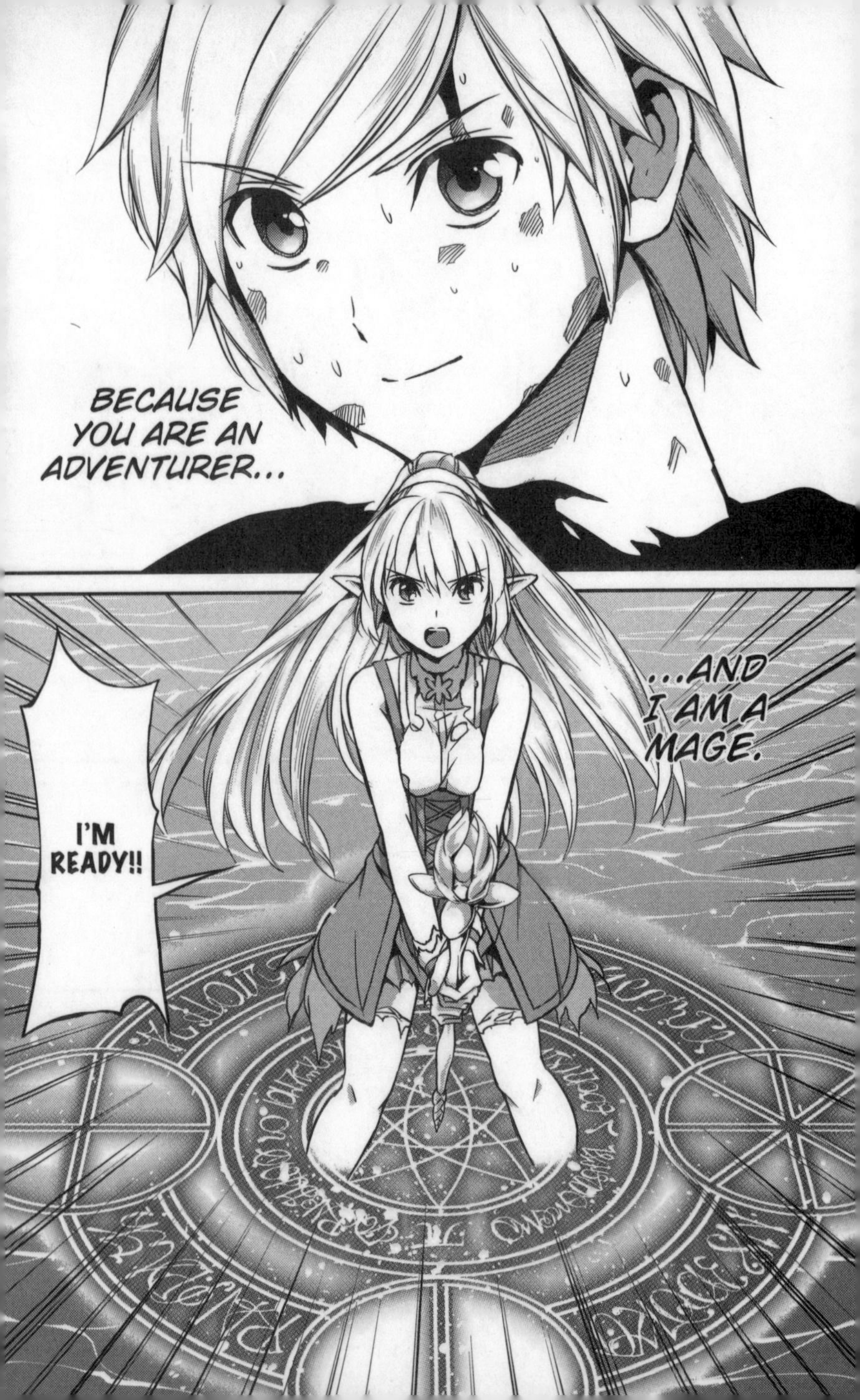
BECAUSE YOU ARE AN ADVENTURER...
...AND I AM A MAGE.
I'M READY!!

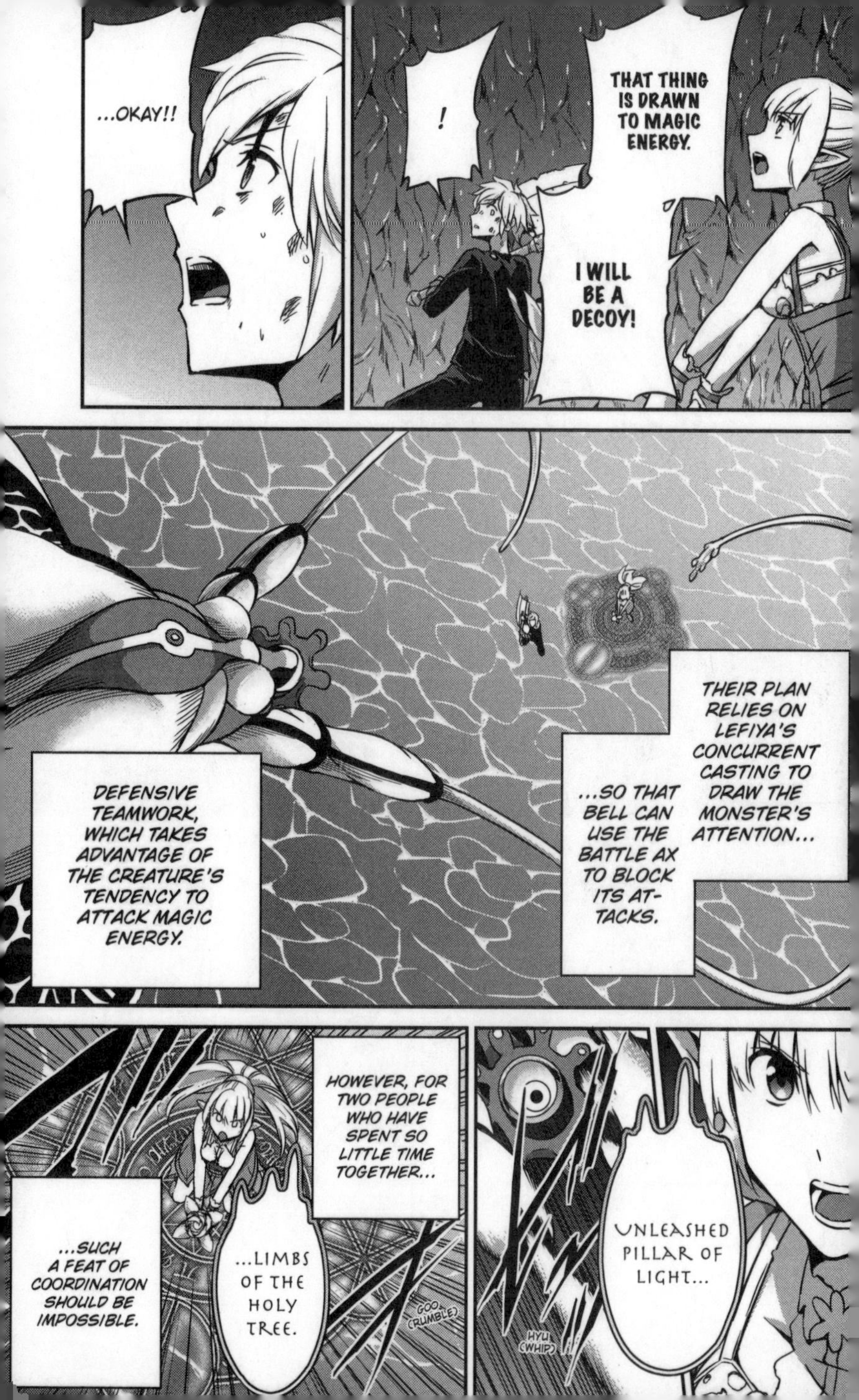
THAT THING IS DRAWN TO MAGIC ENERGY.
I WILL BE A DECOY!
!
...OKAY!!
THEIR PLAN RELIES ON LEFIYA'S CONCURRENT CASTING TO DRAW THE MONSTER'S ATTENTION...
...SO THAT BELL CAN USE THE BATTLE AX TO BLOCK ITS AT-TACKS.
DEFENSIVE TEAMWORK, WHICH TAKES ADVANTAGE OF THE CREATURE'S TENDENCY TO ATTACK MAGIC ENERGY.
UNLEASHED PILLAR OF LIGHT...
HYU (WHIP)
HOWEVER, FOR TWO PEOPLE WHO HAVE SPENT SO LITTLE TIME TOGETHER...
...LIMBS OF THE HOLY TREE.
GOO (RUMBLE)
...SUCH A FEAT OF COORDINATION SHOULD BE IMPOSSIBLE.

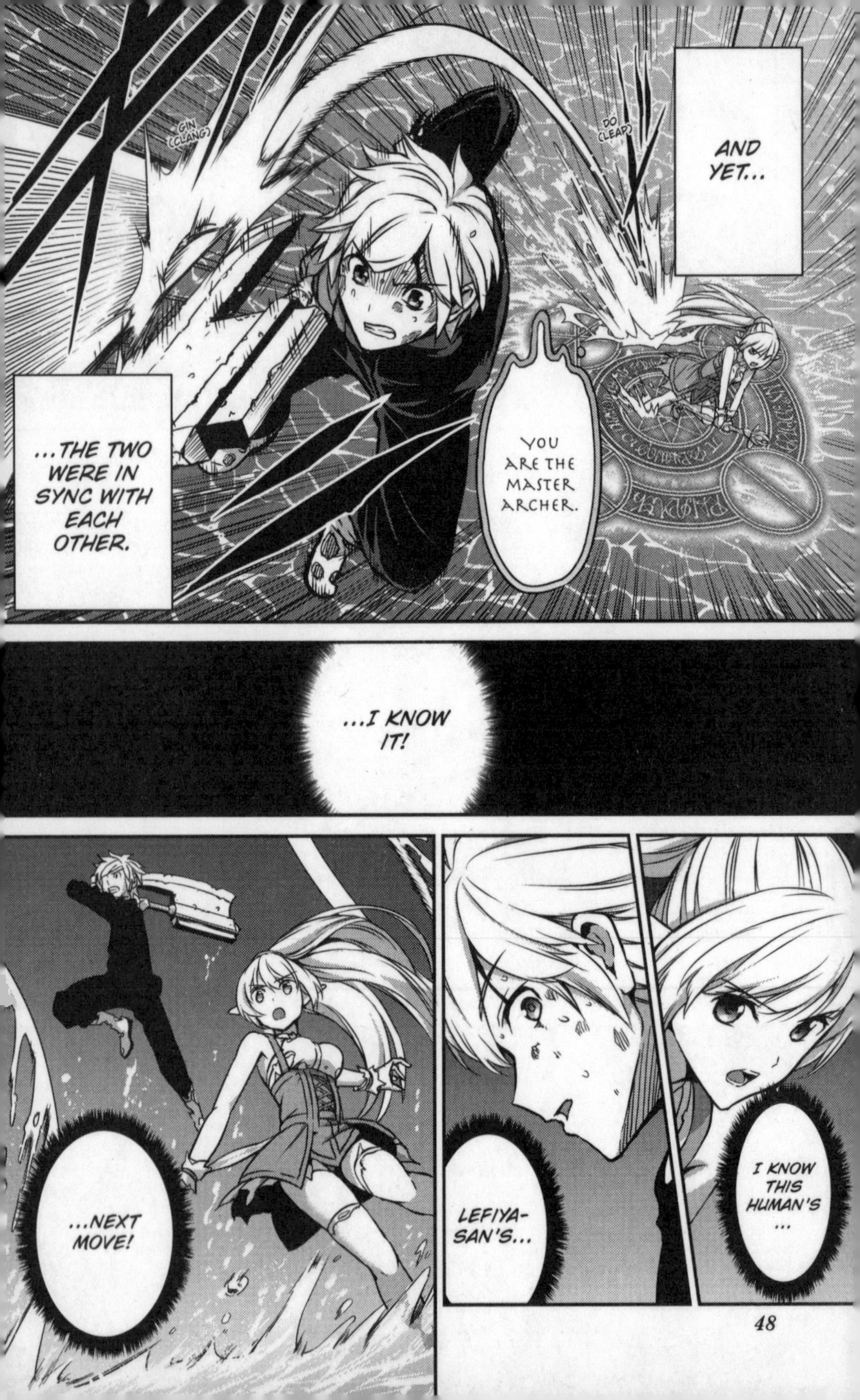
AND YET...
DO (LEAP)
YOU ARE THE MASTER ARCHER.
GIN (CLANG)
...THE TWO WERE IN SYNC WITH EACH OTHER.
...I KNOW IT!
I KNOW THIS HUMAN'S ...
LEFIYA-SAN'S...
...NEXT MOVE!

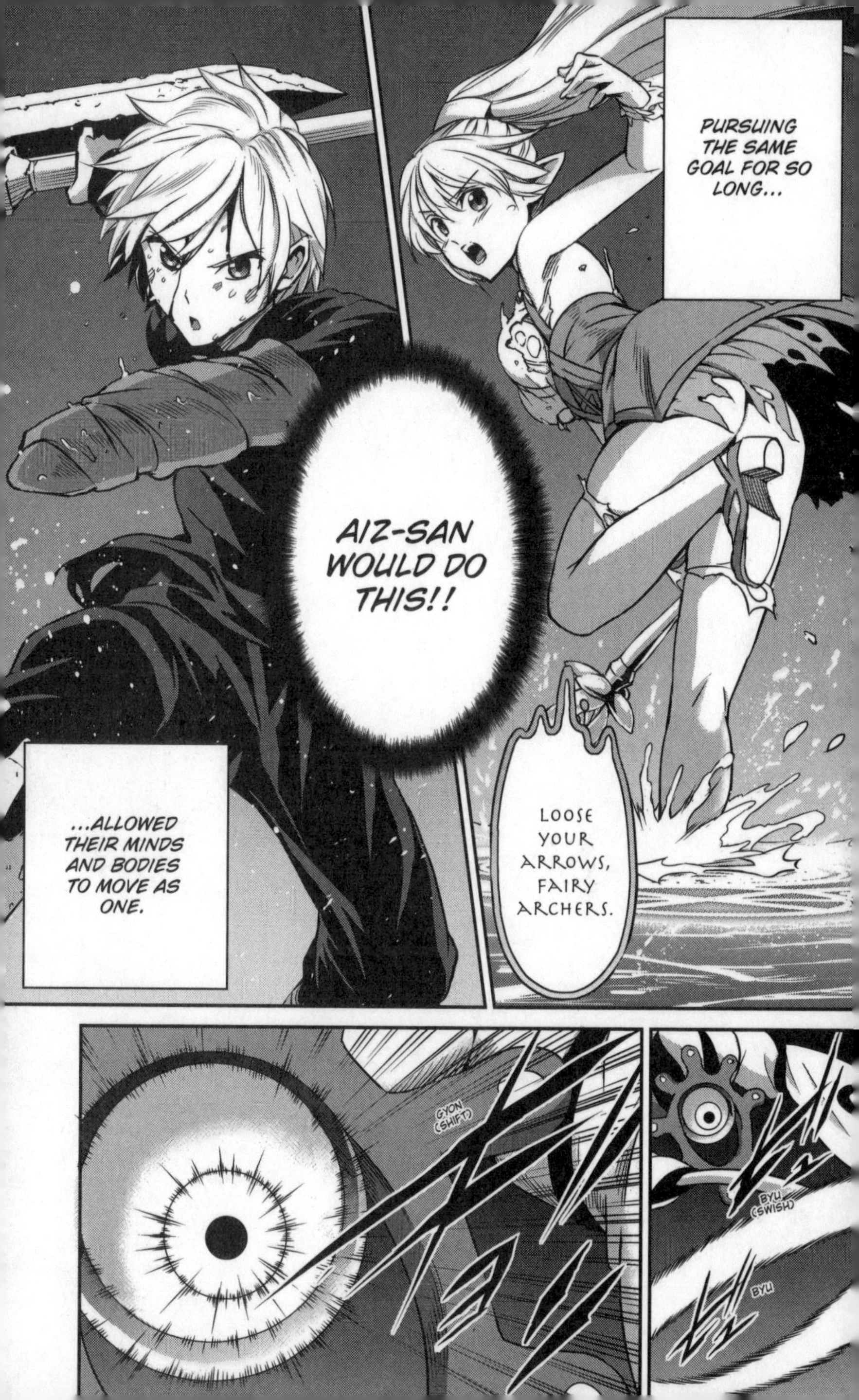
PURSUING THE SAME GOAL FOR SO LONG...
LOOSE YOUR ARROWS, FAIRY ARCHERS.
AIZ-SAN WOULD DO THIS!!
...ALLOWED THEIR MINDS AND BODIES TO MOVE AS ONE.
BYU (SWISH)
BYU
GYON (SHIFT)

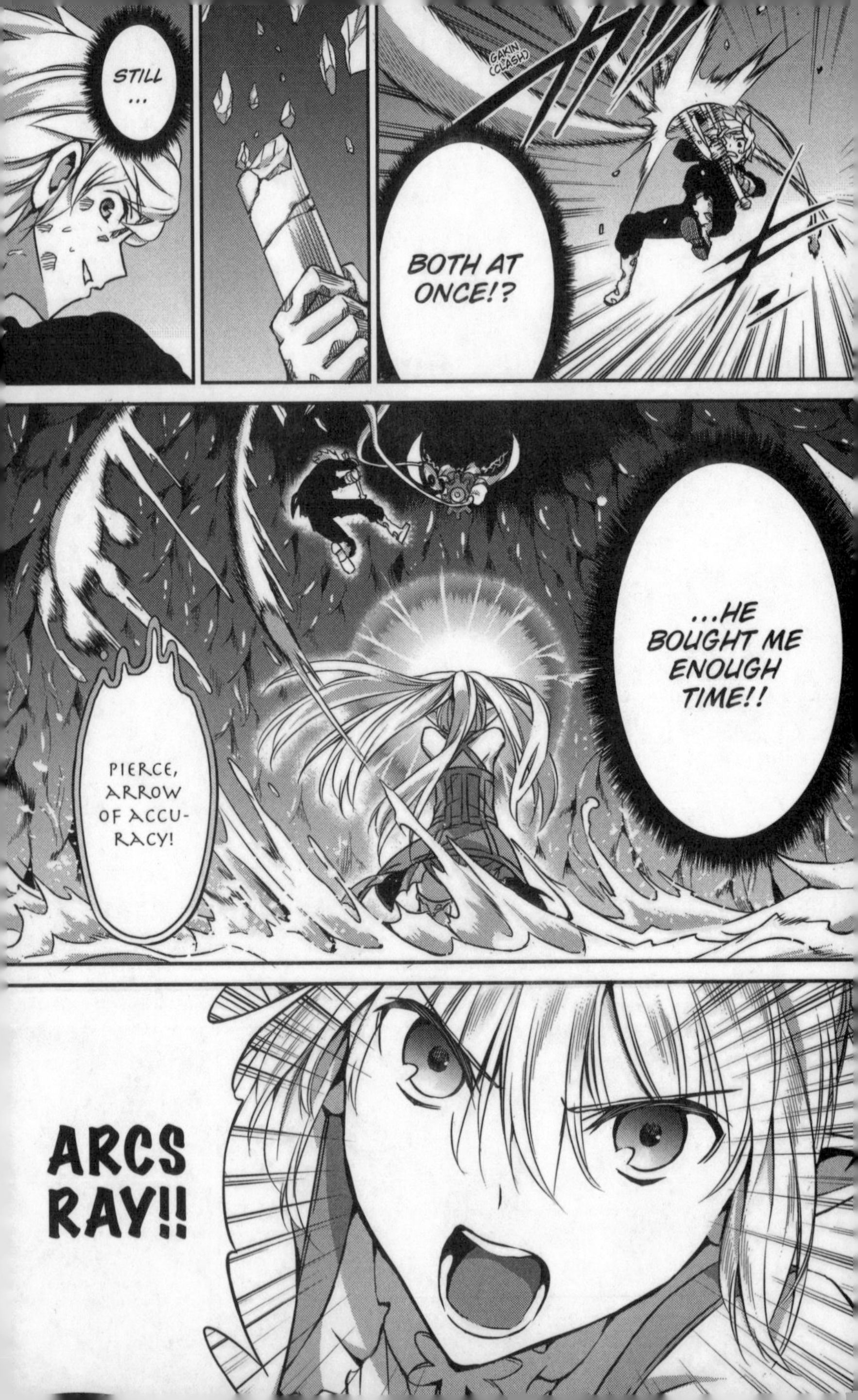
GAKIN (CLASH)
BOTH AT ONCE!?
STILL ...
...HE BOUGHT ME ENOUGH TIME!!
PIERCE, ARROW OF ACCU-RACY!
ARCS RAY!!

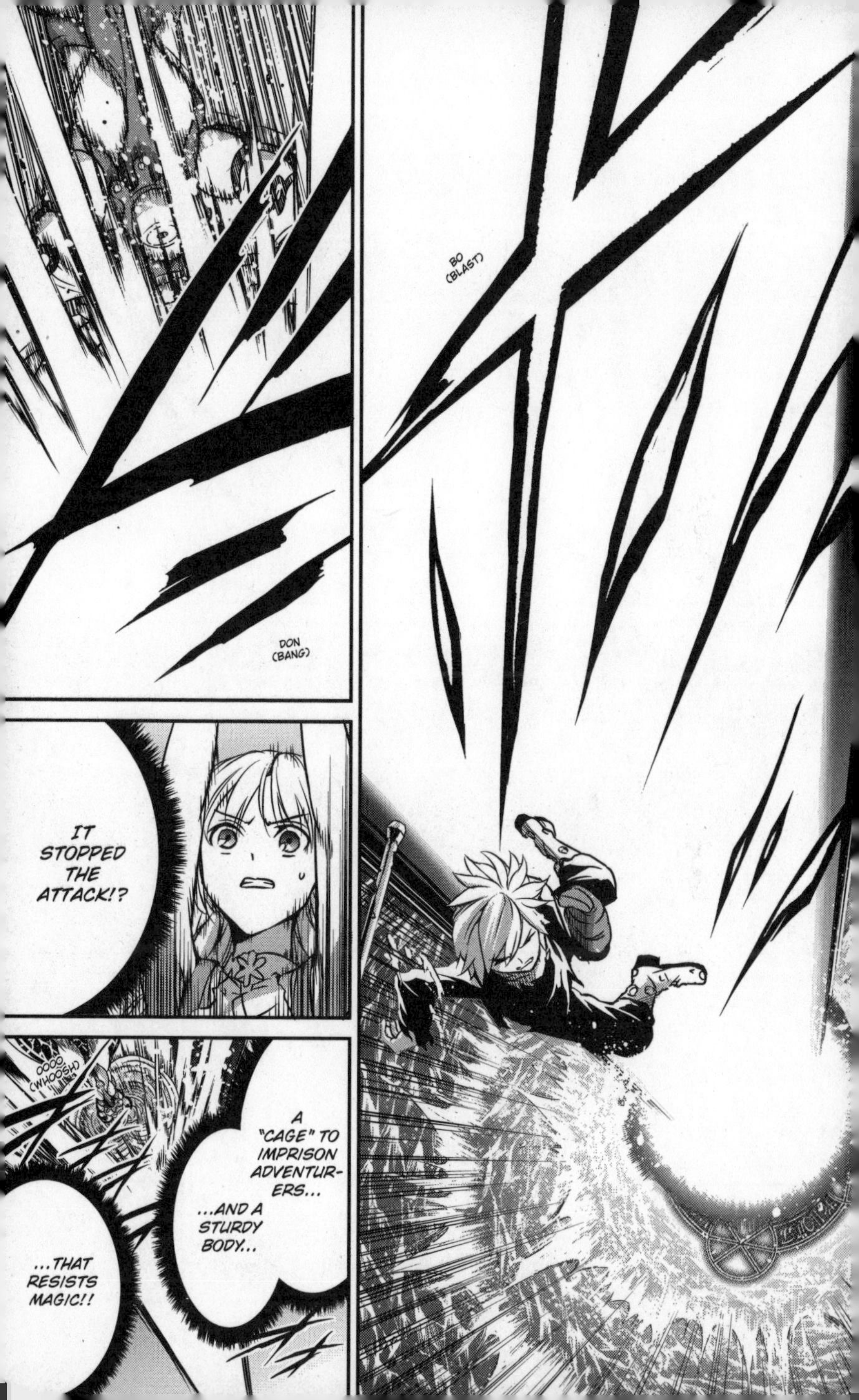
BO (BLAST)
DON (BANG)
IT STOPPED THE ATTACK!?
OOOO (WHOOSH)
A "CAGE" TO IMPRISON ADVENTURERS...
...AND A STURDY BODY...
...THAT RESISTS MAGIC!!

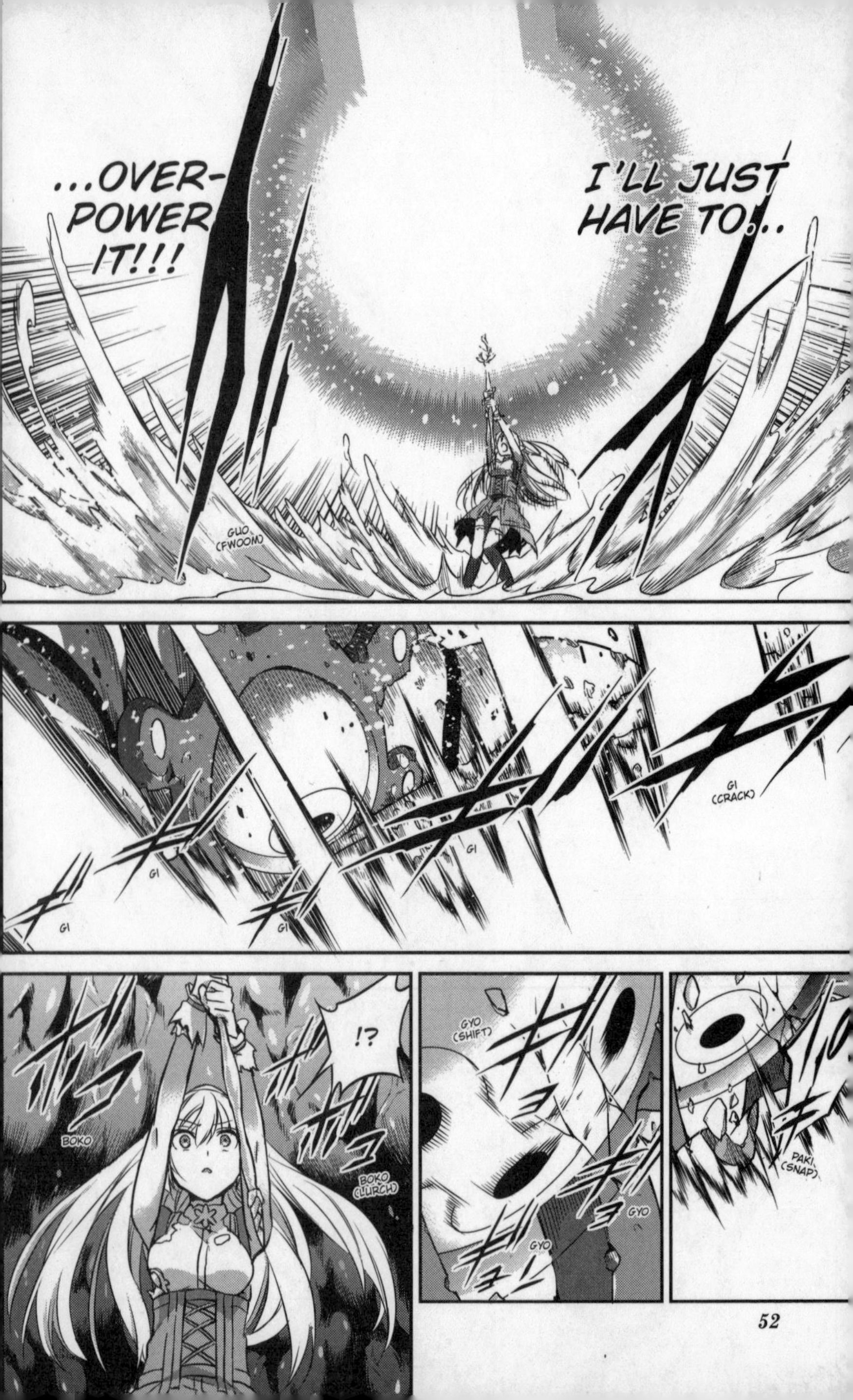
I'LL JUST HAVE TO...
...OVER-POWER IT!!!
GUO (FWOOM)
GI (CRACK)
GI
GI
GI
GI
PAKI (SNAP)
GYO (SHIFT)
GYO
GYO
!?
BOKO (LURCH)
BOKO

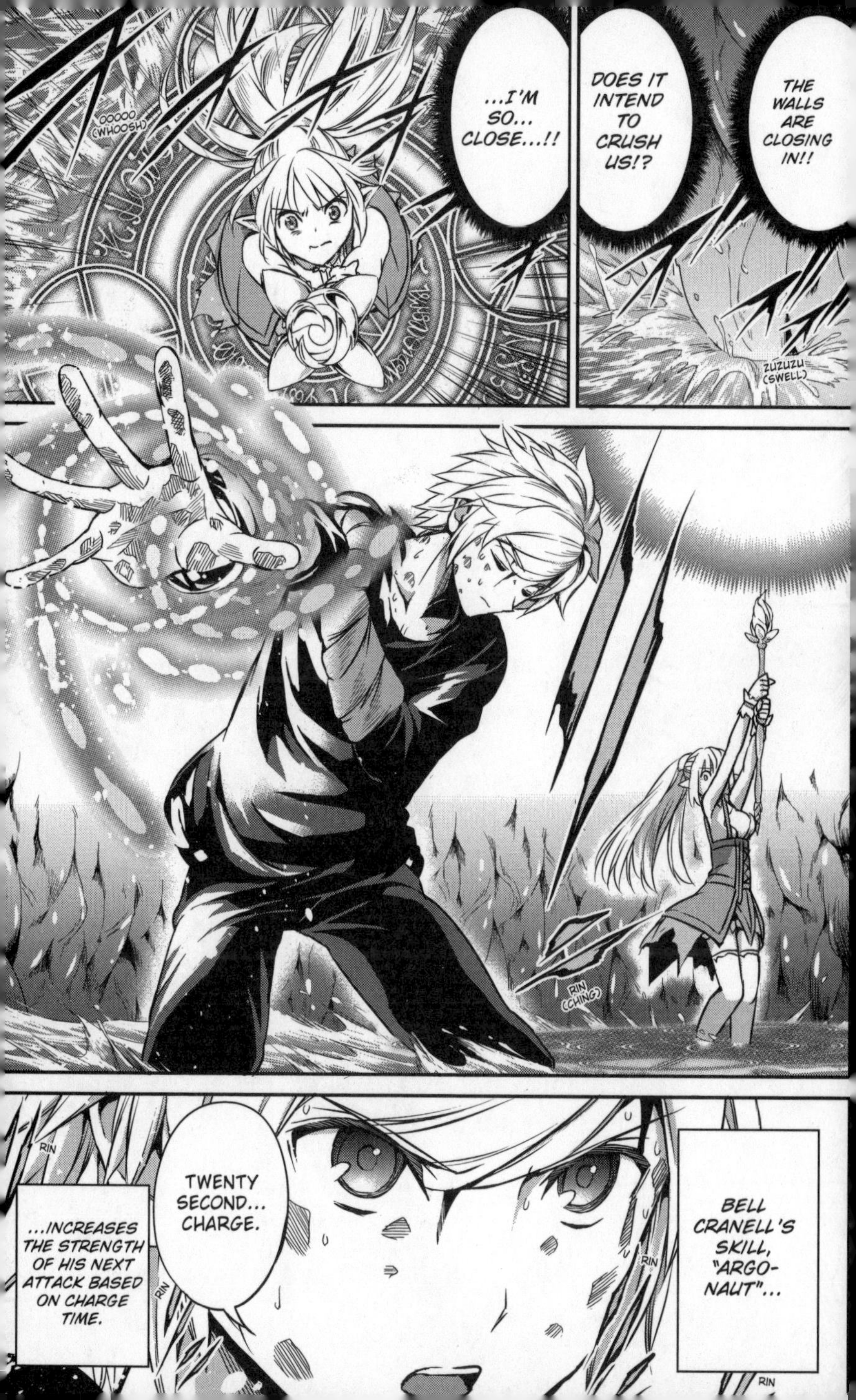
THE WALLS ARE CLOSING IN!!
DOES IT INTEND TO CRUSH US!?
ZUZUZU (SWELL)
...I'M SO... CLOSE...!!
OOOOO (WHOOSH)
RIN (CHING)
BELL CRANELL'S SKILL, "ARGO-NAUT"...
RIN
RIN
TWENTY SECOND... CHARGE.
RIN
RIN
...INCREASES THE STRENGTH OF HIS NEXT ATTACK BASED ON CHARGE TIME.

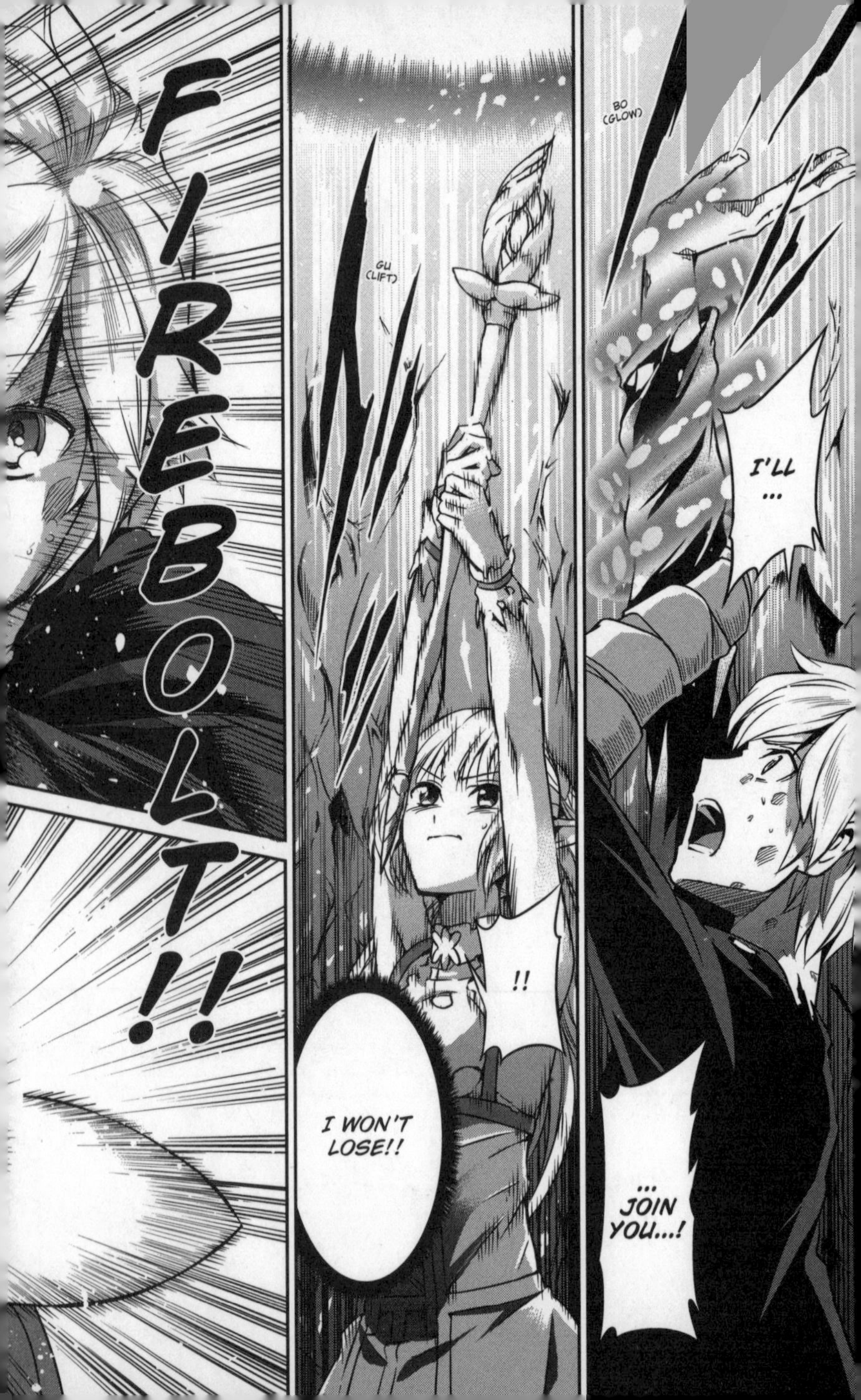
BO
(GLOW)
I'LL...
...JOIN YOU...!
GU
(LIFT)
!!
I WON'T LOSE!!
FIREBOLT!!

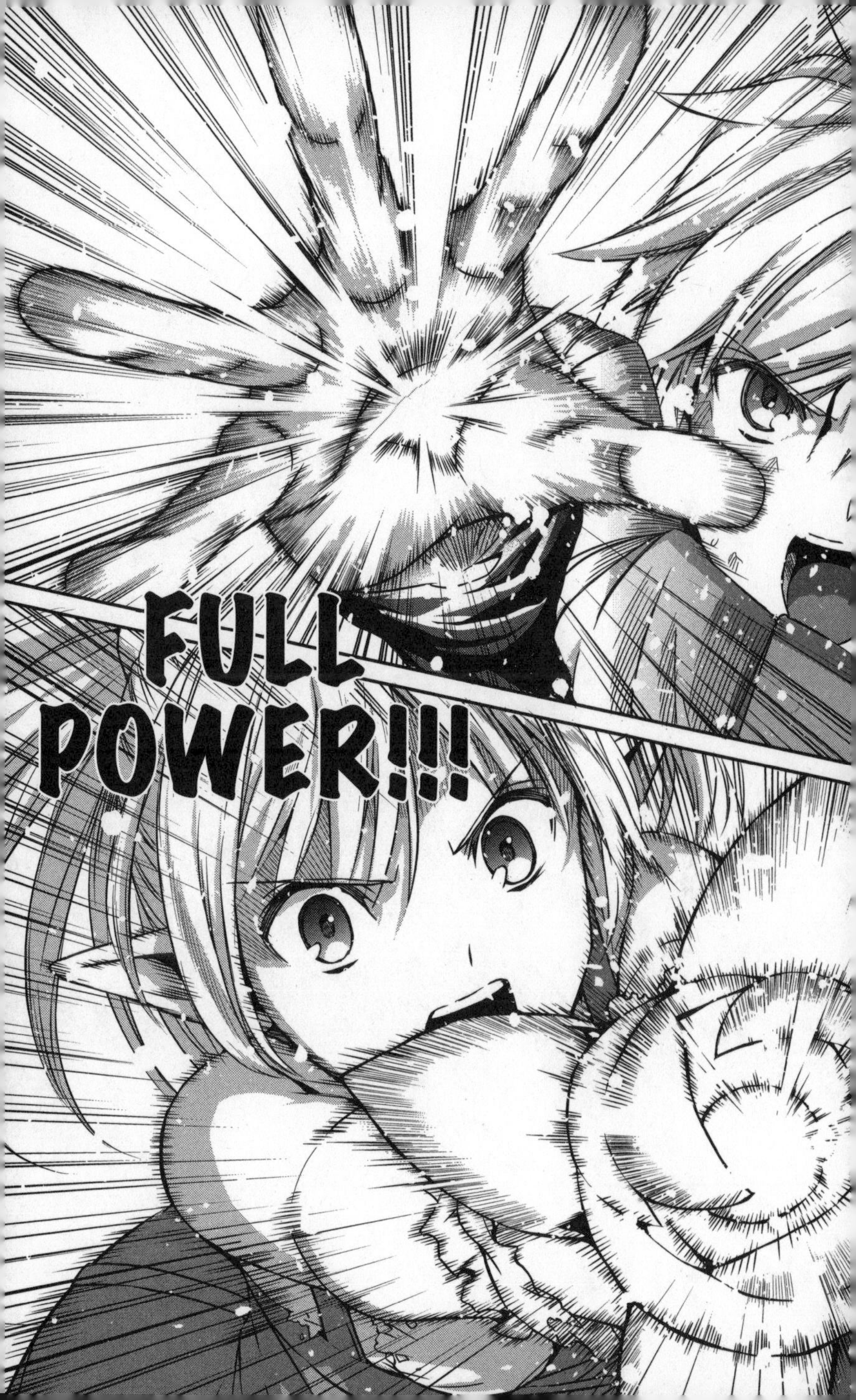
FULL POWER!!!

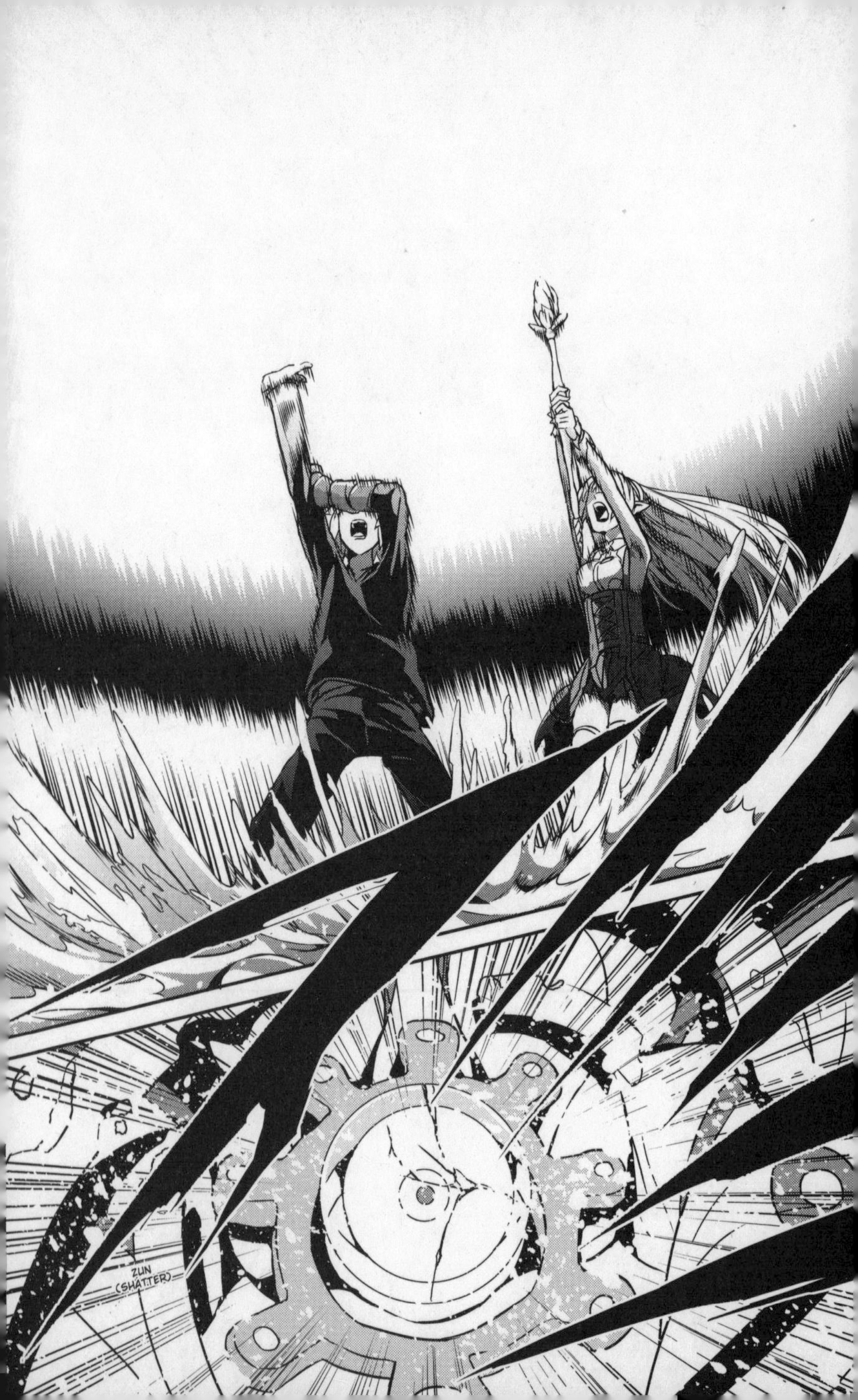
ZUN
(SHATTER)

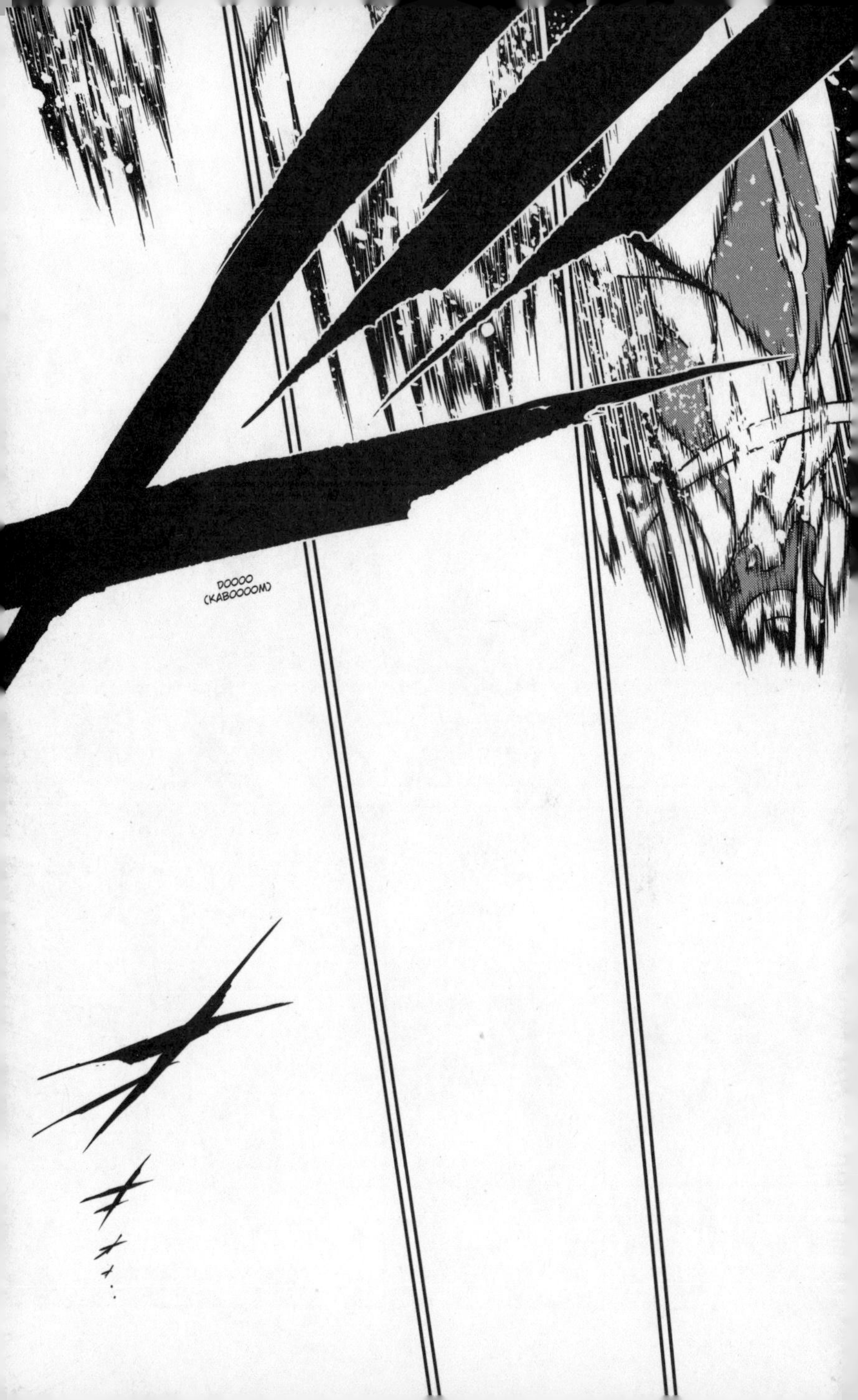
DOOOO
(KABOOOOM)

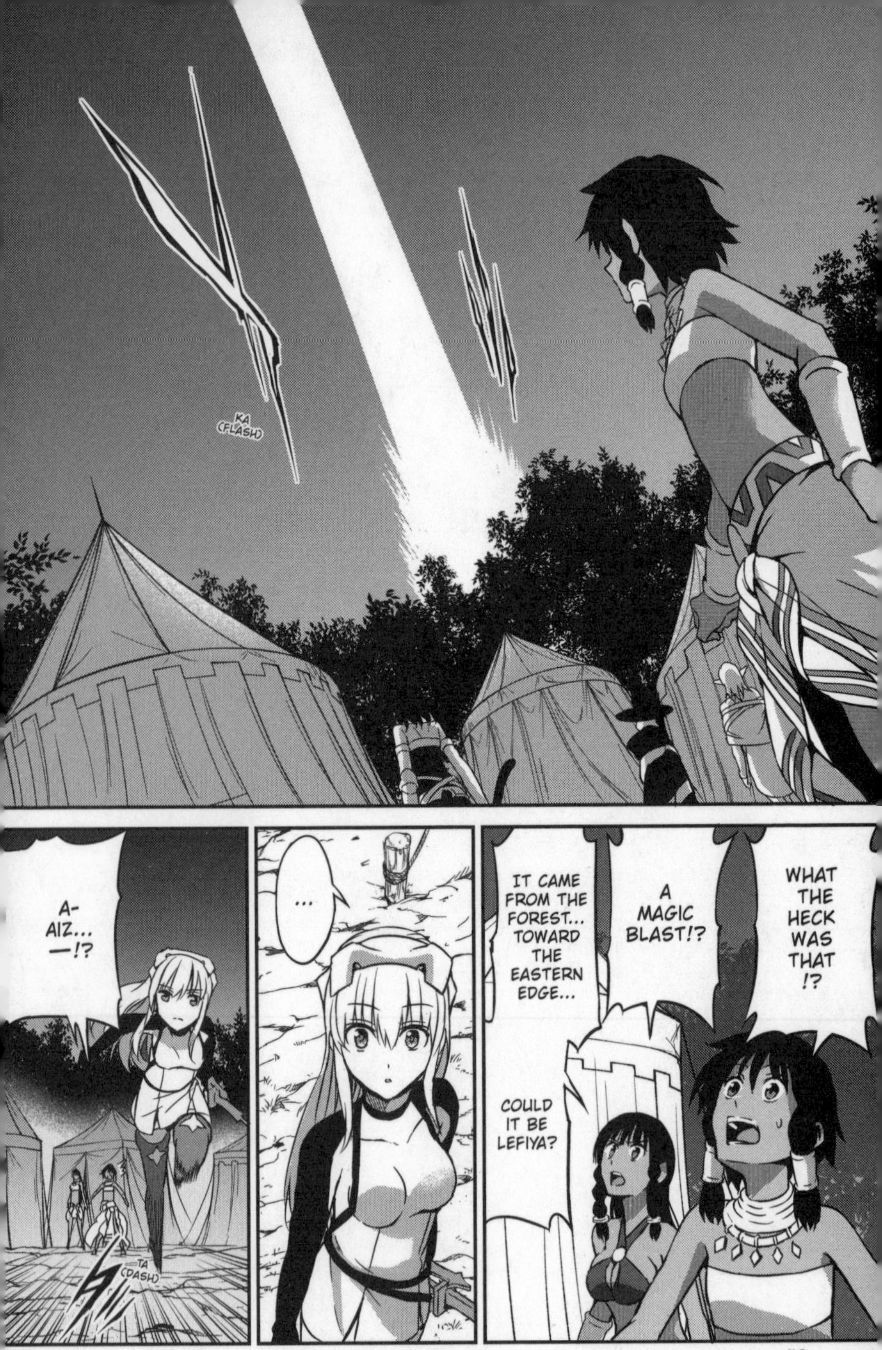
KA (FLASH)
WHAT THE HECK WAS THAT!?
A MAGIC BLAST!?
IT CAME FROM THE FOREST... TOWARD THE EASTERN EDGE...
COULD IT BE LEFIYA?
...
A- AIZ... —!?
TA (DASH)

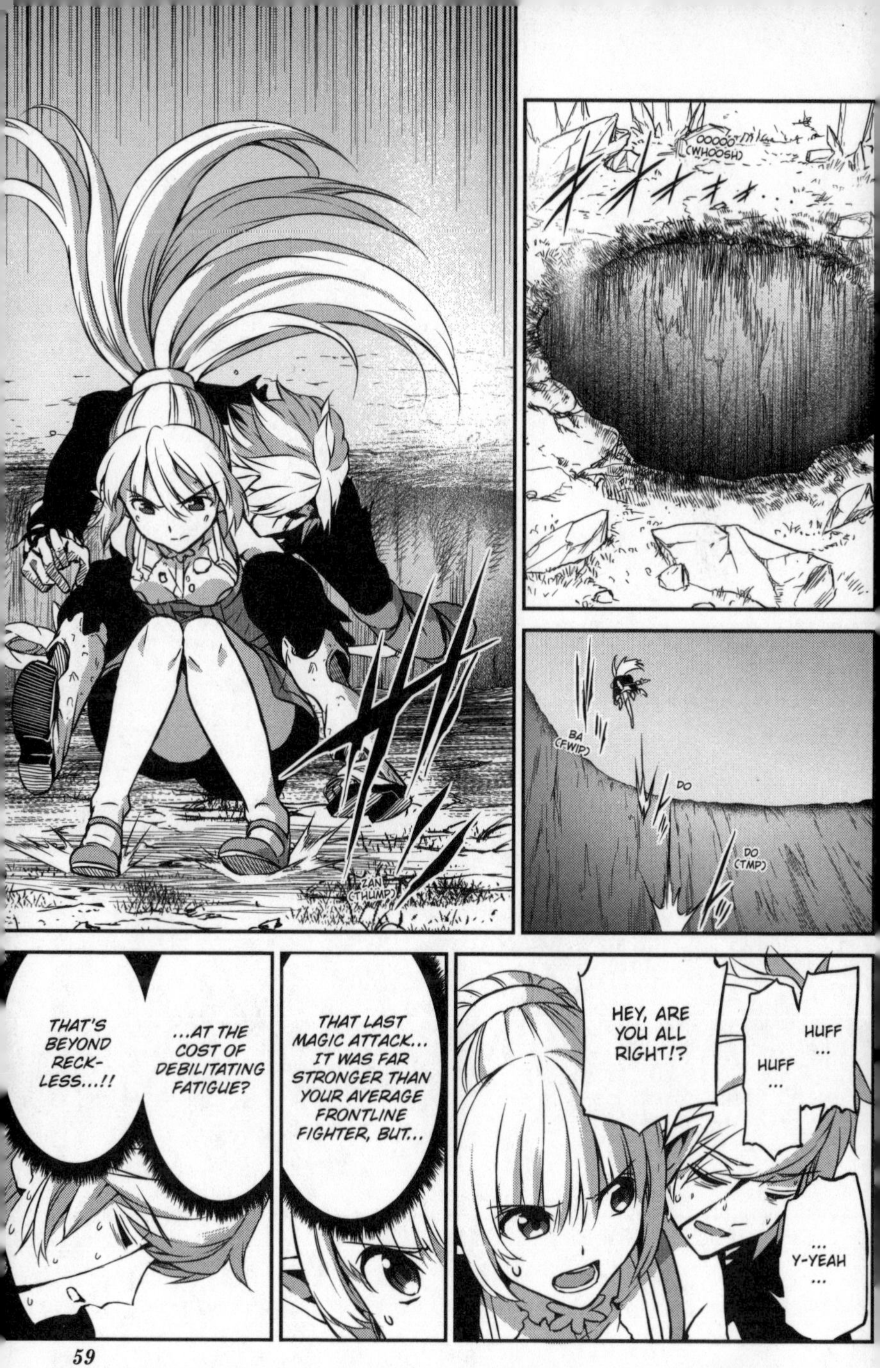
OOOOO (WHOOSH)
BA (FWIP)
DO
DO (TMP)
ZAN (THUMP)
HUFF ...
HUFF ...
HEY, ARE YOU ALL RIGHT!?
... Y-YEAH ...
THAT LAST MAGIC ATTACK... IT WAS FAR STRONGER THAN YOUR AVERAGE FRONTLINE FIGHTER, BUT...
...AT THE COST OF DEBILITATING FATIGUE?
THAT'S BEYOND RECK-LESS...!!

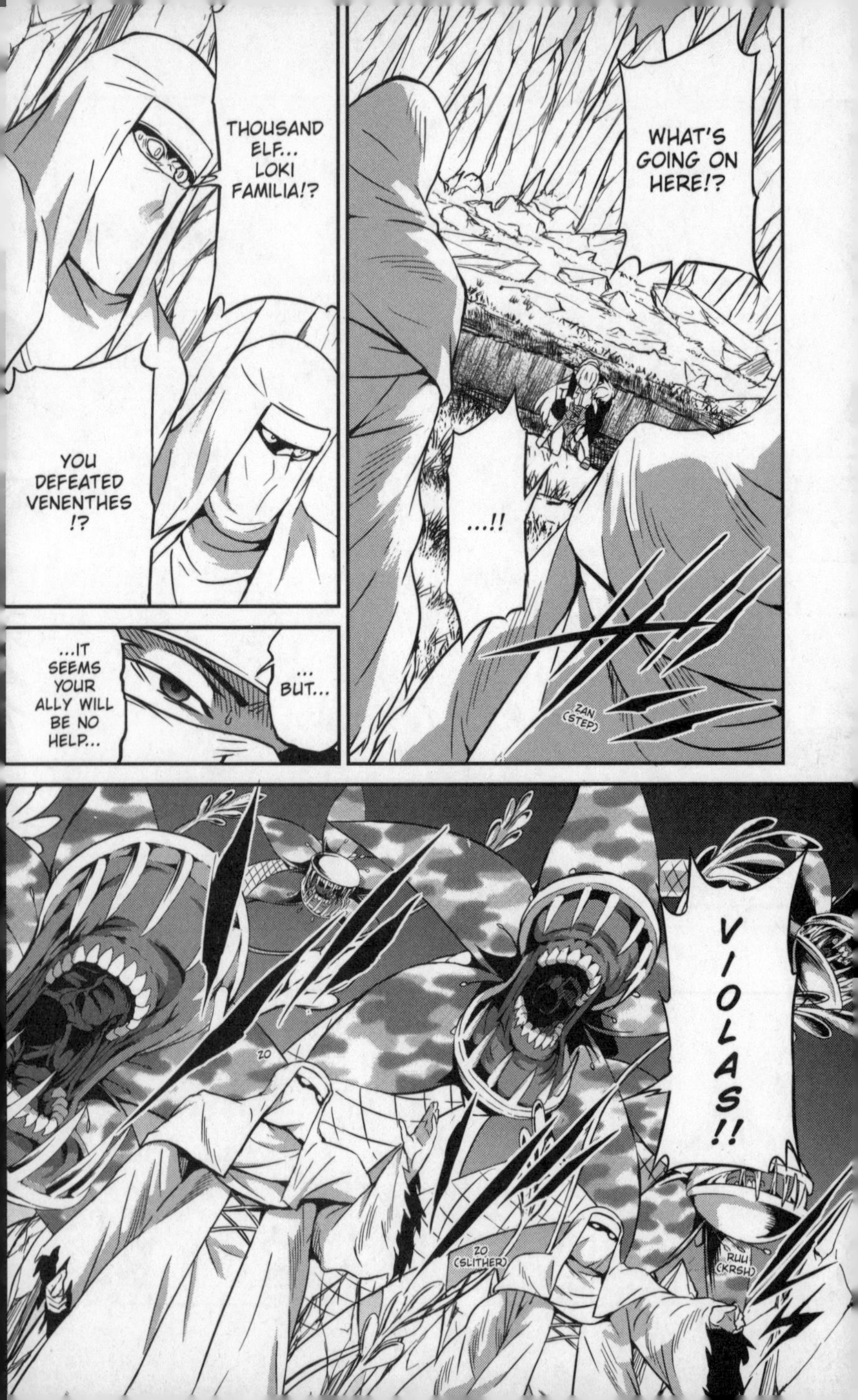
WHAT'S GOING ON HERE!?
...!!
ZAN (STEP)
THOUSAND ELF... LOKI FAMILIA!?
YOU DEFEATED VENENTHES!?
... BUT...
...IT SEEMS YOUR ALLY WILL BE NO HELP...
VIOLAS!!
RUU (KRSH)
ZO (SLITHER)
ZO

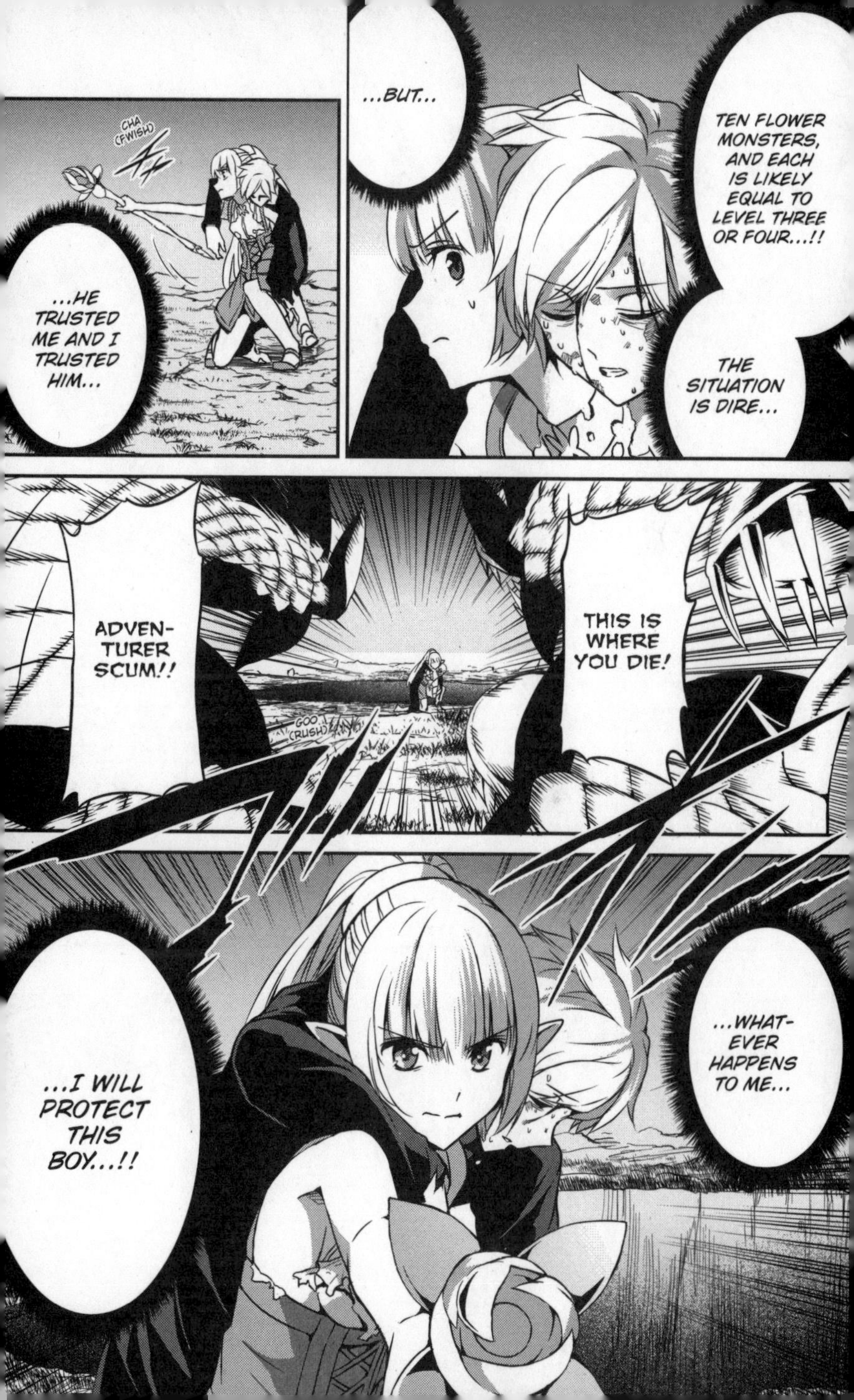
TEN FLOWER MONSTERS, AND EACH IS LIKELY EQUAL TO LEVEL THREE OR FOUR...!!
THE SITUATION IS DIRE...
...BUT...
CHA (F-WISH)
...HE TRUSTED ME AND I TRUSTED HIM...
THIS IS WHERE YOU DIE!
GOO (RUSH)
ADVEN-TURER SCUM!!
...WHAT-EVER HAPPENS TO ME...
...I WILL PROTECT THIS BOY...!!

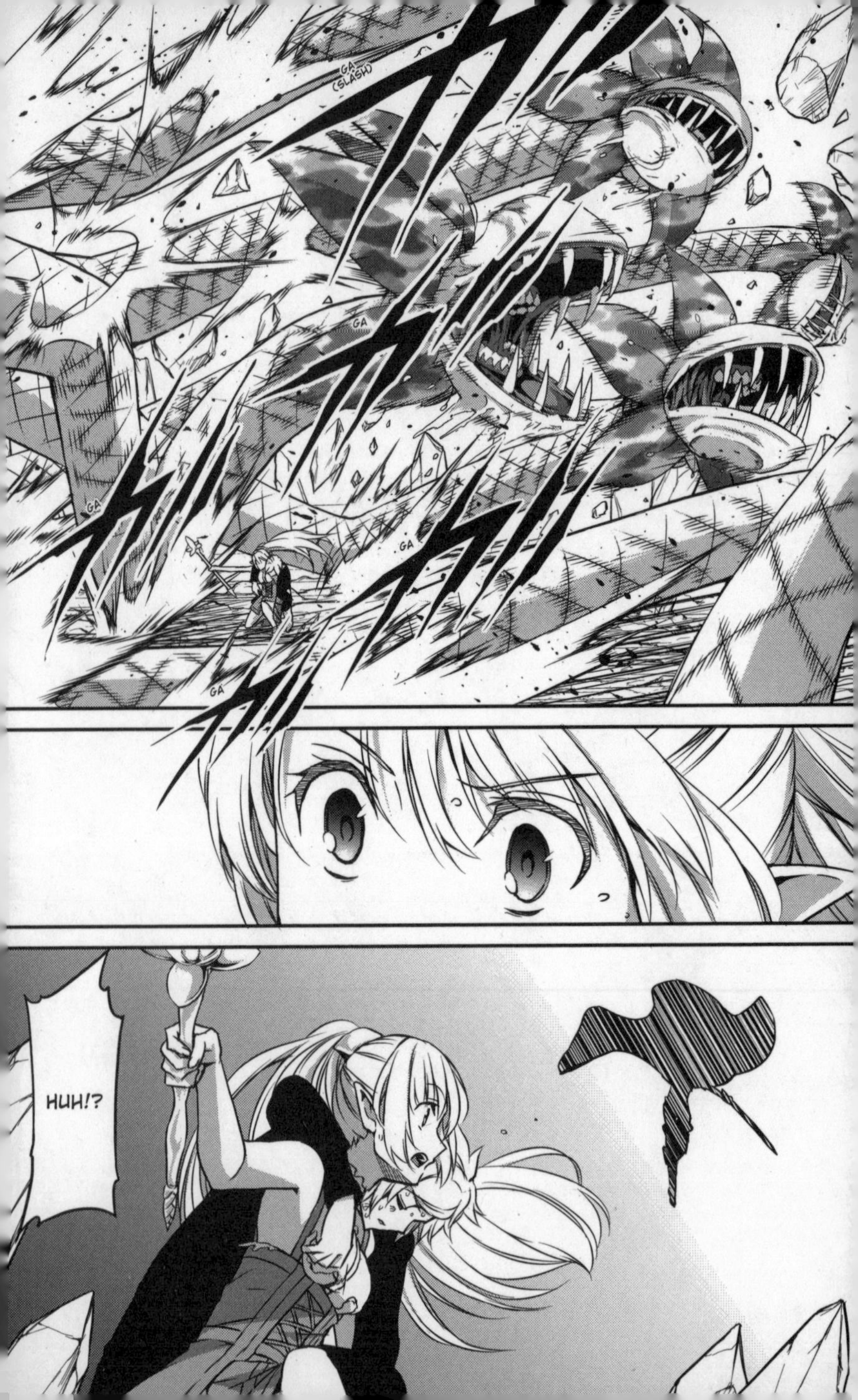
GA (SLASH)
GA
GA
GA
GA
HUH!?

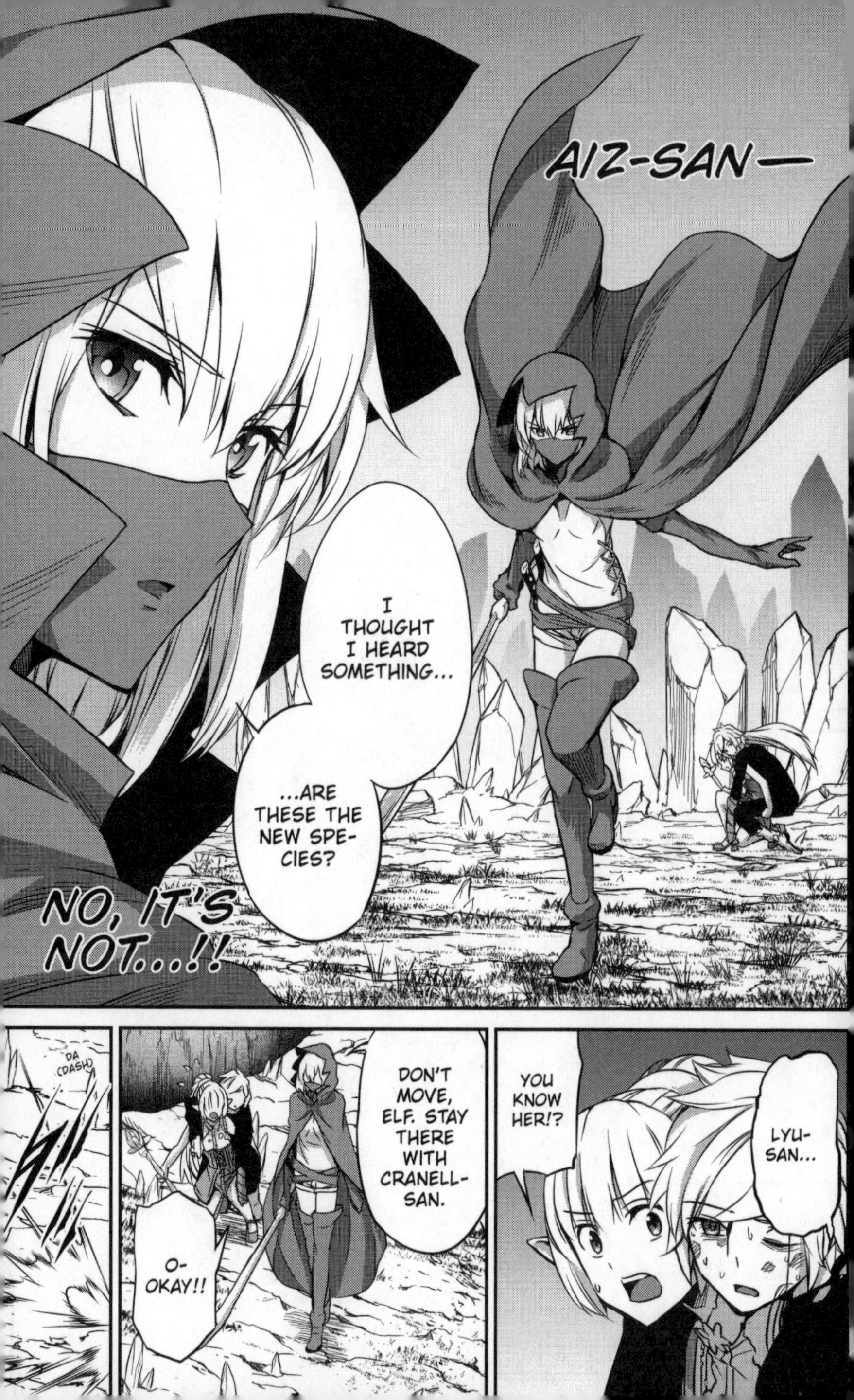
AIZ-SAN—
I THOUGHT I HEARD SOMETHING...
...ARE THESE THE NEW SPECIES?
NO, IT'S NOT...!!
LYU-SAN...
YOU KNOW HER!?
DON'T MOVE, ELF. STAY THERE WITH CRANELL-SAN.
O-OKAY!!
DA (DASH)

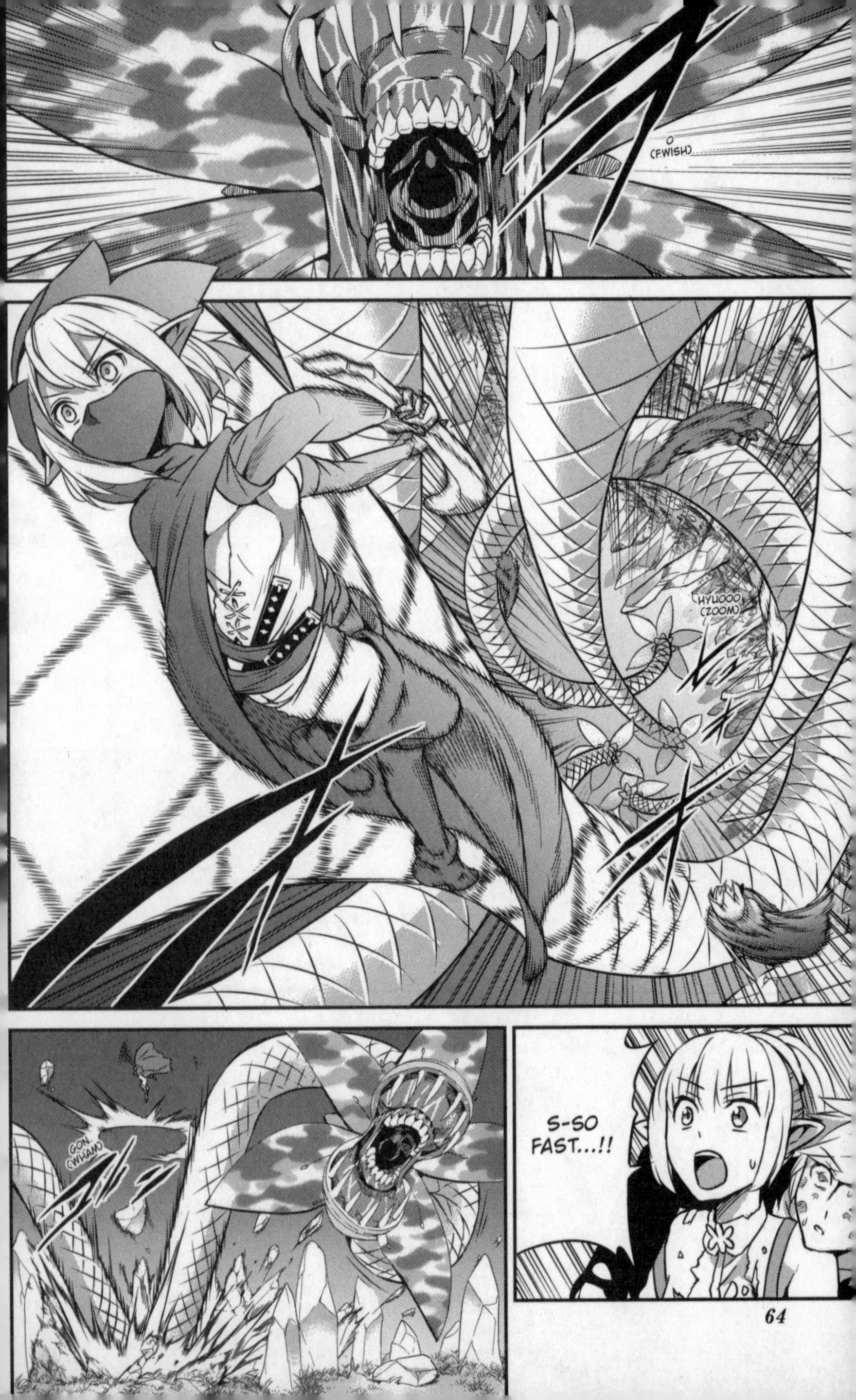
O
(F.WISH)
HYUOOO
(ZOOM)
S-SO FAST...!!
GON
(WHAM)

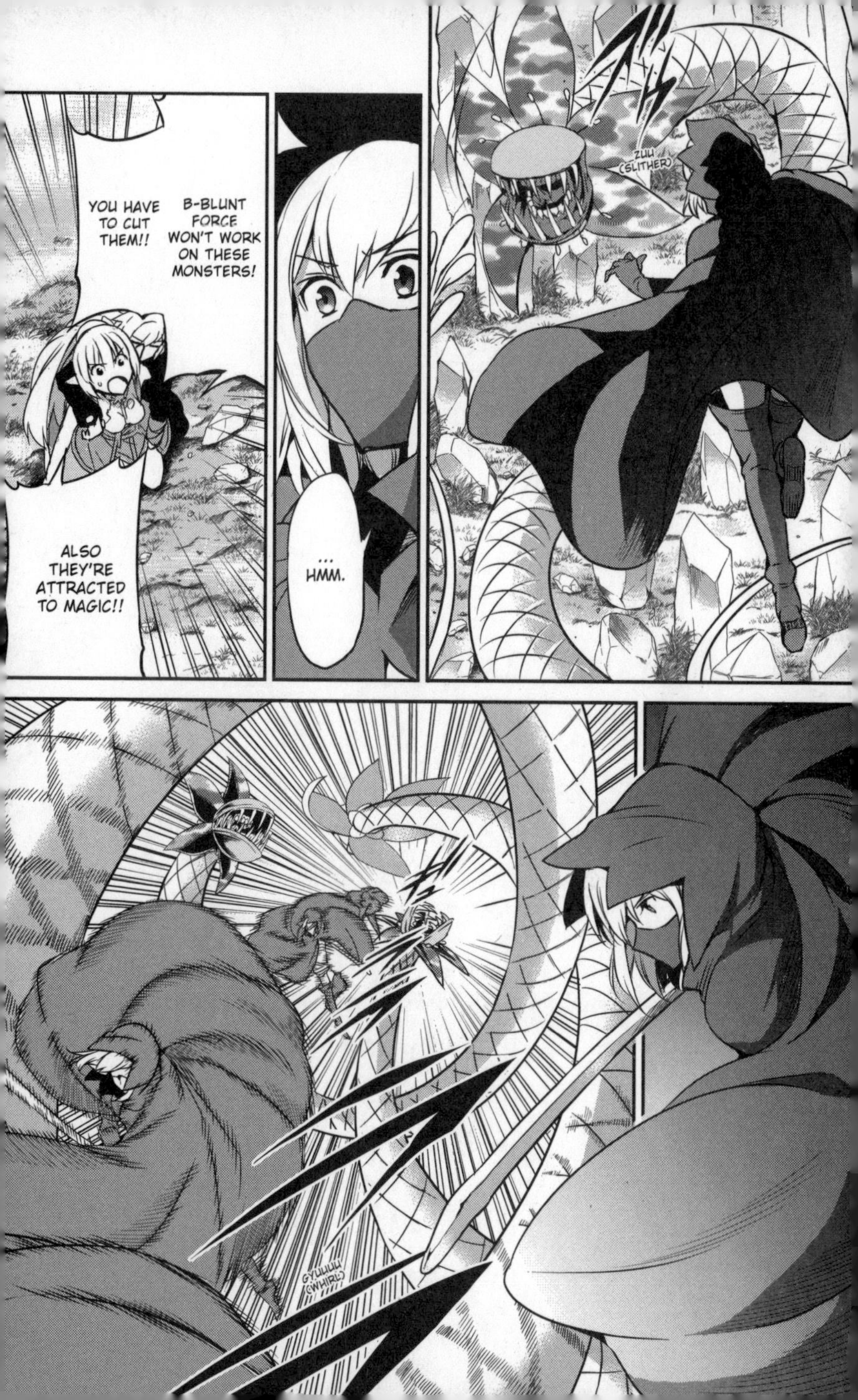
ZUU (SLITHER)
... HMM.
B-BLUNT FORCE WON'T WORK ON THESE MONSTERS!
YOU HAVE TO CUT THEM!!
ALSO THEY'RE ATTRACTED TO MAGIC!!
GYUUUU (WHIRL)

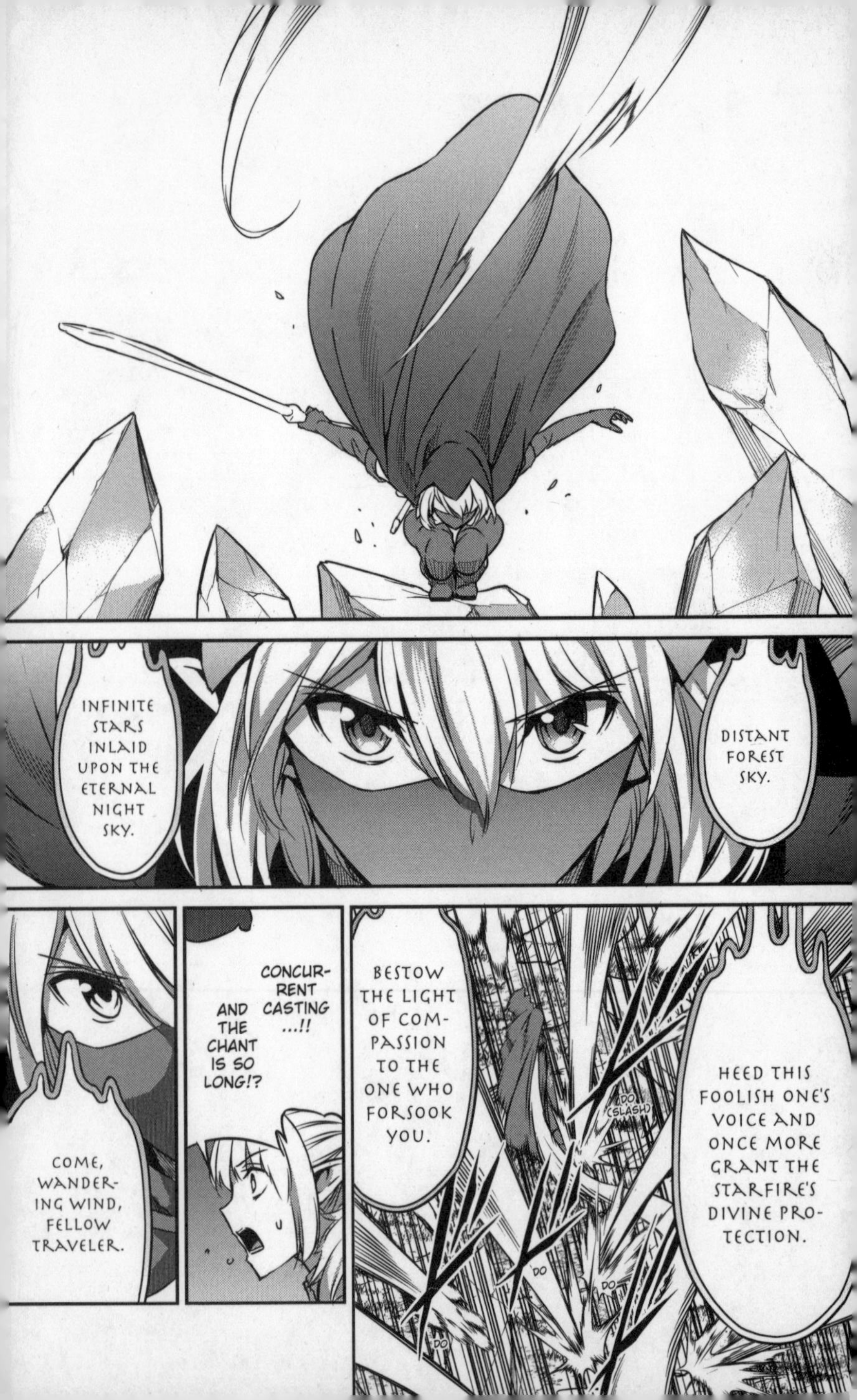
DISTANT FOREST SKY.
INFINITE STARS INLAID UPON THE ETERNAL NIGHT SKY.
HEED THIS FOOLISH ONE'S VOICE AND ONCE MORE GRANT THE STARFIRE'S DIVINE PROTECTION.
BESTOW THE LIGHT OF COMPASSION TO THE ONE WHO FORSOOK YOU.
DO (SLASH)
DO
DO
DO
CONCURRENT CASTING...!!
AND THE CHANT IS SO LONG!?
COME, WANDERING WIND, FELLOW TRAVELER.

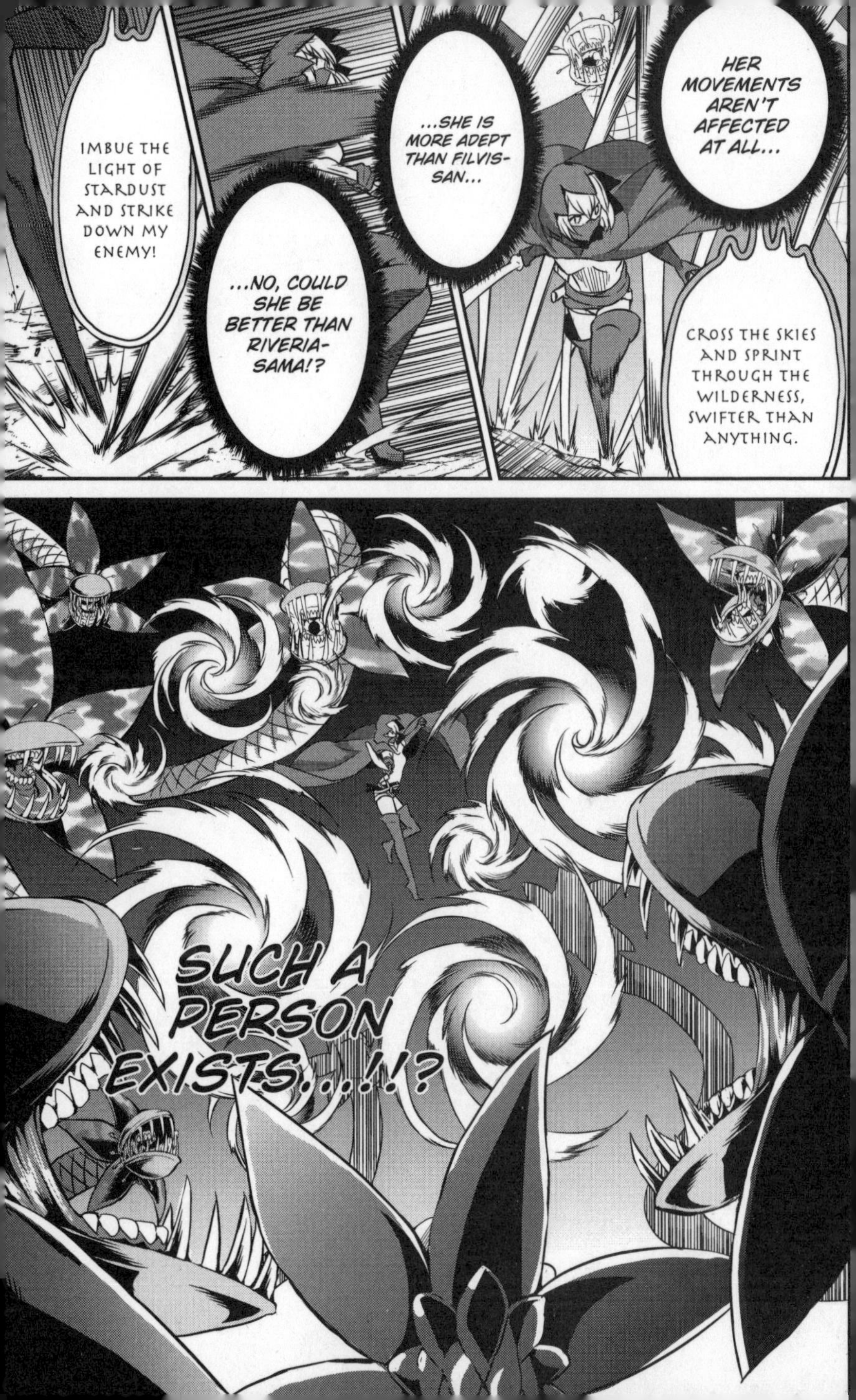
HER MOVEMENTS AREN'T AFFECTED AT ALL...
...SHE IS MORE ADEPT THAN FILVIS-SAN...
CROSS THE SKIES AND SPRINT THROUGH THE WILDERNESS, SWIFTER THAN ANYTHING.
...NO, COULD SHE BE BETTER THAN RIVERIA-SAMA!?
IMBUE THE LIGHT OF STARDUST AND STRIKE DOWN MY ENEMY!
SUCH A PERSON EXISTS...!!?

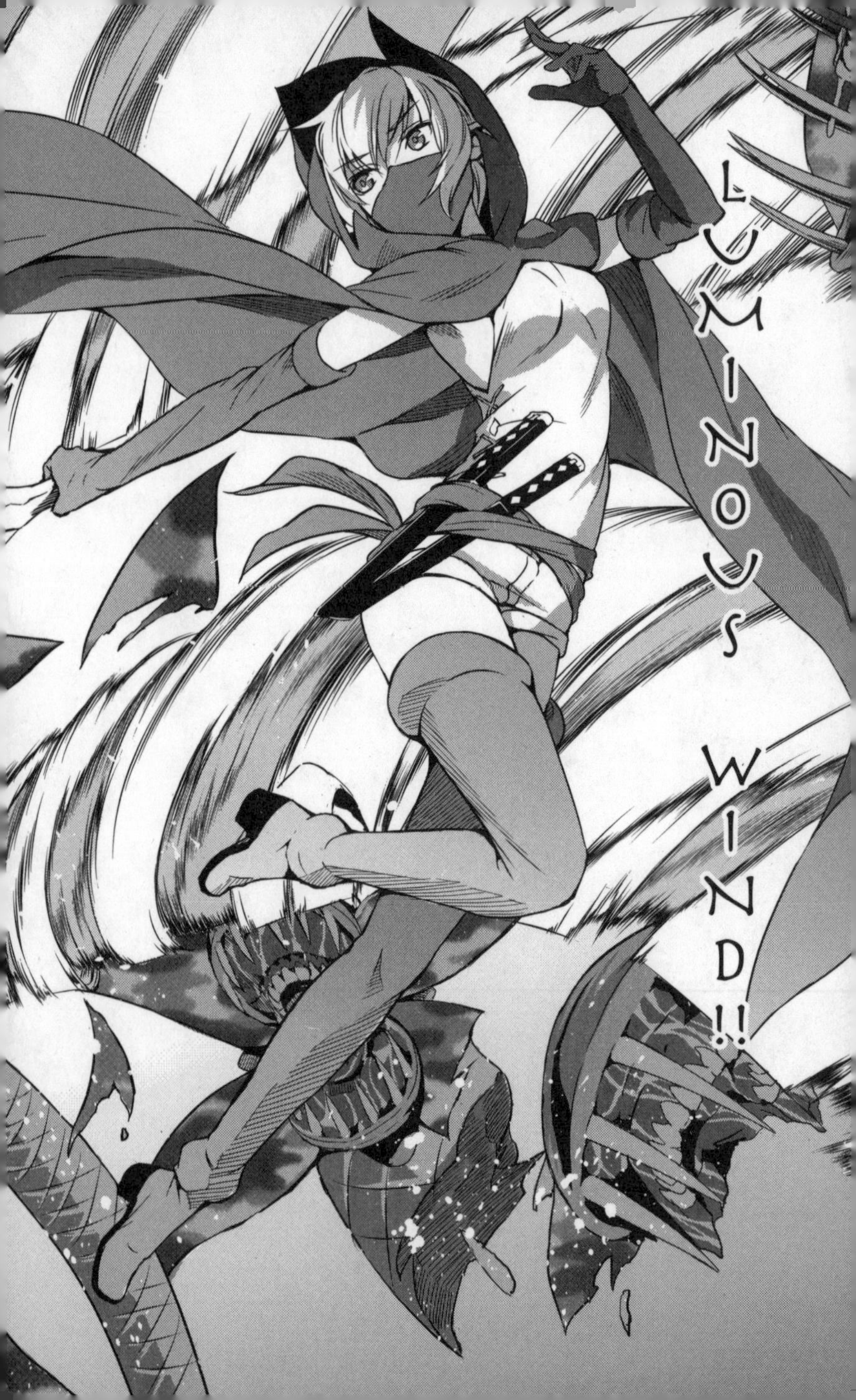
LUMINOUS WIND!!

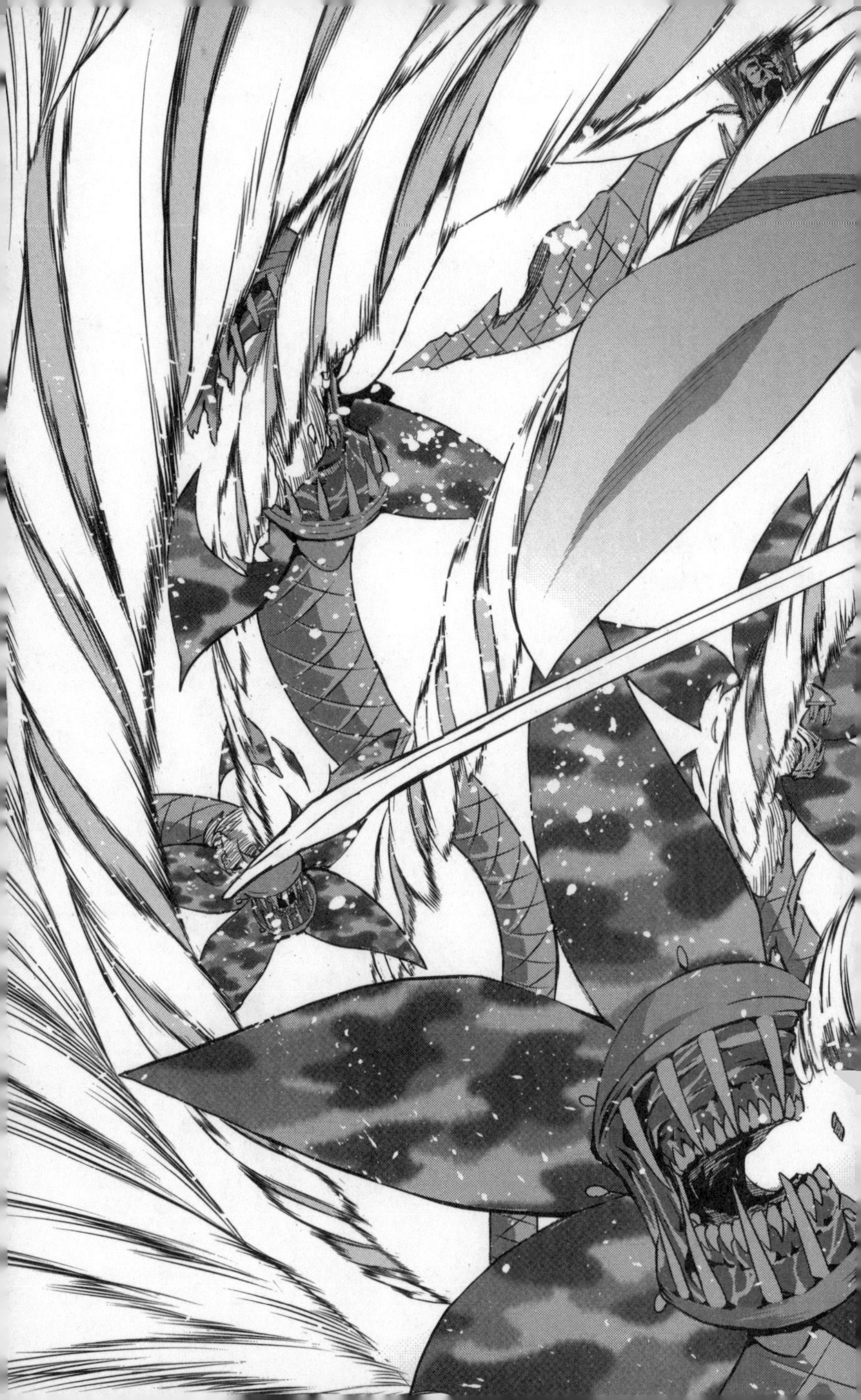

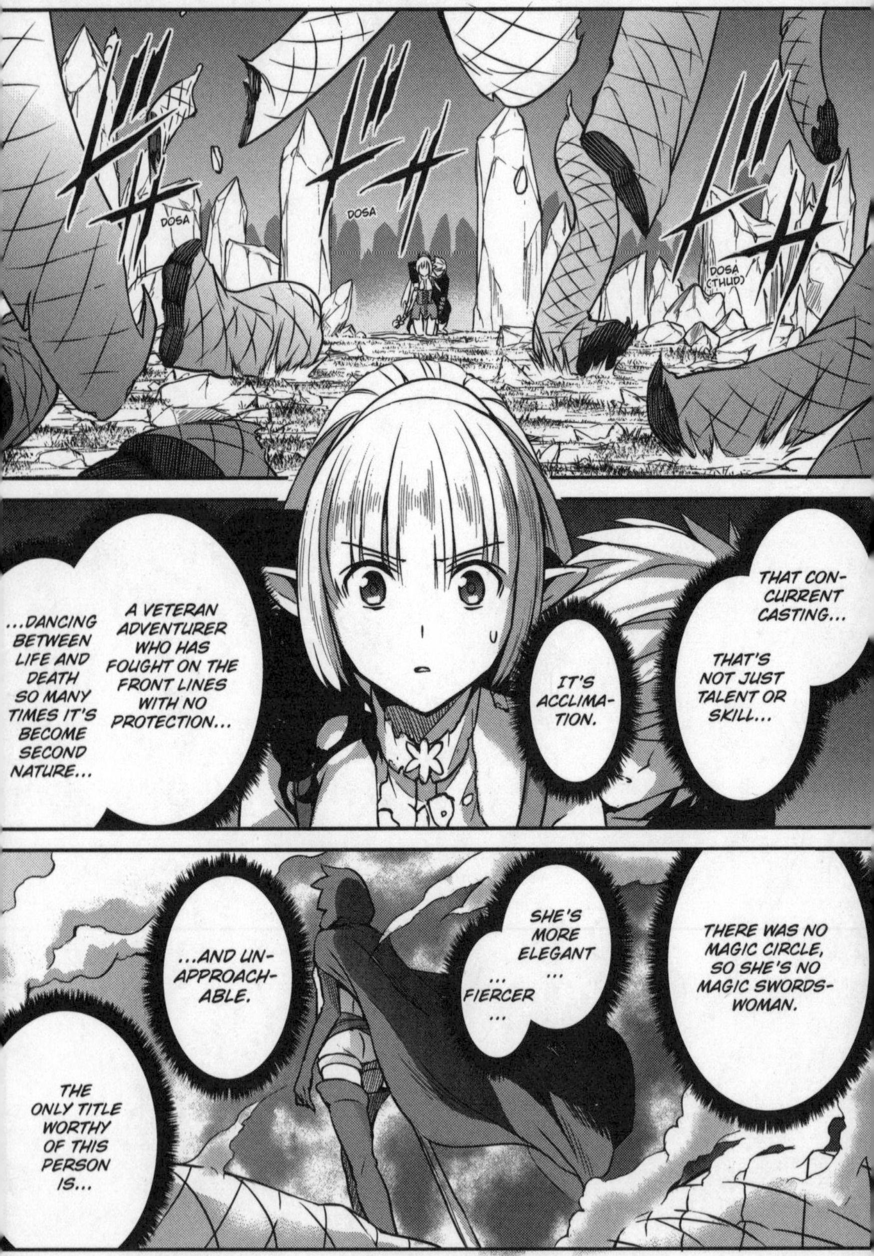
DOSA (THUD)
DOSA
DOSA
THAT CON-CURRENT CASTING...
THAT'S NOT JUST TALENT OR SKILL...
IT'S ACCLIMA-TION.
A VETERAN ADVENTURER WHO HAS FOUGHT ON THE FRONT LINES WITH NO PROTECTION...
...DANCING BETWEEN LIFE AND DEATH SO MANY TIMES IT'S BECOME SECOND NATURE...
THERE WAS NO MAGIC CIRCLE, SO SHE'S NO MAGIC SWORDS-WOMAN.
SHE'S MORE ELEGANT...
...FIERCER...
...AND UN-APPROACH-ABLE.
THE ONLY TITLE WORTHY OF THIS PERSON IS...

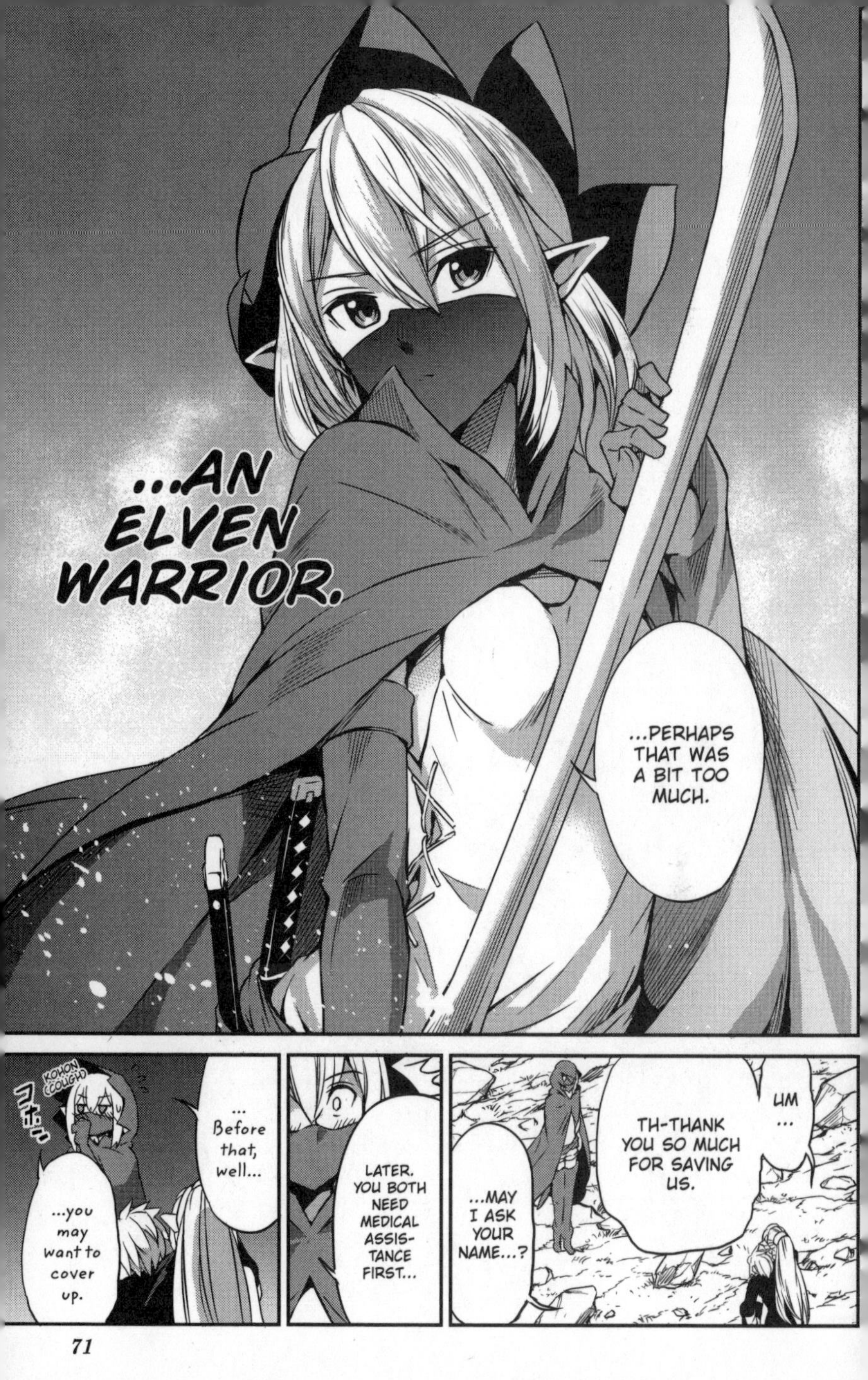
...AN ELVEN WARRIOR.
...PERHAPS THAT WAS A BIT TOO MUCH.
UM ...
TH-THANK YOU SO MUCH FOR SAVING US.
...MAY I ASK YOUR NAME...?
LATER. YOU BOTH NEED MEDICAL ASSIS-TANCE FIRST...
KOHON (COUGH)
... Before that, well...
...you may want to cover up.

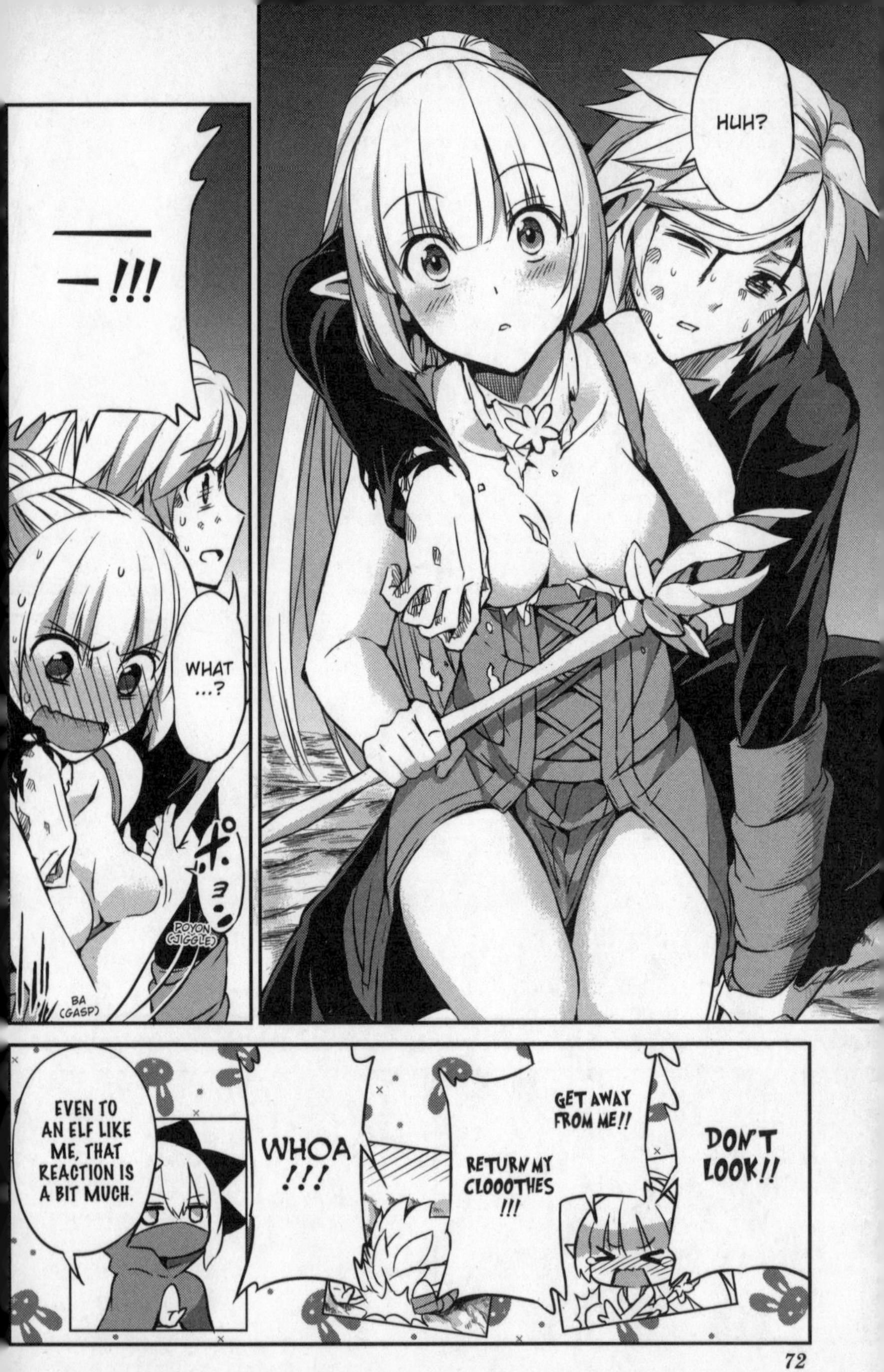
HUH?
———
—!!!
WHAT ...?
POYON (JIGGLE)
BA (GASP)
DON'T LOOK!!
GET AWAY FROM ME!!
RETURN MY CLOOOTHES !!!
WHOA !!!
EVEN TO AN ELF LIKE ME, THAT REACTION IS A BIT MUCH.

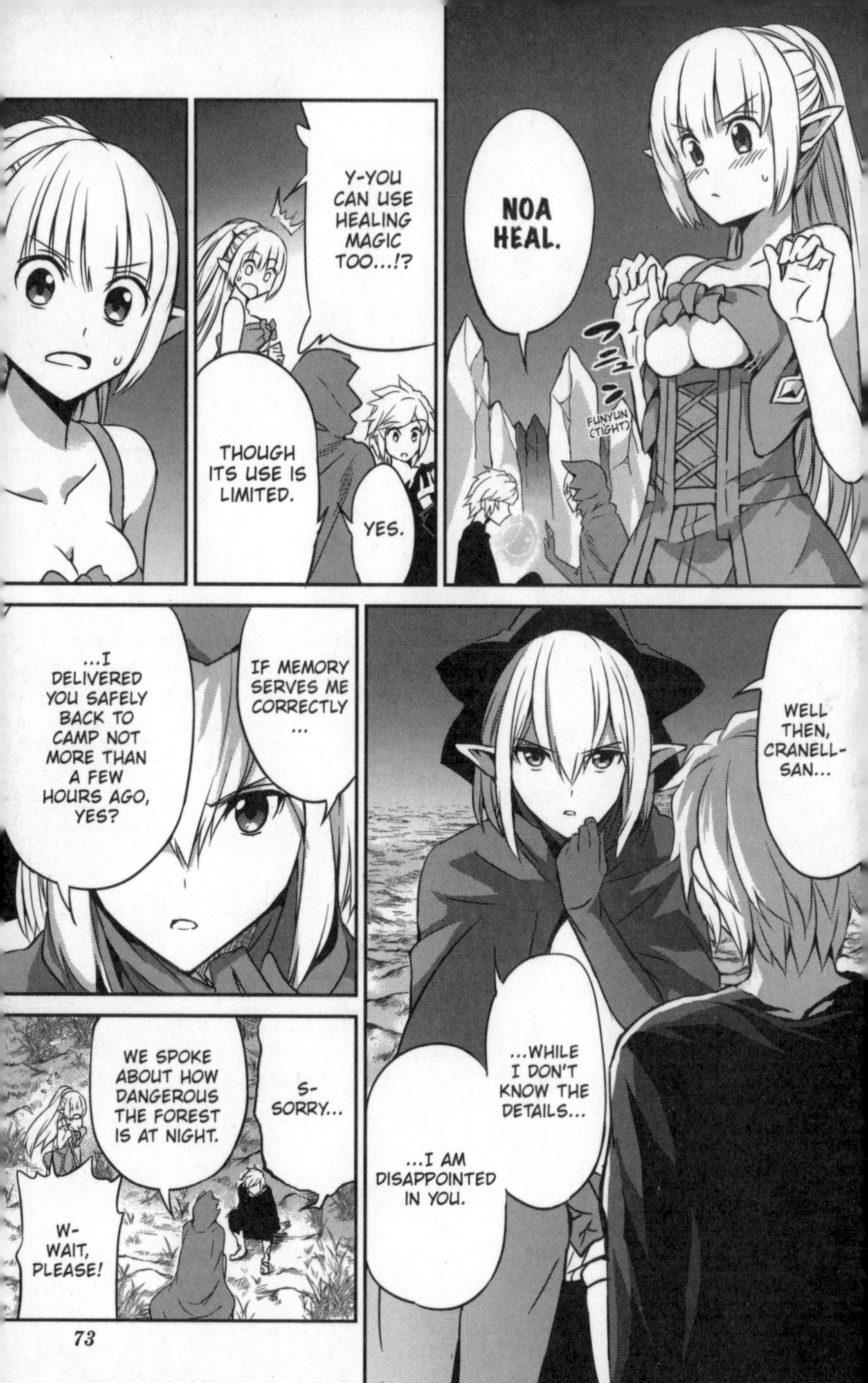
NOA HEAL.
FUNYUN (TIGHT)
Y-YOU CAN USE HEALING MAGIC TOO...!?
THOUGH ITS USE IS LIMITED.
YES.
WELL THEN, CRANELL-SAN...
...WHILE I DON'T KNOW THE DETAILS...
...I AM DISAPPOINTED IN YOU.
IF MEMORY SERVES ME CORRECTLY ...
...I DELIVERED YOU SAFELY BACK TO CAMP NOT MORE THAN A FEW HOURS AGO, YES?
S-SORRY...
WE SPOKE ABOUT HOW DANGEROUS THE FOREST IS AT NIGHT.
W-WAIT, PLEASE!

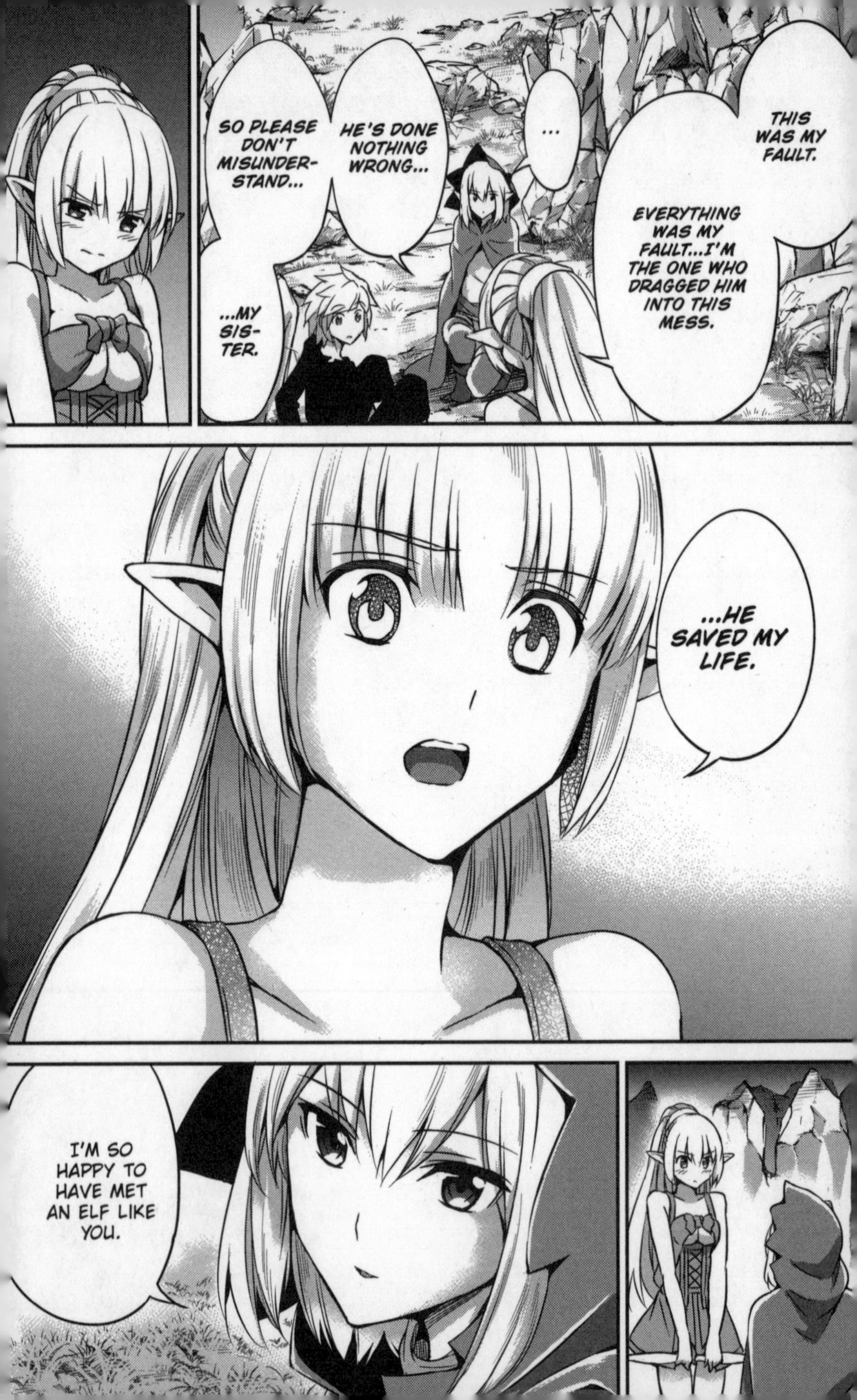
THIS WAS MY FAULT.
EVERYTHING WAS MY FAULT...I'M THE ONE WHO DRAGGED HIM INTO THIS MESS.
...
HE'S DONE NOTHING WRONG...
SO PLEASE DON'T MISUNDER-STAND...
...MY SIS-TER.
...HE SAVED MY LIFE.
I'M SO HAPPY TO HAVE MET AN ELF LIKE YOU.

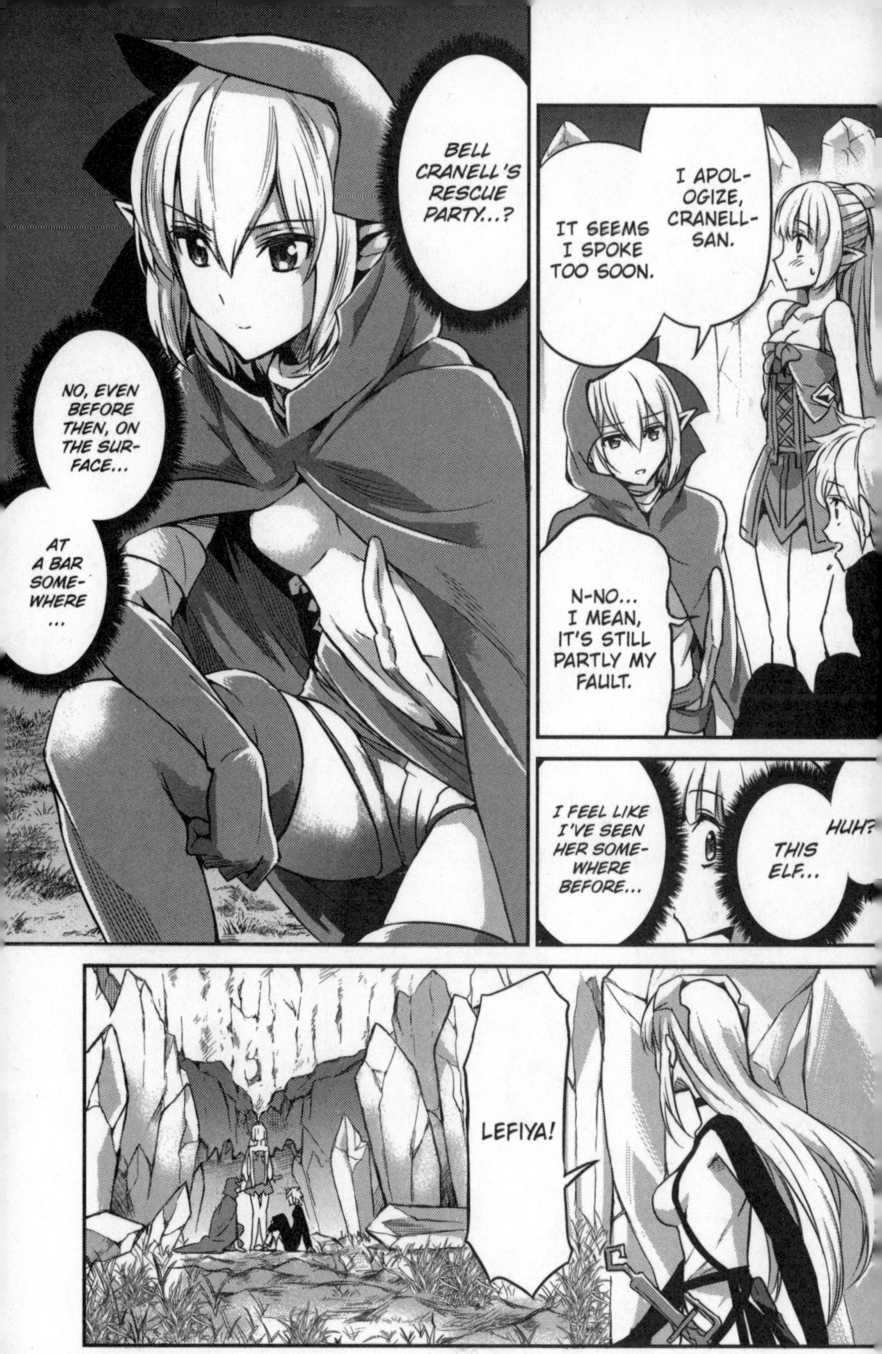
I APOLOGIZE, CRANELL-SAN.
IT SEEMS I SPOKE TOO SOON.
N-NO... I MEAN, IT'S STILL PARTLY MY FAULT.
HUH? THIS ELF...
I FEEL LIKE I'VE SEEN HER SOMEWHERE BEFORE...
BELL CRANELL'S RESCUE PARTY...?
NO, EVEN BEFORE THEN, ON THE SURFACE...
AT A BAR SOMEWHERE...
LEFIYA!

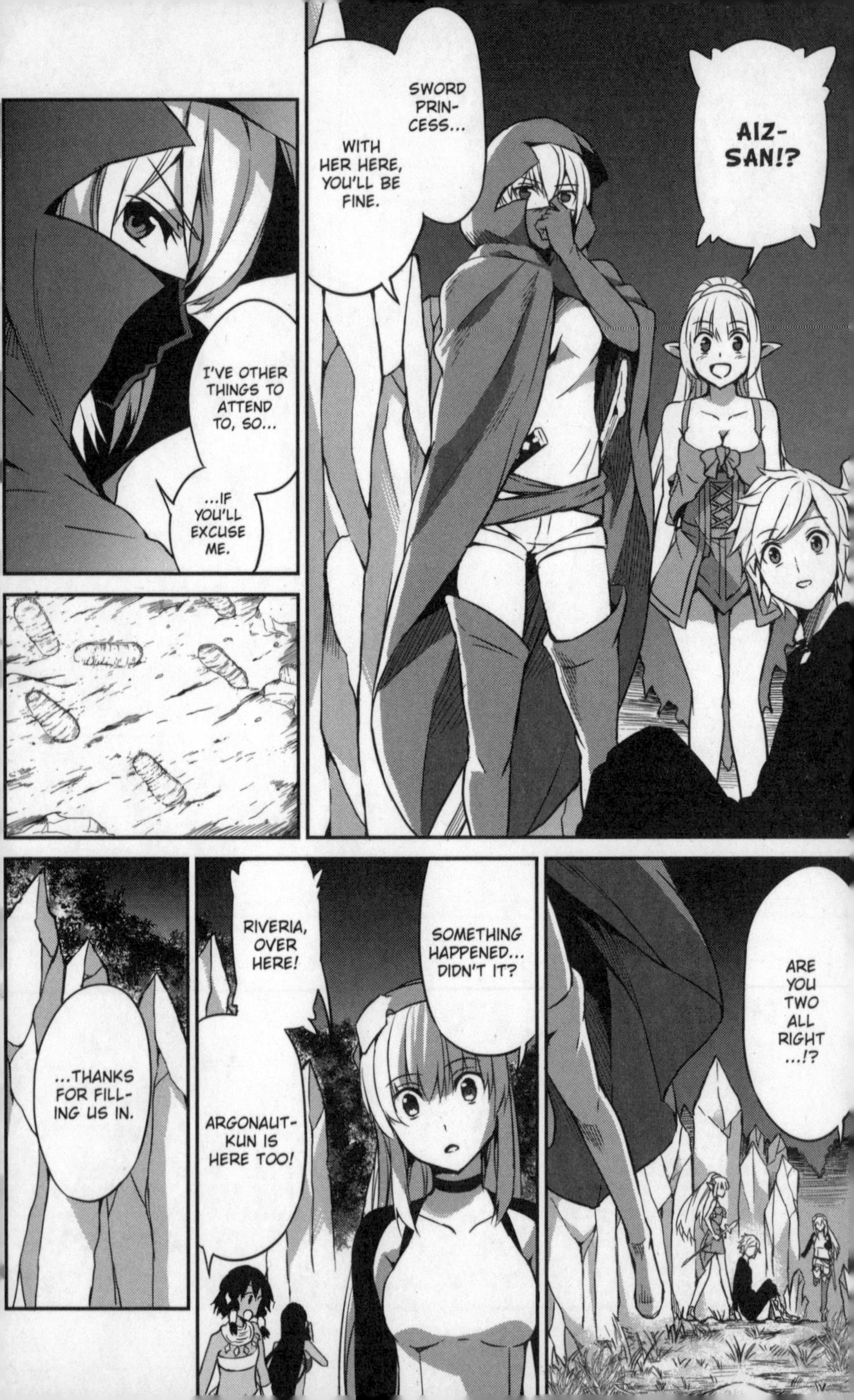
AIZ-SAN!?
SWORD PRINCESS...
WITH HER HERE, YOU'LL BE FINE.
I'VE OTHER THINGS TO ATTEND TO, SO...
...IF YOU'LL EXCUSE ME.
ARE YOU TWO ALL RIGHT...!?
SOMETHING HAPPENED... DIDN'T IT?
RIVERIA, OVER HERE!
ARGONAUT-KUN IS HERE TOO!
...THANKS FOR FILLING US IN.

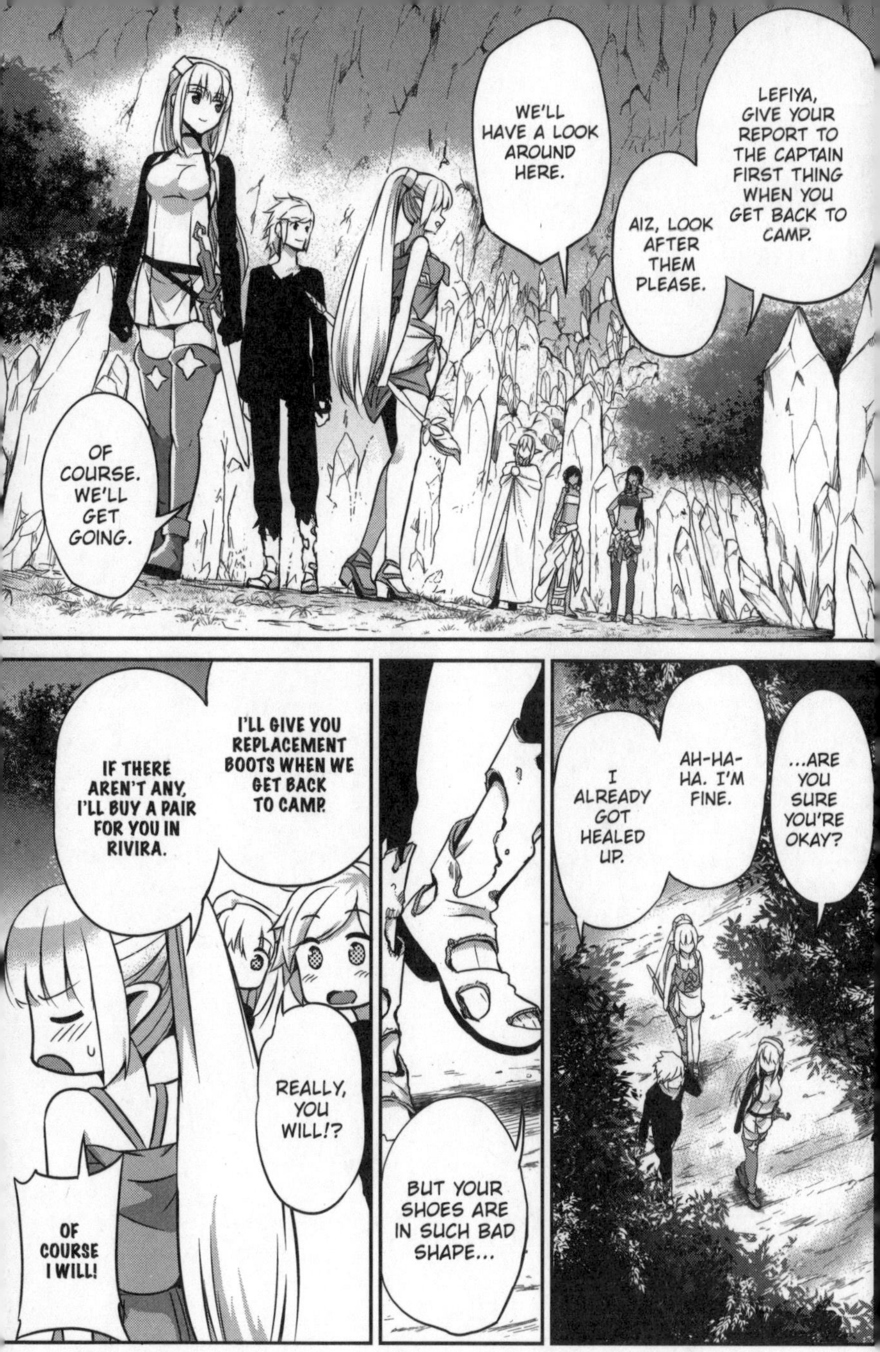
LEFIYA, GIVE YOUR REPORT TO THE CAPTAIN FIRST THING WHEN YOU GET BACK TO CAMP.
AIZ, LOOK AFTER THEM PLEASE.
WE'LL HAVE A LOOK AROUND HERE.
OF COURSE. WE'LL GET GOING.
...ARE YOU SURE YOU'RE OKAY?
AH-HA-HA. I'M FINE.
I ALREADY GOT HEALED UP.
BUT YOUR SHOES ARE IN SUCH BAD SHAPE...
I'LL GIVE YOU REPLACEMENT BOOTS WHEN WE GET BACK TO CAMP.
IF THERE AREN'T ANY, I'LL BUY A PAIR FOR YOU IN RIVIRA.
REALLY, YOU WILL!?
OF COURSE I WILL!

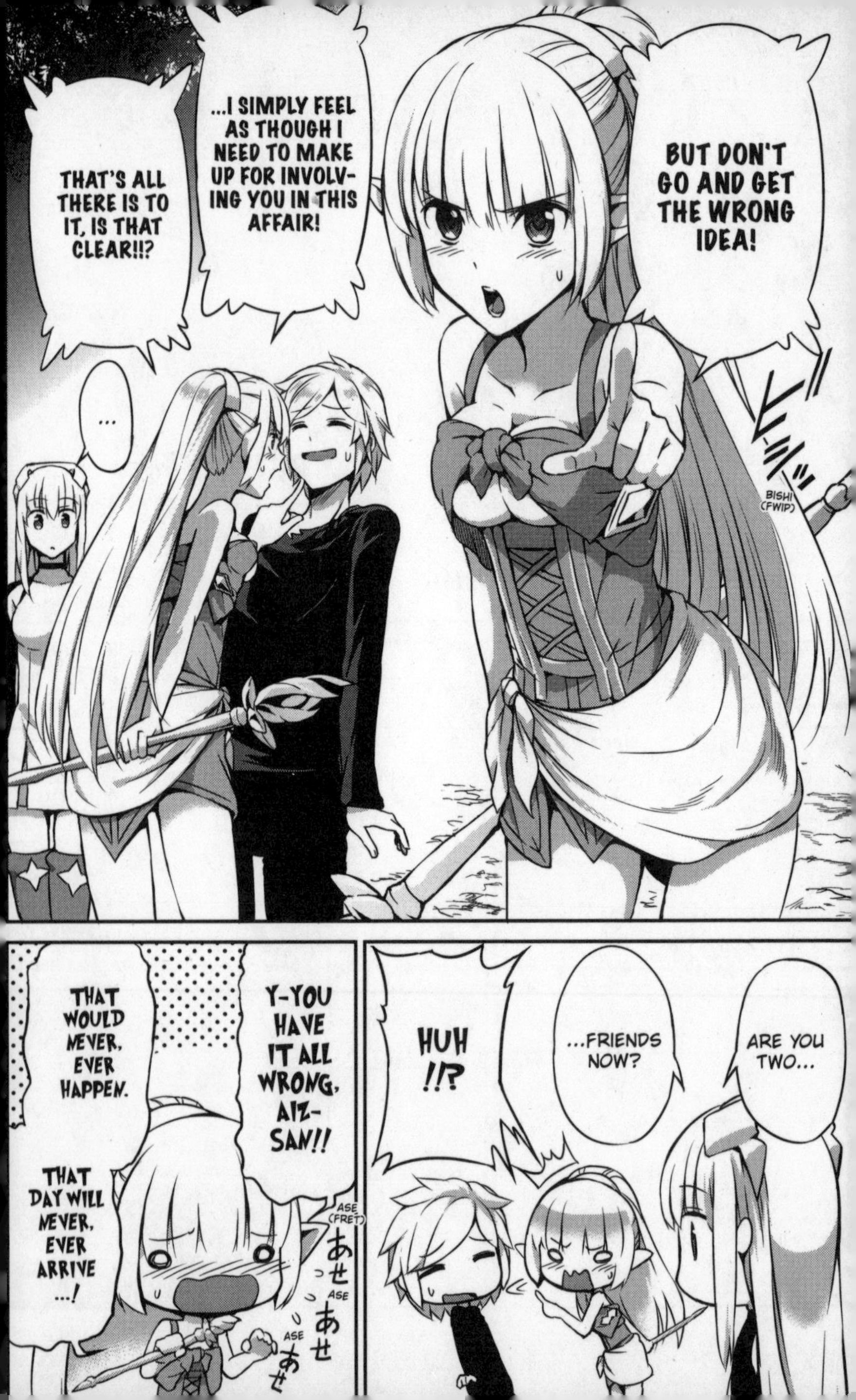
BUT DON'T GO AND GET THE WRONG IDEA!
...I SIMPLY FEEL AS THOUGH I NEED TO MAKE UP FOR INVOLVING YOU IN THIS AFFAIR!
THAT'S ALL THERE IS TO IT, IS THAT CLEAR!!?
BISHI (FWIP)
...
ARE YOU TWO...
...FRIENDS NOW?
HUH!!?
Y-YOU HAVE IT ALL WRONG, AIZ-SAN!!
ASE (FRET)
あせ
ASE
あせ
ASE
あせ
THAT WOULD NEVER, EVER HAPPEN.
THAT DAY WILL NEVER, EVER ARRIVE...!

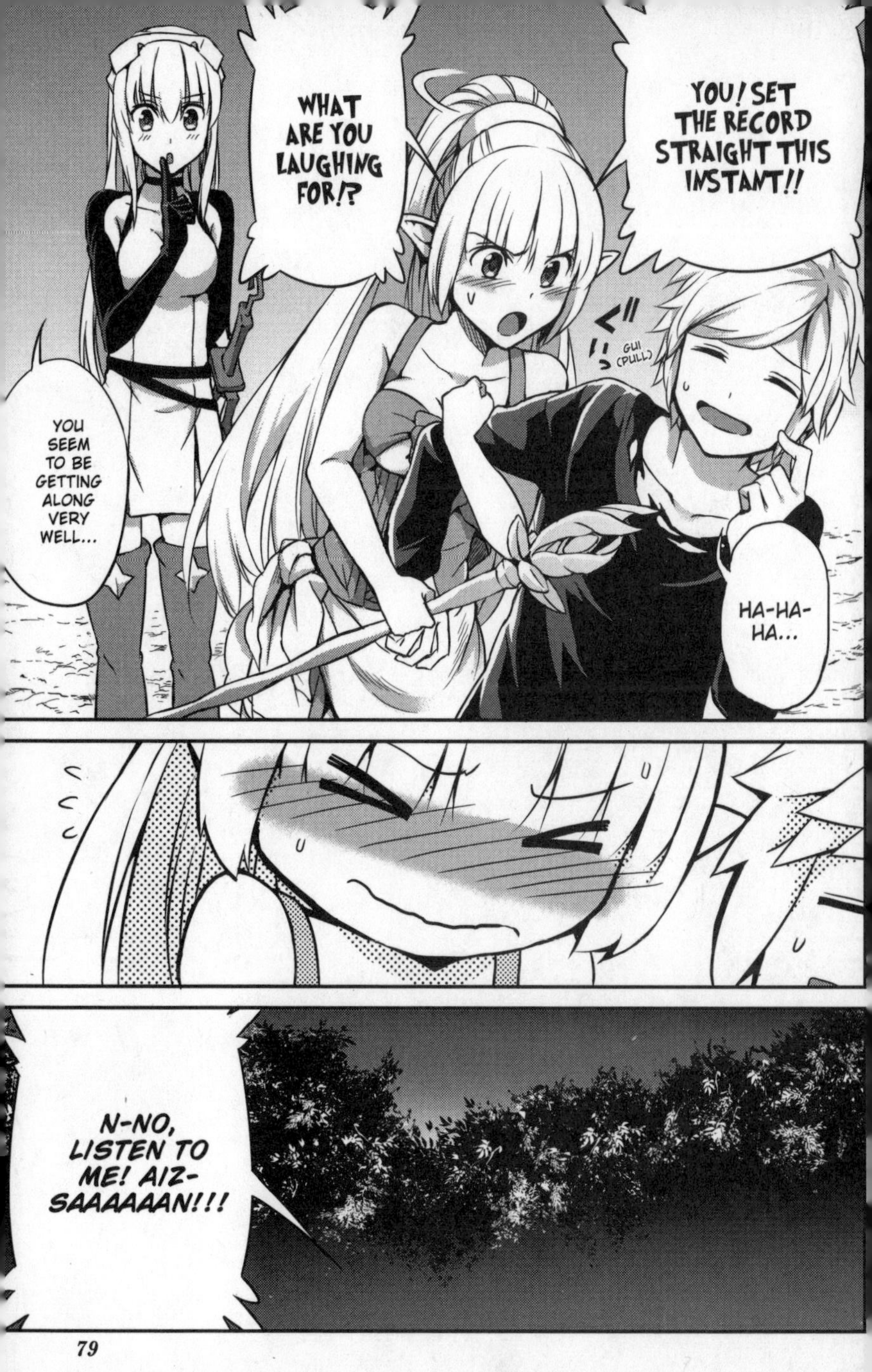
YOU! SET THE RECORD STRAIGHT THIS INSTANT!!
WHAT ARE YOU LAUGHING FOR!?
GUI (PULL)
HA-HA-HA...
YOU SEEM TO BE GETTING ALONG VERY WELL...
N-NO, LISTEN TO ME! AIZ-SAAAAAAN!!!

IS IT WRONG TO TRY TO PICK UP GIRLS IN A DUNGEON? ON THE SIDE

Sword Oratoria

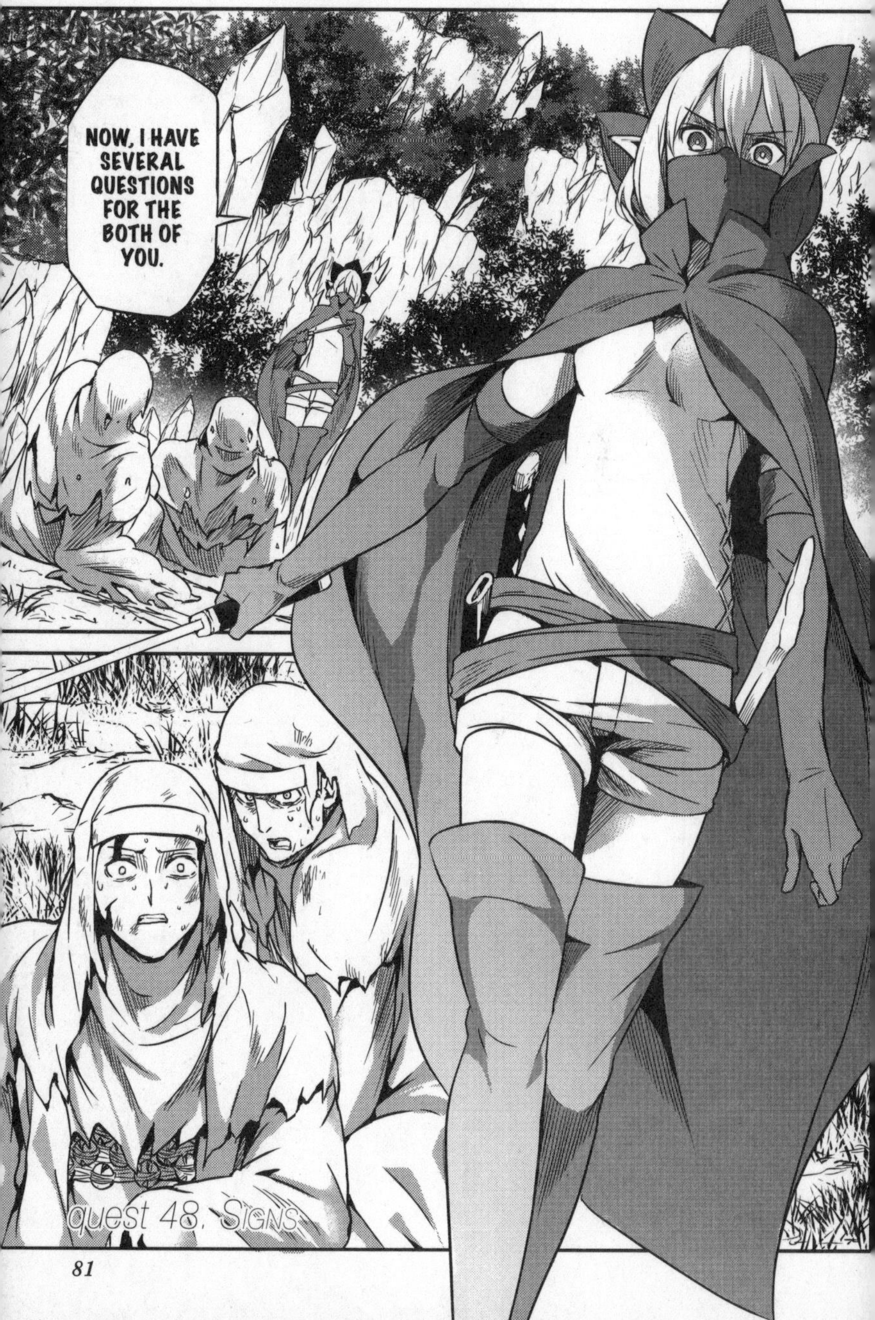
NOW, I HAVE SEVERAL QUESTIONS FOR THE BOTH OF YOU.
quest 48. Signs

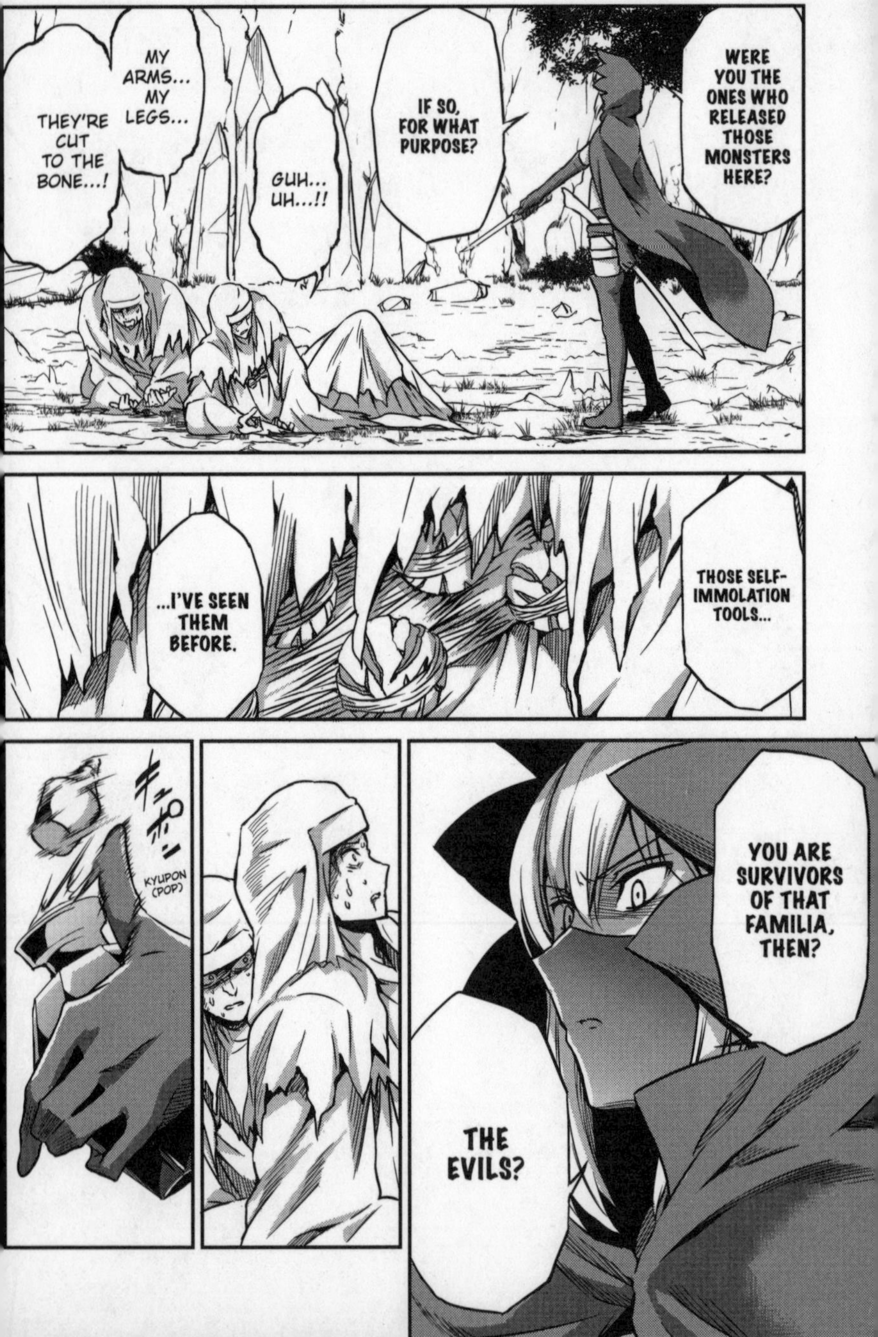
WERE YOU THE ONES WHO RELEASED THOSE MONSTERS HERE?
IF SO, FOR WHAT PURPOSE?
GUH... UH...!!
MY ARMS... MY LEGS...
THEY'RE CUT TO THE BONE...!
THOSE SELF-IMMOLATION TOOLS...
...I'VE SEEN THEM BEFORE.
YOU ARE SURVIVORS OF THAT FAMILIA, THEN?
THE EVILS?
キュポン
KYUPON (POP)

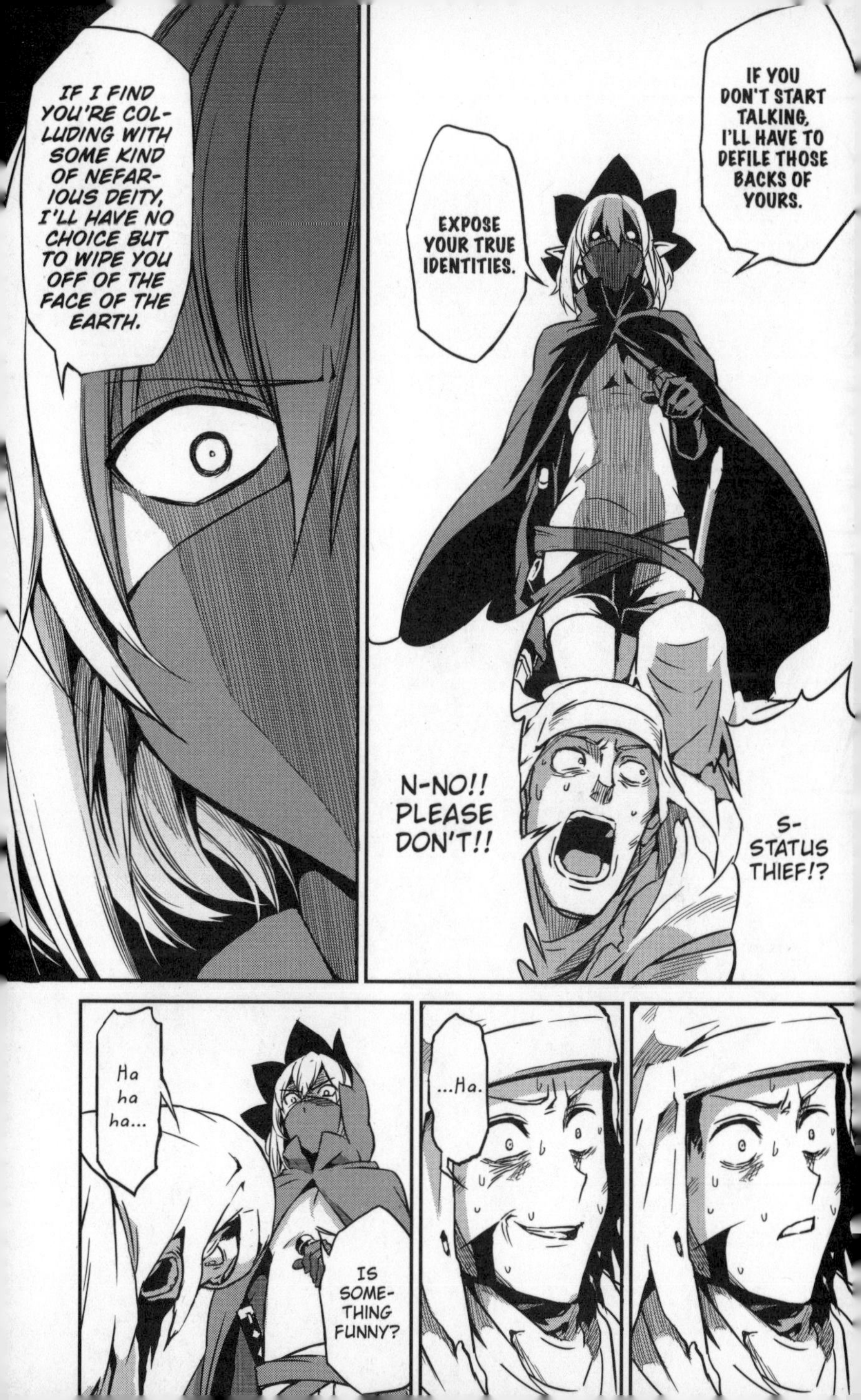
IF YOU DON'T START TALKING, I'LL HAVE TO DEFILE THOSE BACKS OF YOURS.
EXPOSE YOUR TRUE IDENTITIES.
S-STATUS THIEF!?
N-NO!! PLEASE DON'T!!
IF I FIND YOU'RE COLLUDING WITH SOME KIND OF NEFARIOUS DEITY, I'LL HAVE NO CHOICE BUT TO WIPE YOU OFF OF THE FACE OF THE EARTH.
...Ha.
Ha ha ha...
IS SOMETHING FUNNY?

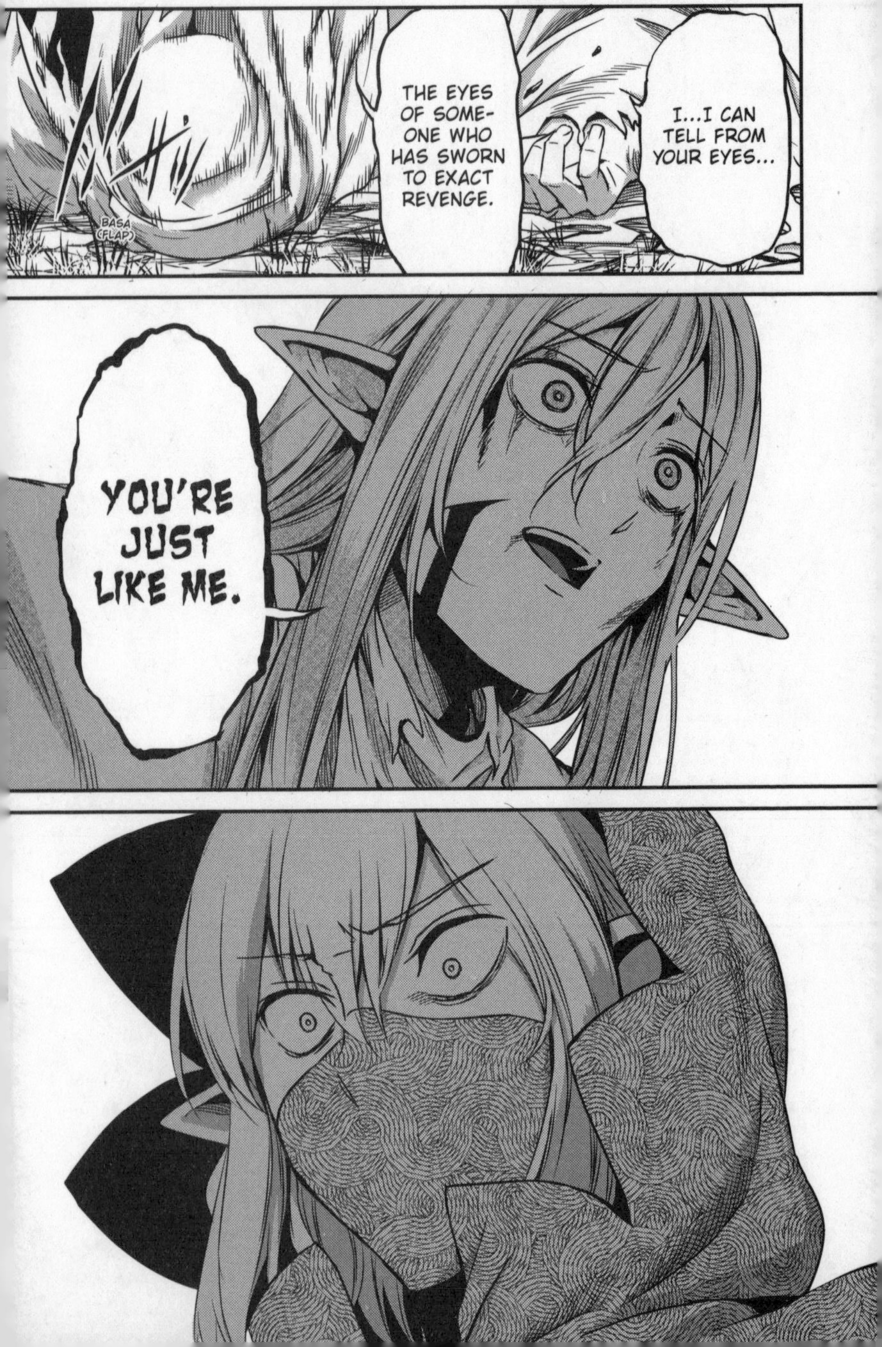
I...I CAN TELL FROM YOUR EYES...
THE EYES OF SOME-ONE WHO HAS SWORN TO EXACT REVENGE.
BASA (FLAP)
YOU'RE JUST LIKE ME.

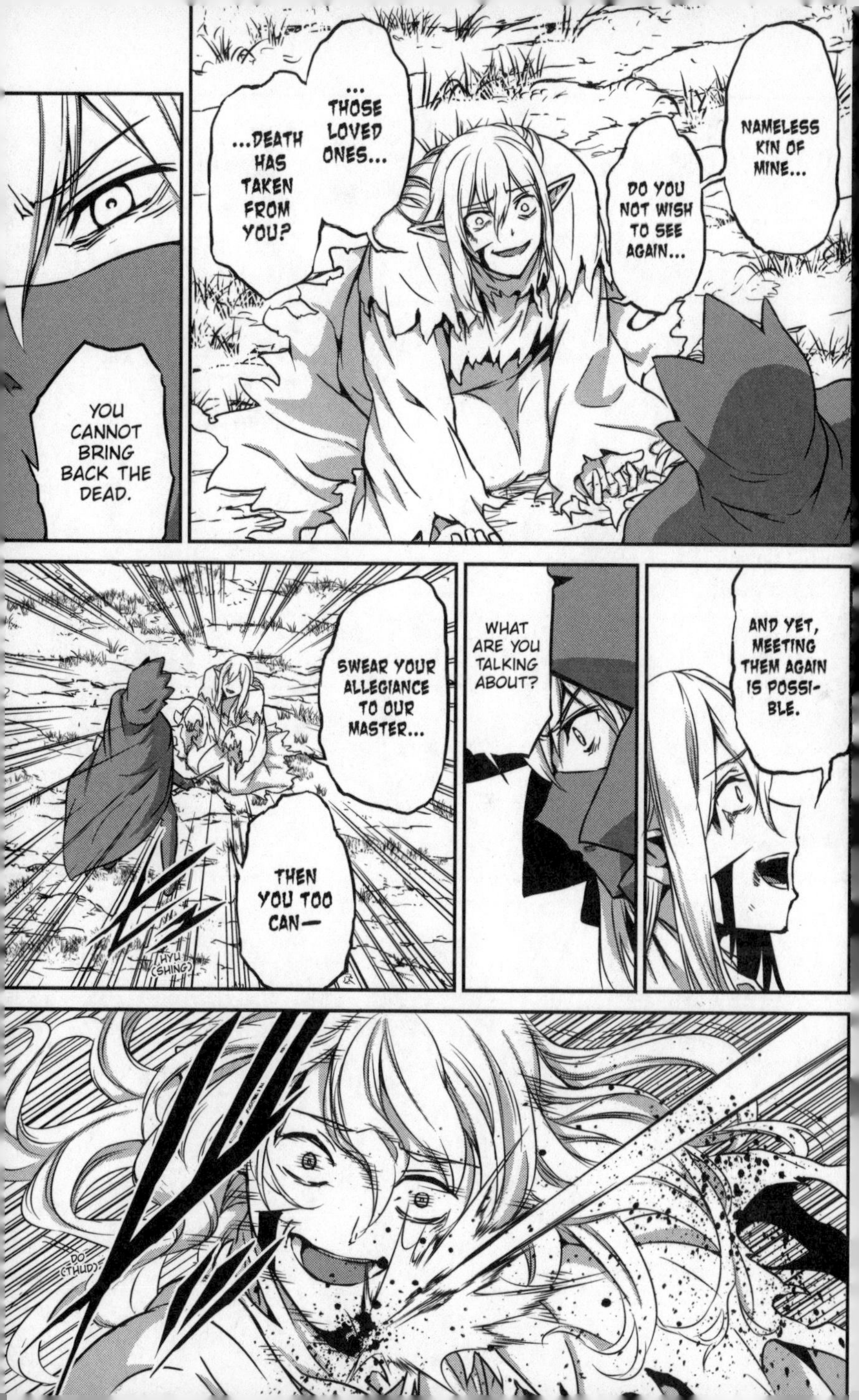
NAMELESS KIN OF MINE...
DO YOU NOT WISH TO SEE AGAIN...
... THOSE LOVED ONES...
...DEATH HAS TAKEN FROM YOU?
YOU CANNOT BRING BACK THE DEAD.
AND YET, MEETING THEM AGAIN IS POSSI-BLE.
WHAT ARE YOU TALKING ABOUT?
SWEAR YOUR ALLEGIANCE TO OUR MASTER...
THEN YOU TOO CAN—
HYU (SHING)
DO (THUD)

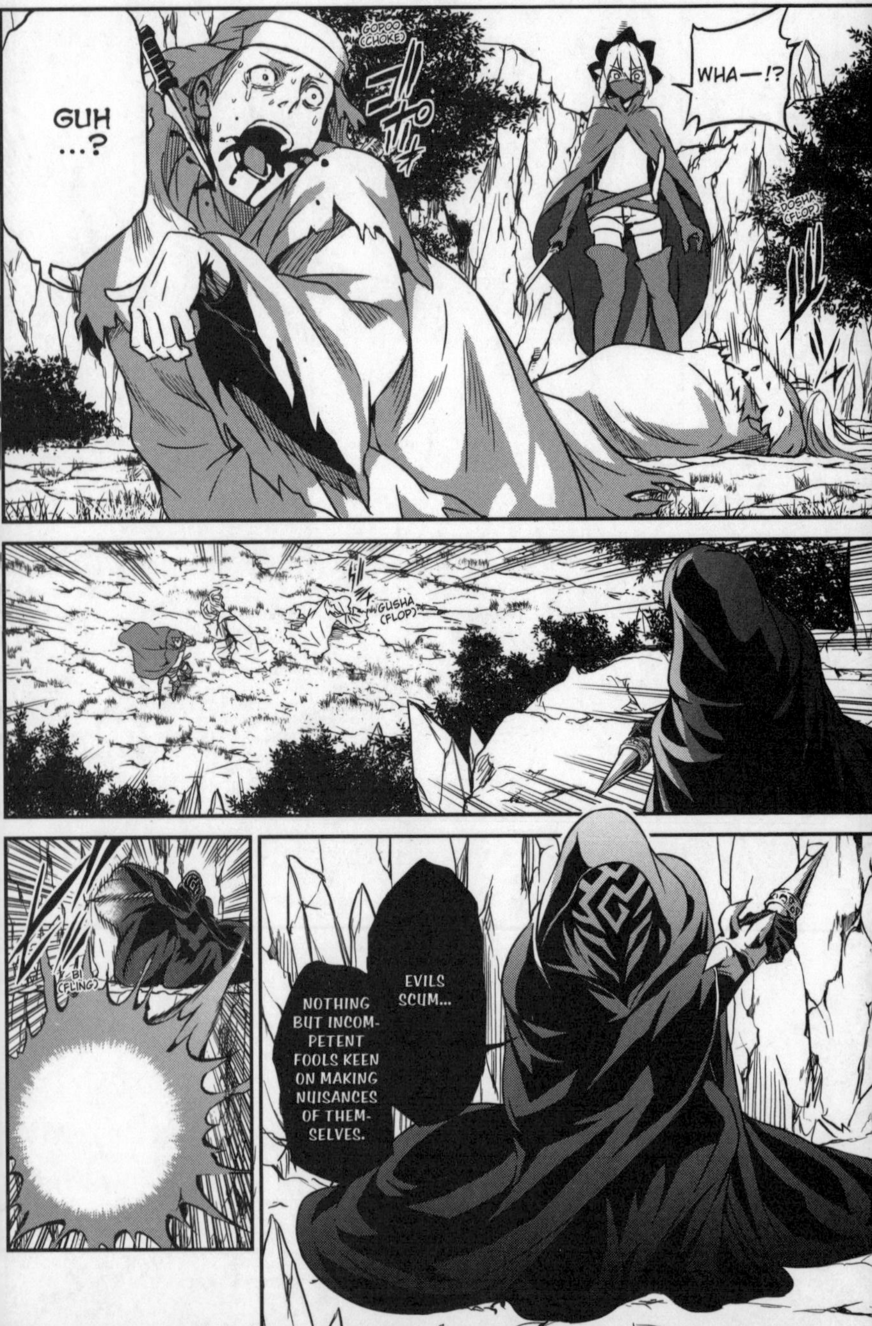
WHA—!?
DOSHA (FLOP)
GOPOO (CHOKE)
GUH ...?
GUSHA (FLOP)
EVILS SCUM...
NOTHING BUT INCOMPETENT FOOLS KEEN ON MAKING NUISANCES OF THEMSELVES.
BI (FLING)

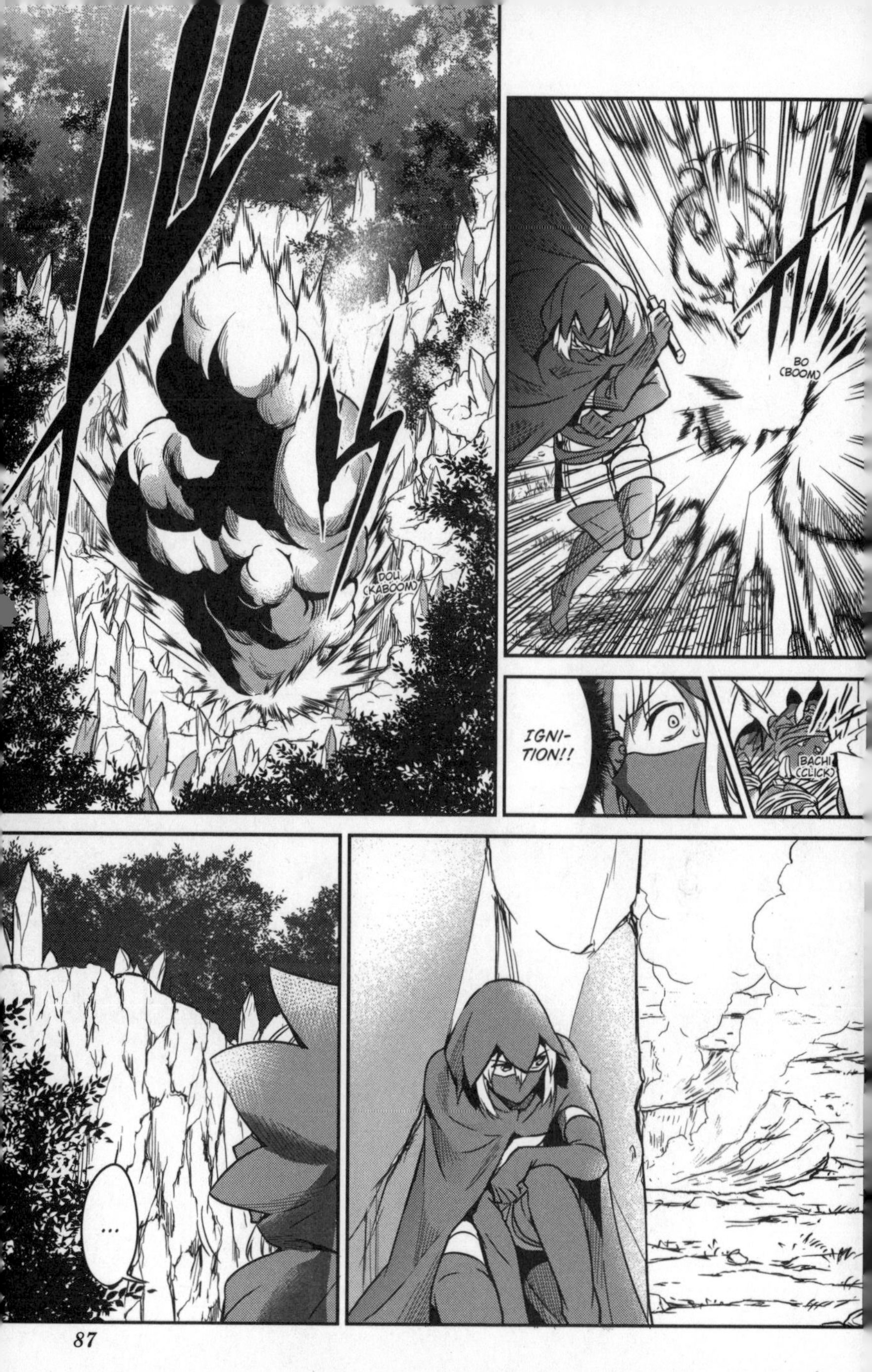
BO
(BOOM)
BACHI
(CLICK)
IGNI-
TION!!
DOU
(KABOOM)
...

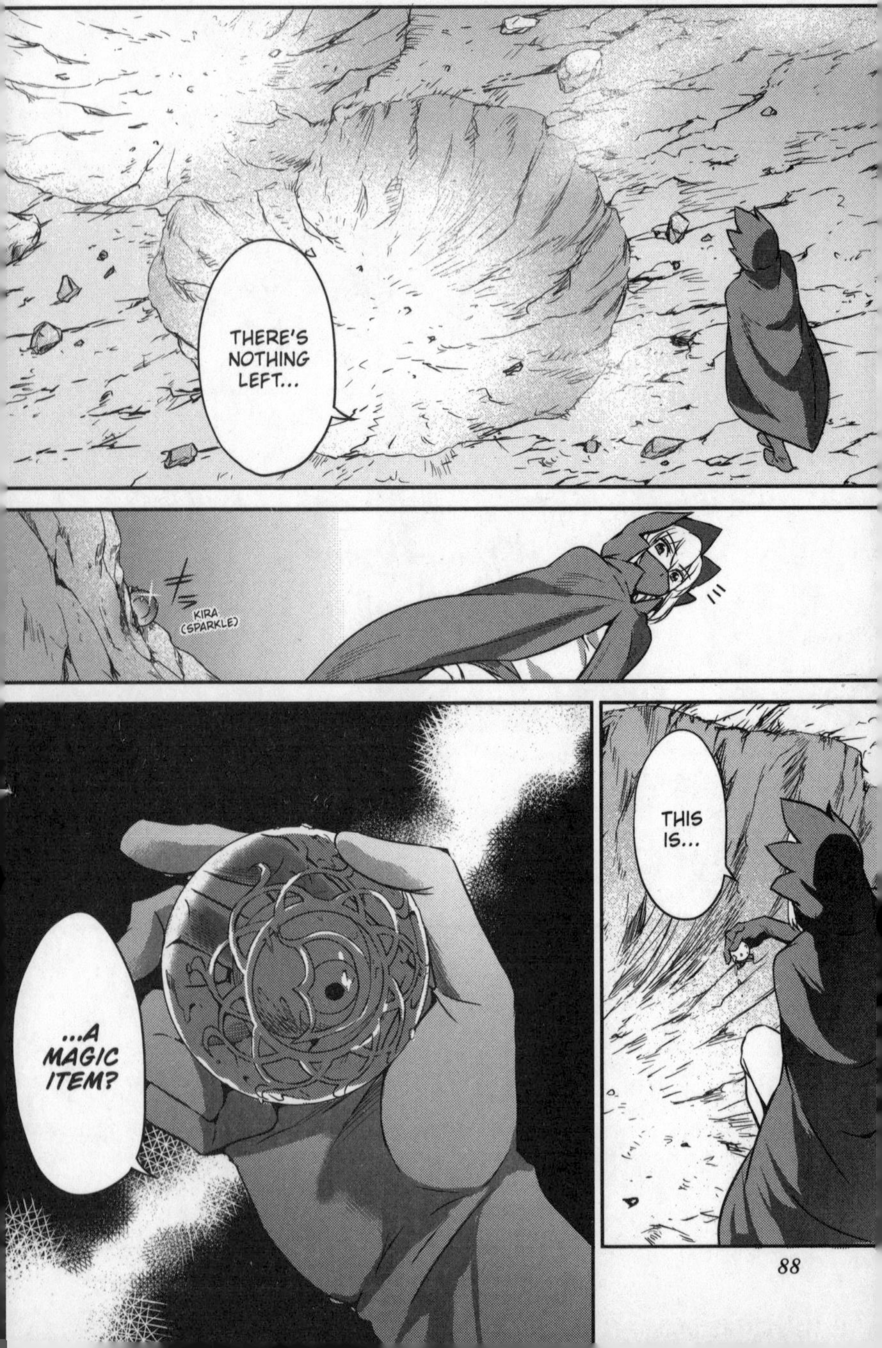
THERE'S NOTHING LEFT...
KIRA (SPARKLE)
THIS IS...
...A MAGIC ITEM?

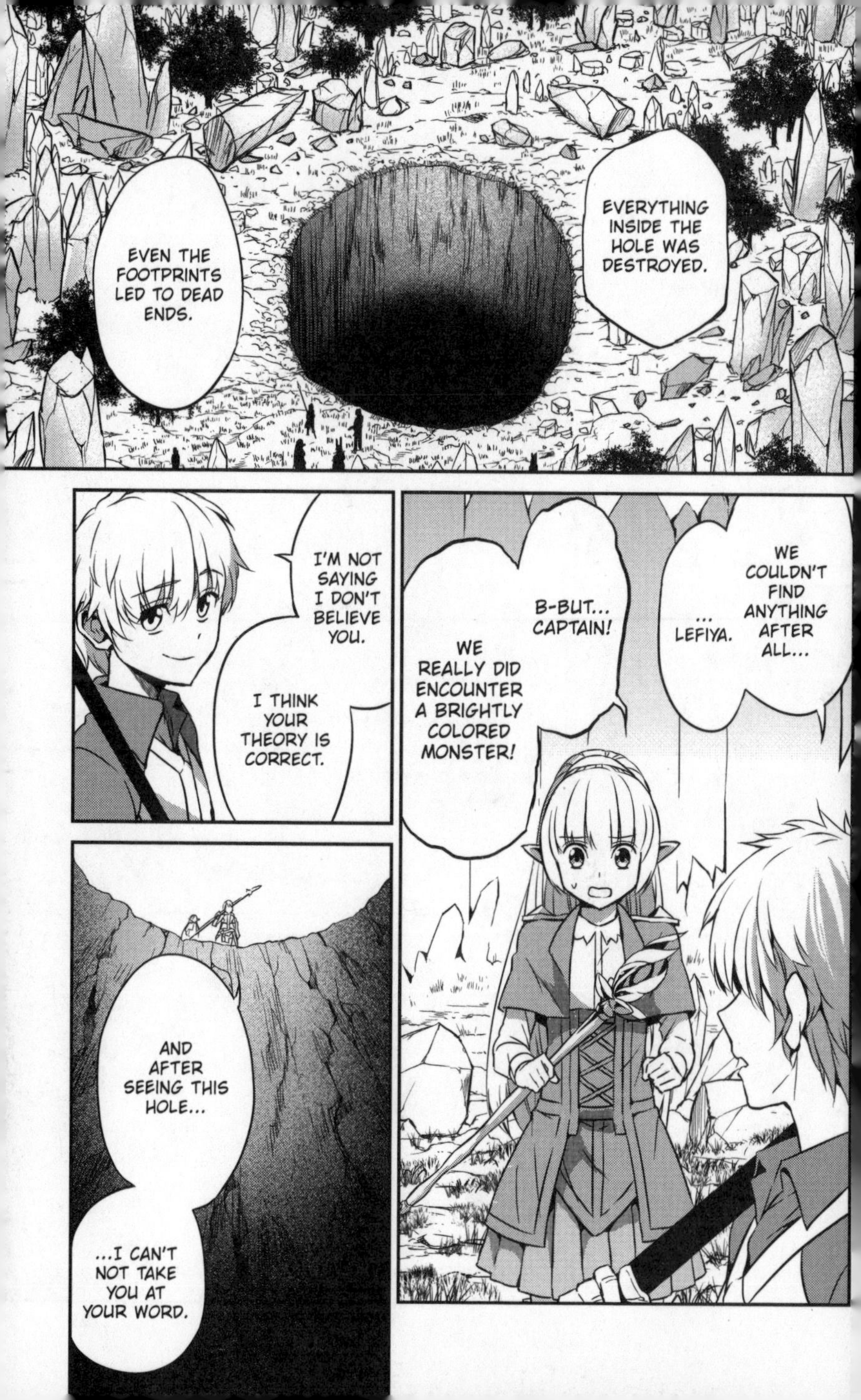
EVERYTHING INSIDE THE HOLE WAS DESTROYED.
EVEN THE FOOTPRINTS LED TO DEAD ENDS.
WE COULDN'T FIND ANYTHING AFTER ALL...
...LEFIYA.
B-BUT... CAPTAIN!
WE REALLY DID ENCOUNTER A BRIGHTLY COLORED MONSTER!
I'M NOT SAYING I DON'T BELIEVE YOU.
I THINK YOUR THEORY IS CORRECT.
AND AFTER SEEING THIS HOLE...
...I CAN'T NOT TAKE YOU AT YOUR WORD.

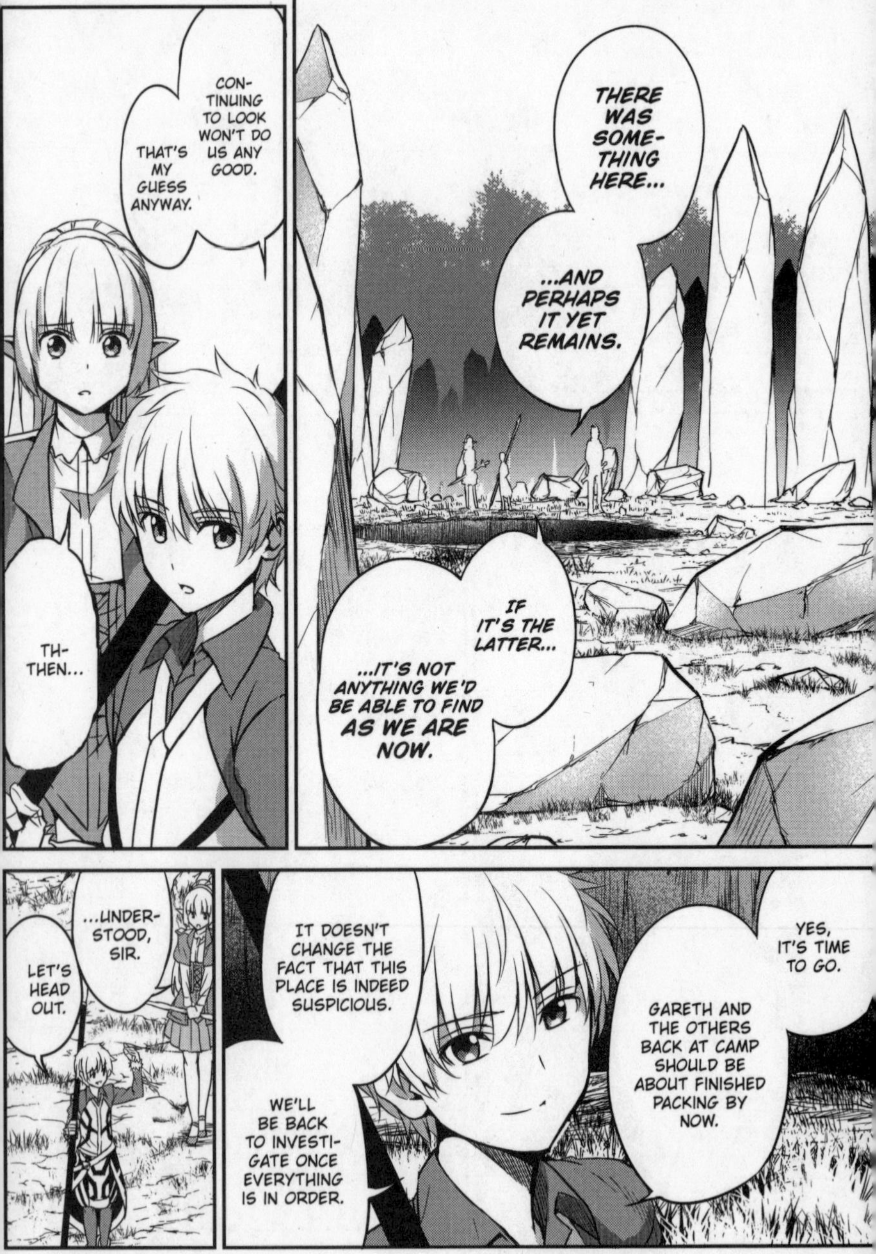
THERE WAS SOME-THING HERE...
...AND PERHAPS IT YET REMAINS.
IF IT'S THE LATTER...
...IT'S NOT ANYTHING WE'D BE ABLE TO FIND AS WE ARE NOW.
CON-TINUING TO LOOK WON'T DO US ANY GOOD.
THAT'S MY GUESS ANYWAY.
TH-THEN...
YES, IT'S TIME TO GO.
GARETH AND THE OTHERS BACK AT CAMP SHOULD BE ABOUT FINISHED PACKING BY NOW.
IT DOESN'T CHANGE THE FACT THAT THIS PLACE IS INDEED SUSPICIOUS.
WE'LL BE BACK TO INVESTI-GATE ONCE EVERYTHING IS IN ORDER.
...UNDER-STOOD, SIR.
LET'S HEAD OUT.

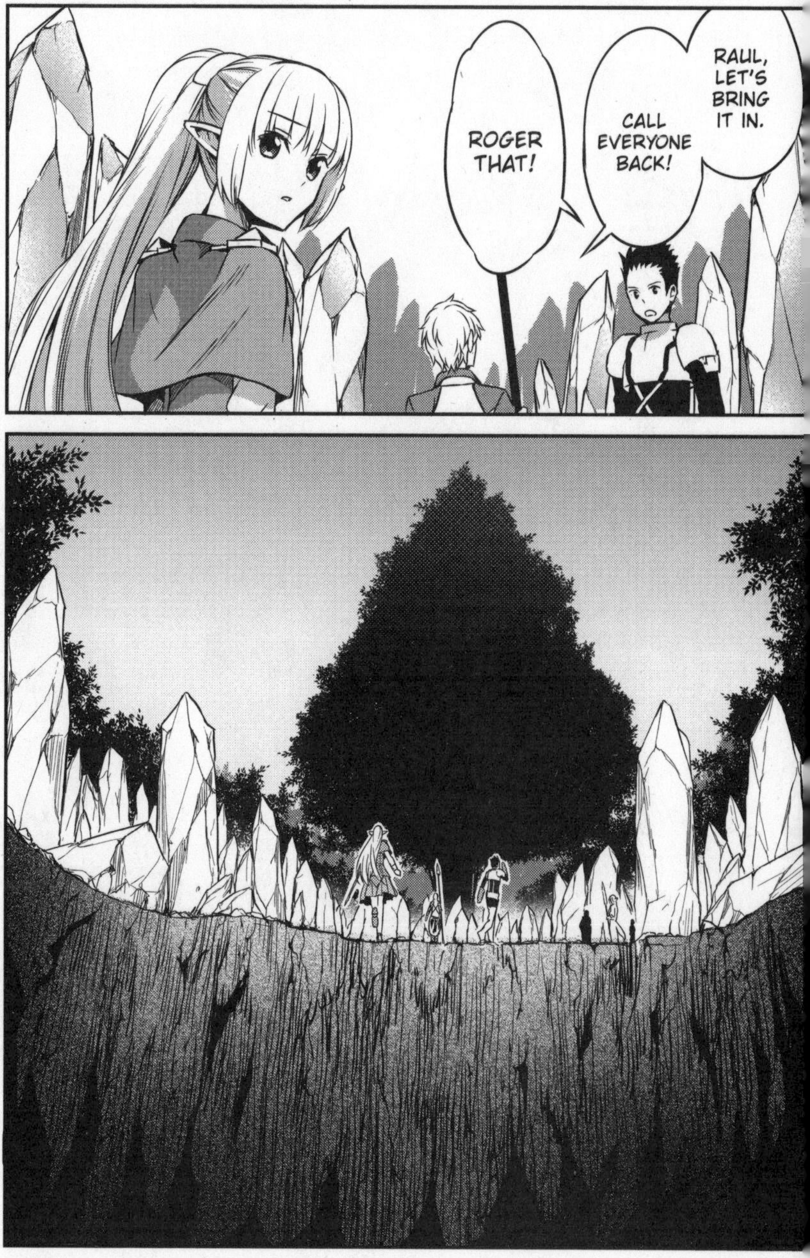
RAUL, LET'S BRING IT IN.
CALL EVERYONE BACK!
ROGER THAT!

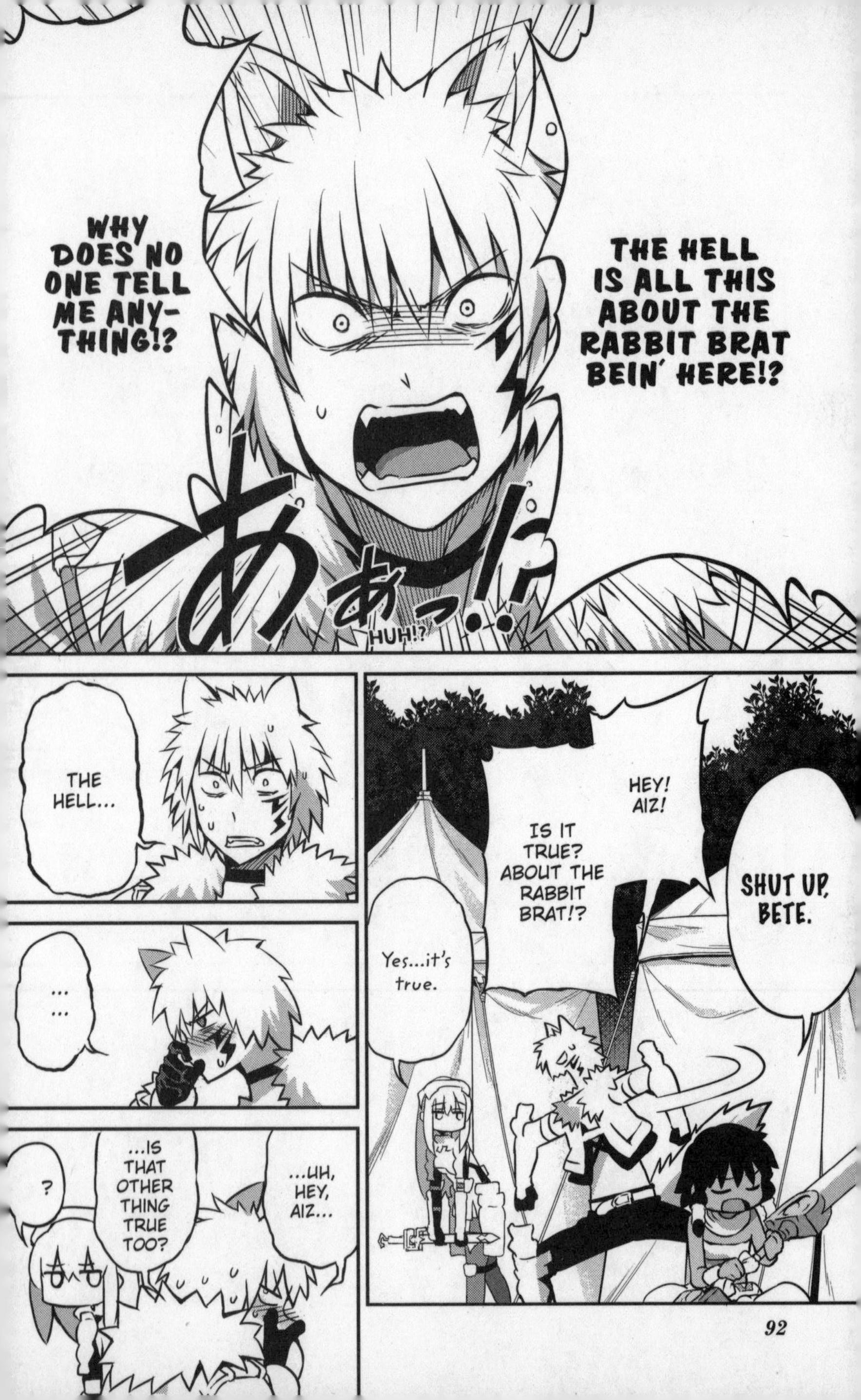
THE HELL IS ALL THIS ABOUT THE RABBIT BRAT BEIN' HERE!?
WHY DOES NO ONE TELL ME ANY-THING!?
あぁっ!?
HUH!?
HEY! AIZ!
IS IT TRUE? ABOUT THE RABBIT BRAT!?
SHUT UP, BETE.
Yes...it's true.
THE HELL...
......
...UH, HEY, AIZ...
...IS THAT OTHER THING TRUE TOO?
?

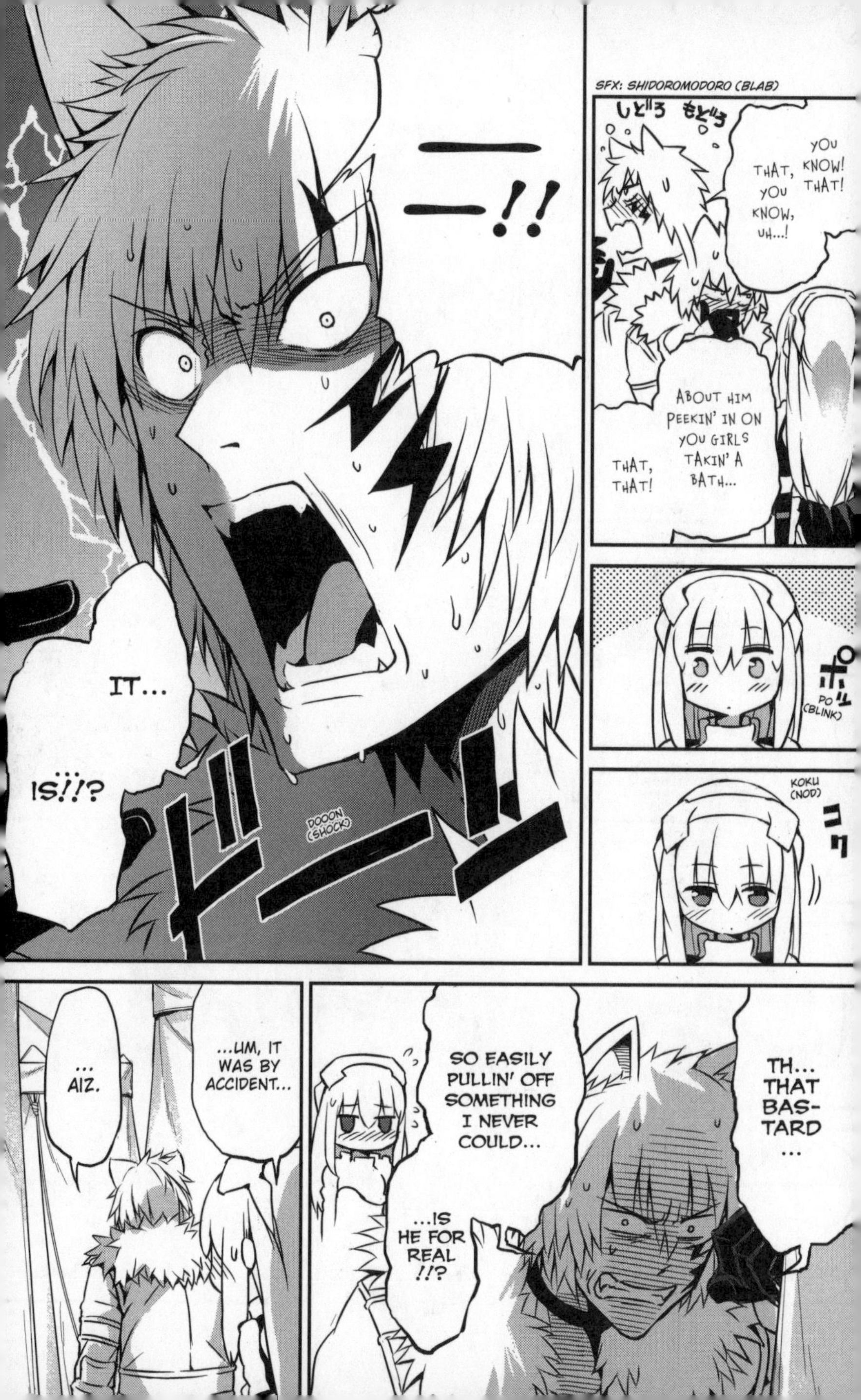
SFX: SHIDOROMODORO (BLAB)
しどろ もどろ
YOU KNOW! THAT!
THAT, YOU KNOW, UH...!
ABOUT HIM PEEKIN' IN ON YOU GIRLS TAKIN' A BATH...
THAT, THAT!
PO (BLINK)
KOKU (NOD)
——— —!!
IT...
IS!!?
DOOON (SHOCK)
TH... THAT BAS-TARD ...
SO EASILY PULLIN' OFF SOMETHING I NEVER COULD...
...IS HE FOR REAL!!?
...UM, IT WAS BY ACCIDENT...
... AIZ.

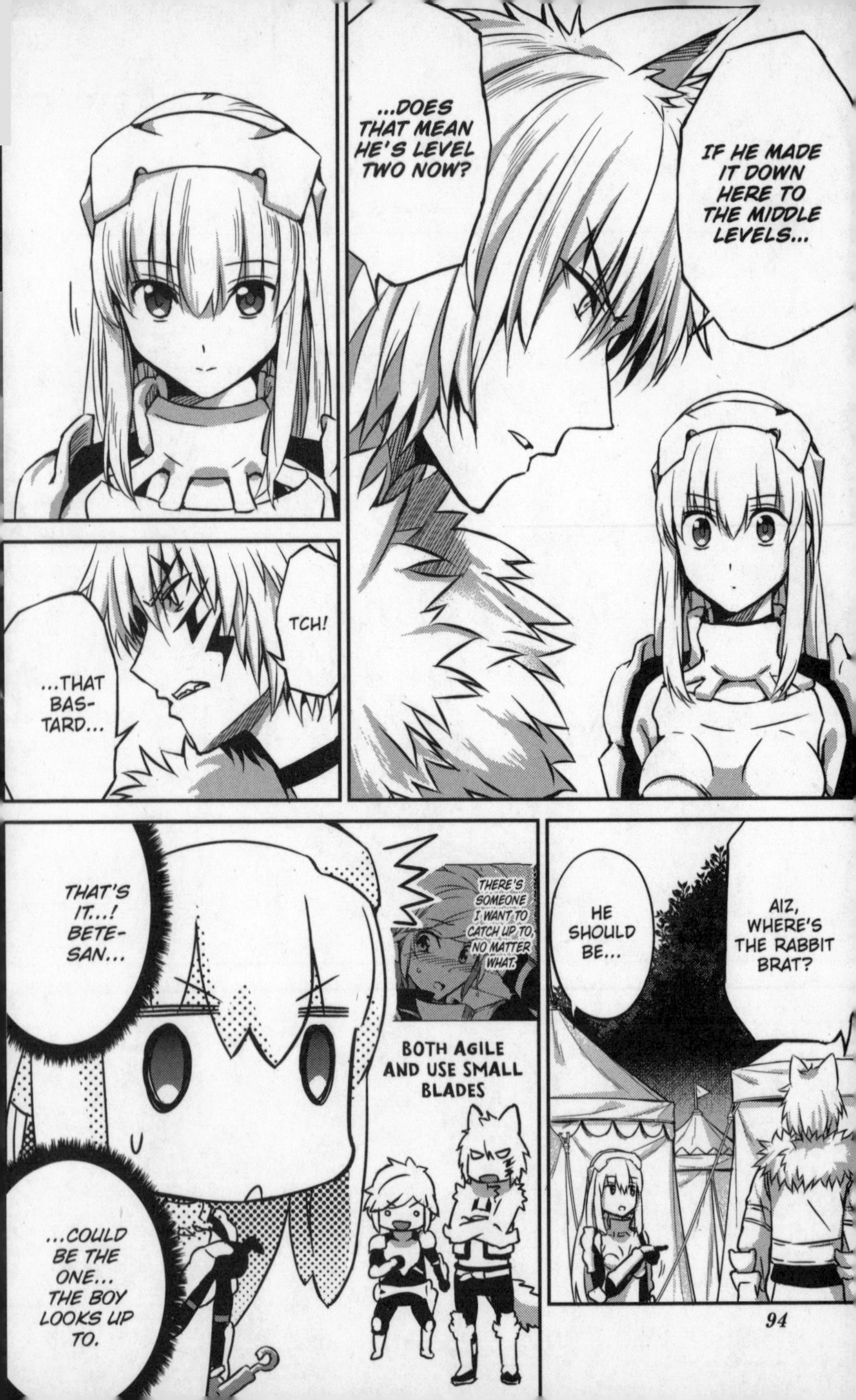

IF HE MADE IT DOWN HERE TO THE MIDDLE LEVELS...
...DOES THAT MEAN HE'S LEVEL TWO NOW?
TCH!
...THAT BAS-TARD...
AIZ, WHERE'S THE RABBIT BRAT?
HE SHOULD BE...
THERE'S SOMEONE I WANT TO CATCH UP TO, NO MATTER WHAT.
THAT'S IT...! BETE-SAN...
BOTH AGILE AND USE SMALL BLADES
...COULD BE THE ONE... THE BOY LOOKS UP TO.

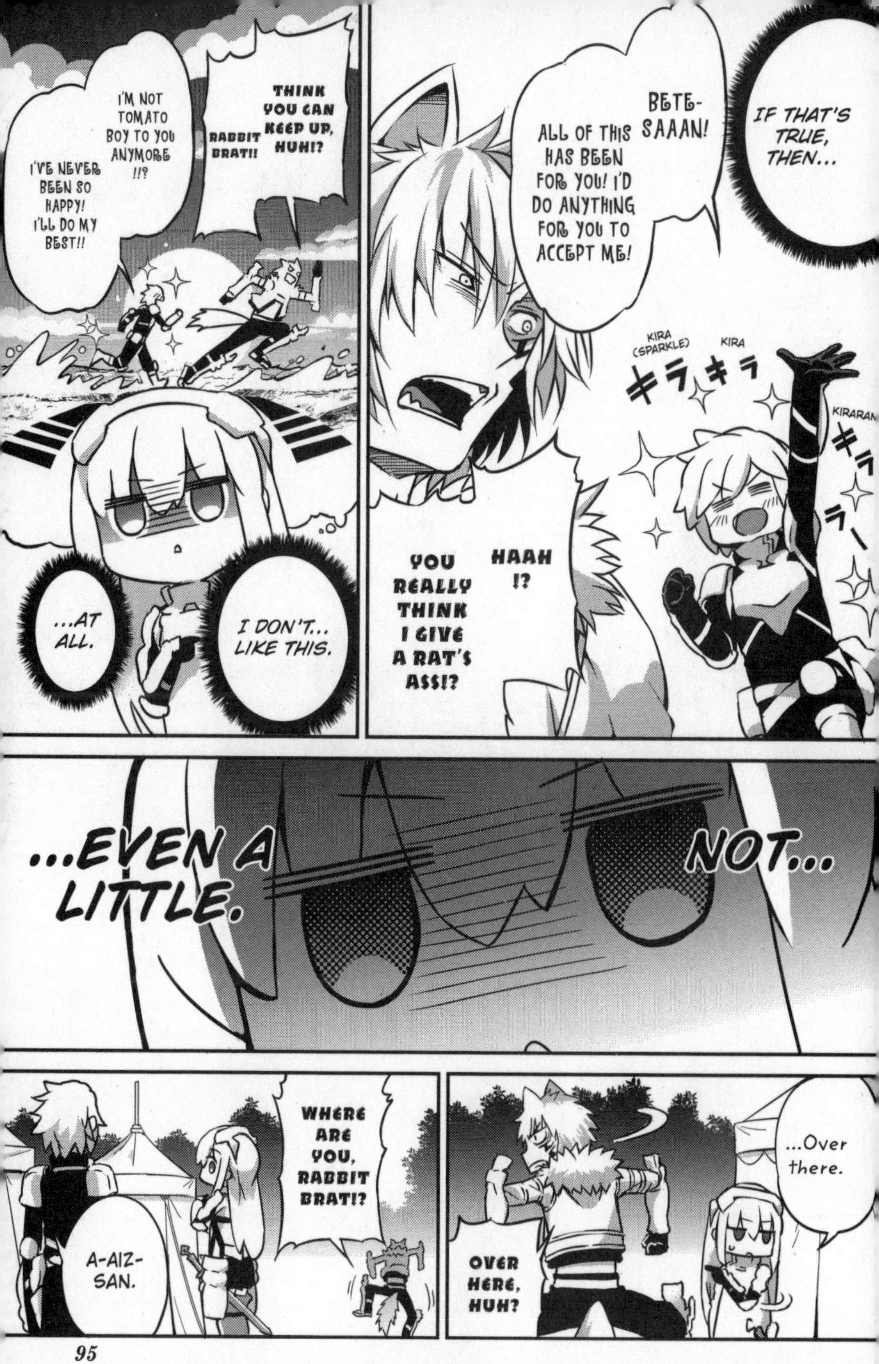

IF THAT'S TRUE, THEN...
BETE-SAAAN!
ALL OF THIS HAS BEEN FOR YOU! I'D DO ANYTHING FOR YOU TO ACCEPT ME!
KIRA (SPARKLE)
KIRA
キラキラ
KIRARAN
キララ～
HAAH!?
YOU REALLY THINK I GIVE A RAT'S ASS!?
THINK YOU CAN KEEP UP, HUH!?
RABBIT BRAT!!
I'M NOT TOMATO BOY TO YOU ANYMORE!!?
I'VE NEVER BEEN SO HAPPY! I'LL DO MY BEST!!
I DON'T... LIKE THIS.
...AT ALL.
NOT...
...EVEN A LITTLE.
...Over there.
OVER HERE, HUH?
WHERE ARE YOU, RABBIT BRAT!?
A-AIZ-SAN.

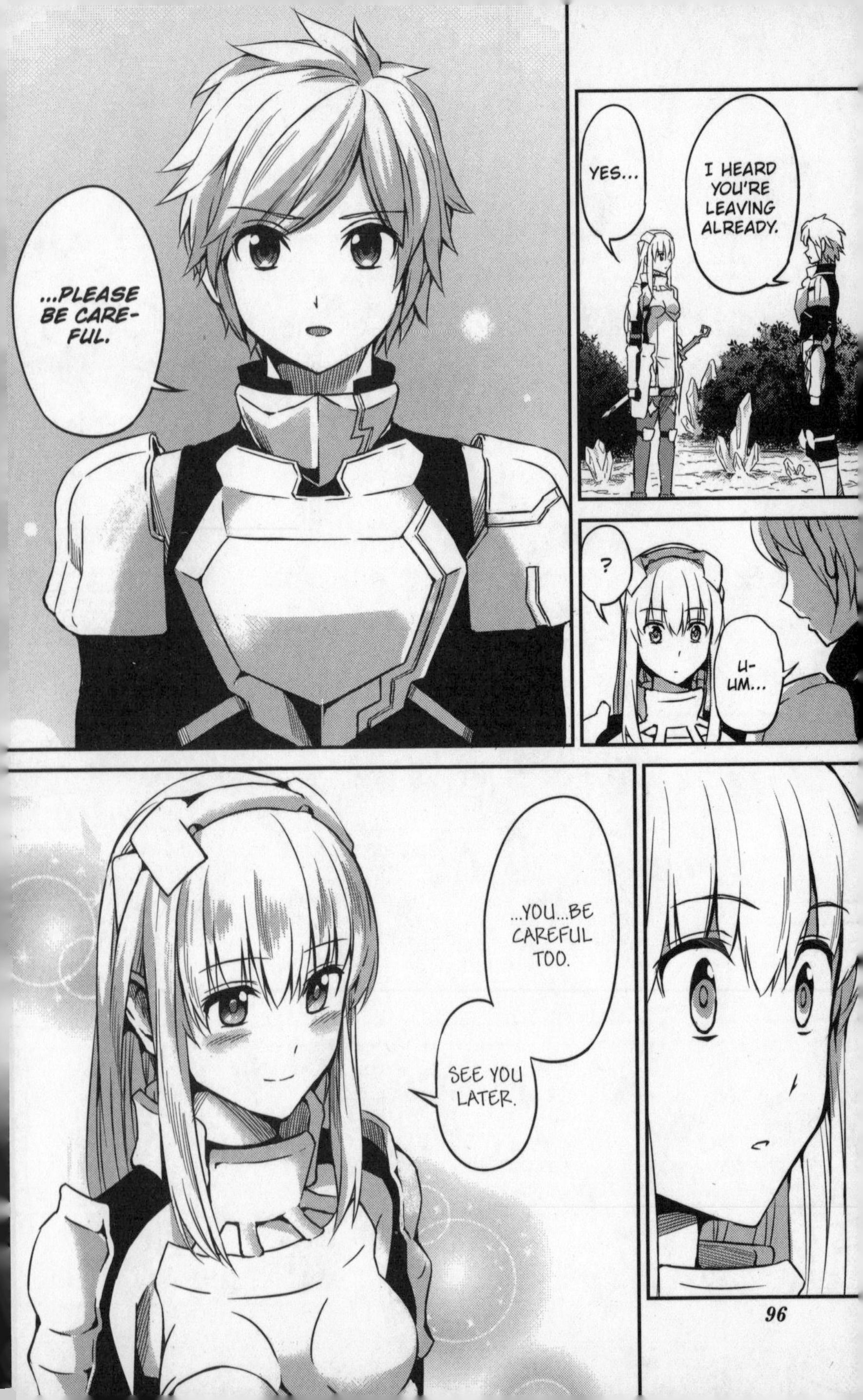
I HEARD YOU'RE LEAVING ALREADY.
YES...
U-UM...
?
...PLEASE BE CARE-FUL.
...YOU...BE CAREFUL TOO.
SEE YOU LATER.

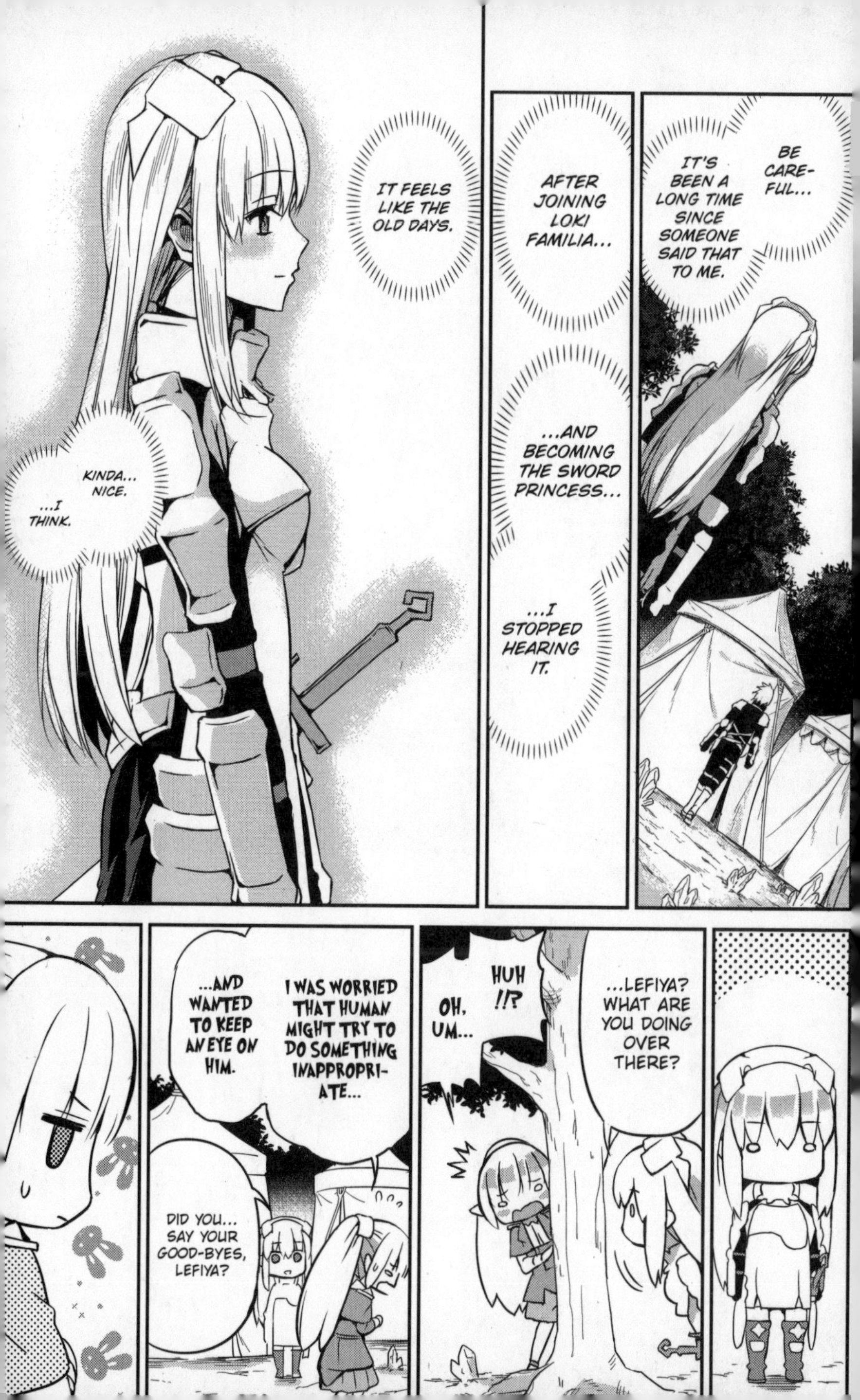
BE CAREFUL...
IT'S BEEN A LONG TIME SINCE SOMEONE SAID THAT TO ME.
AFTER JOINING LOKI FAMILIA...
...AND BECOMING THE SWORD PRINCESS...
...I STOPPED HEARING IT.
IT FEELS LIKE THE OLD DAYS.
KINDA... NICE.
...I THINK.
...LEFIYA? WHAT ARE YOU DOING OVER THERE?
HUH !!?
OH, UM...
MM
I WAS WORRIED THAT HUMAN MIGHT TRY TO DO SOMETHING INAPPROPRIATE...
...AND WANTED TO KEEP AN EYE ON HIM.
DID YOU... SAY YOUR GOOD-BYES, LEFIYA?

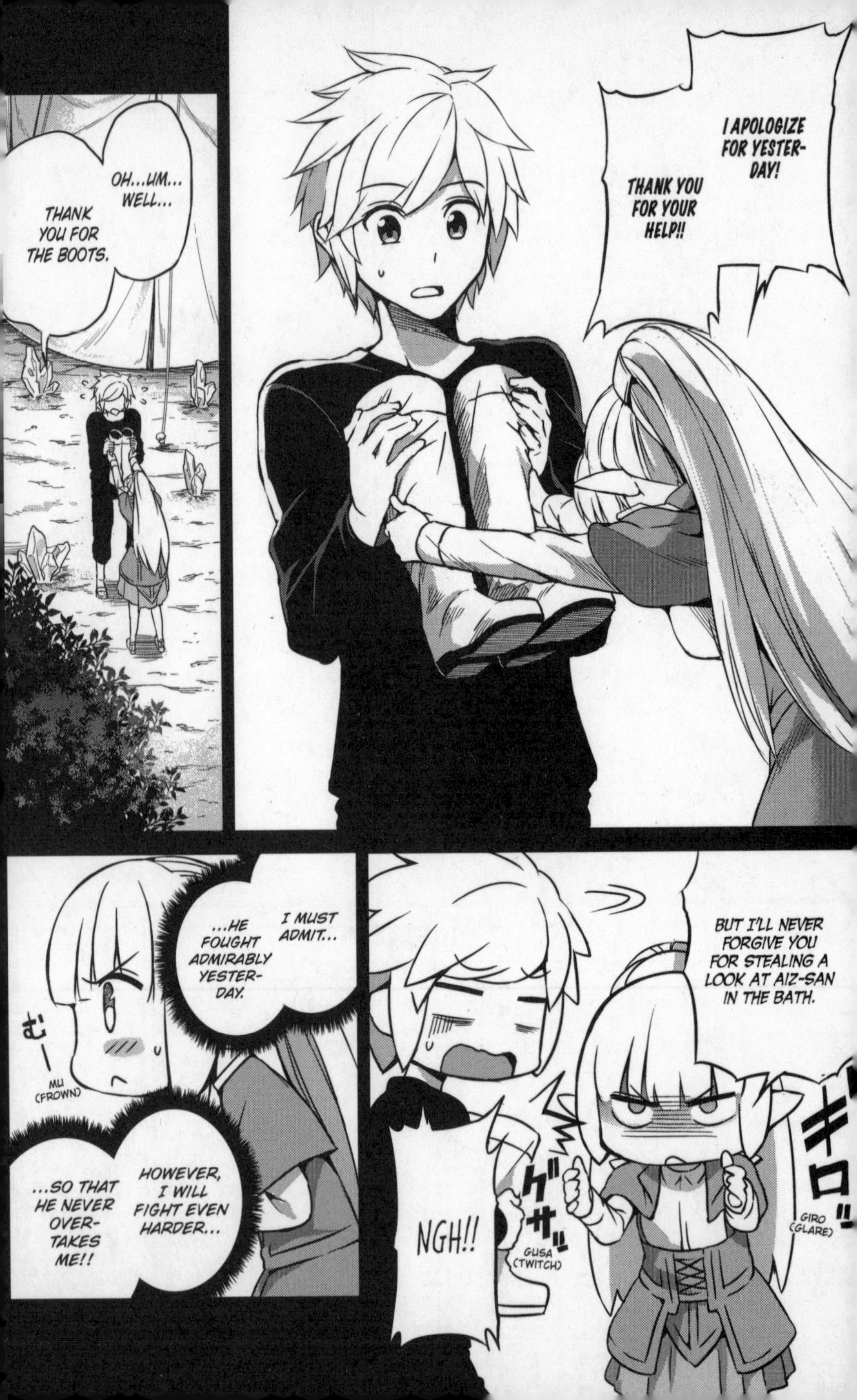
I APOLOGIZE FOR YESTER-DAY!
THANK YOU FOR YOUR HELP!!
OH...UM... WELL...
THANK YOU FOR THE BOOTS.
BUT I'LL NEVER FORGIVE YOU FOR STEALING A LOOK AT AIZ-SAN IN THE BATH.
ギロッ
GIRO (GLARE)
グサッ
GUSA (TWITCH)
NGH!!
I MUST ADMIT...
...HE FOUGHT ADMIRABLY YESTER-DAY.
むー
MU (FROWN)
HOWEVER, I WILL FIGHT EVEN HARDER...
...SO THAT HE NEVER OVER-TAKES ME!!

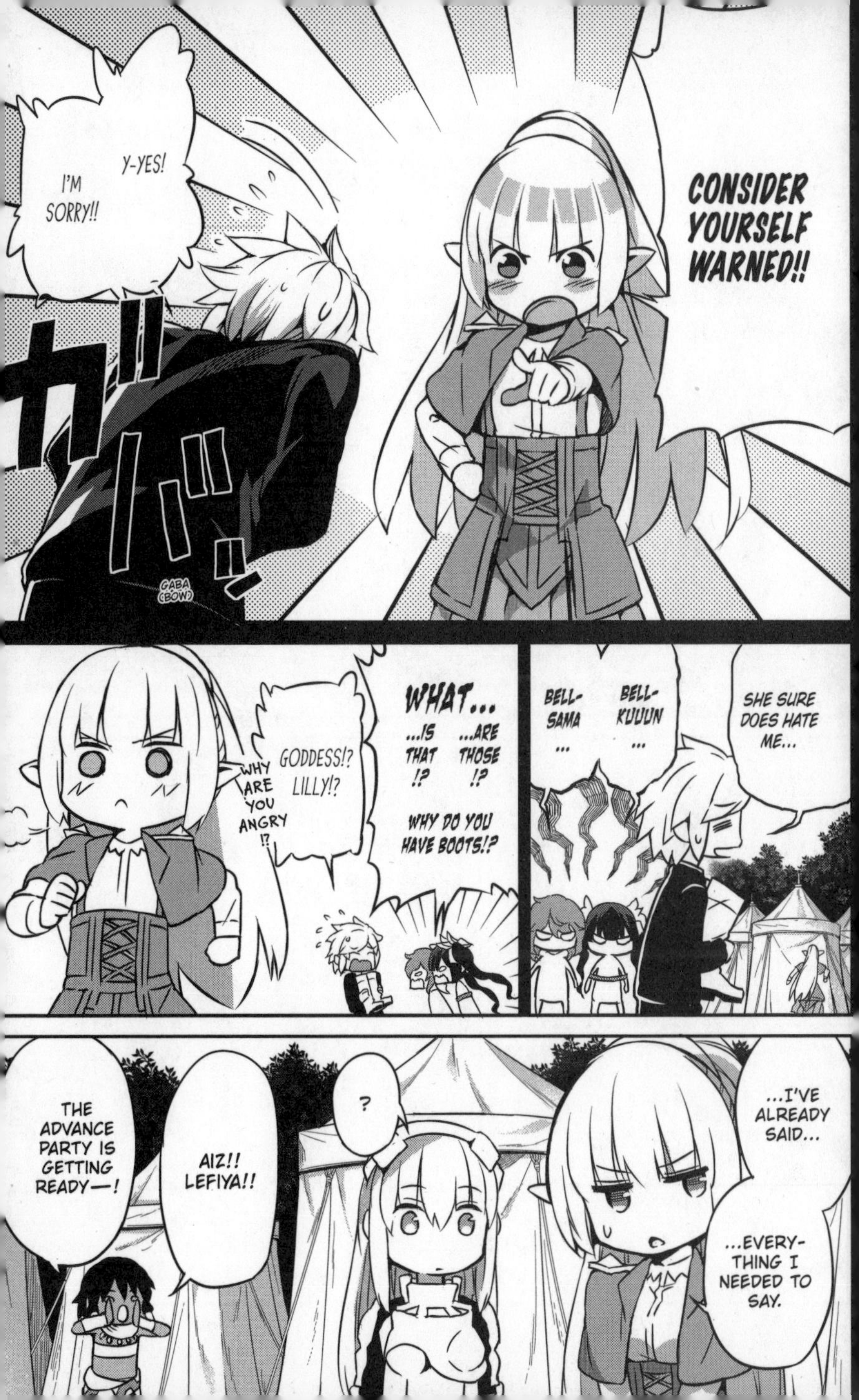
CONSIDER YOURSELF WARNED!!
Y-YES! I'M SORRY!!
GABA (BOW)
SHE SURE DOES HATE ME...
BELL-KUUUN ...
BELL-SAMA ...
WHAT...
...ARE THOSE!?
...IS THAT!?
WHY DO YOU HAVE BOOTS!?
GODDESS!? LILLY!?
WHY ARE YOU ANGRY!?
...I'VE ALREADY SAID...
...EVERYTHING I NEEDED TO SAY.
?
AIZ!! LEFIYA!!
THE ADVANCE PARTY IS GETTING READY—!

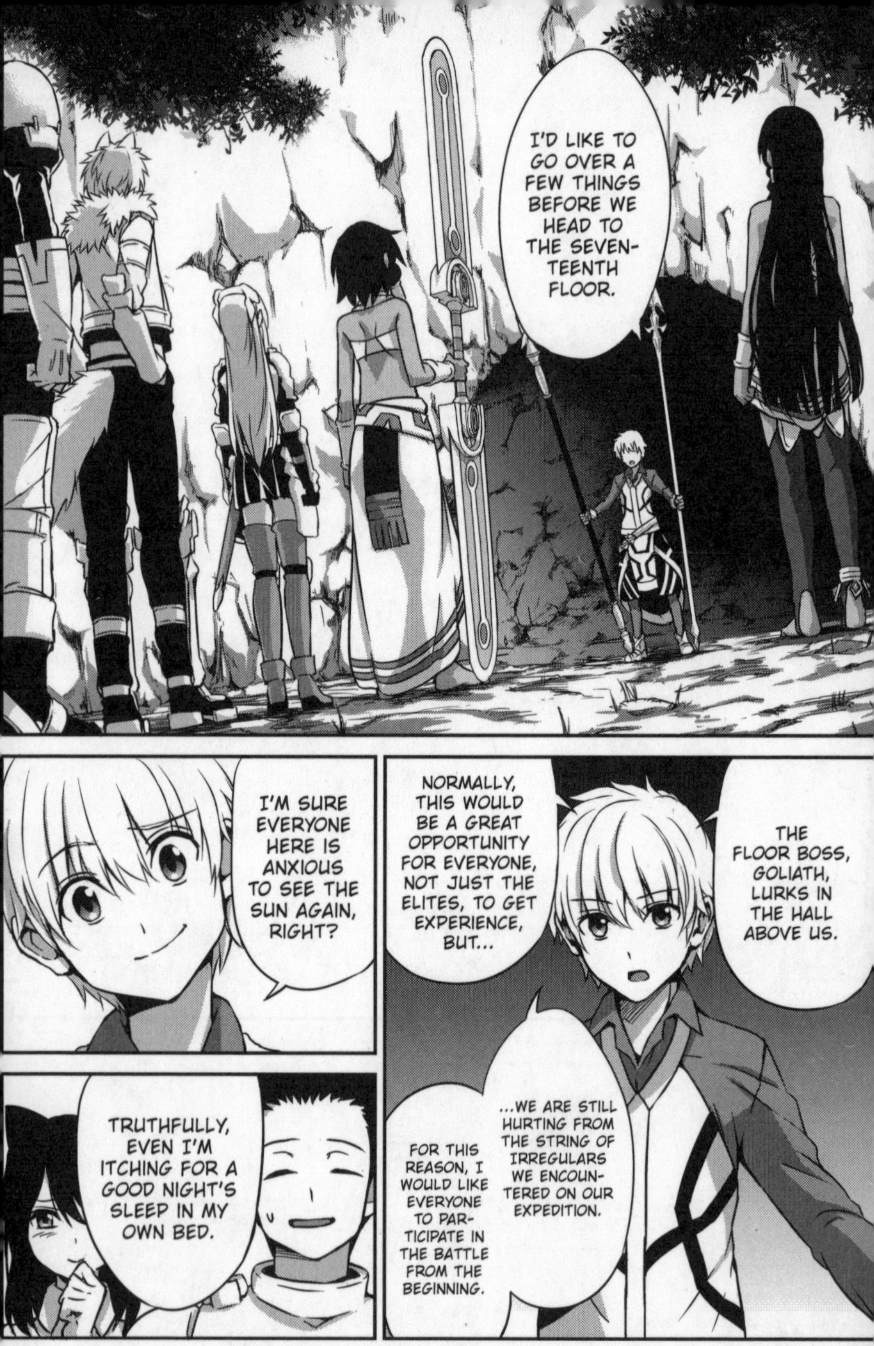
I'D LIKE TO GO OVER A FEW THINGS BEFORE WE HEAD TO THE SEVEN-TEENTH FLOOR.
THE FLOOR BOSS, GOLIATH, LURKS IN THE HALL ABOVE US.
NORMALLY, THIS WOULD BE A GREAT OPPORTUNITY FOR EVERYONE, NOT JUST THE ELITES, TO GET EXPERIENCE, BUT...
...WE ARE STILL HURTING FROM THE STRING OF IRREGULARS WE ENCOUN-TERED ON OUR EXPEDITION.
FOR THIS REASON, I WOULD LIKE EVERYONE TO PAR-TICIPATE IN THE BATTLE FROM THE BEGINNING.
I'M SURE EVERYONE HERE IS ANXIOUS TO SEE THE SUN AGAIN, RIGHT?
TRUTHFULLY, EVEN I'M ITCHING FOR A GOOD NIGHT'S SLEEP IN MY OWN BED.

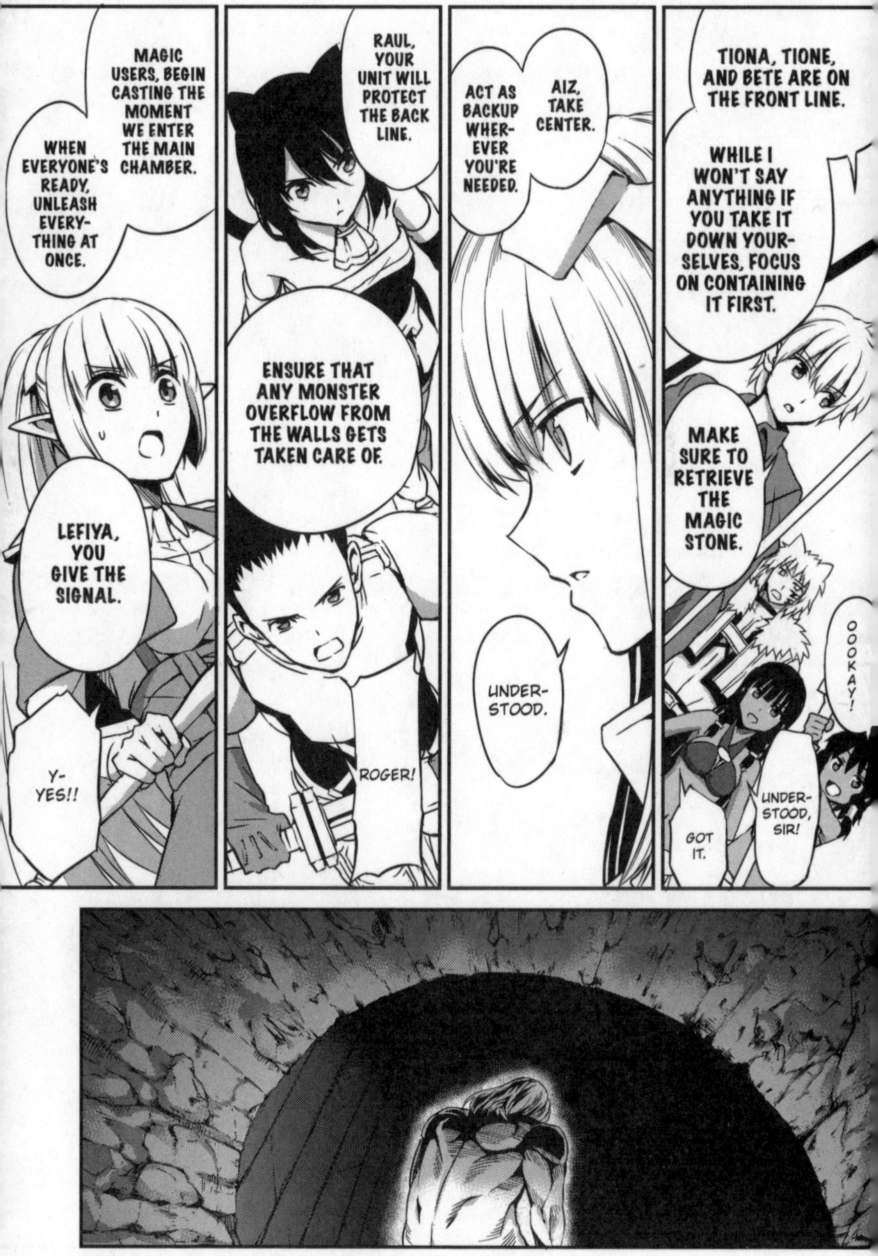

TIONA, TIONE, AND BETE ARE ON THE FRONT LINE.
WHILE I WON'T SAY ANYTHING IF YOU TAKE IT DOWN YOURSELVES, FOCUS ON CONTAINING IT FIRST.
MAKE SURE TO RETRIEVE THE MAGIC STONE.
OOOKAY!
UNDERSTOOD, SIR!
GOT IT.
AIZ, TAKE CENTER.
ACT AS BACKUP WHEREVER YOU'RE NEEDED.
UNDERSTOOD.
RAUL, YOUR UNIT WILL PROTECT THE BACK LINE.
ENSURE THAT ANY MONSTER OVERFLOW FROM THE WALLS GETS TAKEN CARE OF.
ROGER!
MAGIC USERS, BEGIN CASTING THE MOMENT WE ENTER THE MAIN CHAMBER.
WHEN EVERYONE'S READY, UNLEASH EVERYTHING AT ONCE.
LEFIYA, YOU GIVE THE SIGNAL.
Y-YES!!

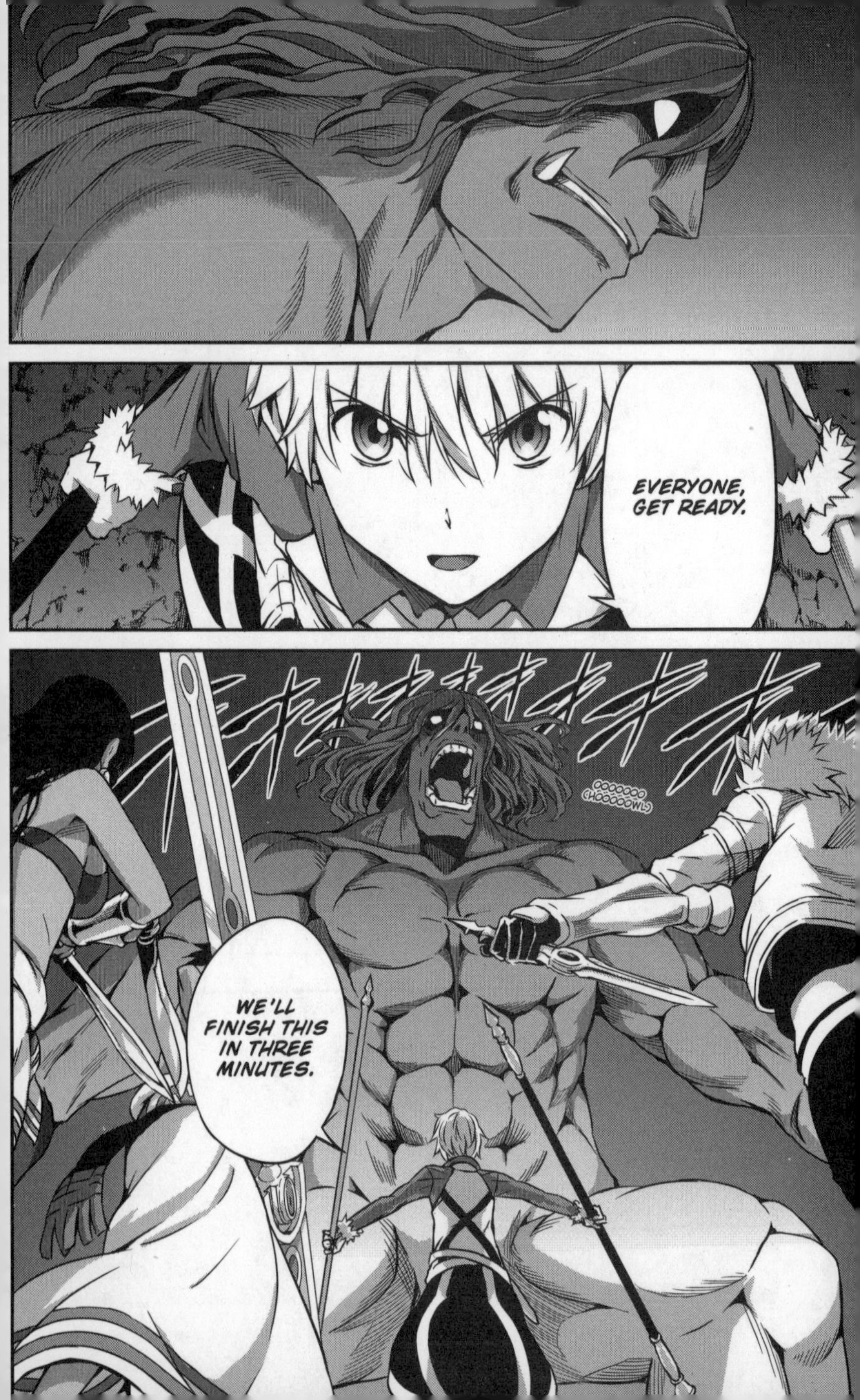
EVERYONE, GET READY.
OOOOOOO (HOOOOOWL)
WE'LL FINISH THIS IN THREE MINUTES.

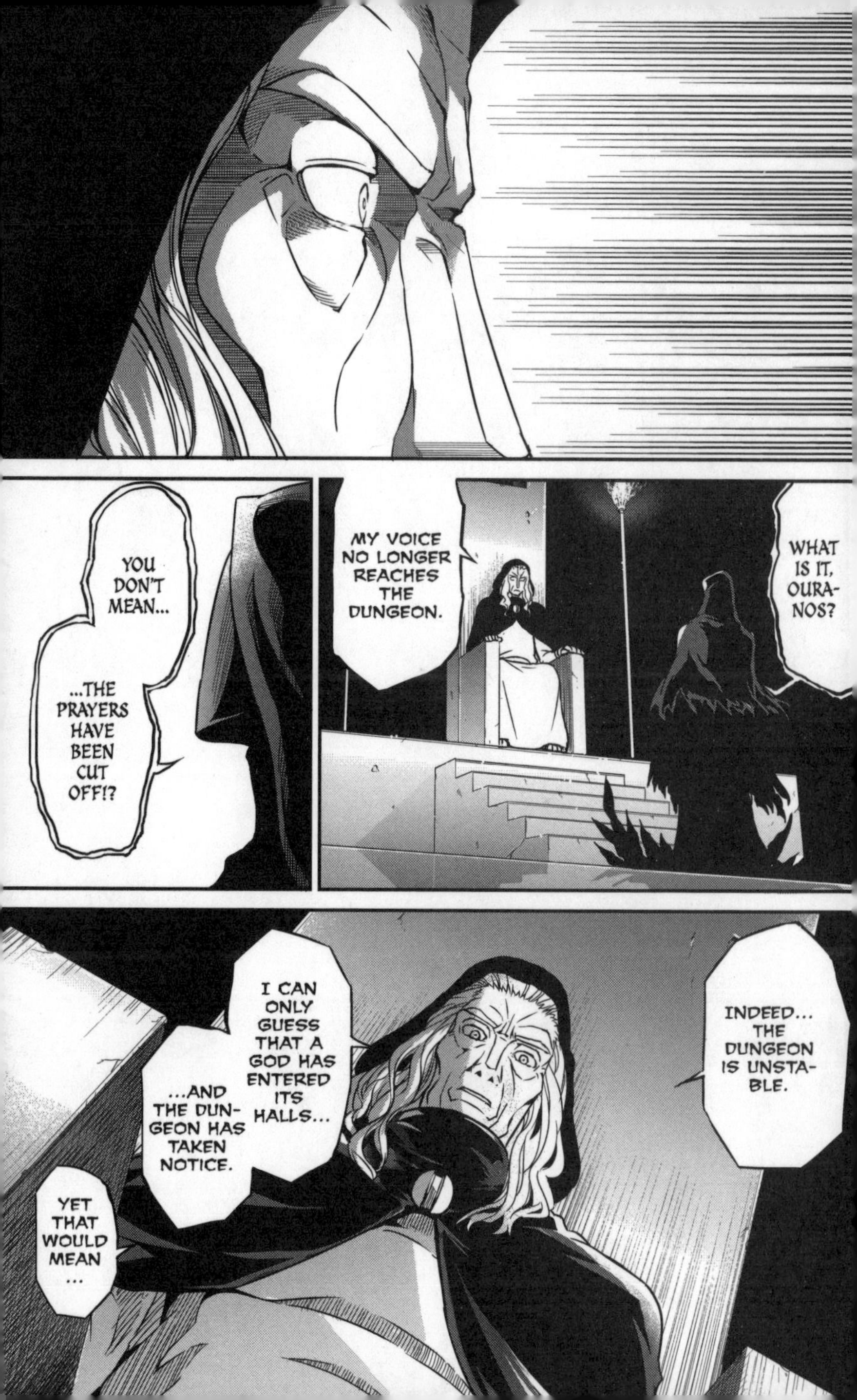
WHAT IS IT, OURANOS?
MY VOICE NO LONGER REACHES THE DUNGEON.
YOU DON'T MEAN...
...THE PRAYERS HAVE BEEN CUT OFF!?
INDEED... THE DUNGEON IS UNSTABLE.
I CAN ONLY GUESS THAT A GOD HAS ENTERED ITS HALLS...
...AND THE DUNGEON HAS TAKEN NOTICE.
YET THAT WOULD MEAN...

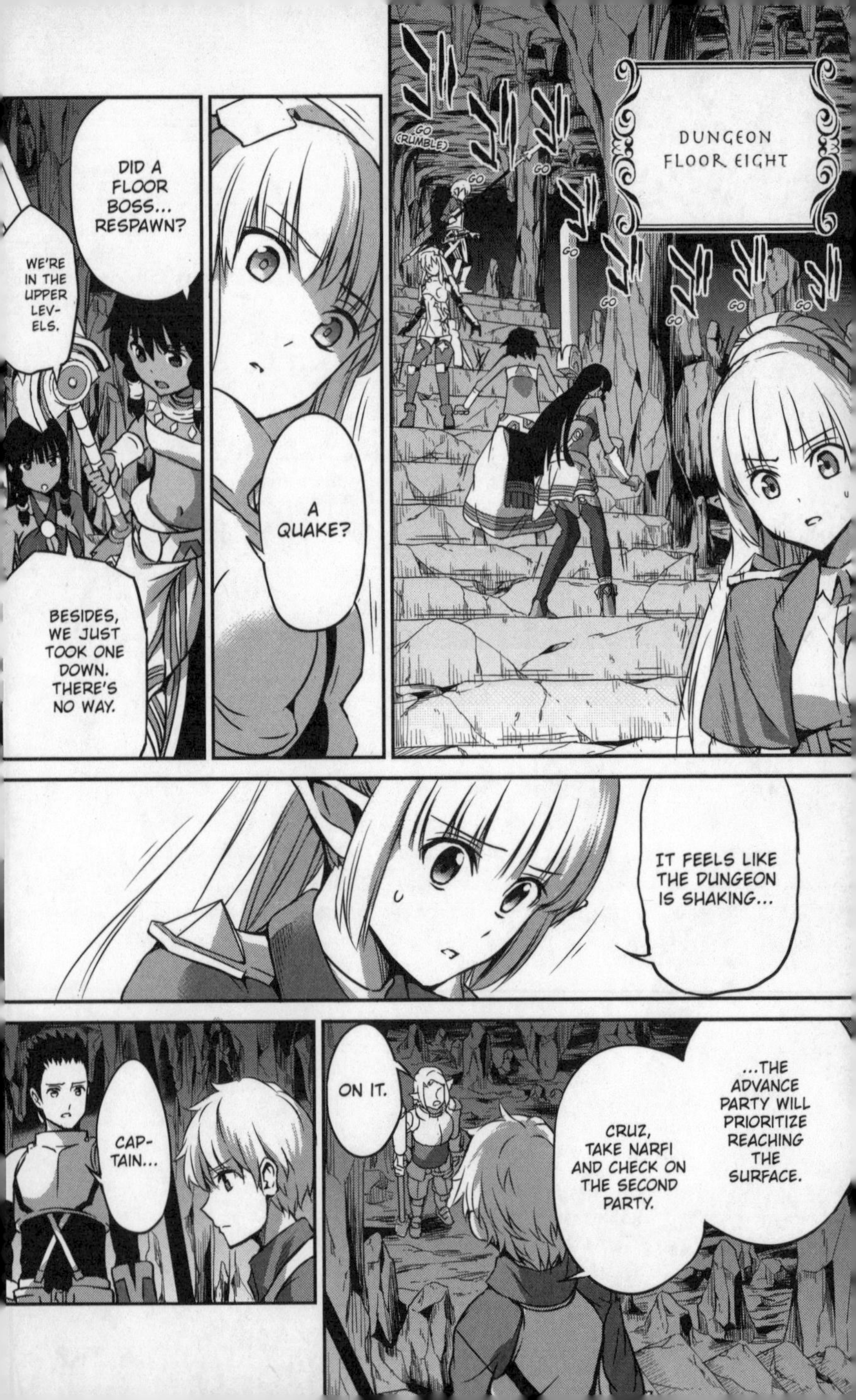
DUNGEON FLOOR EIGHT
GO (RUMBLE)
GO
GO
GO
GO
GO
GO
GO
A QUAKE?
DID A FLOOR BOSS... RESPAWN?
WE'RE IN THE UPPER LEV-ELS.
BESIDES, WE JUST TOOK ONE DOWN. THERE'S NO WAY.
IT FEELS LIKE THE DUNGEON IS SHAKING...
...THE ADVANCE PARTY WILL PRIORITIZE REACHING THE SURFACE.
CRUZ, TAKE NARFI AND CHECK ON THE SECOND PARTY.
ON IT.
CAP-TAIN...

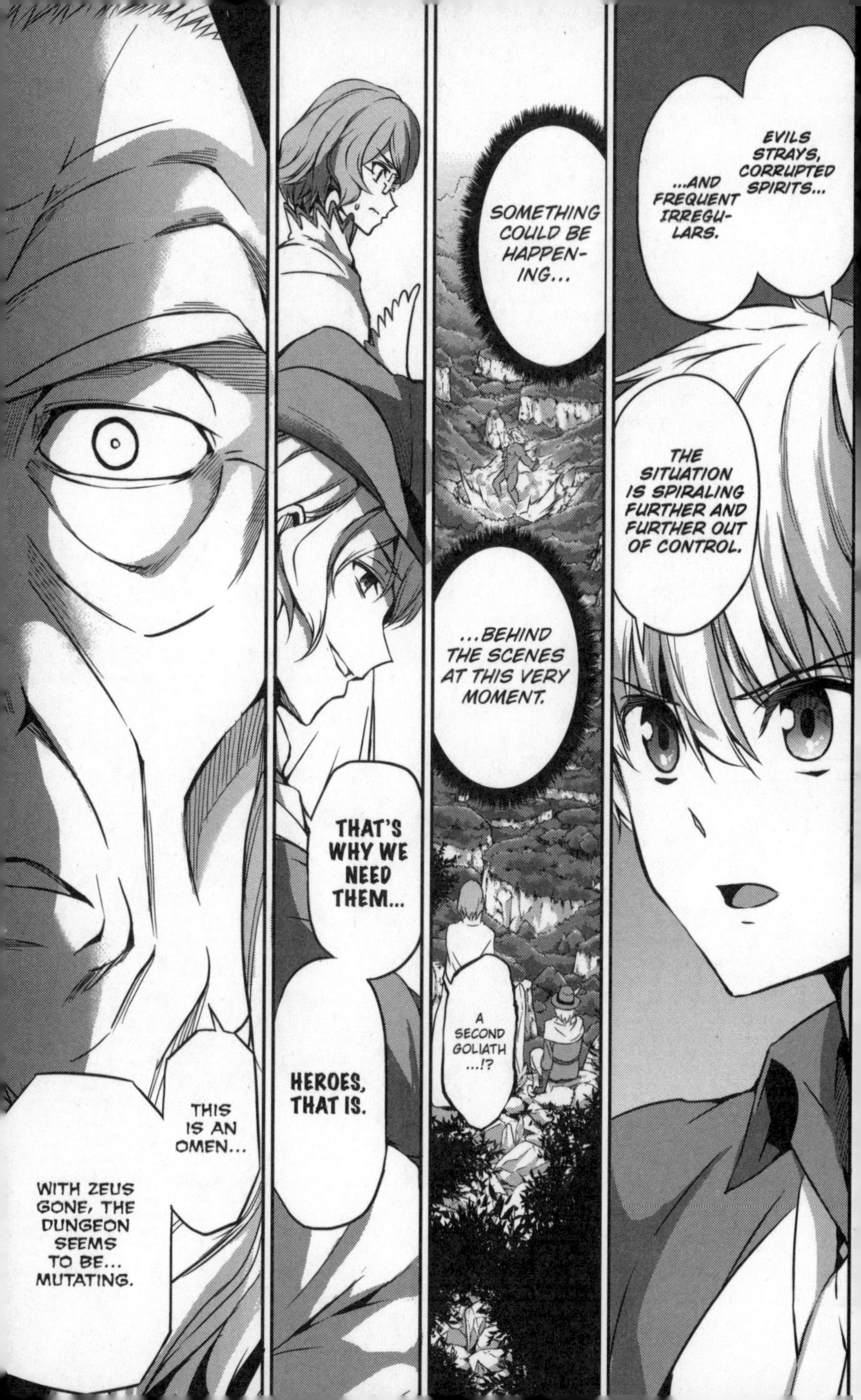
EVILS STRAYS, CORRUPTED SPIRITS...
...AND FREQUENT IRREGU-LARS.
THE SITUATION IS SPIRALING FURTHER AND FURTHER OUT OF CONTROL.
SOMETHING COULD BE HAPPEN-ING...
...BEHIND THE SCENES AT THIS VERY MOMENT.
A SECOND GOLIATH ...!?
THAT'S WHY WE NEED THEM...
HEROES, THAT IS.
THIS IS AN OMEN...
WITH ZEUS GONE, THE DUNGEON SEEMS TO BE... MUTATING.

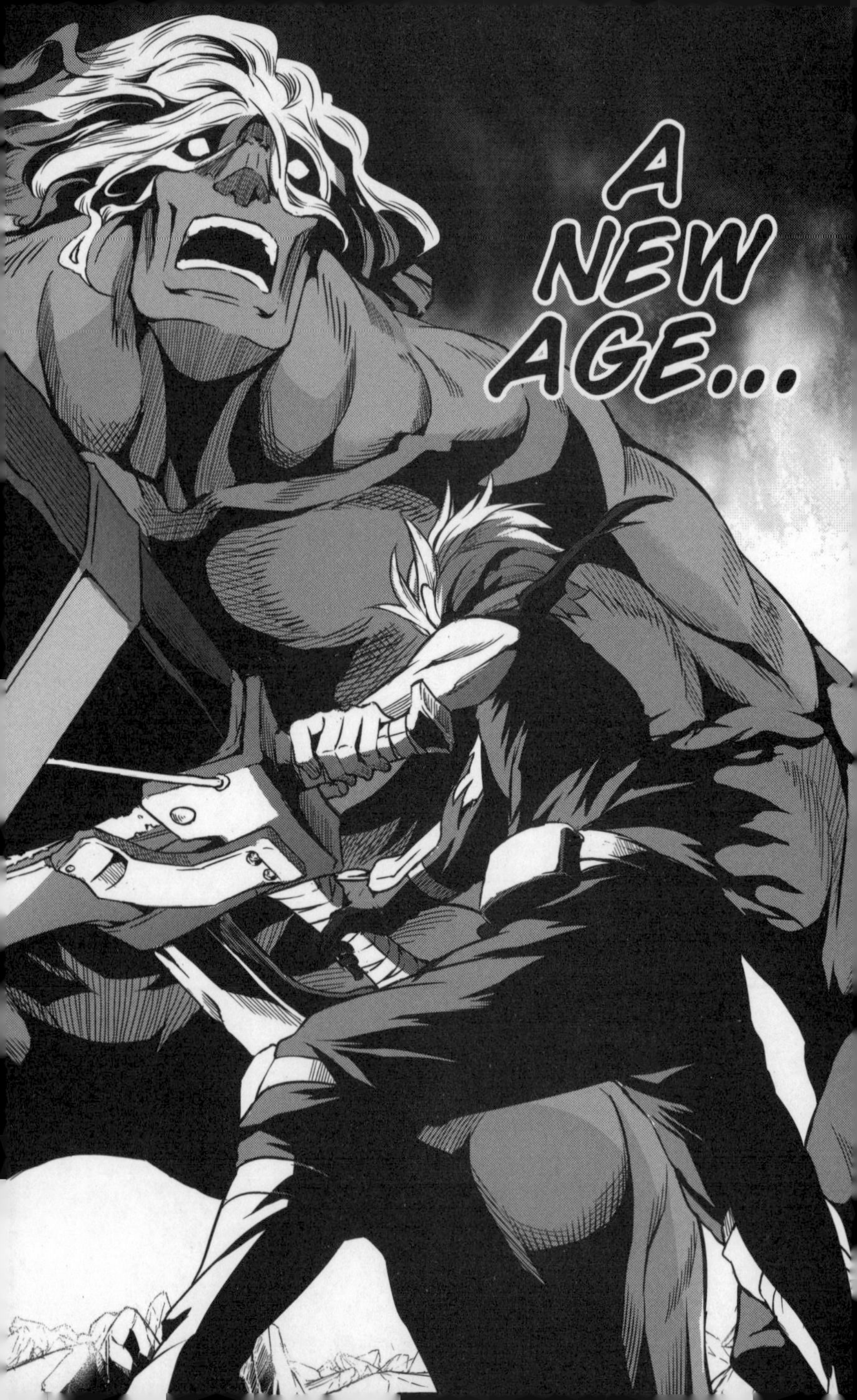
A NEW AGE...

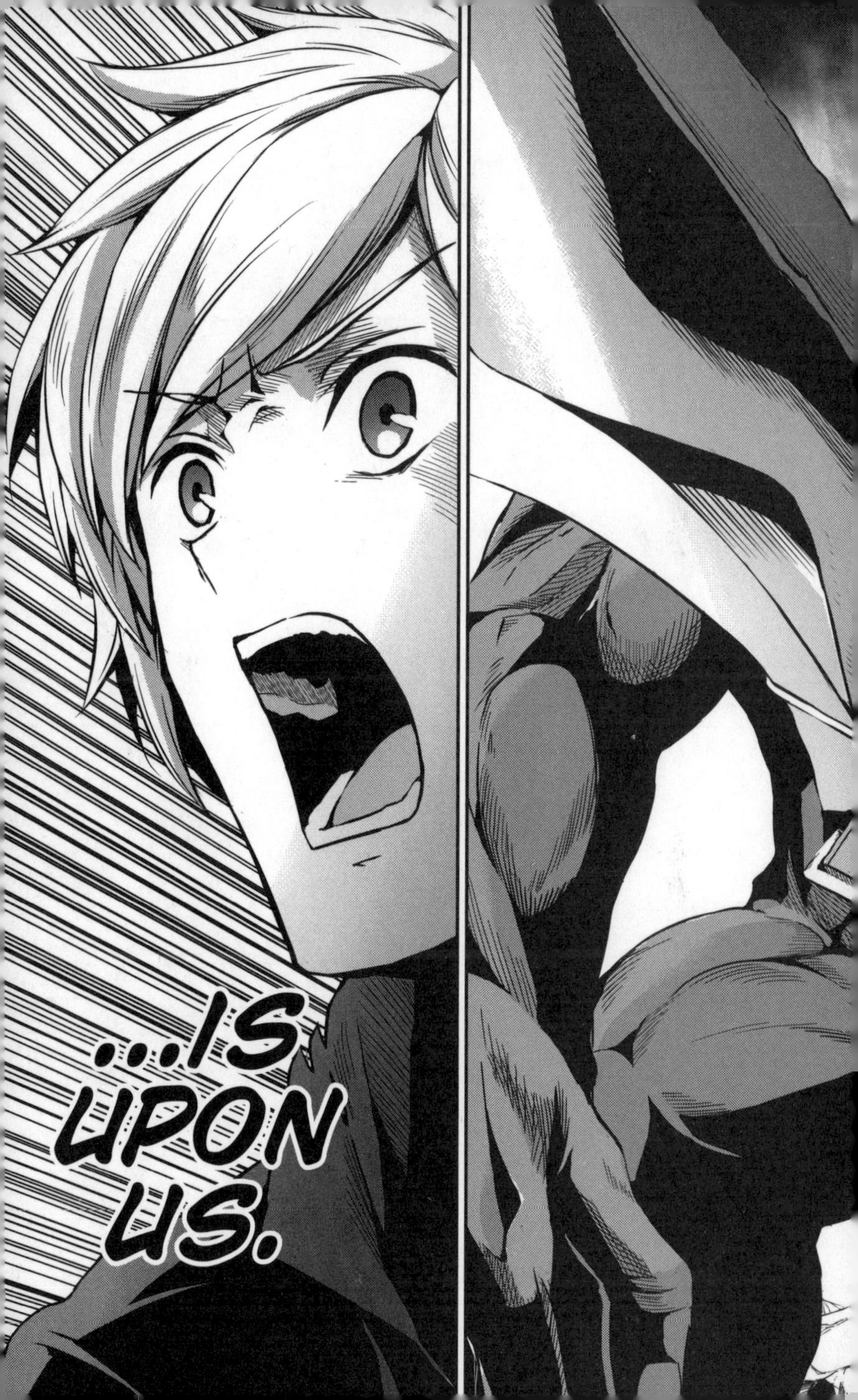
...IS UPON US.

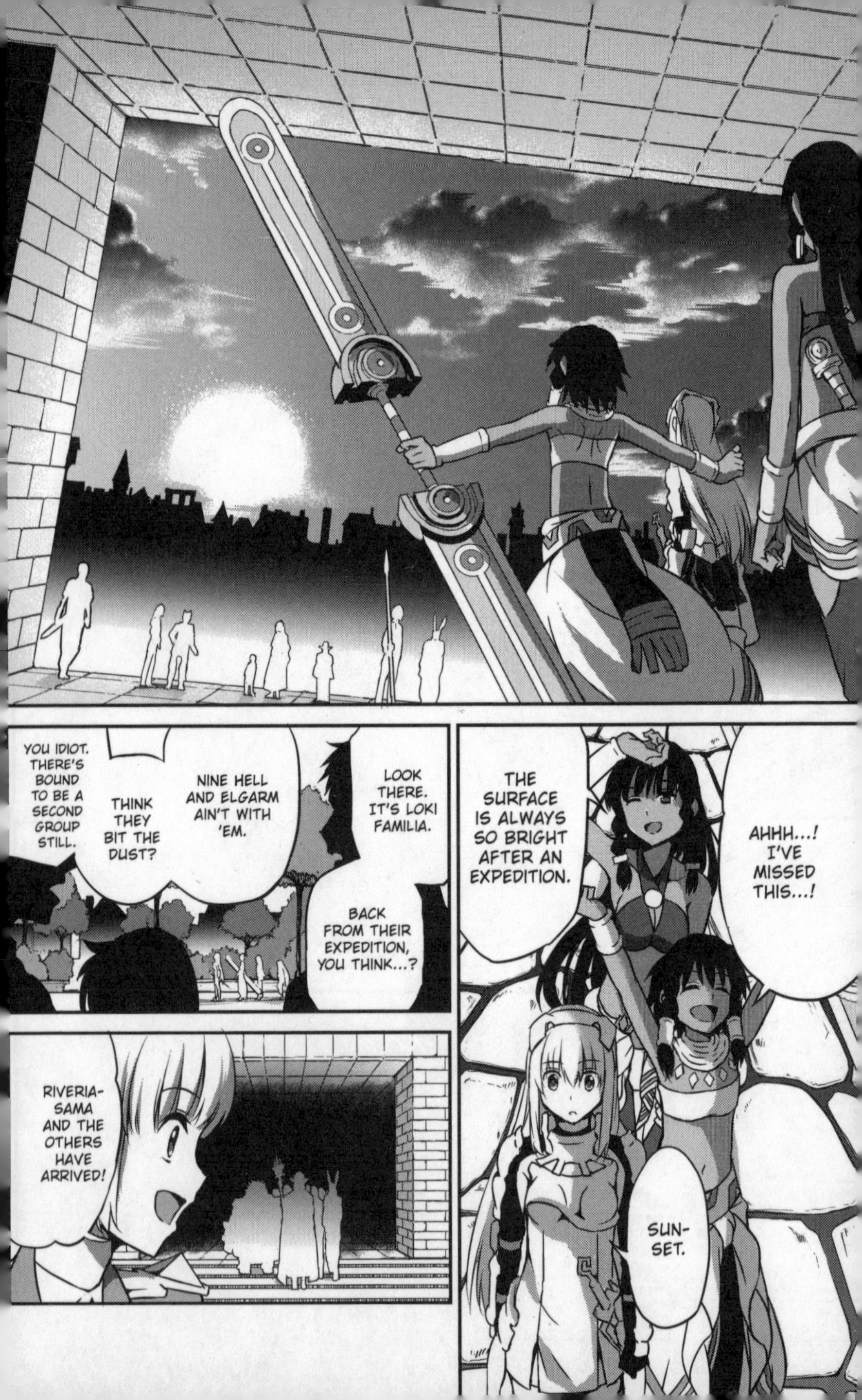
AHHH...! I'VE MISSED THIS...!
THE SURFACE IS ALWAYS SO BRIGHT AFTER AN EXPEDITION.
SUN-SET.
LOOK THERE. IT'S LOKI FAMILIA.
BACK FROM THEIR EXPEDITION, YOU THINK...?
NINE HELL AND ELGARM AIN'T WITH 'EM.
THINK THEY BIT THE DUST?
YOU IDIOT. THERE'S BOUND TO BE A SECOND GROUP STILL.
RIVERIA-SAMA AND THE OTHERS HAVE ARRIVED!

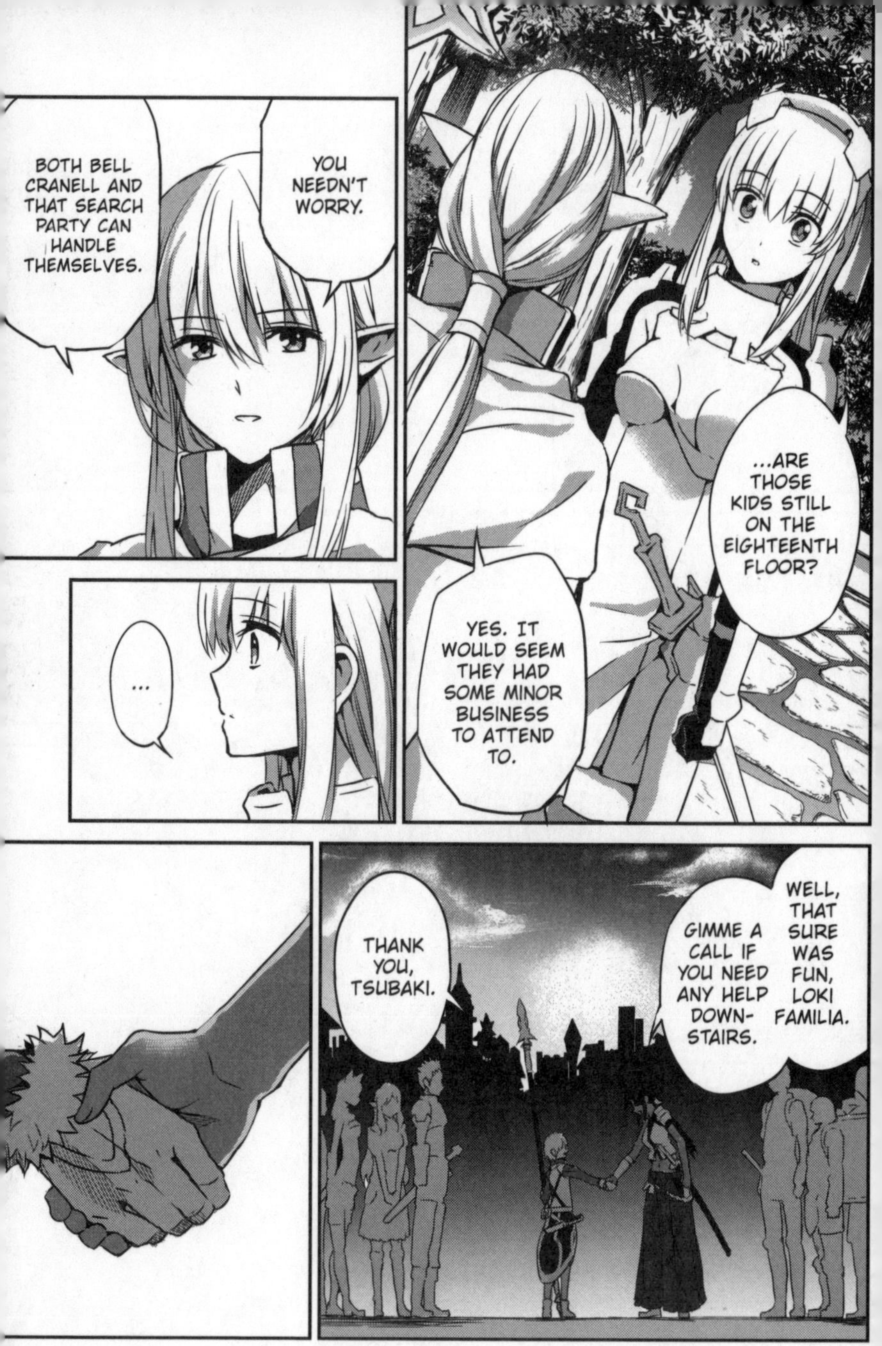
...ARE THOSE KIDS STILL ON THE EIGHTEENTH FLOOR?
YES. IT WOULD SEEM THEY HAD SOME MINOR BUSINESS TO ATTEND TO.
YOU NEEDN'T WORRY.
BOTH BELL CRANELL AND THAT SEARCH PARTY CAN HANDLE THEMSELVES.
...
WELL, THAT SURE WAS FUN, LOKI FAMILIA.
GIMME A CALL IF YOU NEED ANY HELP DOWN-STAIRS.
THANK YOU, TSUBAKI.

WE
MADE
IT...

HM?

WEL

DO

DO (TMP)

DO

COME

DO

DO

DO

DO

DO

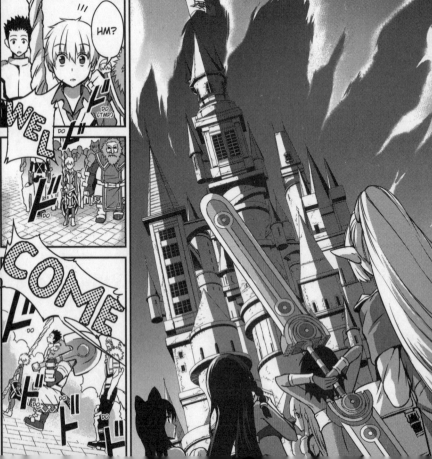

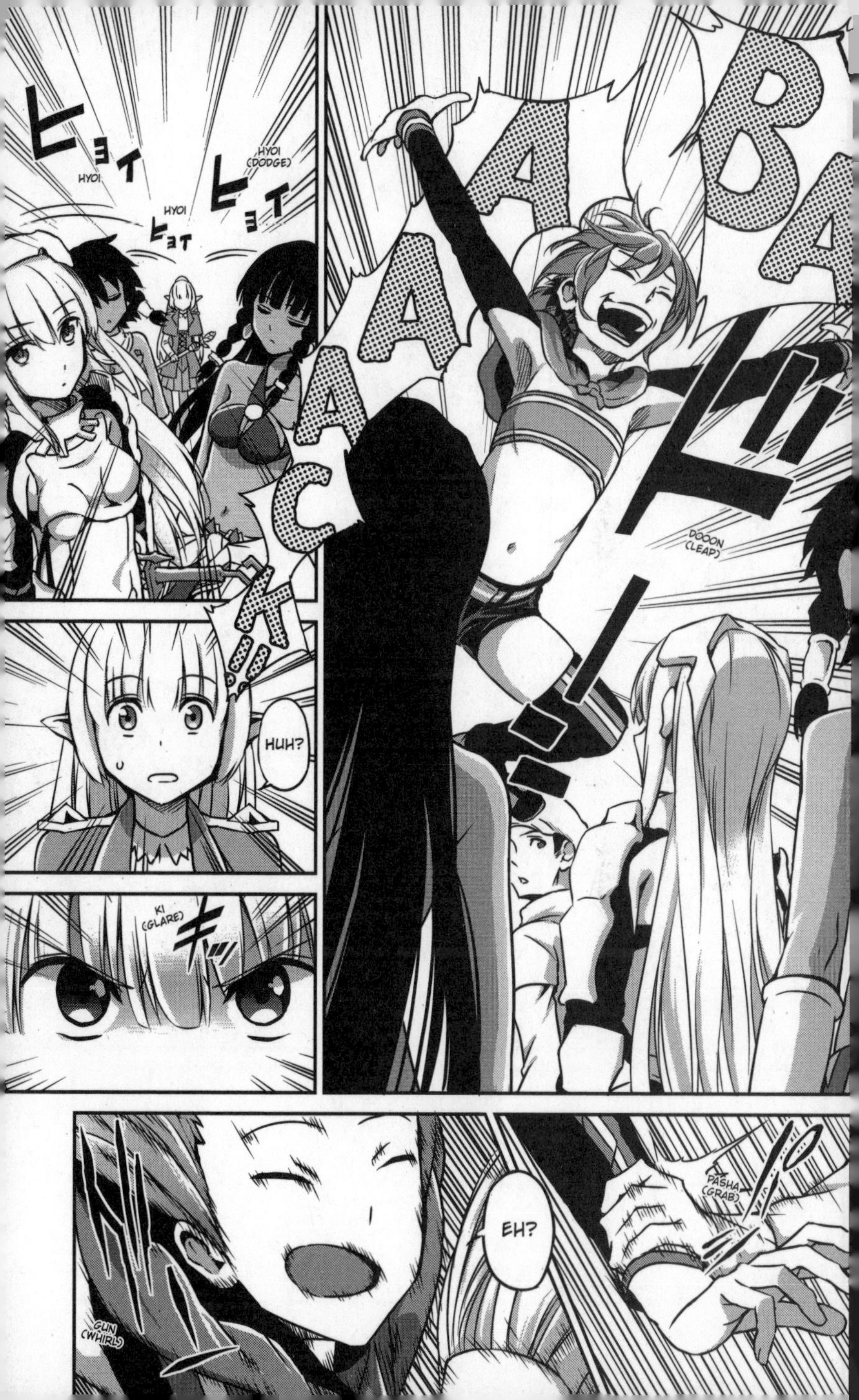
DOOON (LEAP)
HYOI (DODGE)
HYOI
HYOI
HUH?
KI (GLARE)
PASHA (GRAB)
EH?
GUN (WHIRL)

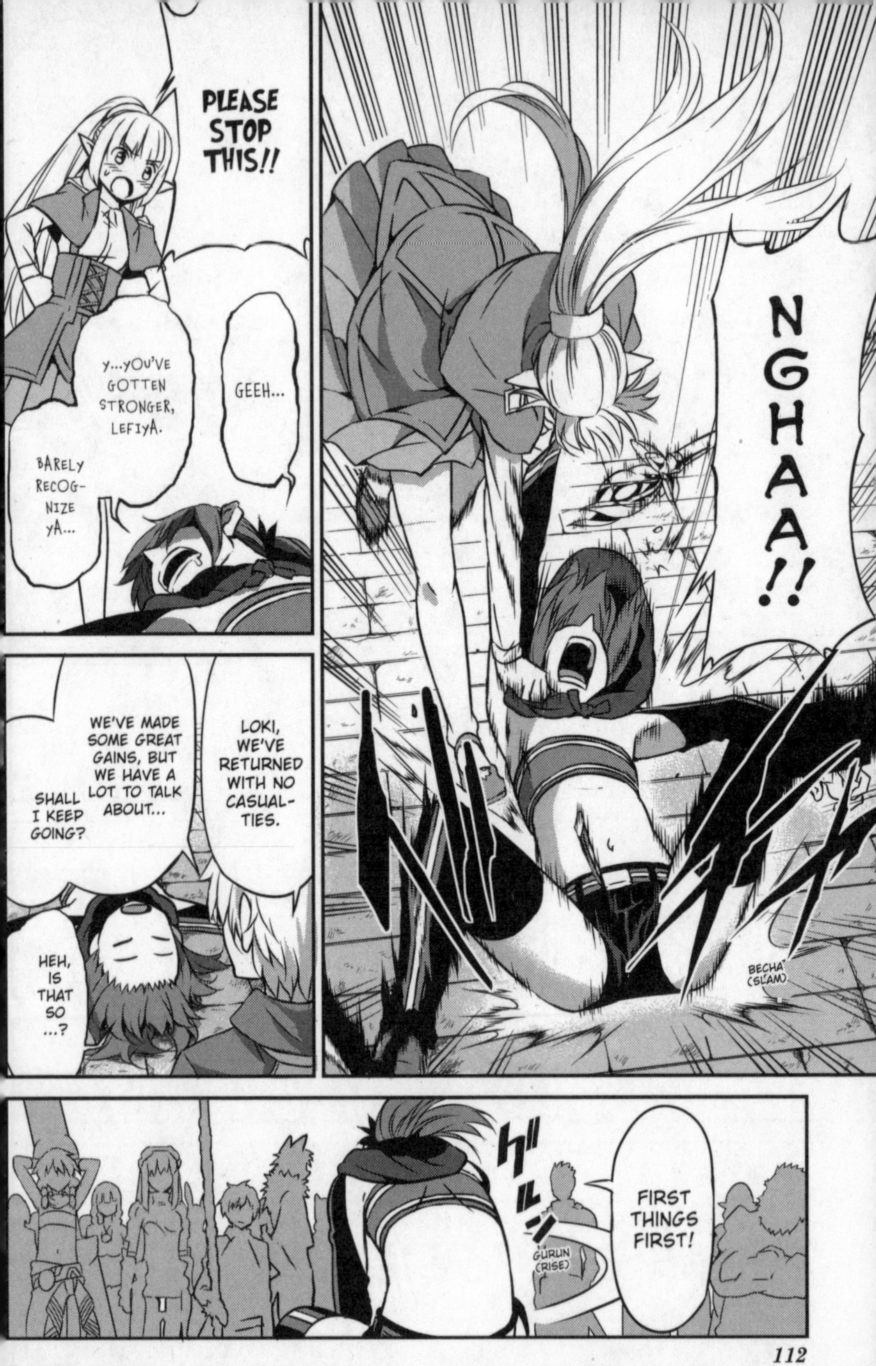
NGHAA!!
BECHA (SLAM)
PLEASE STOP THIS!!
GEEH...
Y...YOU'VE GOTTEN STRONGER, LEFIYA.
BARELY RECOG-NIZE YA...
LOKI, WE'VE RETURNED WITH NO CASUAL-TIES.
WE'VE MADE SOME GREAT GAINS, BUT WE HAVE A LOT TO TALK ABOUT...
SHALL I KEEP GOING?
HEH, IS THAT SO ...?
FIRST THINGS FIRST!
GURUN (RISE)

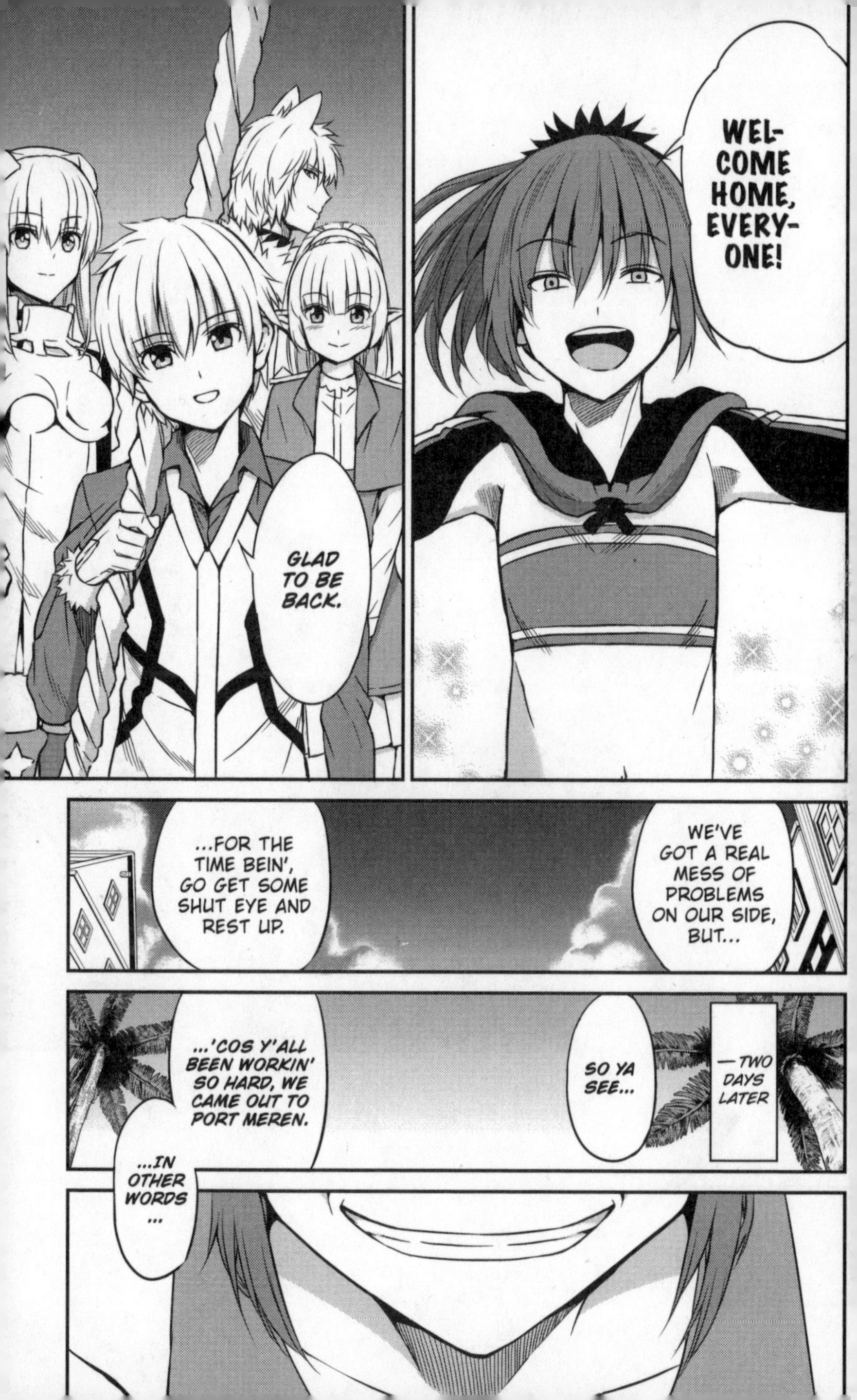
WEL-COME HOME, EVERY-ONE!
GLAD TO BE BACK.
WE'VE GOT A REAL MESS OF PROBLEMS ON OUR SIDE, BUT...
...FOR THE TIME BEIN', GO GET SOME SHUT EYE AND REST UP.
—TWO DAYS LATER
SO YA SEE...
...'COS Y'ALL BEEN WORKIN' SO HARD, WE CAME OUT TO PORT MEREN.
...IN OTHER WORDS ...

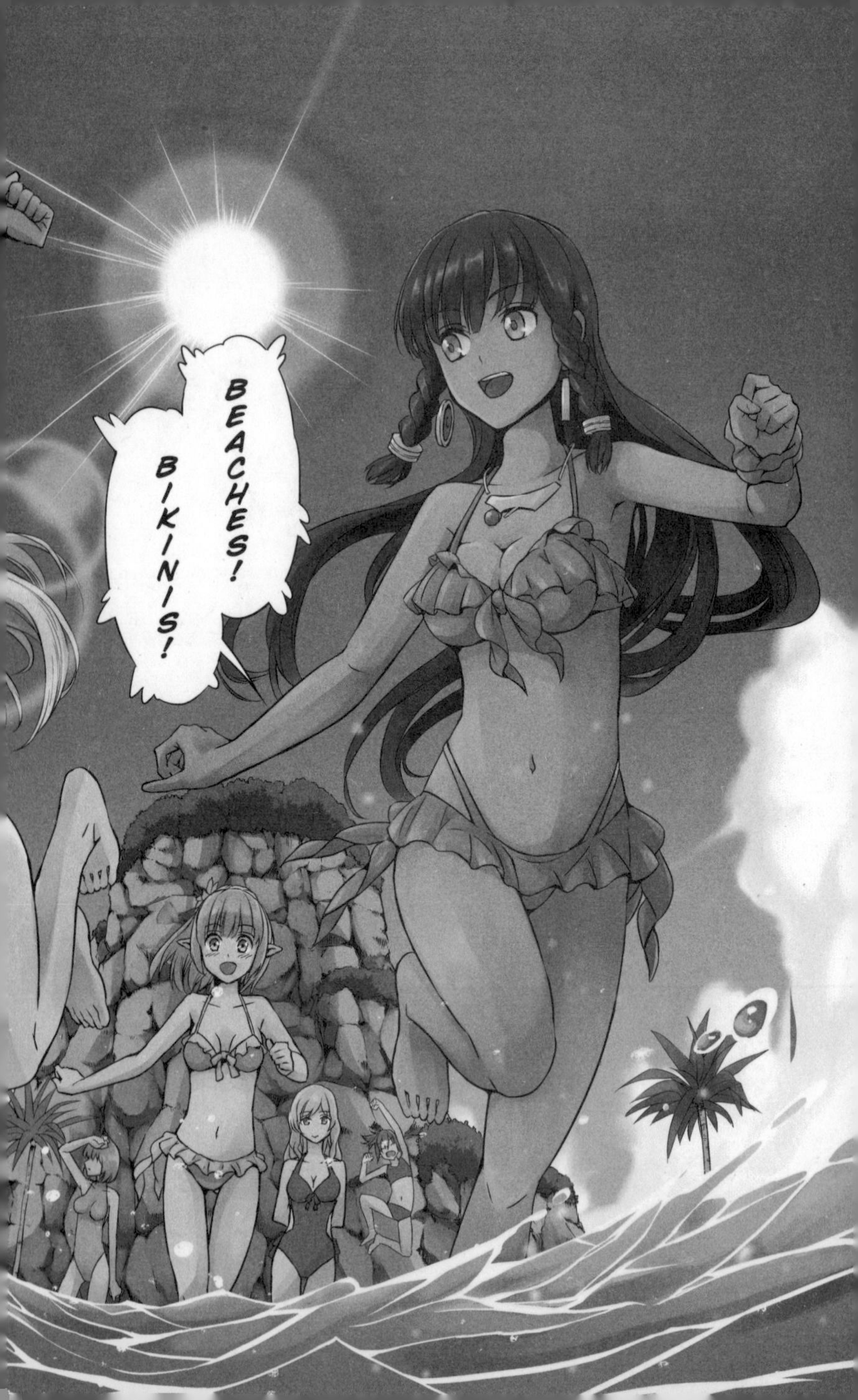
BEACHES!
BIKINIS!

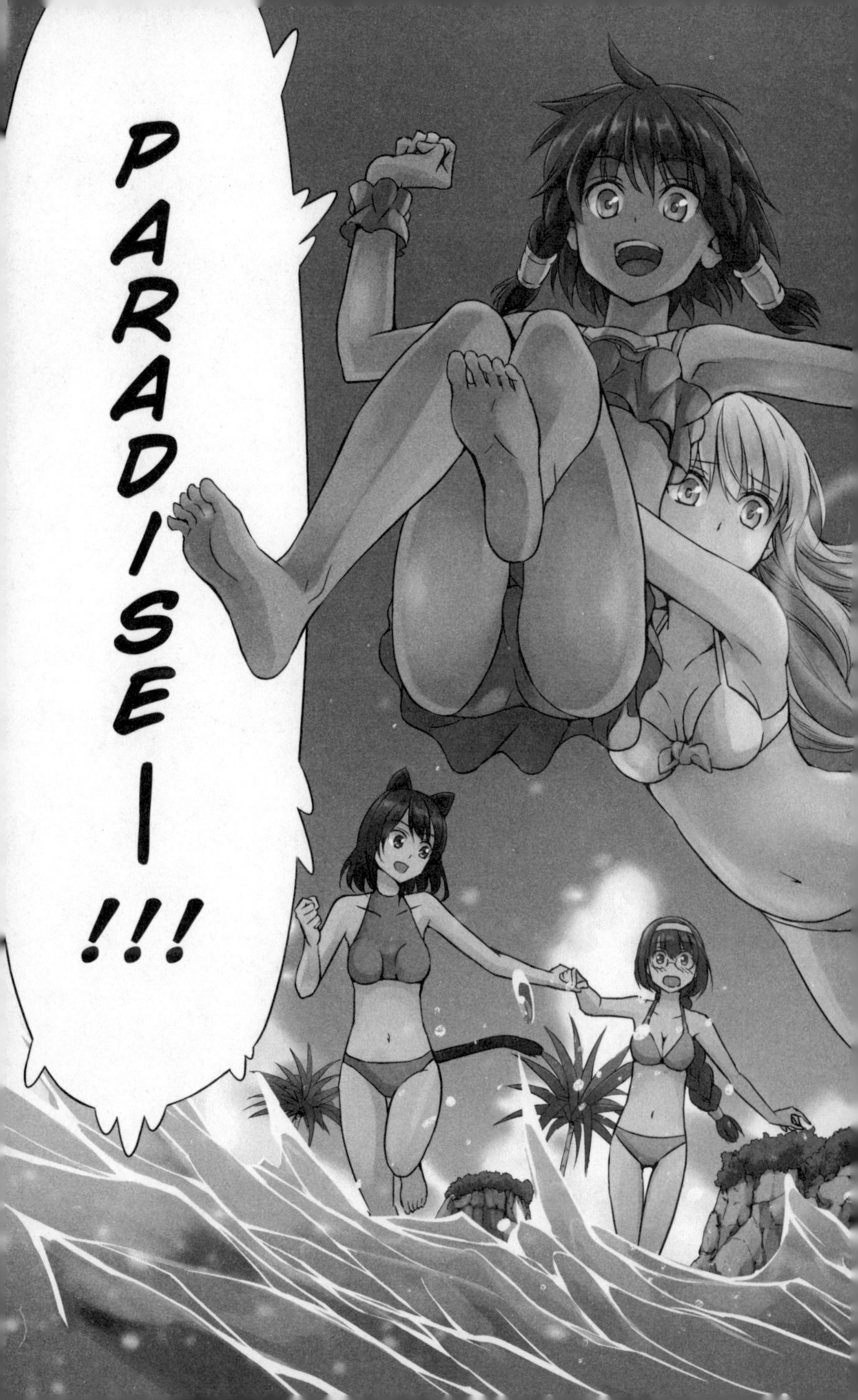
PARADISE!!!

Is it WRONG to TRY to PICK UP GIRLS IN A DUNGEON? ON THE SIDE

Sword Oratoria

quest 49. Travel Trouble

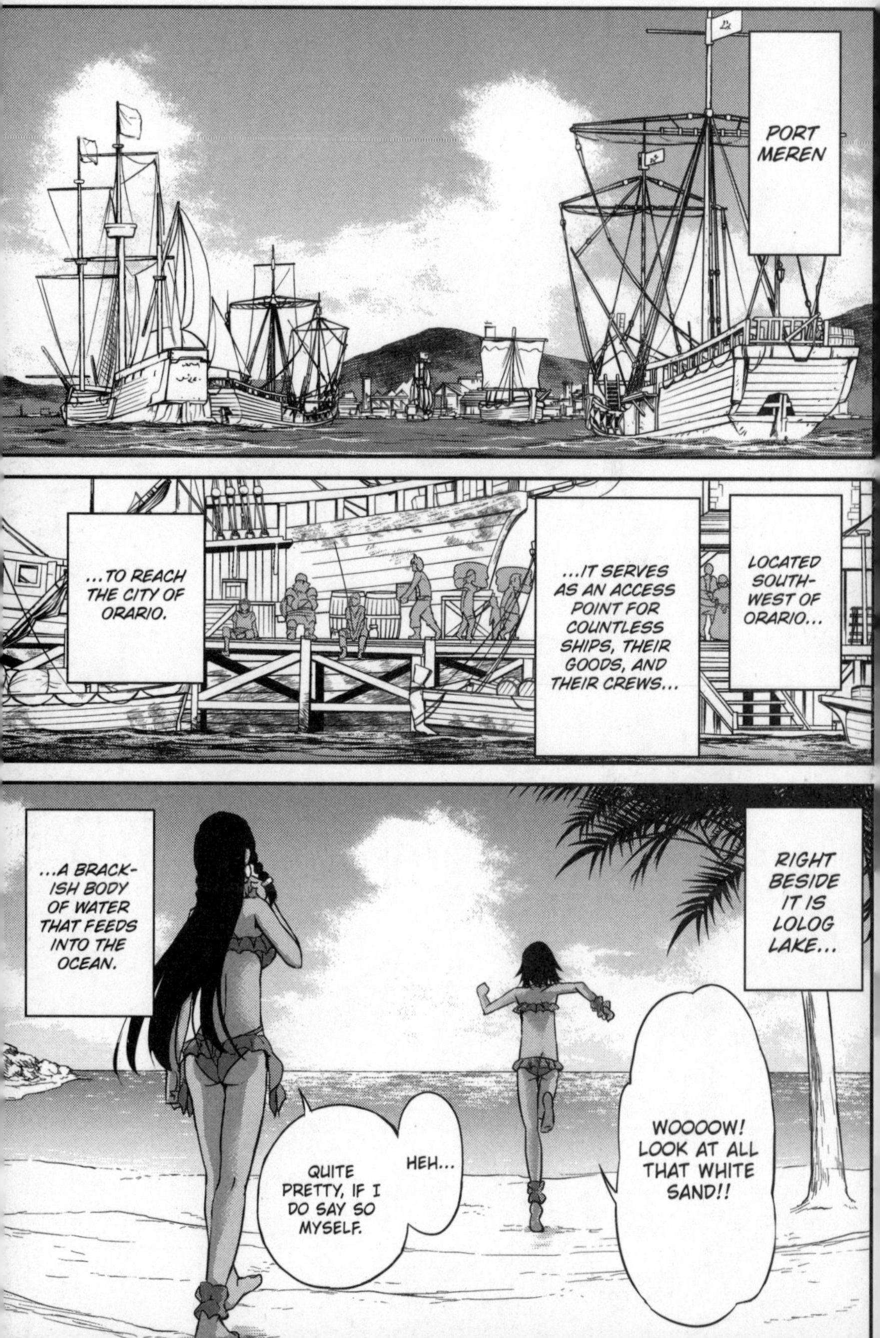
PORT MEREN
LOCATED SOUTH-WEST OF ORARIO...
...IT SERVES AS AN ACCESS POINT FOR COUNTLESS SHIPS, THEIR GOODS, AND THEIR CREWS...
...TO REACH THE CITY OF ORARIO.
RIGHT BESIDE IT IS LOLOG LAKE...
...A BRACK-ISH BODY OF WATER THAT FEEDS INTO THE OCEAN.
WOOOOW! LOOK AT ALL THAT WHITE SAND!!
HEH...
QUITE PRETTY, IF I DO SAY SO MYSELF.

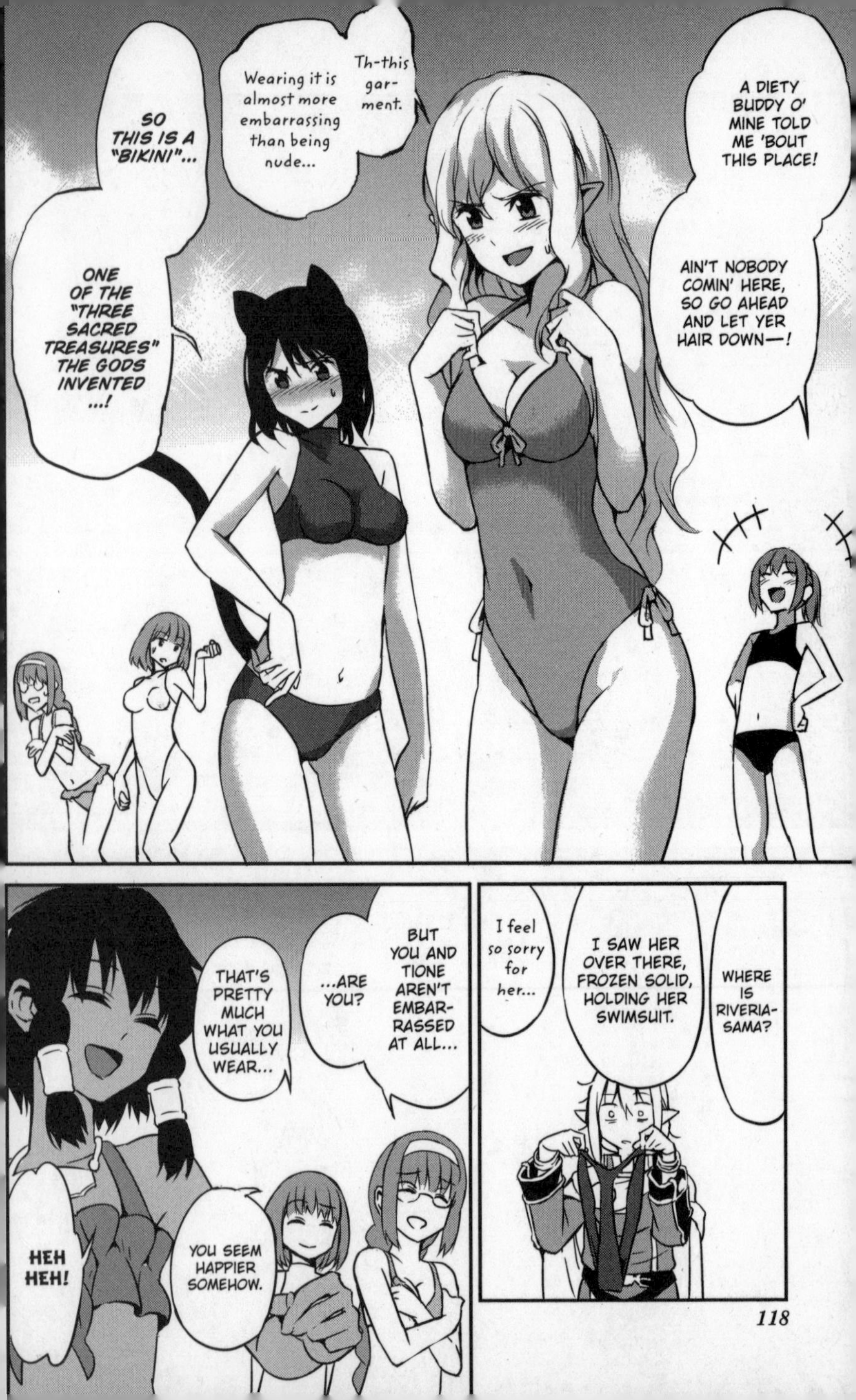
A DIETY BUDDY O' MINE TOLD ME 'BOUT THIS PLACE!
AIN'T NOBODY COMIN' HERE, SO GO AHEAD AND LET YER HAIR DOWN—!
Th-this garment.
Wearing it is almost more embarrassing than being nude...
SO THIS IS A "BIKINI"...
ONE OF THE "THREE SACRED TREASURES" THE GODS INVENTED ...!
WHERE IS RIVERIA-SAMA?
I SAW HER OVER THERE, FROZEN SOLID, HOLDING HER SWIMSUIT.
I feel so sorry for her...
BUT YOU AND TIONE AREN'T EMBARRASSED AT ALL...
...ARE YOU?
THAT'S PRETTY MUCH WHAT YOU USUALLY WEAR...
YOU SEEM HAPPIER SOMEHOW.
HEH HEH!

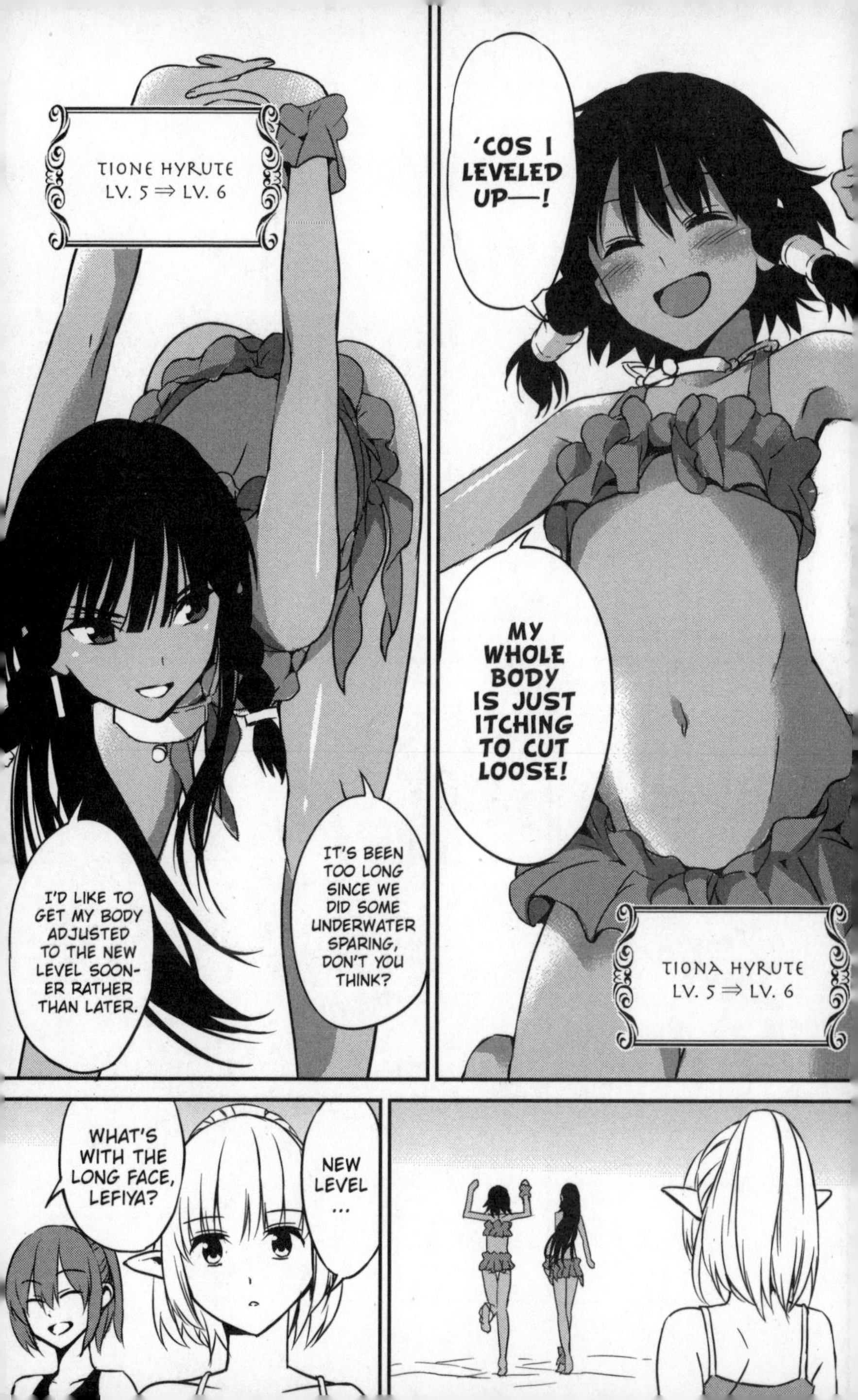
'COS I LEVELED UP—!
MY WHOLE BODY IS JUST ITCHING TO CUT LOOSE!
TIONA HYRUTE LV. 5 ⇒ LV. 6
TIONE HYRUTE LV. 5 ⇒ LV. 6
IT'S BEEN TOO LONG SINCE WE DID SOME UNDERWATER SPARING, DON'T YOU THINK?
I'D LIKE TO GET MY BODY ADJUSTED TO THE NEW LEVEL SOONER RATHER THAN LATER.
NEW LEVEL ...
WHAT'S WITH THE LONG FACE, LEFIYA?

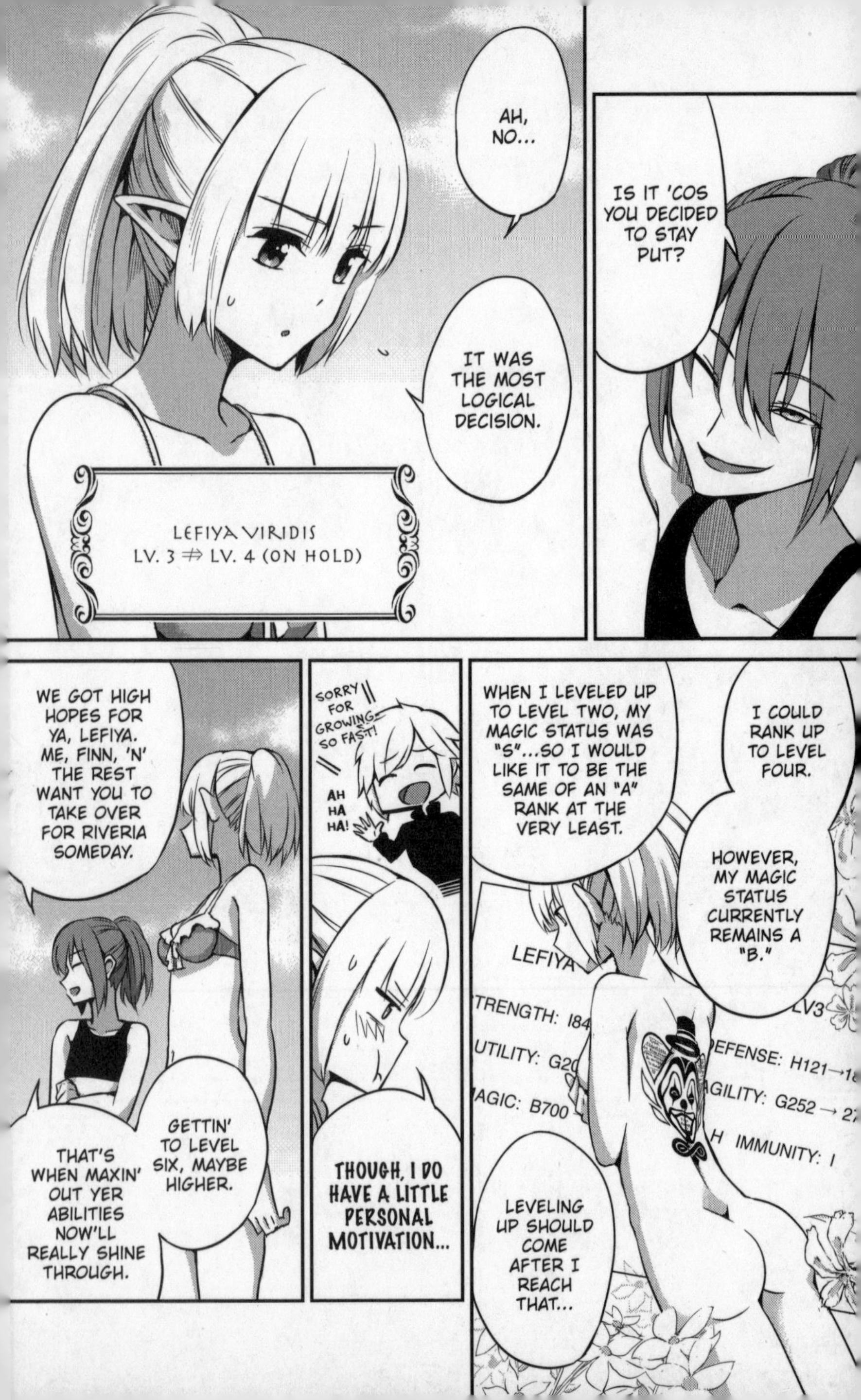
IS IT 'COS YOU DECIDED TO STAY PUT?
AH, NO...
IT WAS THE MOST LOGICAL DECISION.
LEFIYA VIRIDIS LV. 3 ⇏ LV. 4 (ON HOLD)
I COULD RANK UP TO LEVEL FOUR.
HOWEVER, MY MAGIC STATUS CURRENTLY REMAINS A "B."
WHEN I LEVELED UP TO LEVEL TWO, MY MAGIC STATUS WAS "S"...SO I WOULD LIKE IT TO BE THE SAME OF AN "A" RANK AT THE VERY LEAST.
LEFIYA
LV3
TRENGTH: I84
UTILITY: G2
DEFENSE: H121→1
AGIC: B700
AGILITY: G252 → 2
H IMMUNITY: I
LEVELING UP SHOULD COME AFTER I REACH THAT...
SORRY FOR GROWING SO FAST!
AH HA HA!
THOUGH, I DO HAVE A LITTLE PERSONAL MOTIVATION...
WE GOT HIGH HOPES FOR YA, LEFIYA. ME, FINN, 'N' THE REST WANT YOU TO TAKE OVER FOR RIVERIA SOMEDAY.
GETTIN' TO LEVEL SIX, MAYBE HIGHER.
THAT'S WHEN MAXIN' OUT YER ABILITIES NOW'LL REALLY SHINE THROUGH.

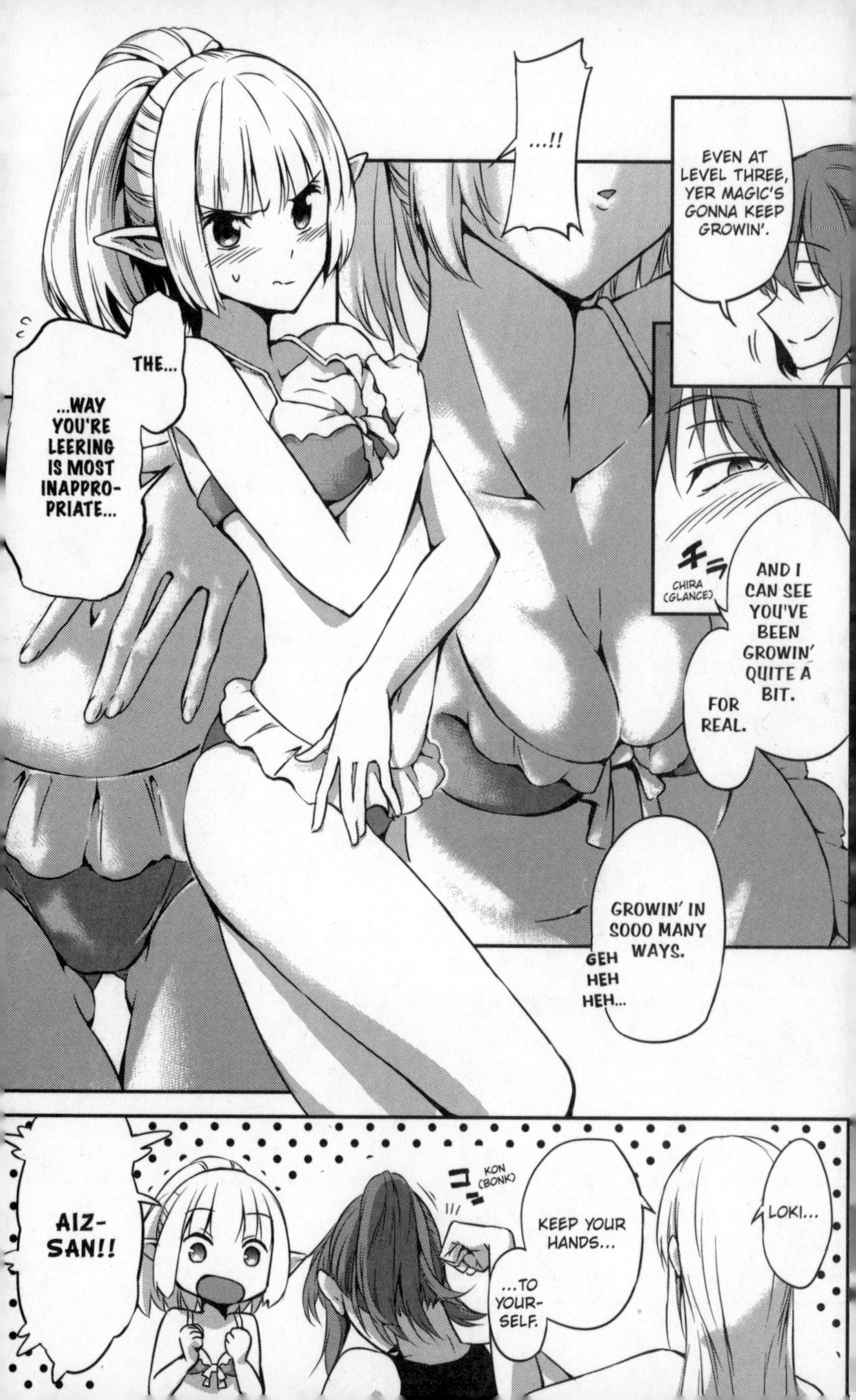

EVEN AT LEVEL THREE, YER MAGIC'S GONNA KEEP GROWIN'.
チラ
CHIRA (GLANCE)
AND I CAN SEE YOU'VE BEEN GROWIN' QUITE A BIT.
FOR REAL.
GROWIN' IN SOOO MANY WAYS.
GEH HEH HEH...
...!!
THE...
...WAY YOU'RE LEERING IS MOST INAPPROPRIATE...
LOKI...
KEEP YOUR HANDS...
...TO YOURSELF.
コン
KON (BONK)
AIZ-SAN!!

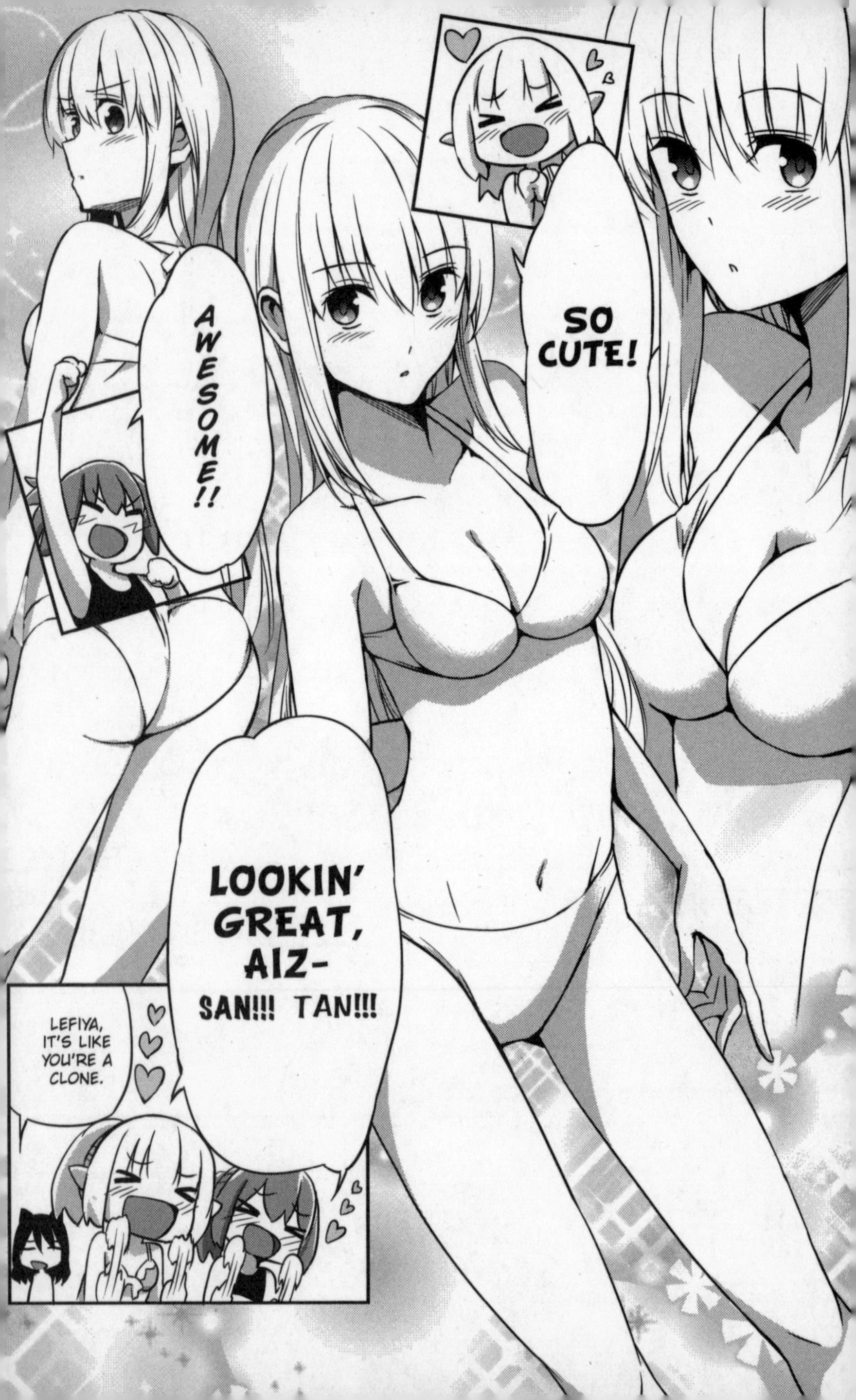
SO CUTE!
AWESOME!!
LOOKIN' GREAT, AIZ-SAN!!! TAN!!!
LEFIYA, IT'S LIKE YOU'RE A CLONE.

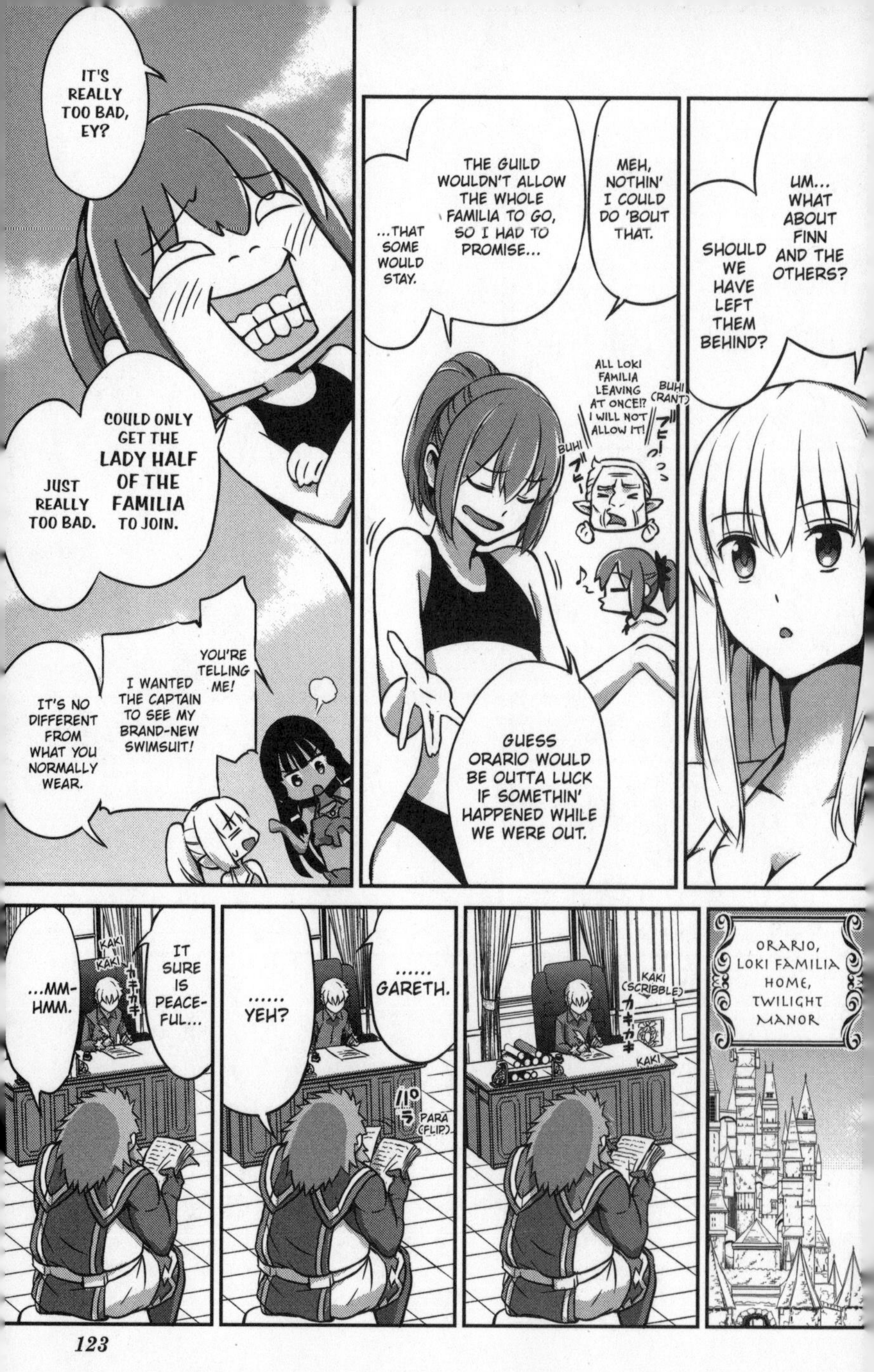
UM... WHAT ABOUT FINN AND THE OTHERS?
SHOULD WE HAVE LEFT THEM BEHIND?
MEH, NOTHIN' I COULD DO 'BOUT THAT.
THE GUILD WOULDN'T ALLOW THE WHOLE FAMILIA TO GO, SO I HAD TO PROMISE...
...THAT SOME WOULD STAY.
BUHI (RANT)
ALL LOKI FAMILIA LEAVING AT ONCE!? I WILL NOT ALLOW IT!
BUHI
GUESS ORARIO WOULD BE OUTTA LUCK IF SOMETHIN' HAPPENED WHILE WE WERE OUT.
IT'S REALLY TOO BAD, EY?
COULD ONLY GET THE LADY HALF OF THE FAMILIA TO JOIN.
JUST REALLY TOO BAD.
YOU'RE TELLING ME!
I WANTED THE CAPTAIN TO SEE MY BRAND-NEW SWIMSUIT!
IT'S NO DIFFERENT FROM WHAT YOU NORMALLY WEAR.
ORARIO, LOKI FAMILIA HOME, TWILIGHT MANOR
KAKI (SCRIBBLE)
KAKI
......GARETH.
......YEH?
PARA (FLIP)
IT SURE IS PEACEFUL...
KAKI KAKI
...MM-HMM.

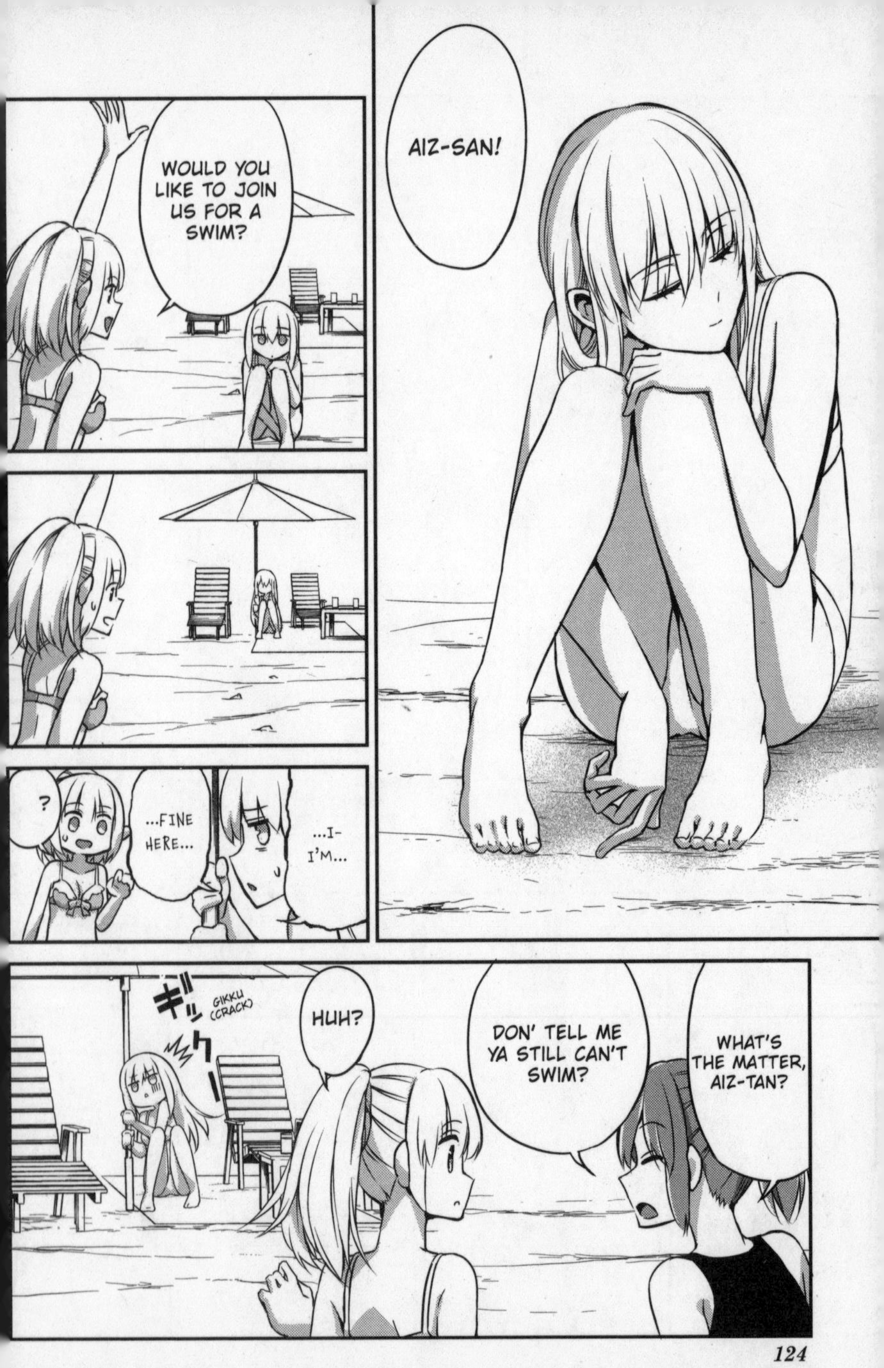
AIZ-SAN!
WOULD YOU LIKE TO JOIN US FOR A SWIM?
...I- I'M...
...FINE HERE...
?
WHAT'S THE MATTER, AIZ-TAN?
DON' TELL ME YA STILL CAN'T SWIM?
HUH?
ギクッ
GIKKU (CRACK)

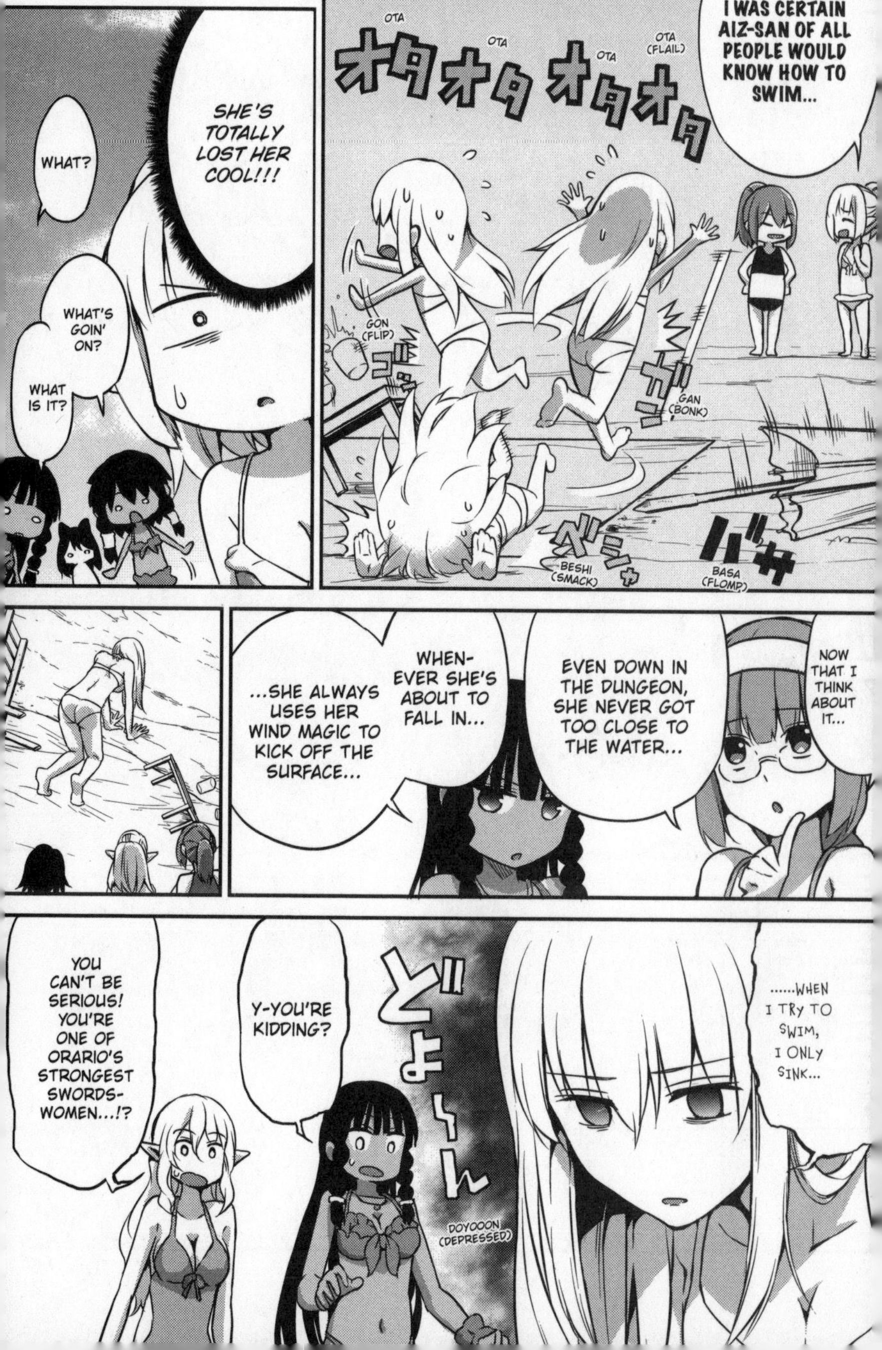
I WAS CERTAIN AIZ-SAN OF ALL PEOPLE WOULD KNOW HOW TO SWIM...
OTA
OTA
OTA
OTA (FLAIL)
GAN (BONK)
GON (FLIP)
BASA (FLOMP)
BESHI (SMACK)
SHE'S TOTALLY LOST HER COOL!!!
WHAT?
WHAT'S GOIN' ON?
WHAT IS IT?
NOW THAT I THINK ABOUT IT...
EVEN DOWN IN THE DUNGEON, SHE NEVER GOT TOO CLOSE TO THE WATER...
WHEN-EVER SHE'S ABOUT TO FALL IN...
...SHE ALWAYS USES HER WIND MAGIC TO KICK OFF THE SURFACE...
......WHEN I TRY TO SWIM, I ONLY SINK...
DOYOOON (DEPRESSED)
Y-YOU'RE KIDDING?
YOU CAN'T BE SERIOUS! YOU'RE ONE OF ORARIO'S STRONGEST SWORDS-WOMEN...!?

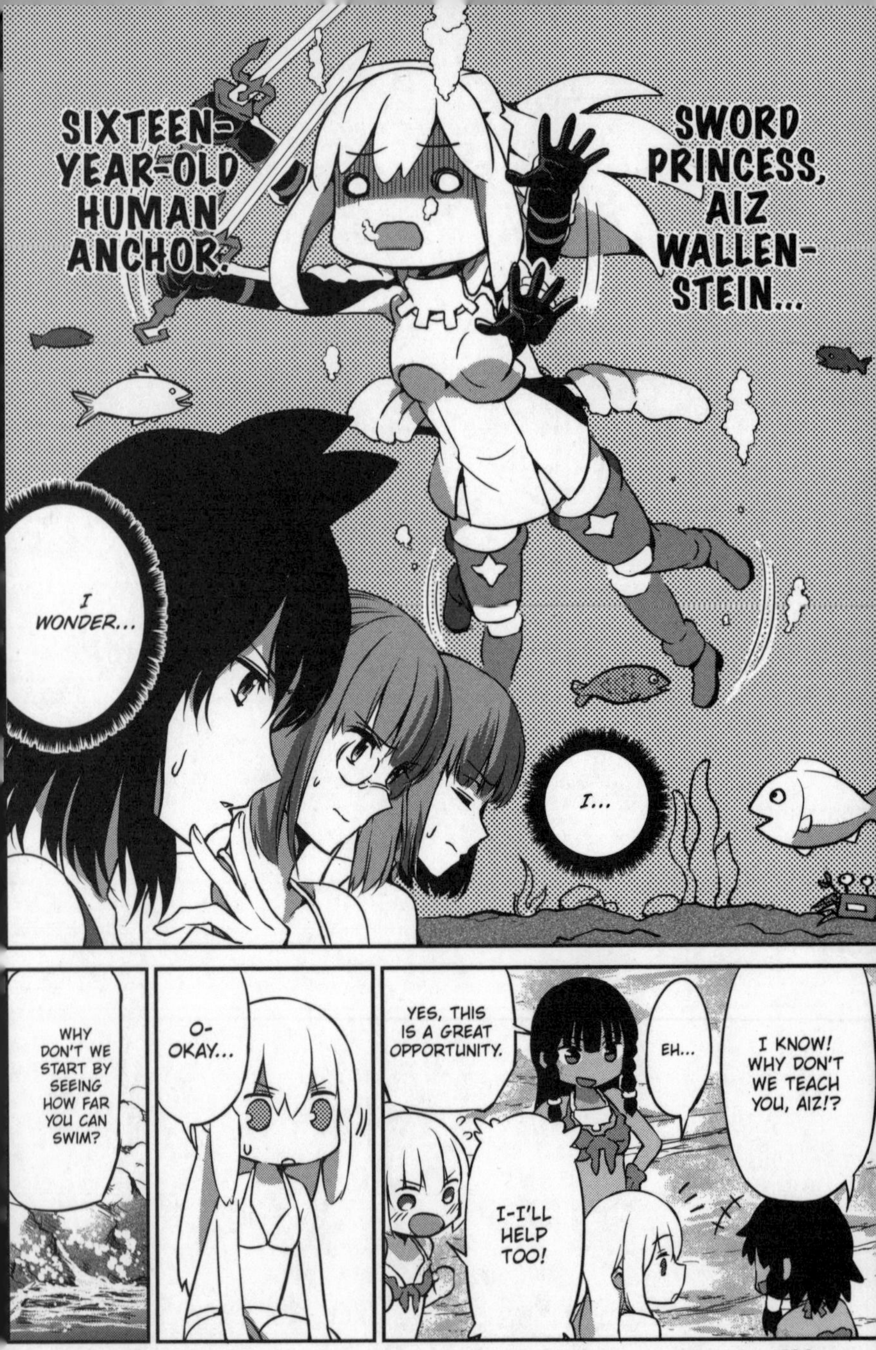
SWORD PRINCESS, AIZ WALLEN-STEIN...
SIXTEEN-YEAR-OLD HUMAN ANCHOR.
I...
I WONDER...
I KNOW! WHY DON'T WE TEACH YOU, AIZ!?
EH...
YES, THIS IS A GREAT OPPORTUNITY.
I-I'LL HELP TOO!
O-OKAY...
WHY DON'T WE START BY SEEING HOW FAR YOU CAN SWIM?

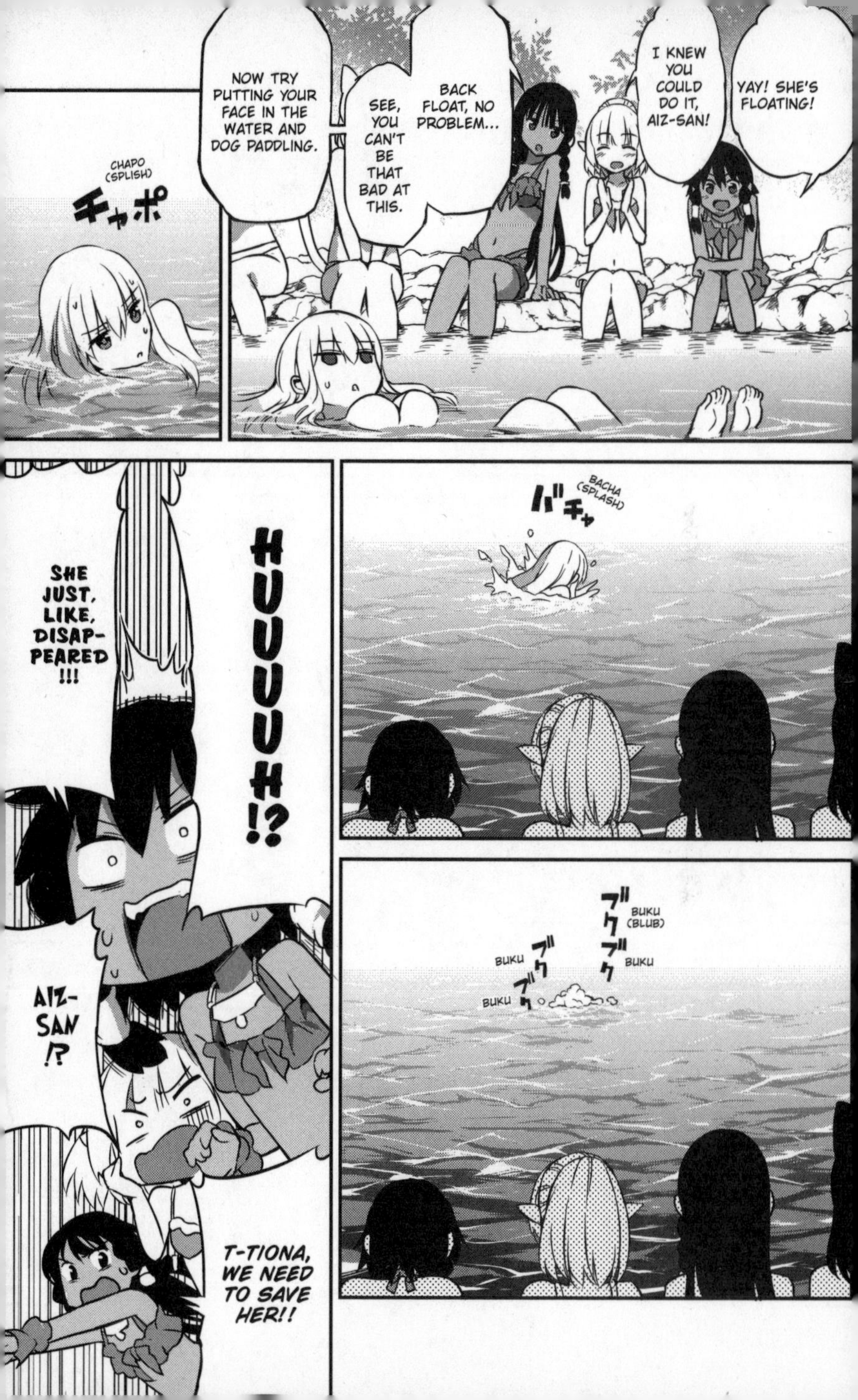
YAY! SHE'S FLOATING!
I KNEW YOU COULD DO IT, AIZ-SAN!
BACK FLOAT, NO PROBLEM...
SEE, YOU CAN'T BE THAT BAD AT THIS.
NOW TRY PUTTING YOUR FACE IN THE WATER AND DOG PADDLING.
チャポ
CHAPO (SPLASH)
バチャ
BACHA (SPLASH)
ブクブク
BUKU (BLUB)
ブク
BUKU
ブク
BUKU
ブク
BUKU
HUUUUUH!?
SHE JUST, LIKE, DISAPPEARED!!!
AIZ-SAN!?
T-TIONA, WE NEED TO SAVE HER!!

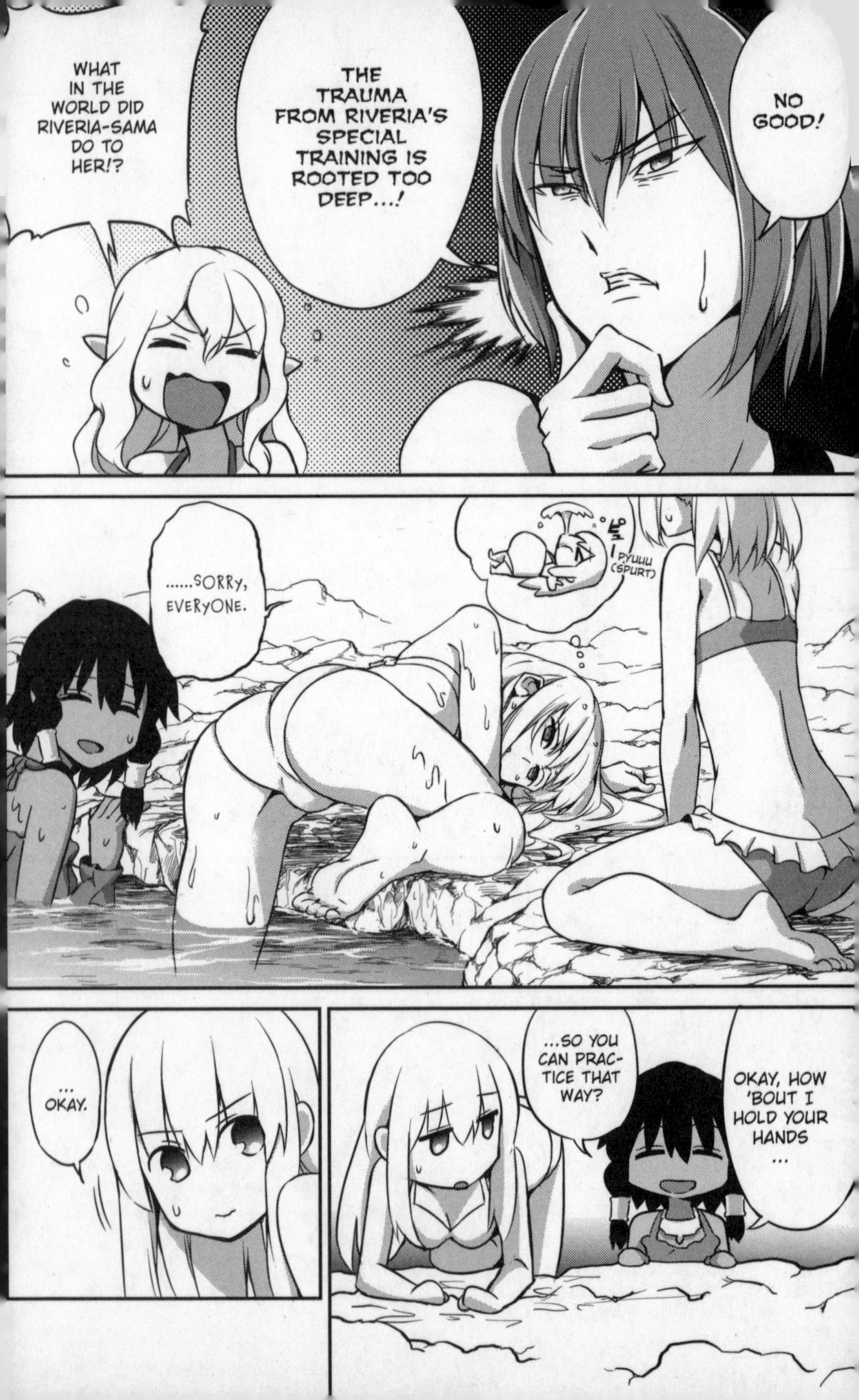
NO GOOD!
THE TRAUMA FROM RIVERIA'S SPECIAL TRAINING IS ROOTED TOO DEEP...!
WHAT IN THE WORLD DID RIVERIA-SAMA DO TO HER!?
PYUUU (SPURT)
......SORRY, EVERYONE.
OKAY, HOW 'BOUT I HOLD YOUR HANDS ...
...SO YOU CAN PRAC-TICE THAT WAY?
... OKAY.

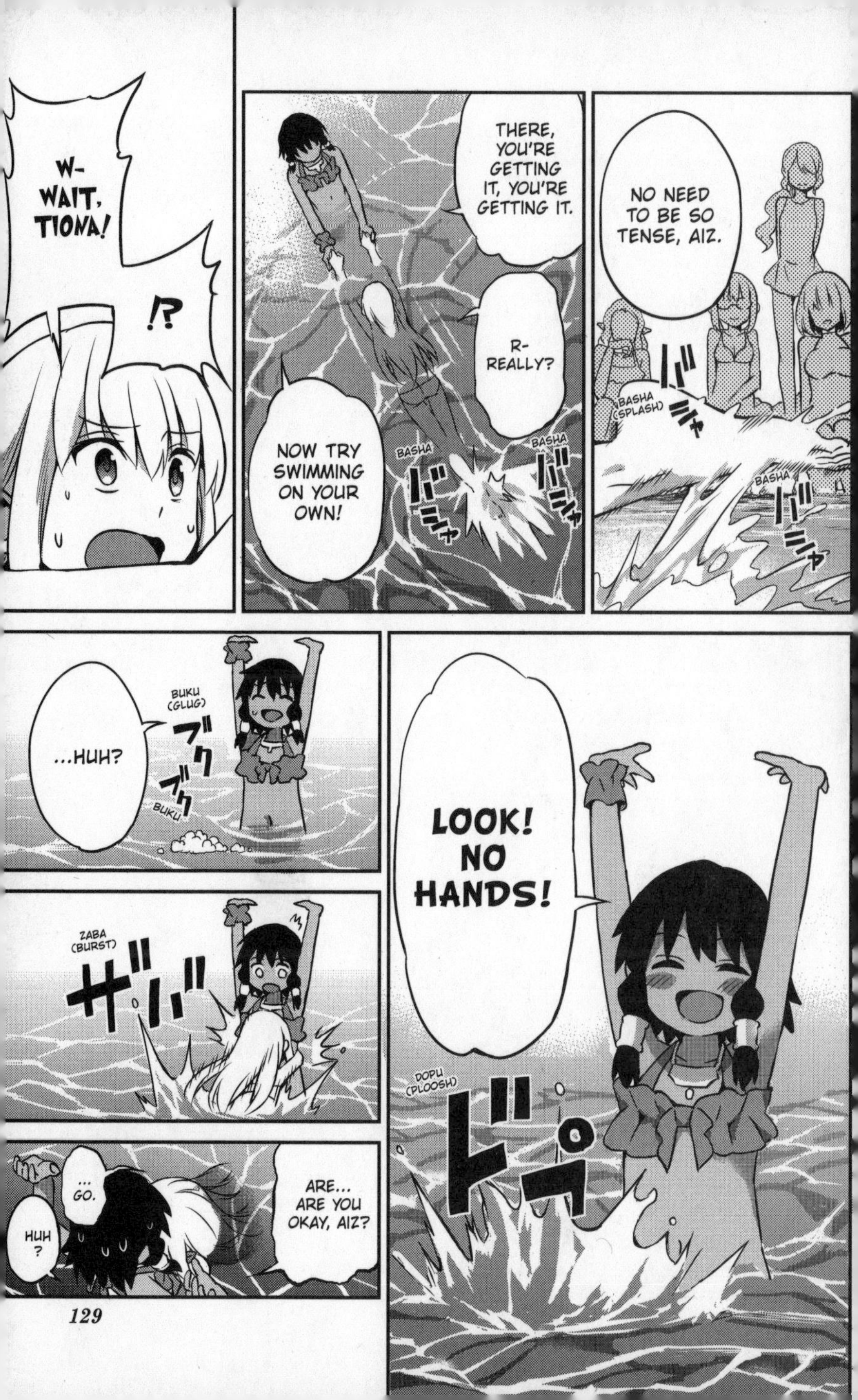
NO NEED TO BE SO TENSE, AIZ.
BASHA (SPLASH)
BASHA
THERE, YOU'RE GETTING IT, YOU'RE GETTING IT.
R- REALLY?
BASHA
BASHA
NOW TRY SWIMMING ON YOUR OWN!
W- WAIT, TIONA!
!?
LOOK! NO HANDS!
DOPU (PLOOSH)
BUKU (GLUG)
BUKU
...HUH?
ZABA (BURST)
ARE... ARE YOU OKAY, AIZ?
... GO.
HUH ?

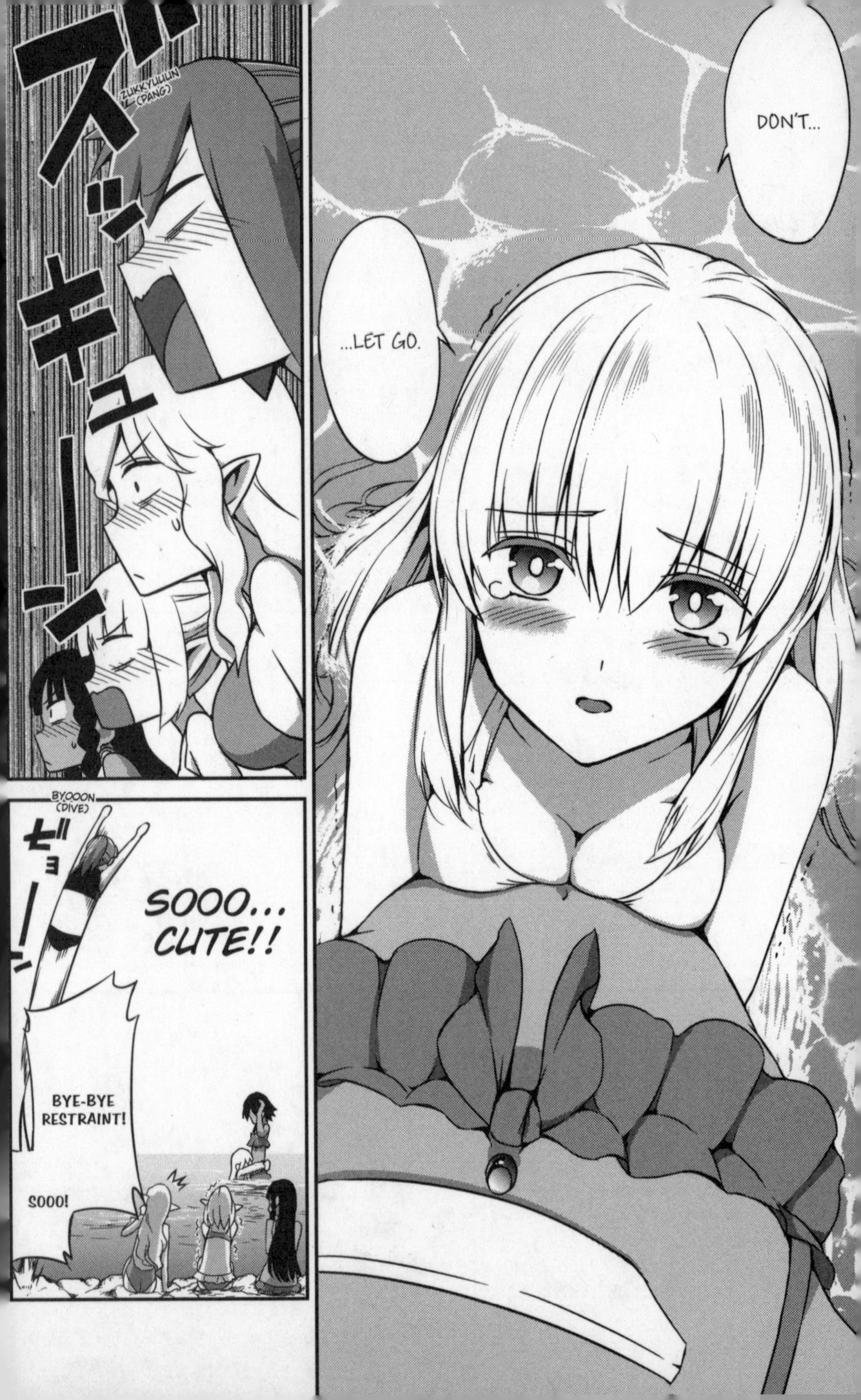
DON'T...
...LET GO.
ZUKKYUUUN (PANG)
BYOOON (DIVE)
SOOO... CUTE!!
BYE-BYE RESTRAINT!
SOOO!

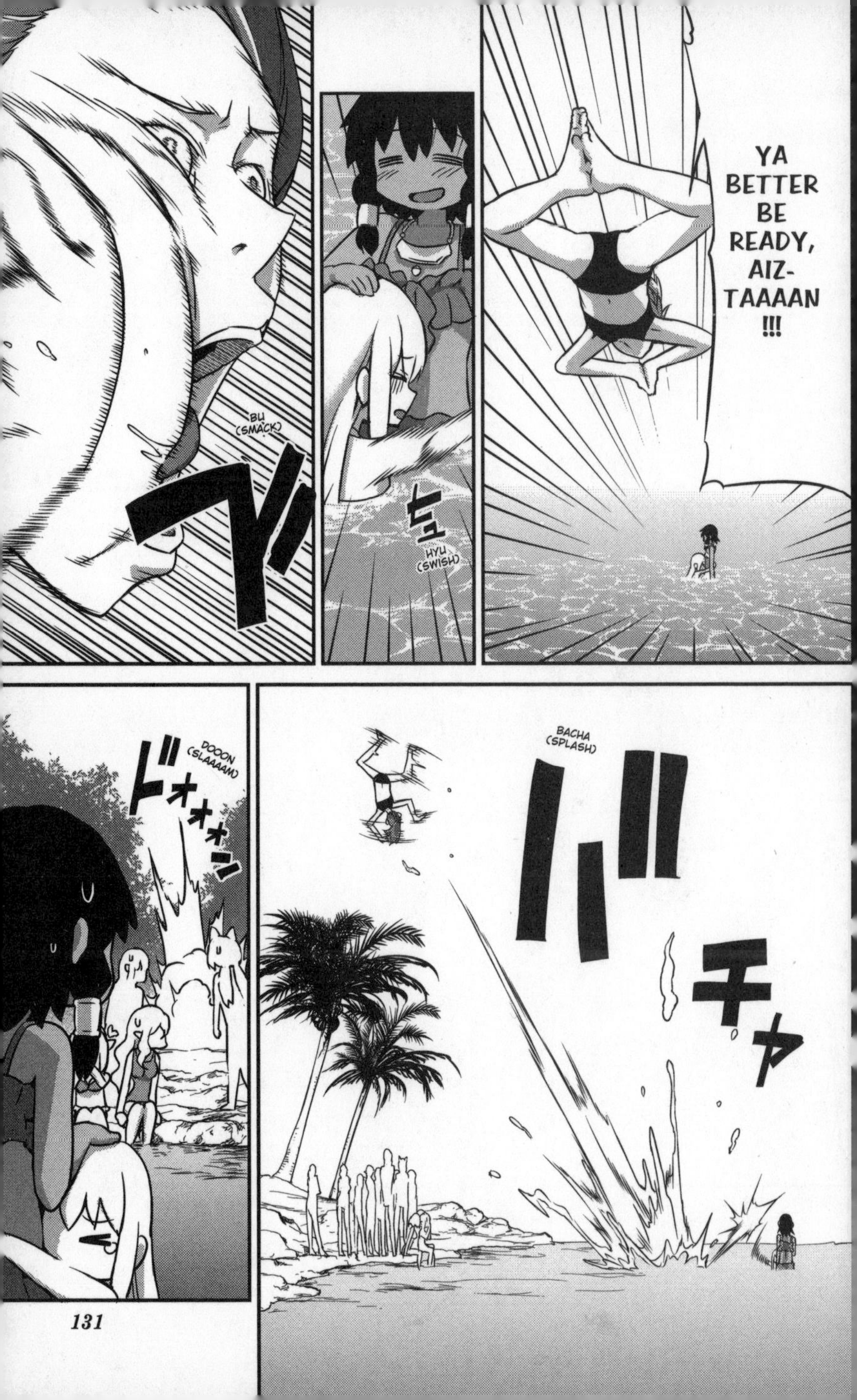
YA BETTER BE READY, AIZ-TAAAAN!!!
ヒュ
HYU (SWISH)
ブ
BU (SMACK)
バチャ
BACHA (SPLASH)
ドォォォン
DOOON (SLAAAAM)

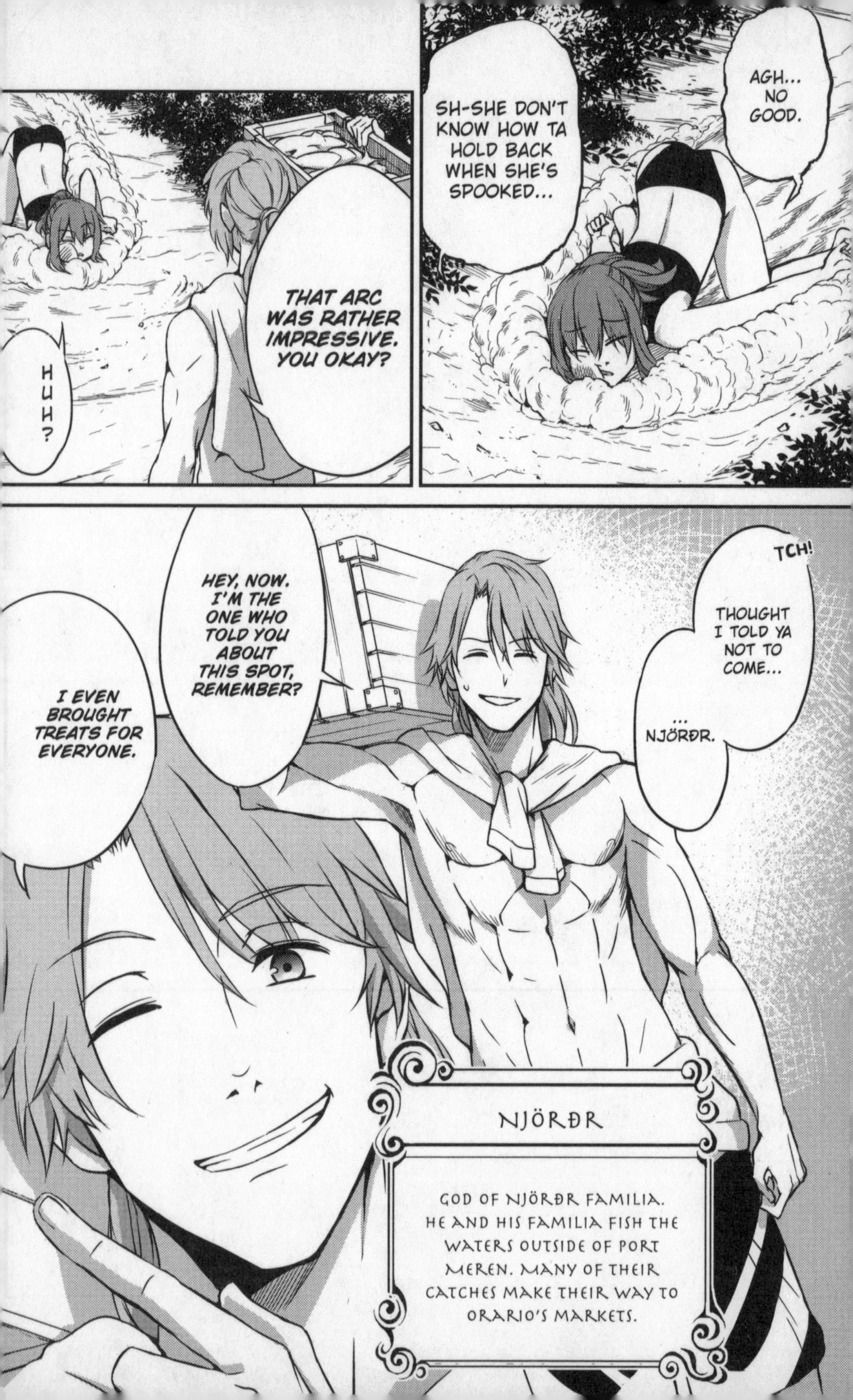
AGH... NO GOOD.
SH-SHE DON'T KNOW HOW TA HOLD BACK WHEN SHE'S SPOOKED...
THAT ARC WAS RATHER IMPRESSIVE. YOU OKAY?
HUH?
TCH!
THOUGHT I TOLD YA NOT TO COME...
... NJÖRÐR.
HEY, NOW. I'M THE ONE WHO TOLD YOU ABOUT THIS SPOT, REMEMBER?
I EVEN BROUGHT TREATS FOR EVERYONE.
NJÖRÐR
GOD OF NJÖRÐR FAMILIA. HE AND HIS FAMILIA FISH THE WATERS OUTSIDE OF PORT MEREN. MANY OF THEIR CATCHES MAKE THEIR WAY TO ORARIO'S MARKETS.

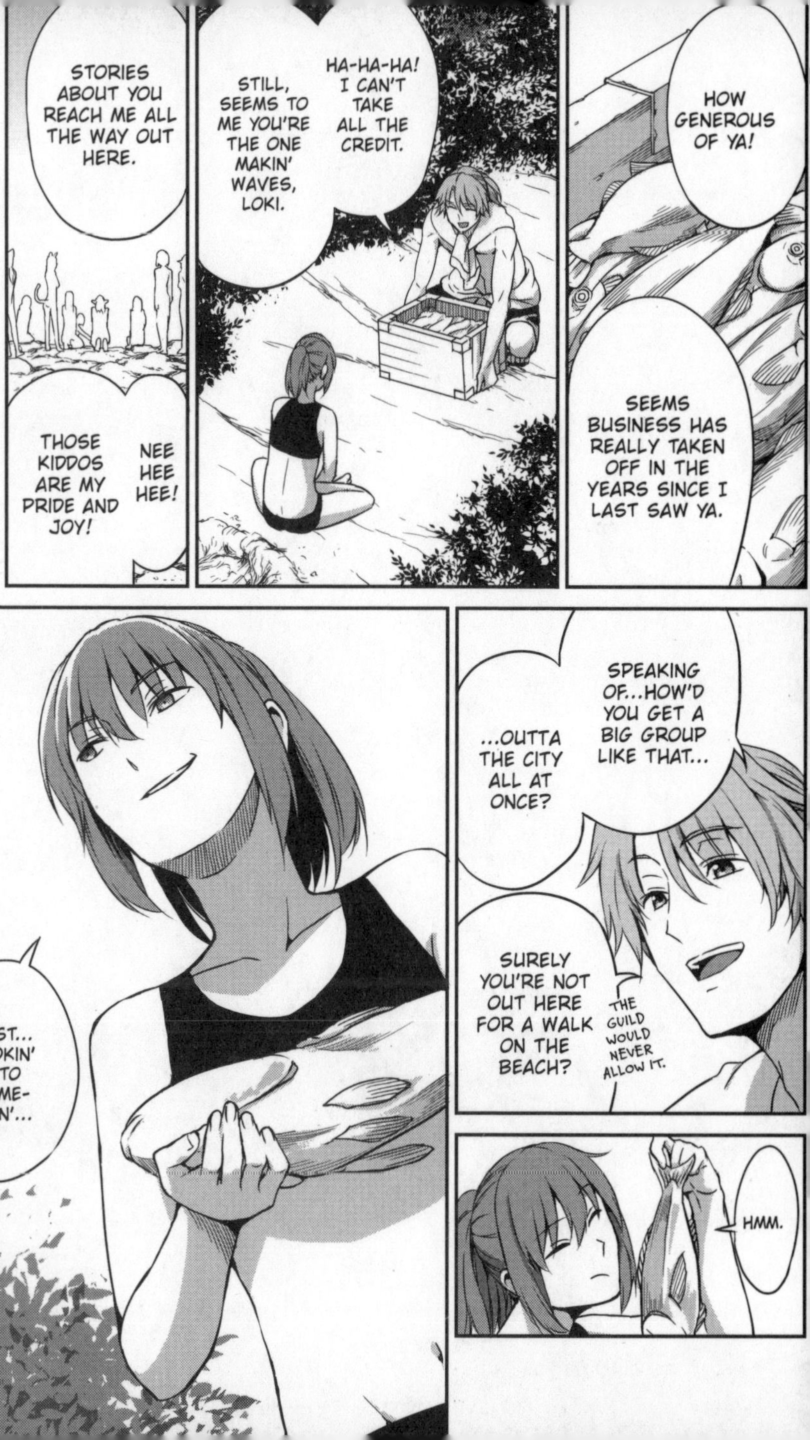
HOW GENEROUS OF YA!
SEEMS BUSINESS HAS REALLY TAKEN OFF IN THE YEARS SINCE I LAST SAW YA.
HA-HA-HA! I CAN'T TAKE ALL THE CREDIT.
STILL, SEEMS TO ME YOU'RE THE ONE MAKIN' WAVES, LOKI.
STORIES ABOUT YOU REACH ME ALL THE WAY OUT HERE.
NEE HEE HEE!
THOSE KIDDOS ARE MY PRIDE AND JOY!
SPEAKING OF...HOW'D YOU GET A BIG GROUP LIKE THAT...
...OUTTA THE CITY ALL AT ONCE?
SURELY YOU'RE NOT OUT HERE FOR A WALK ON THE BEACH?
THE GUILD WOULD NEVER ALLOW IT.
HMM.
JUST... LOOKIN' INTO SOME-THIN'...

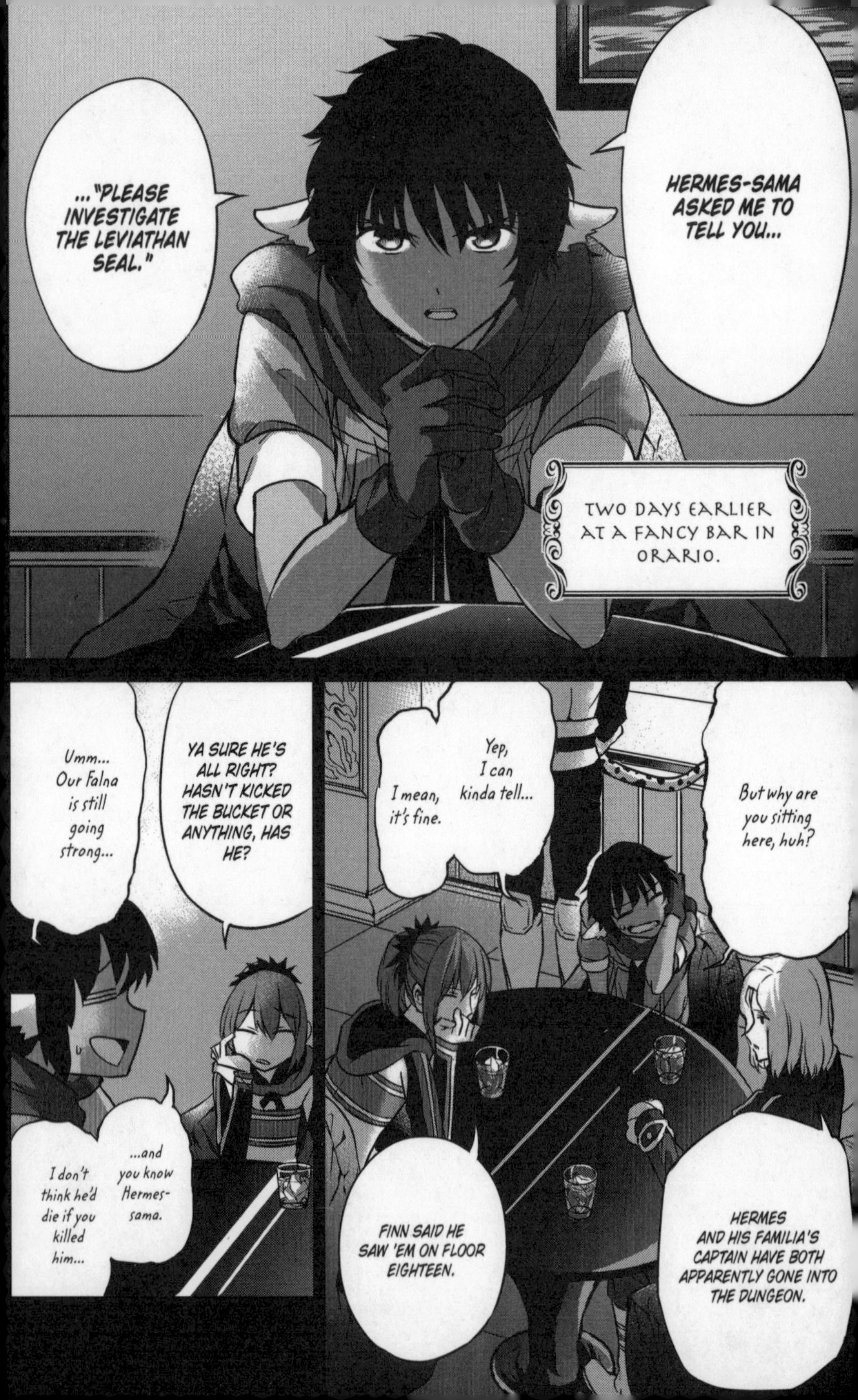
HERMES-SAMA ASKED ME TO TELL YOU...
..."PLEASE INVESTIGATE THE LEVIATHAN SEAL."
TWO DAYS EARLIER AT A FANCY BAR IN ORARIO.
But why are you sitting here, huh?
Yep, I can kinda tell...
I mean, it's fine.
HERMES AND HIS FAMILIA'S CAPTAIN HAVE BOTH APPARENTLY GONE INTO THE DUNGEON.
FINN SAID HE SAW 'EM ON FLOOR EIGHTEEN.
YA SURE HE'S ALL RIGHT? HASN'T KICKED THE BUCKET OR ANYTHING, HAS HE?
Umm... Our Falna is still going strong...
...and you know Hermes-sama.
I don't think he'd die if you killed him...

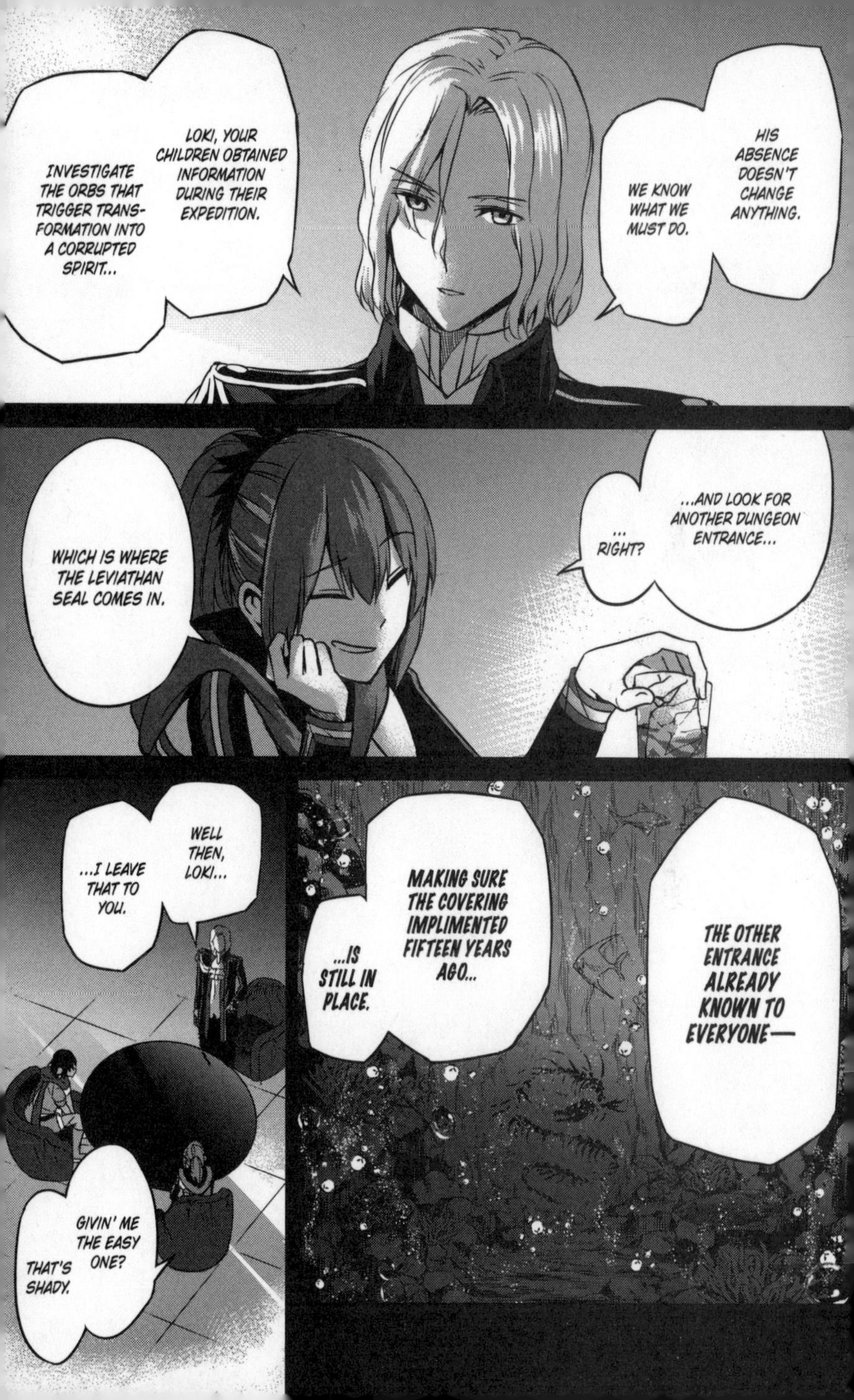
HIS ABSENCE DOESN'T CHANGE ANYTHING.
WE KNOW WHAT WE MUST DO.
LOKI, YOUR CHILDREN OBTAINED INFORMATION DURING THEIR EXPEDITION.
INVESTIGATE THE ORBS THAT TRIGGER TRANS-FORMATION INTO A CORRUPTED SPIRIT...
...AND LOOK FOR ANOTHER DUNGEON ENTRANCE...
... RIGHT?
WHICH IS WHERE THE LEVIATHAN SEAL COMES IN.
THE OTHER ENTRANCE ALREADY KNOWN TO EVERYONE—
MAKING SURE THE COVERING IMPLIMENTED FIFTEEN YEARS AGO...
...IS STILL IN PLACE.
WELL THEN, LOKI...
...I LEAVE THAT TO YOU.
GIVIN' ME THE EASY ONE?
THAT'S SHADY.

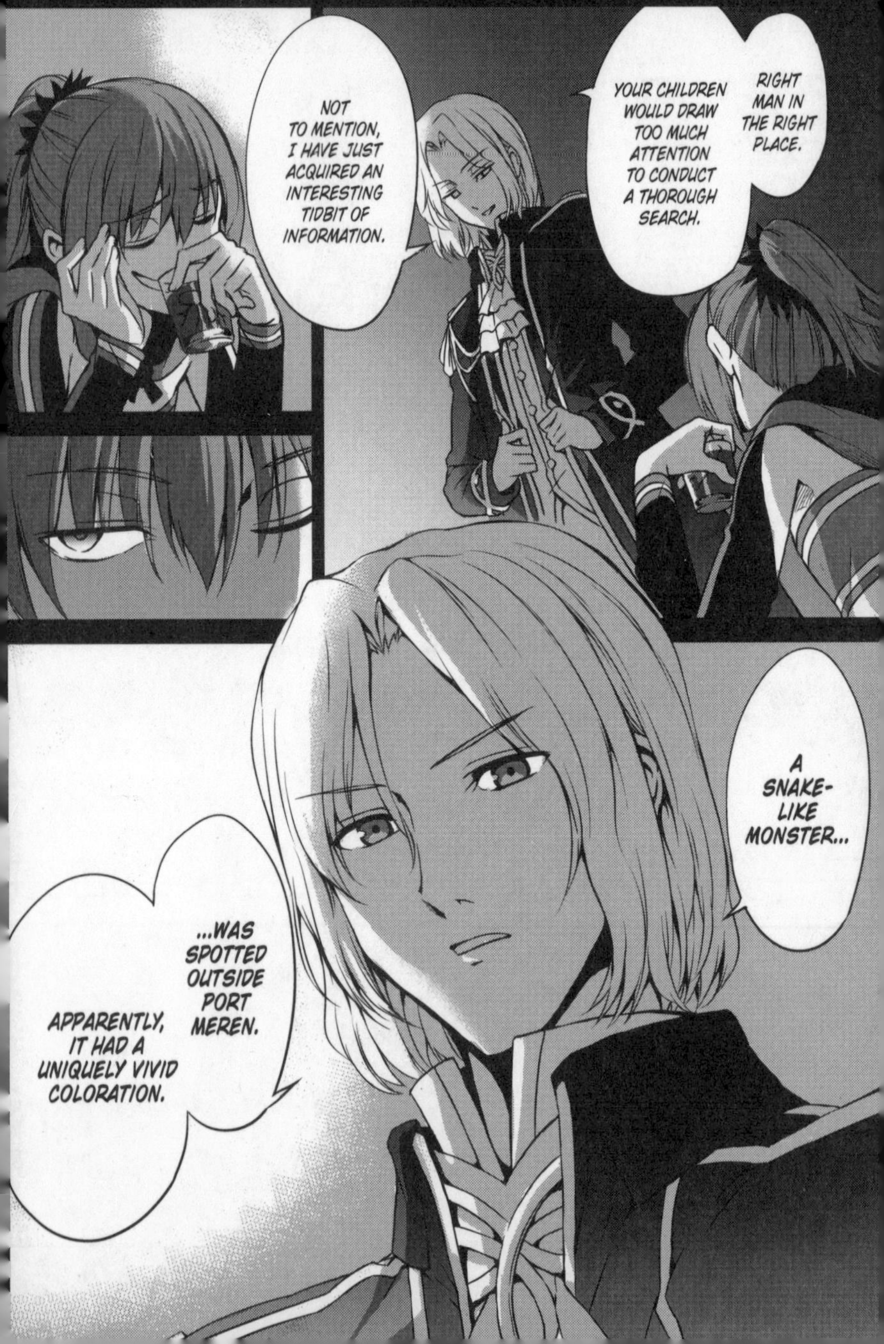
RIGHT MAN IN THE RIGHT PLACE.
YOUR CHILDREN WOULD DRAW TOO MUCH ATTENTION TO CONDUCT A THOROUGH SEARCH.
NOT TO MENTION, I HAVE JUST ACQUIRED AN INTERESTING TIDBIT OF INFORMATION.
A SNAKE-LIKE MONSTER...
...WAS SPOTTED OUTSIDE PORT MEREN.
APPARENTLY, IT HAD A UNIQUELY VIVID COLORATION.

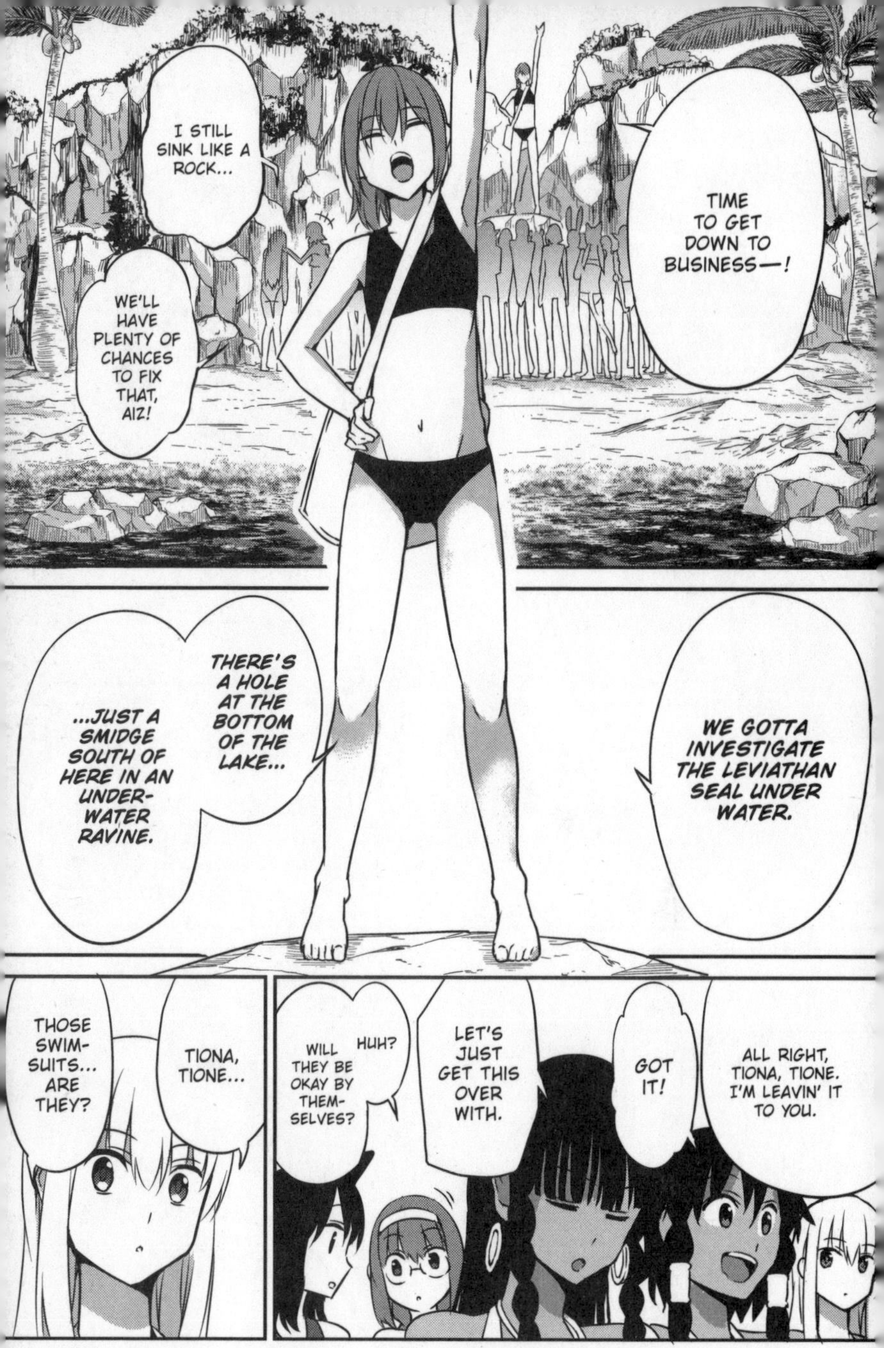
TIME TO GET DOWN TO BUSINESS—!
I STILL SINK LIKE A ROCK...
WE'LL HAVE PLENTY OF CHANCES TO FIX THAT, AIZ!
WE GOTTA INVESTIGATE THE LEVIATHAN SEAL UNDER WATER.
THERE'S A HOLE AT THE BOTTOM OF THE LAKE...
...JUST A SMIDGE SOUTH OF HERE IN AN UNDER-WATER RAVINE.
ALL RIGHT, TIONA, TIONE. I'M LEAVIN' IT TO YOU.
GOT IT!
LET'S JUST GET THIS OVER WITH.
HUH?
WILL THEY BE OKAY BY THEM-SELVES?
TIONA, TIONE...
THOSE SWIM-SUITS... ARE THEY?

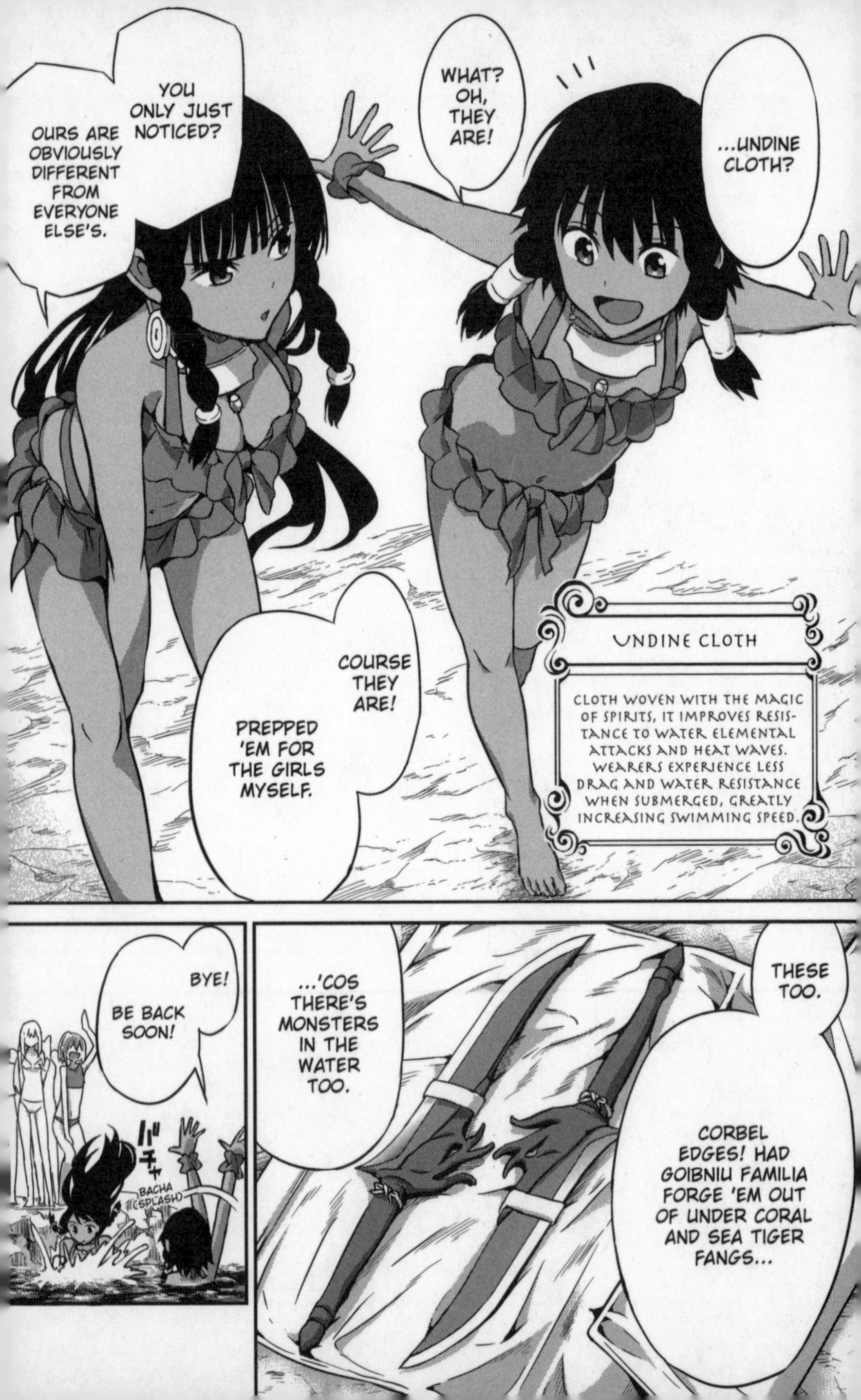
...UNDINE CLOTH?
WHAT? OH, THEY ARE!
YOU ONLY JUST NOTICED?
OURS ARE OBVIOUSLY DIFFERENT FROM EVERYONE ELSE'S.
UNDINE CLOTH
CLOTH WOVEN WITH THE MAGIC OF SPIRITS, IT IMPROVES RESISTANCE TO WATER ELEMENTAL ATTACKS AND HEAT WAVES. WEARERS EXPERIENCE LESS DRAG AND WATER RESISTANCE WHEN SUBMERGED, GREATLY INCREASING SWIMMING SPEED.
COURSE THEY ARE!
PREPPED 'EM FOR THE GIRLS MYSELF.
THESE TOO.
CORBEL EDGES! HAD GOIBNIU FAMILIA FORGE 'EM OUT OF UNDER CORAL AND SEA TIGER FANGS...
...'COS THERE'S MONSTERS IN THE WATER TOO.
BYE!
BE BACK SOON!
バチャ
BACHA (SPLASH)

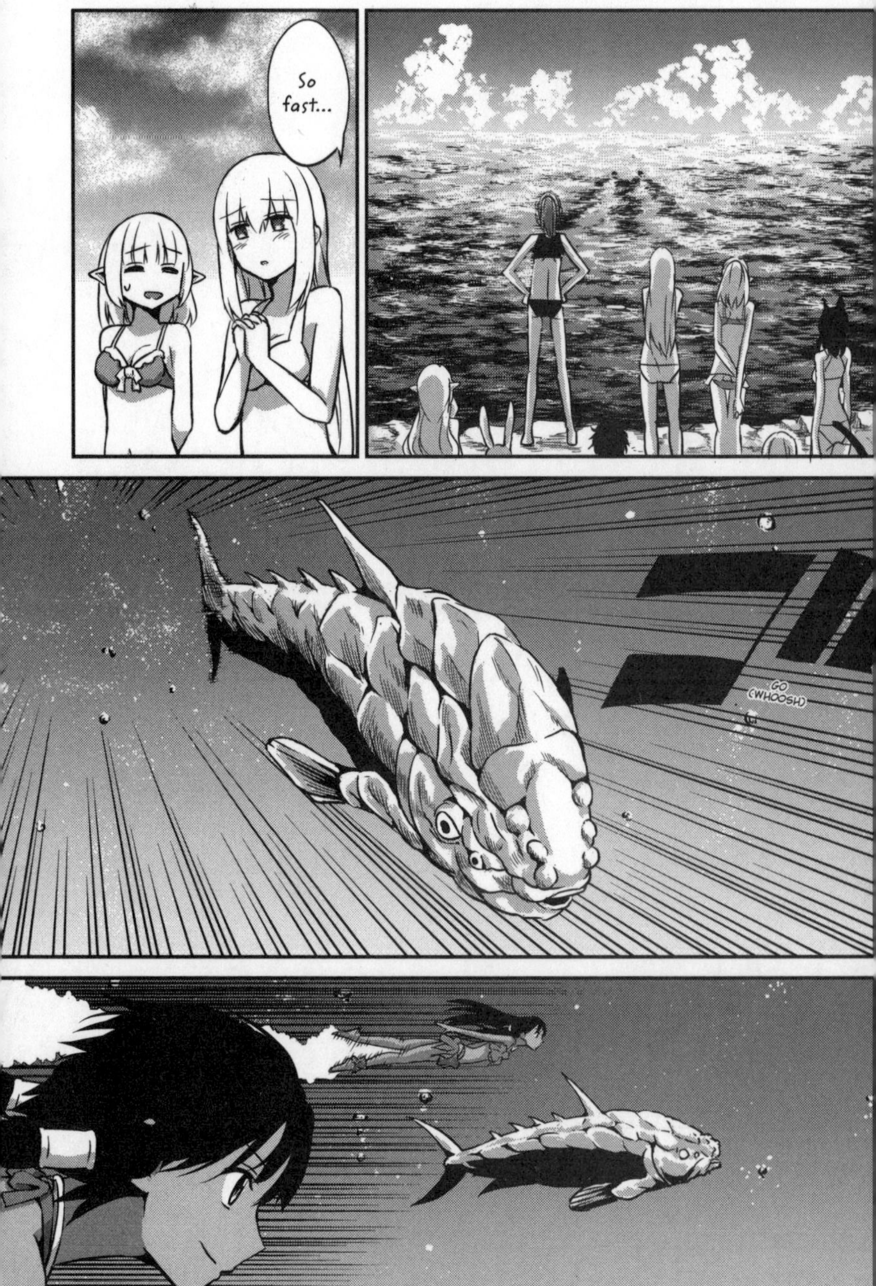
So fast...
GO (WHOOSH)

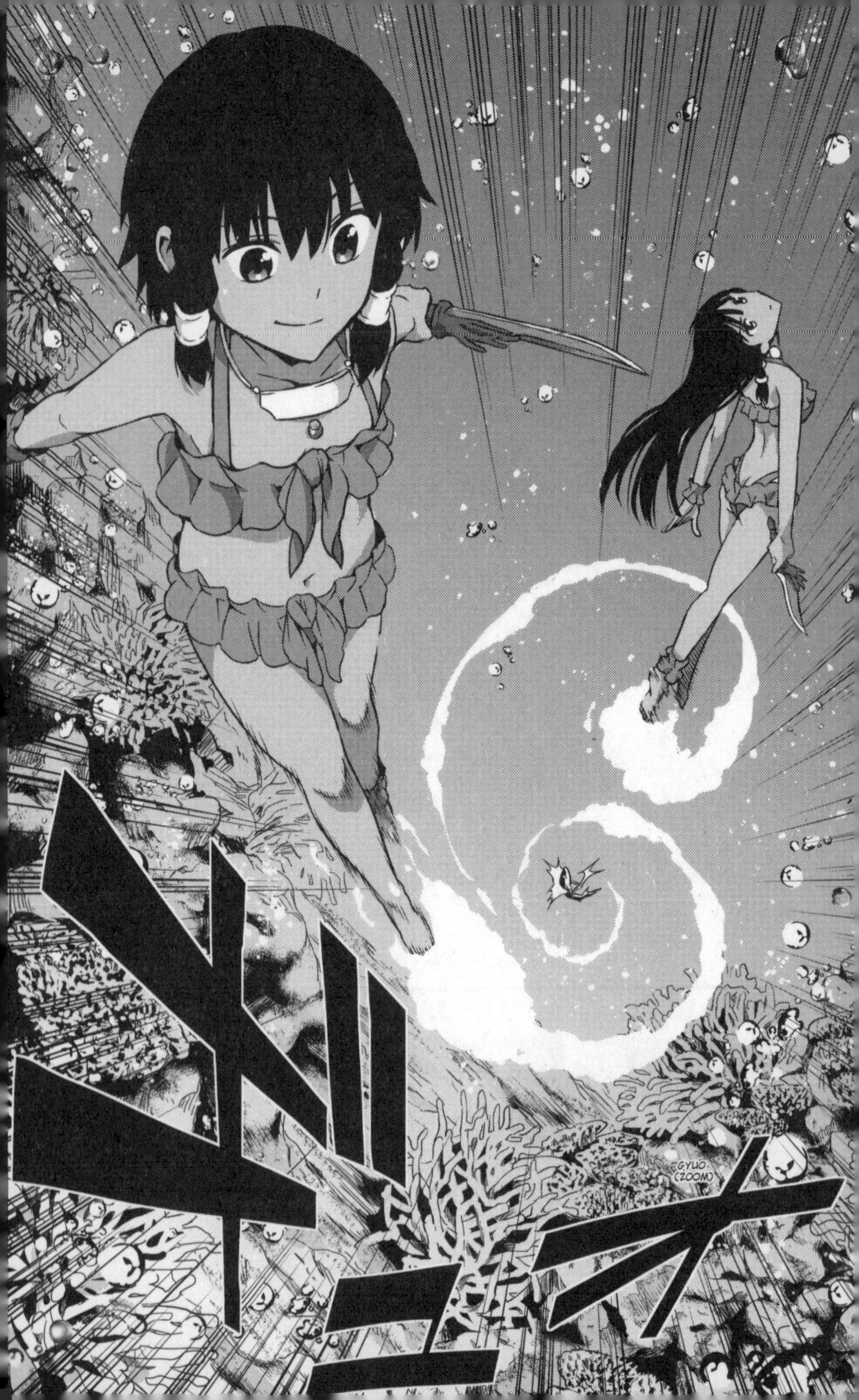
GYUO
(ZOOM)

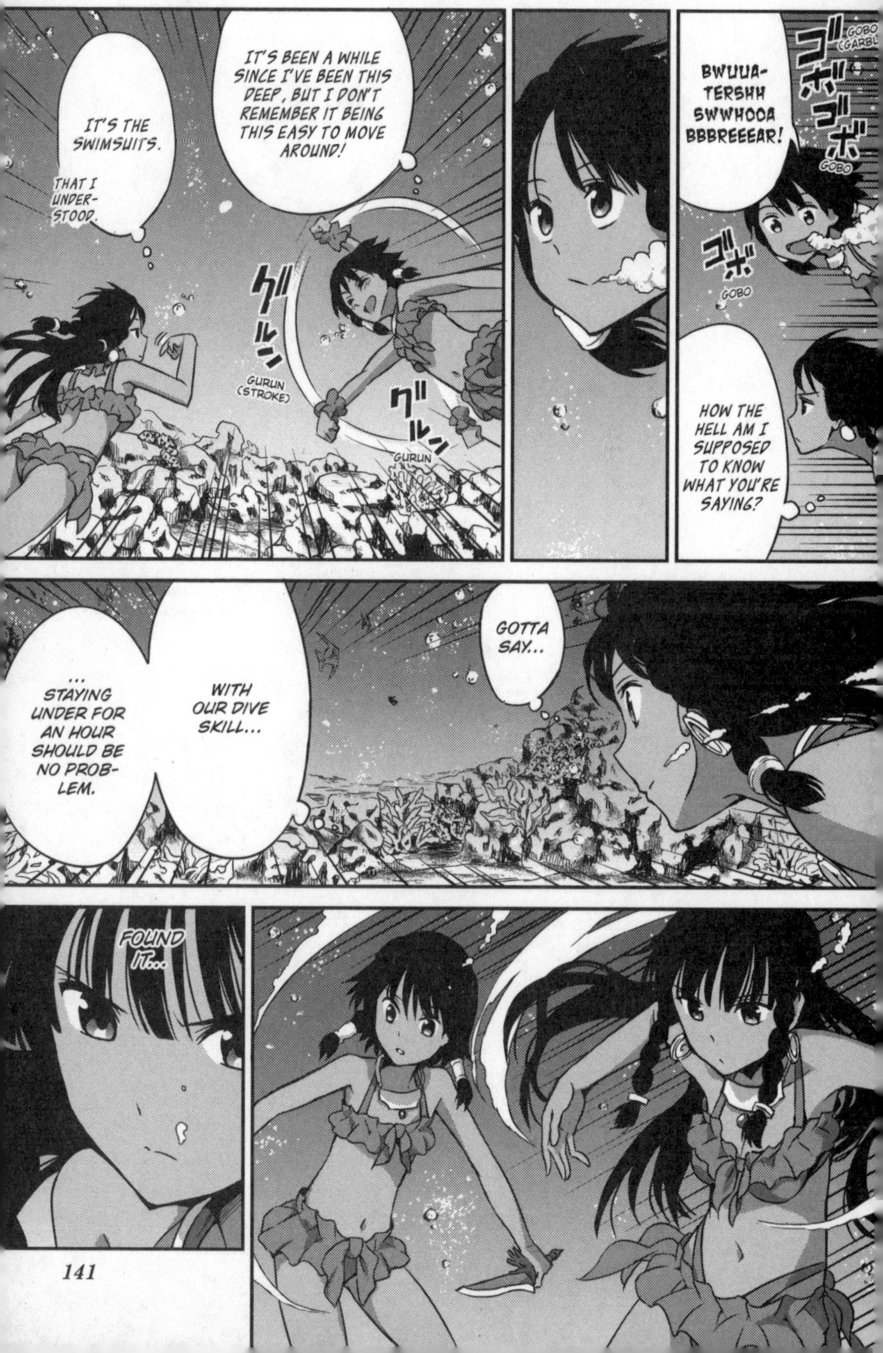
ゴボ
GOBO (GARBL
BWUUA-TERSHH SWWHOOA BBBREEEAR!
ゴボ
GOBO
ゴボ
GOBO
HOW THE HELL AM I SUPPOSED TO KNOW WHAT YOU'RE SAYING?
IT'S BEEN A WHILE SINCE I'VE BEEN THIS DEEP, BUT I DON'T REMEMBER IT BEING THIS EASY TO MOVE AROUND!
IT'S THE SWIMSUITS.
THAT I UNDER-STOOD.
グルン
GURUN (STROKE)
グルン
GURUN
GOTTA SAY...
WITH OUR DIVE SKILL...
...STAYING UNDER FOR AN HOUR SHOULD BE NO PROB-LEM.
FOUND IT...

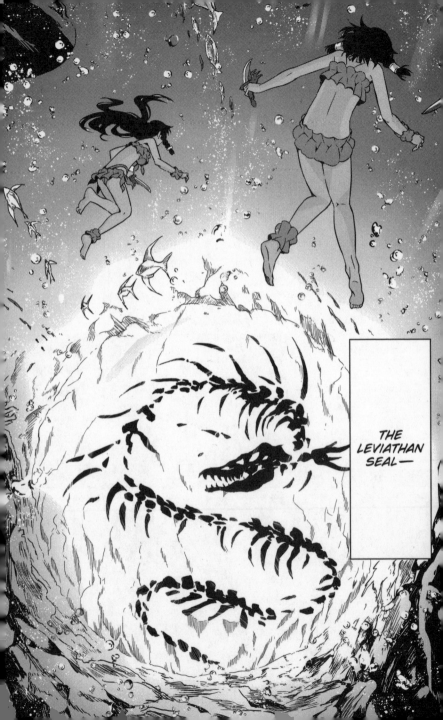

THE
LEVIATHAN
SEAL—

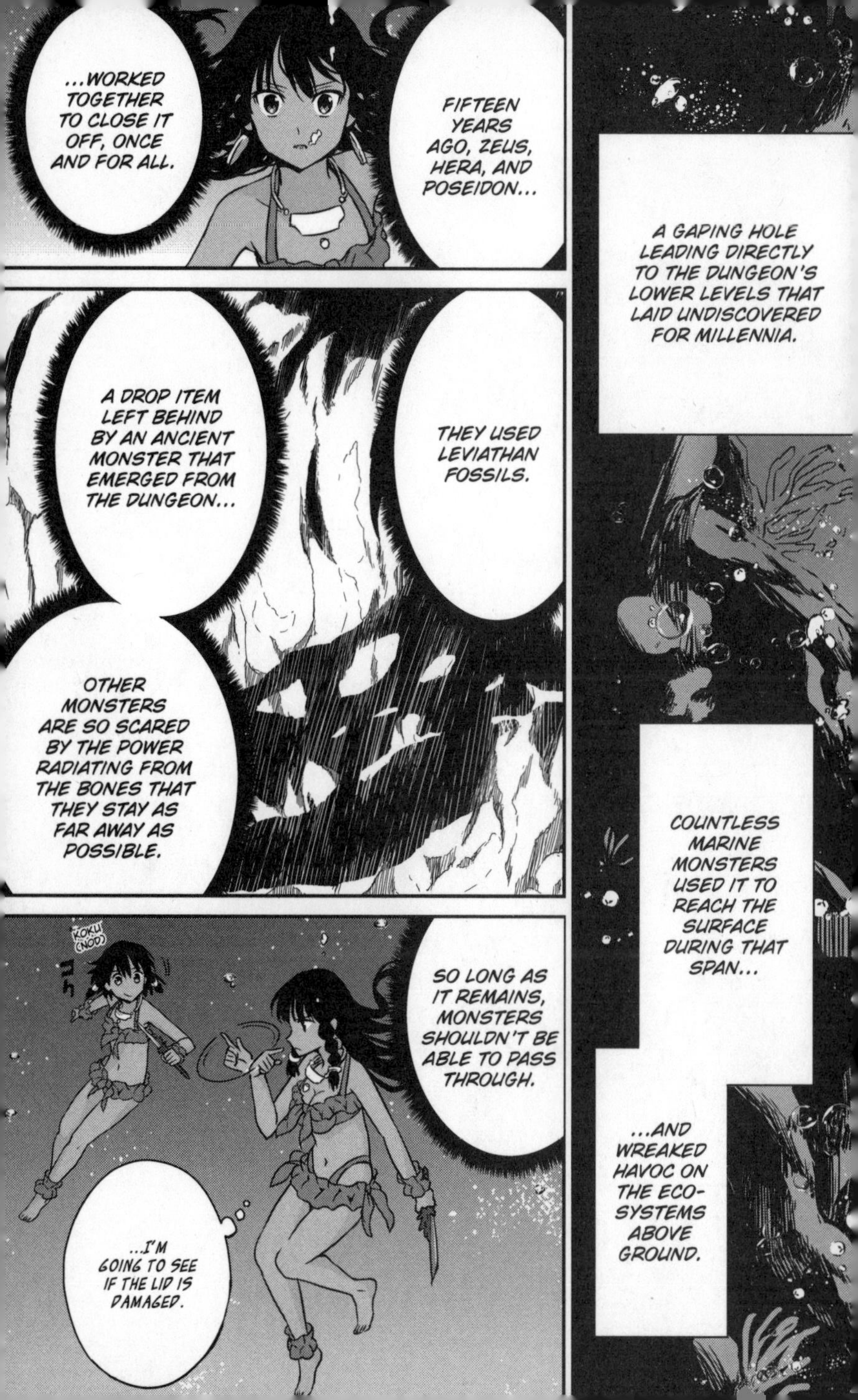
A GAPING HOLE LEADING DIRECTLY TO THE DUNGEON'S LOWER LEVELS THAT LAID UNDISCOVERED FOR MILLENNIA.
COUNTLESS MARINE MONSTERS USED IT TO REACH THE SURFACE DURING THAT SPAN...
...AND WREAKED HAVOC ON THE ECO-SYSTEMS ABOVE GROUND.
FIFTEEN YEARS AGO, ZEUS, HERA, AND POSEIDON...
...WORKED TOGETHER TO CLOSE IT OFF, ONCE AND FOR ALL.
THEY USED LEVIATHAN FOSSILS.
A DROP ITEM LEFT BEHIND BY AN ANCIENT MONSTER THAT EMERGED FROM THE DUNGEON...
OTHER MONSTERS ARE SO SCARED BY THE POWER RADIATING FROM THE BONES THAT THEY STAY AS FAR AWAY AS POSSIBLE.
SO LONG AS IT REMAINS, MONSTERS SHOULDN'T BE ABLE TO PASS THROUGH.
KOKU (NOD)
...I'M GOING TO SEE IF THE LID IS DAMAGED.

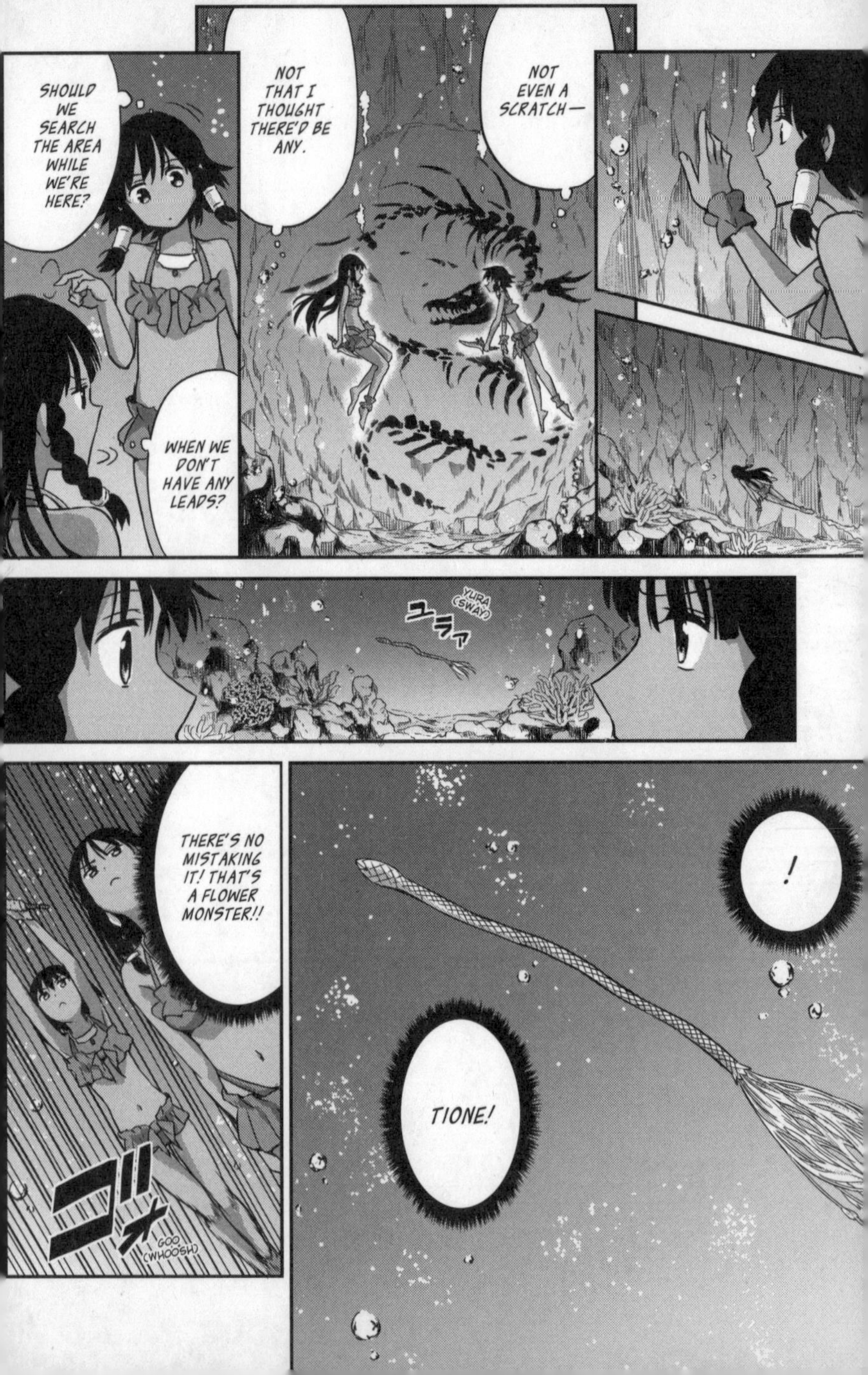
NOT EVEN A SCRATCH—
NOT THAT I THOUGHT THERE'D BE ANY.
SHOULD WE SEARCH THE AREA WHILE WE'RE HERE?
WHEN WE DON'T HAVE ANY LEADS?
YURA (SWAY)
!
TIONE!
THERE'S NO MISTAKING IT! THAT'S A FLOWER MONSTER!!
GOO (WHOOSH)

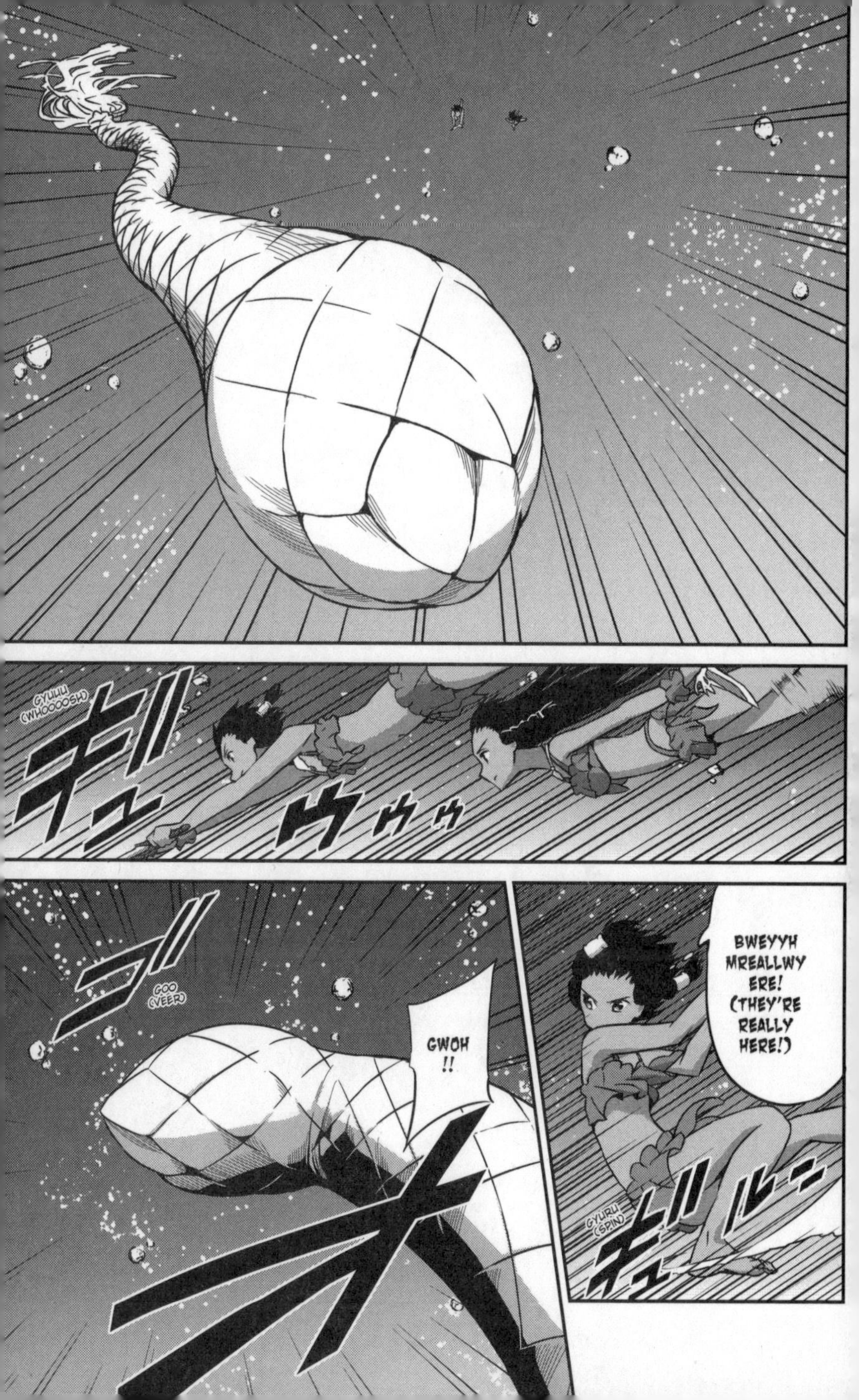
GYUUU (WHOOOOSH)
BWEYYH MREALLWY ERE! (THEY'RE REALLY HERE!)
GYURU (SPIN)
GOO (VEER)
GWOH !!

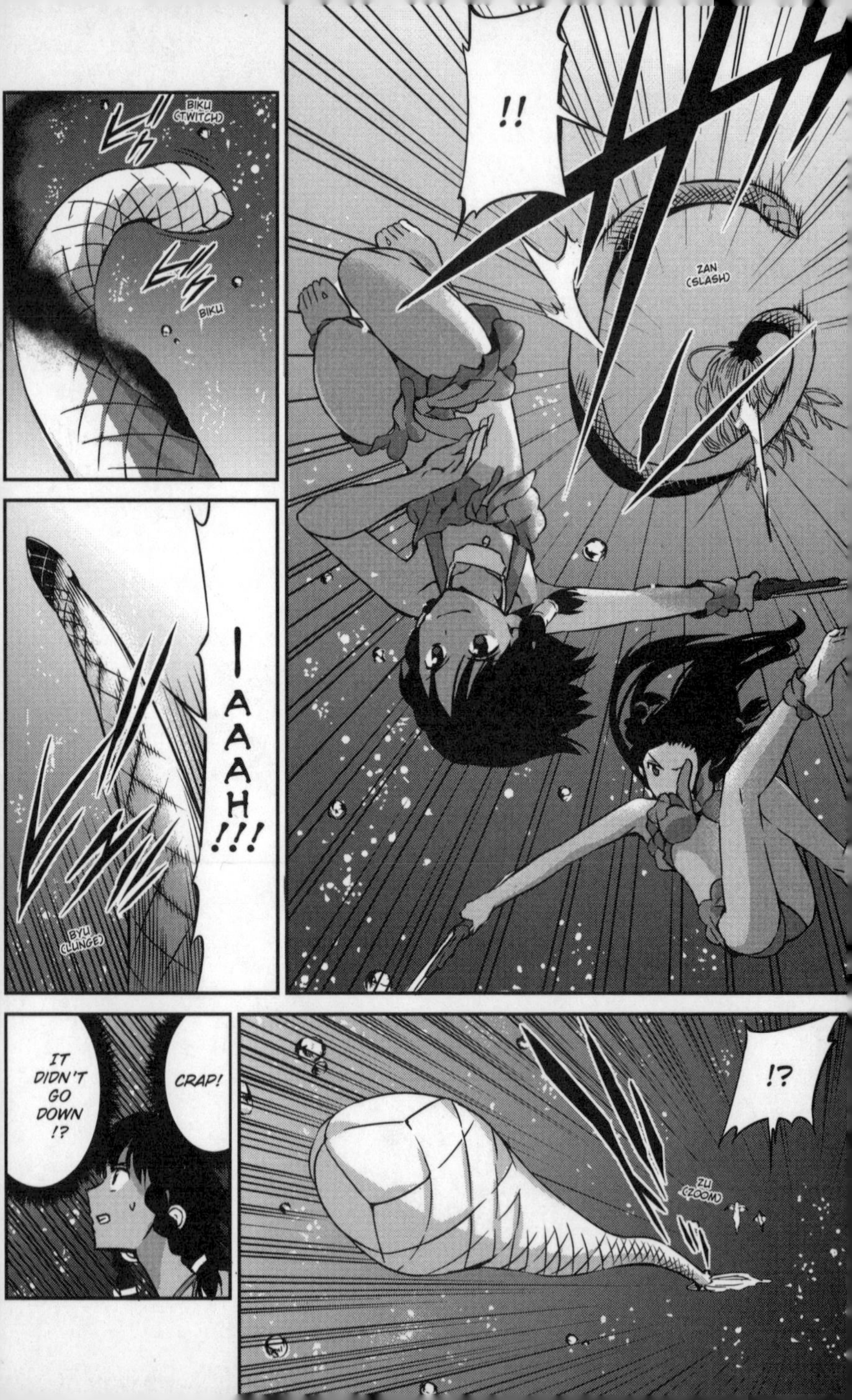
!!
ZAN (SLASH)
BIKU (TWITCH)
BIKU
IAAAAH!!!
BYU (LUNGE)
!?
ZU (ZOOM)
CRAP!
IT DIDN'T GO DOWN !?

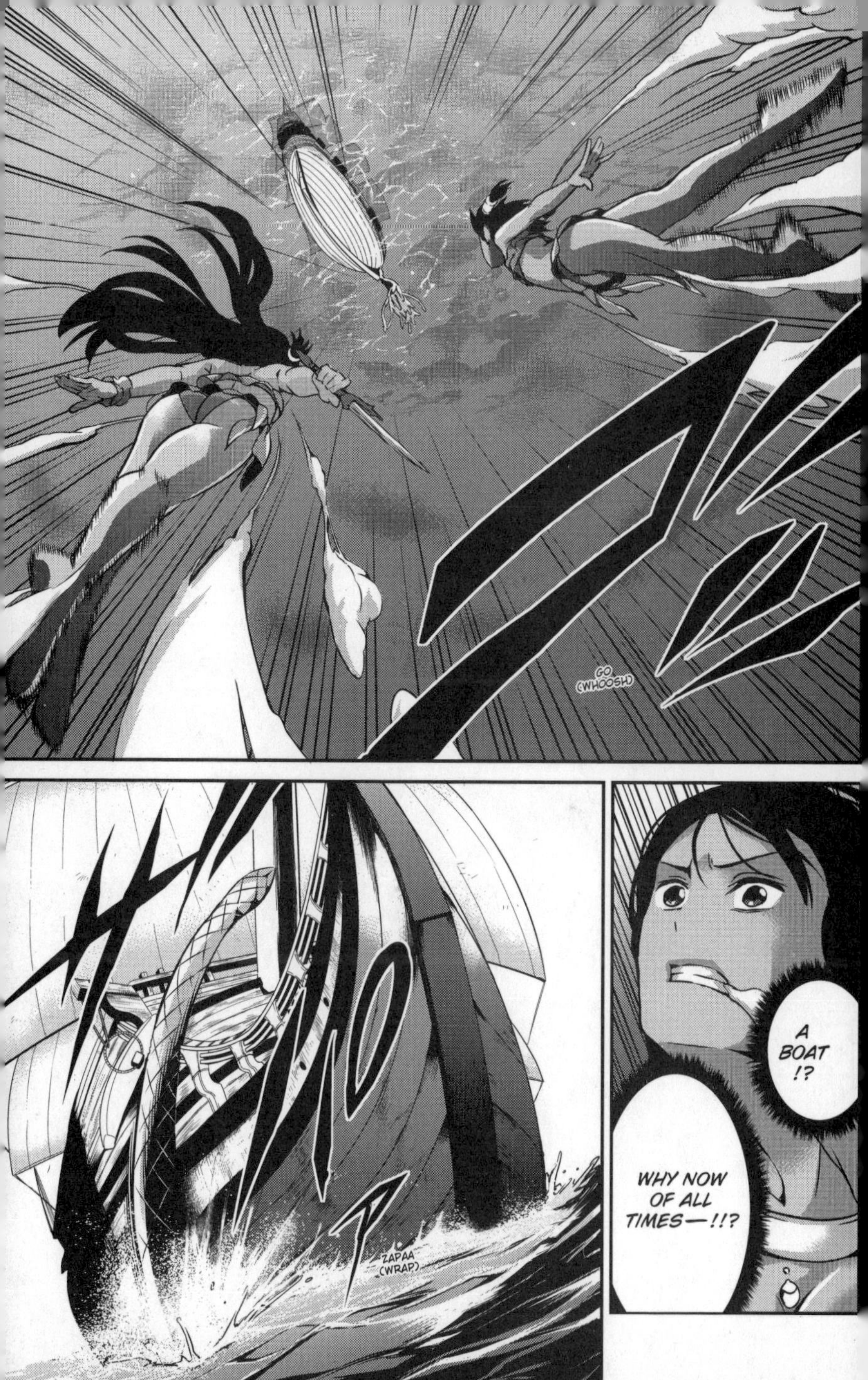
GO (WHOOSH)
A BOAT !?
WHY NOW OF ALL TIMES—!!?
ZAPAA (WRAP)

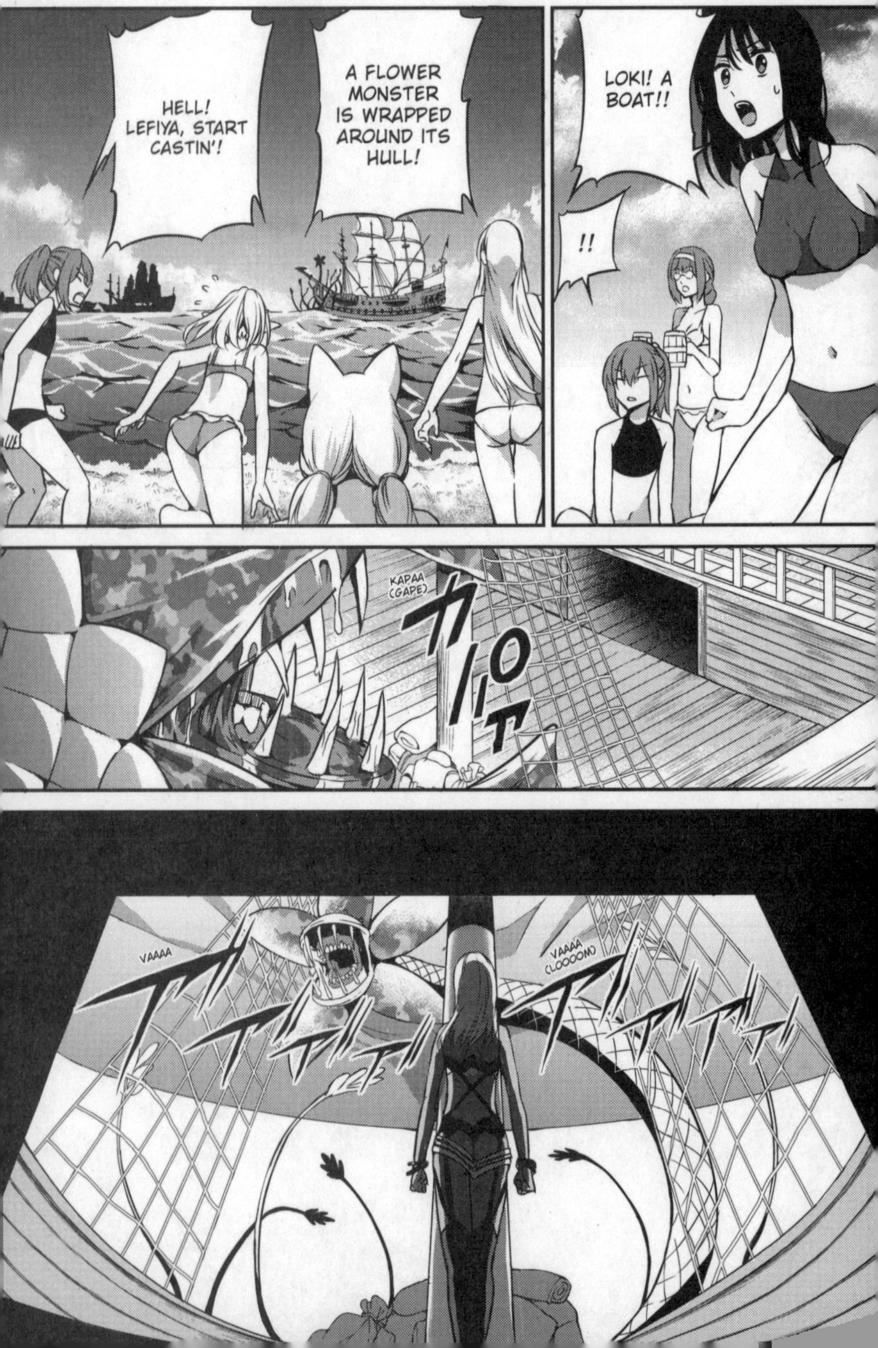
LOKI! A BOAT!!
!!
A FLOWER MONSTER IS WRAPPED AROUND ITS HULL!
HELL! LEFIYA, START CASTIN'!
KAPAA (GAPE)
VAAAA (LOOOOM)
VAAAA

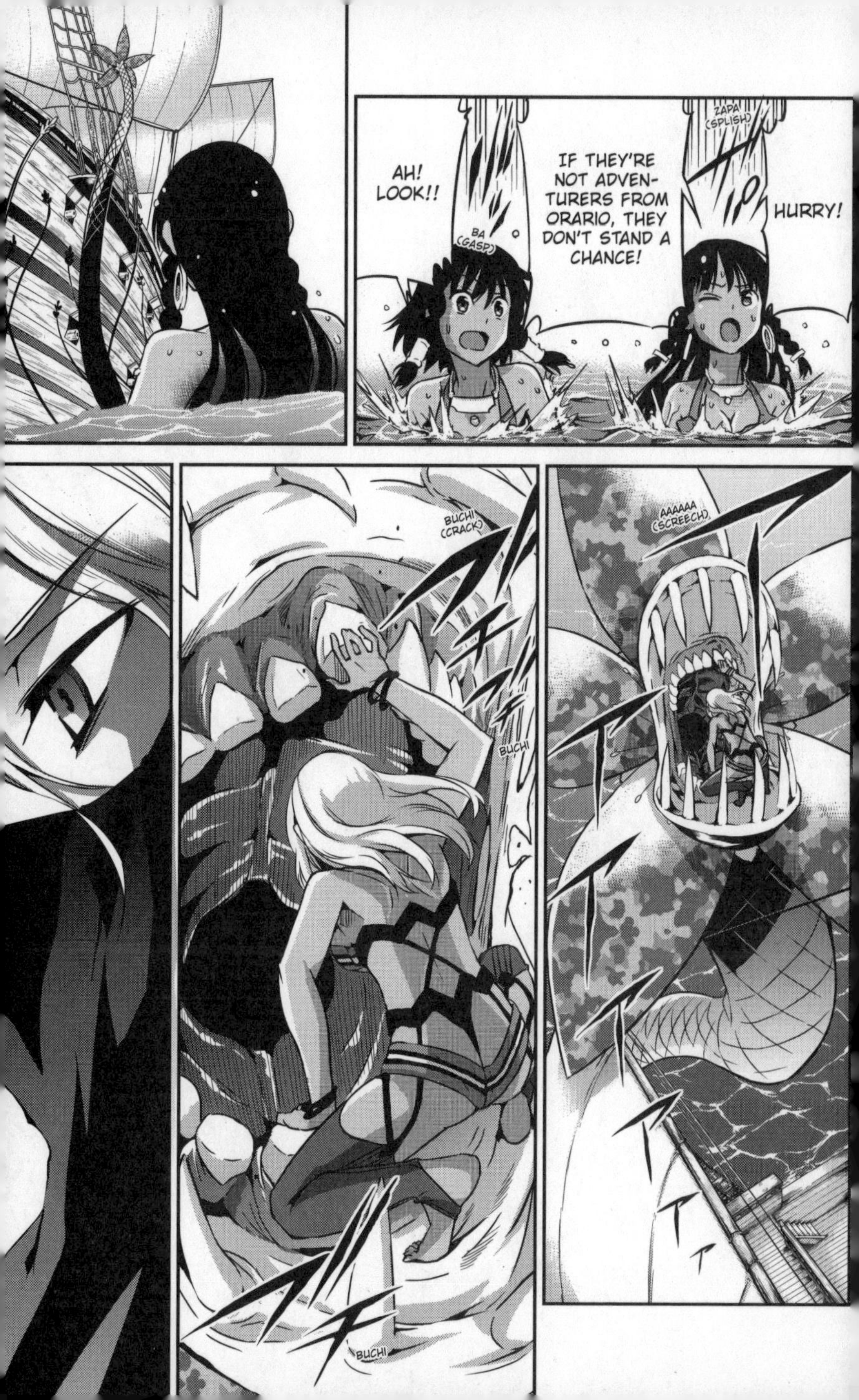
ZAPA (SPLISH)
HURRY!
IF THEY'RE NOT ADVENTURERS FROM ORARIO, THEY DON'T STAND A CHANCE!
AH! LOOK!!
BA (GASP)
AAAAAA (SCREECH)
BUCHI (CRACK)
BUCHI
BUCHI

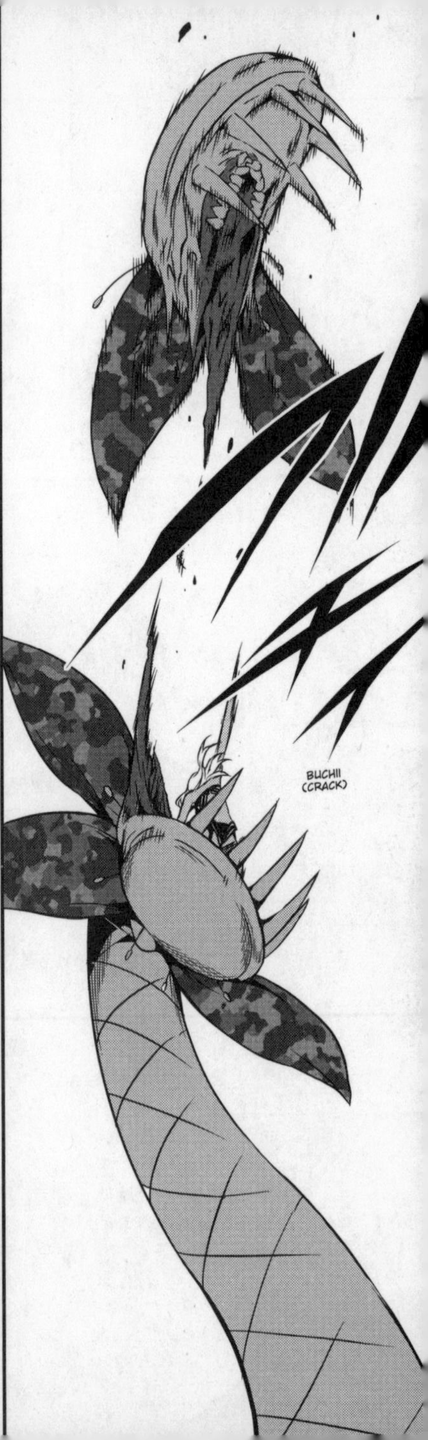
BUCHII (CRACK)
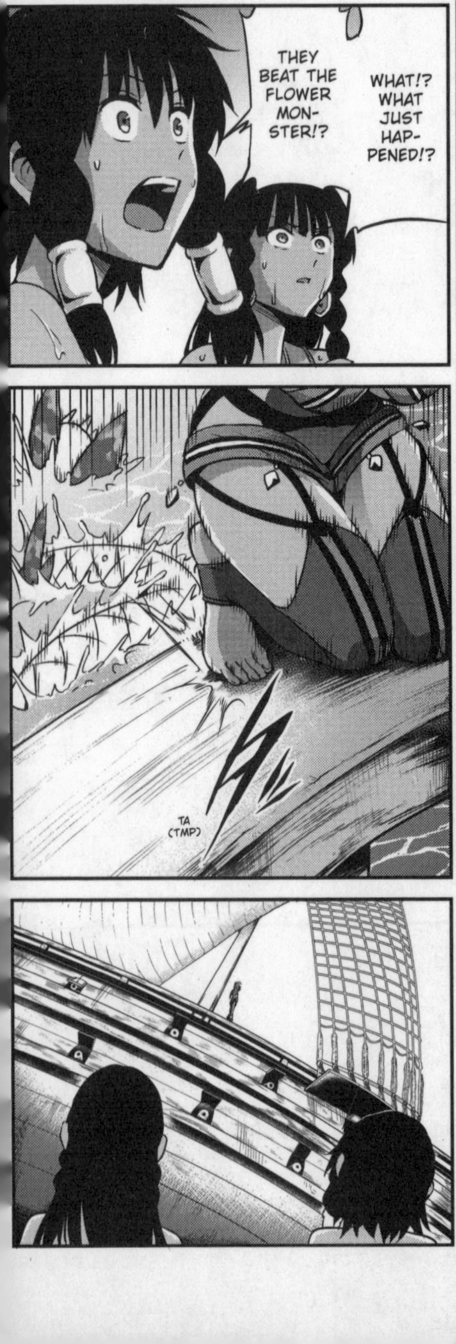
WHAT!? WHAT JUST HAP-PENED!?
THEY BEAT THE FLOWER MON-STER!?
TA (TMP)

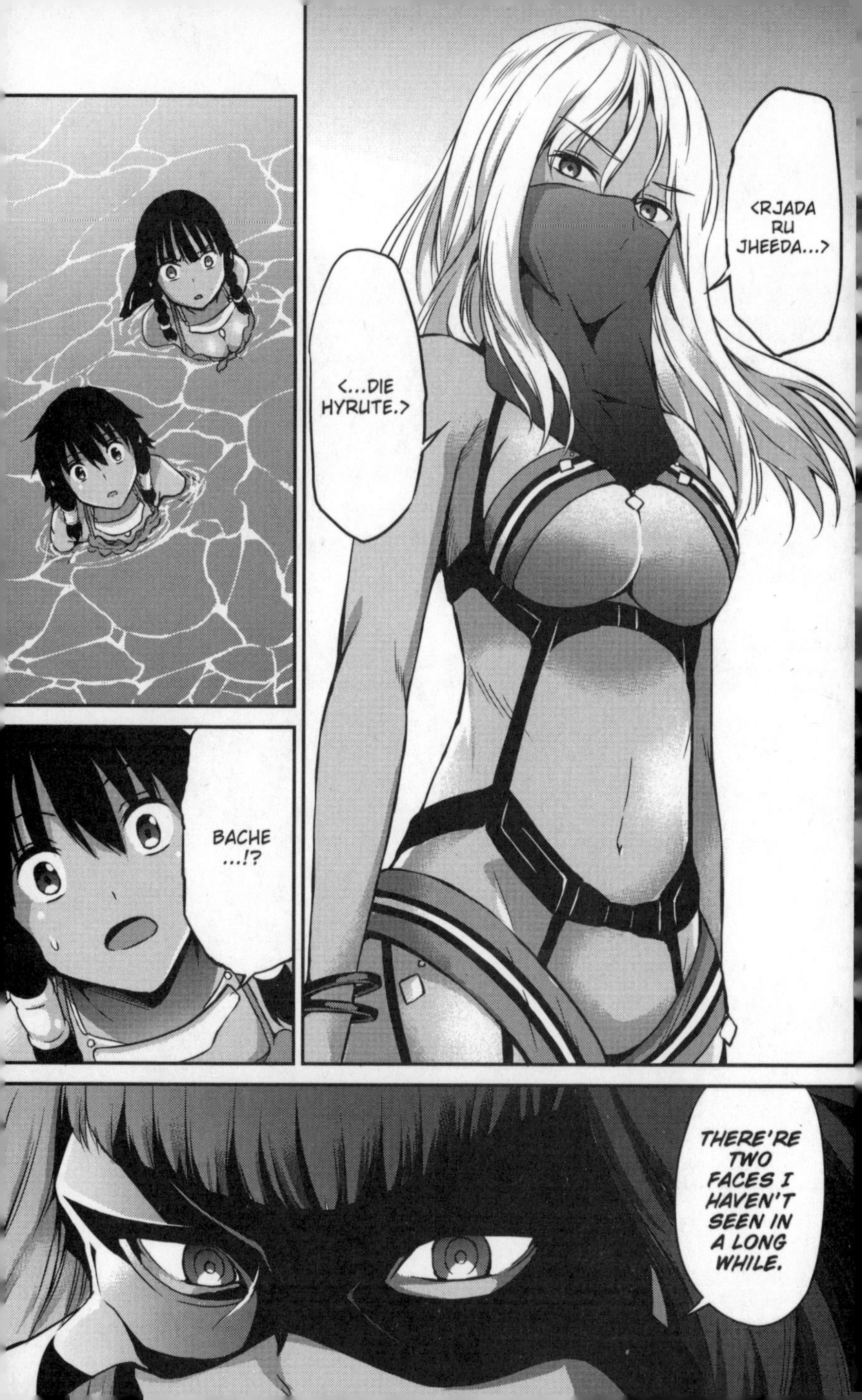
<RJADA RU JHEEDA...>
<...DIE HYRUTE.>
BACHE ...!?
THERE'RE TWO FACES I HAVEN'T SEEN IN A LONG WHILE.

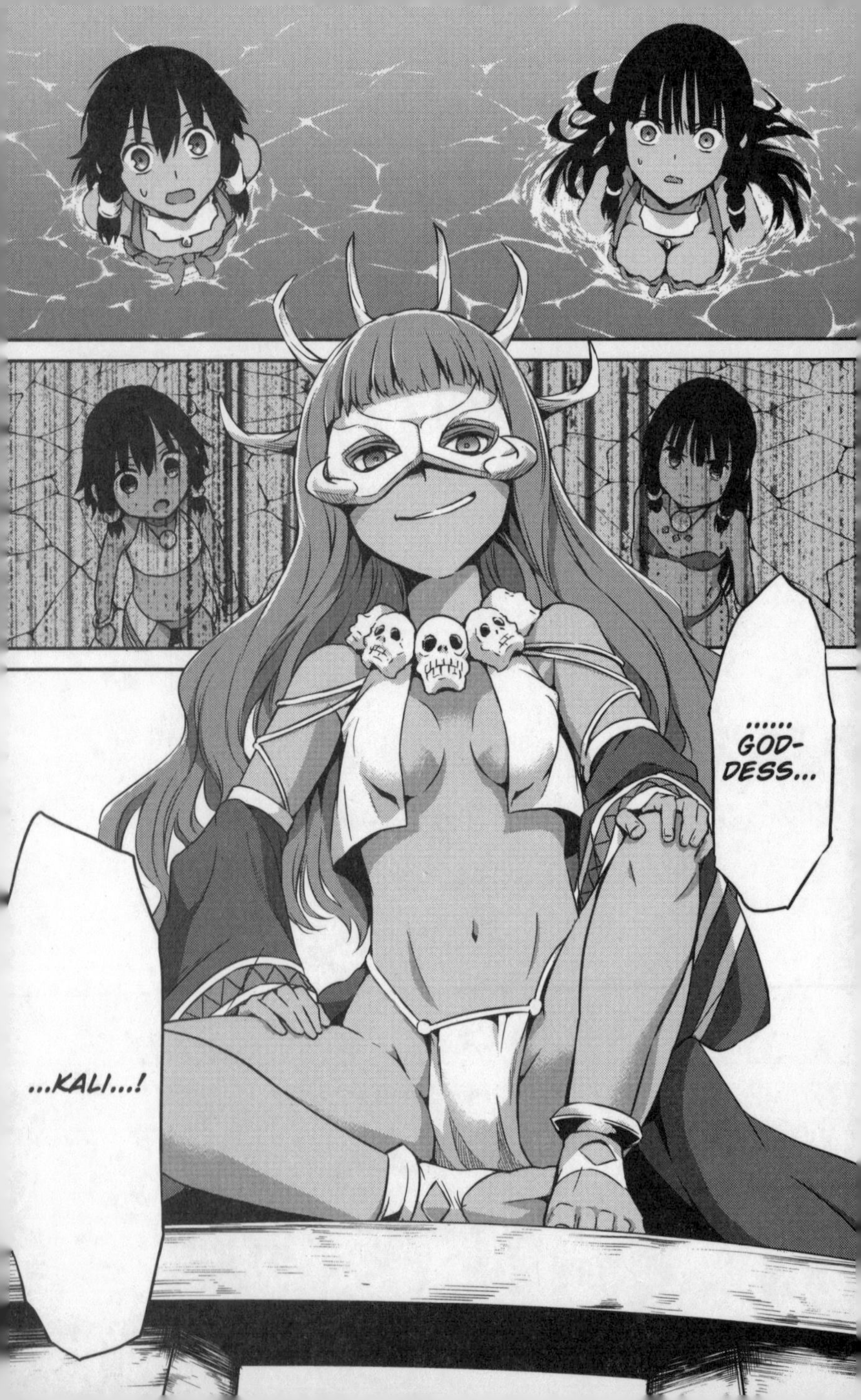
......
GOD-
DESS...
...KALI...!

Is it WRONG
to TRY to
PICK UP GIRLS
in a DUNGEON?
ON THE
SIDE

Sword
Oratoria

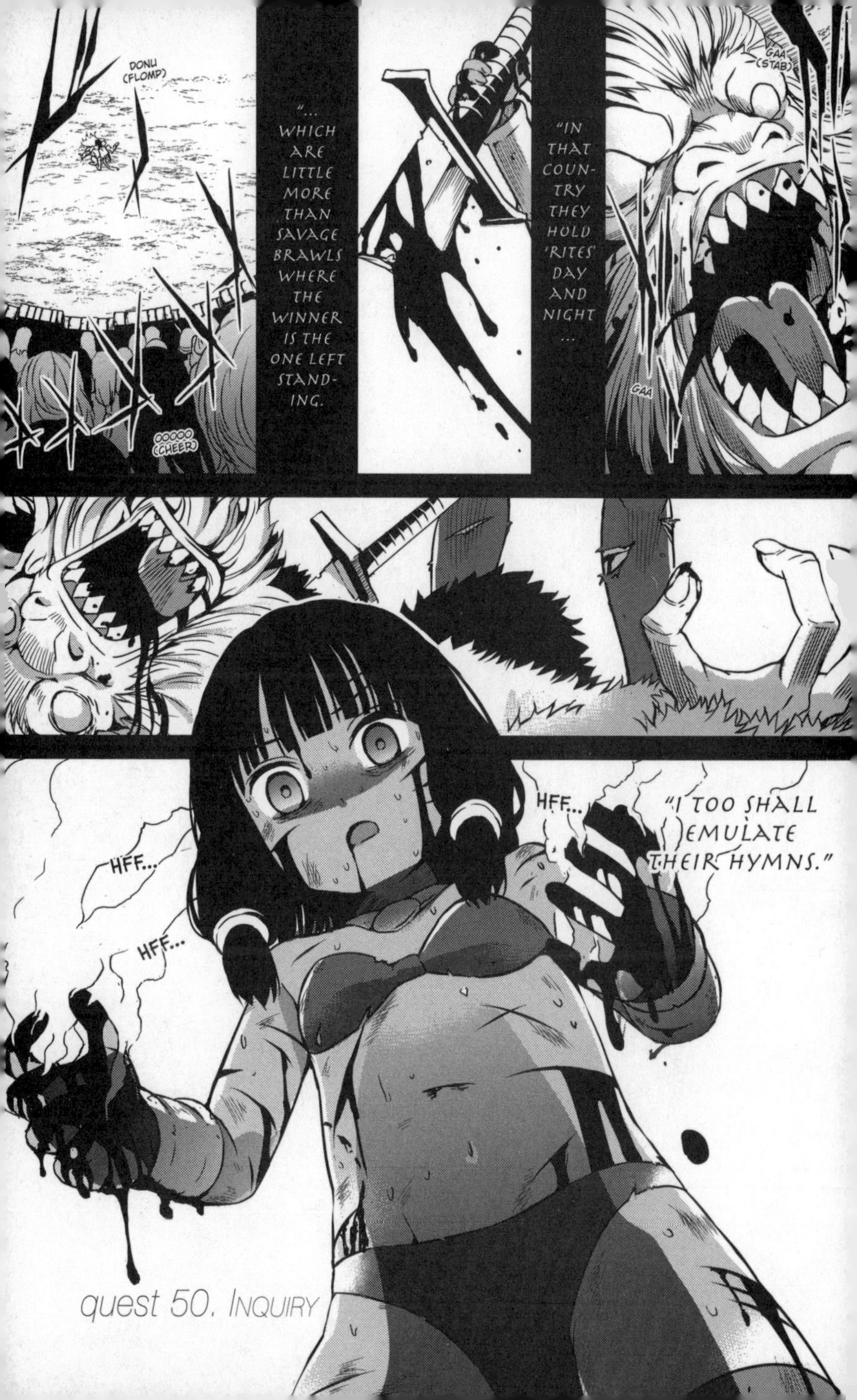
GAA (STAB)
GAA
"IN THAT COUNTRY THEY HOLD 'RITES' DAY AND NIGHT...
"...WHICH ARE LITTLE MORE THAN SAVAGE BRAWLS WHERE THE WINNER IS THE ONE LEFT STANDING.
DONU (FLOMP)
OOOOO (CHEER)
"I TOO SHALL EMULATE THEIR HYMNS."
HFF...
HFF...
HFF...
quest 50. Inquiry

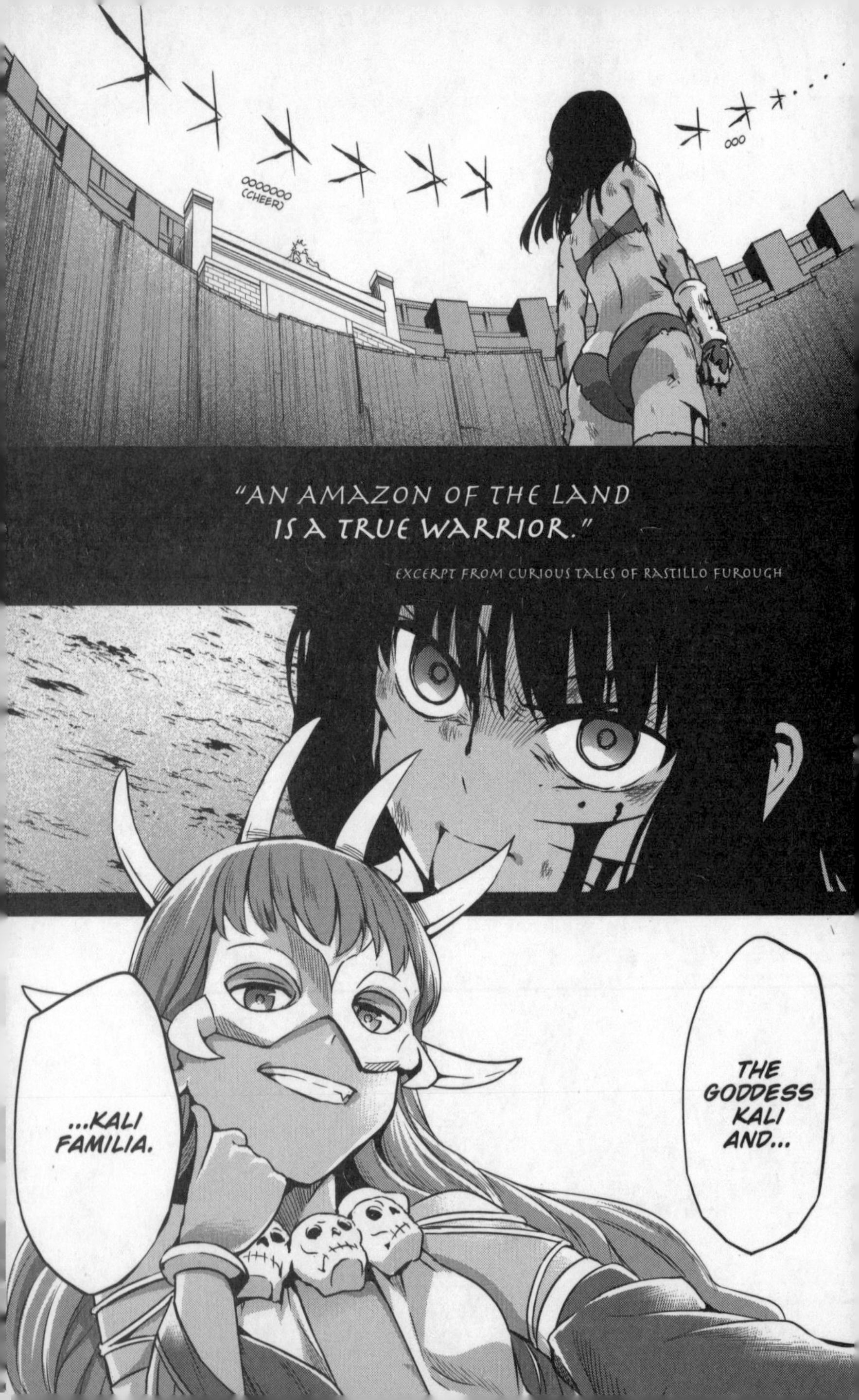
OOO
OOOOOOO (CHEER)
"AN AMAZON OF THE LAND IS A TRUE WARRIOR."
EXCERPT FROM CURIOUS TALES OF RASTILLO FUROUGH
THE GODDESS KALI AND...
...KALI FAMILIA.

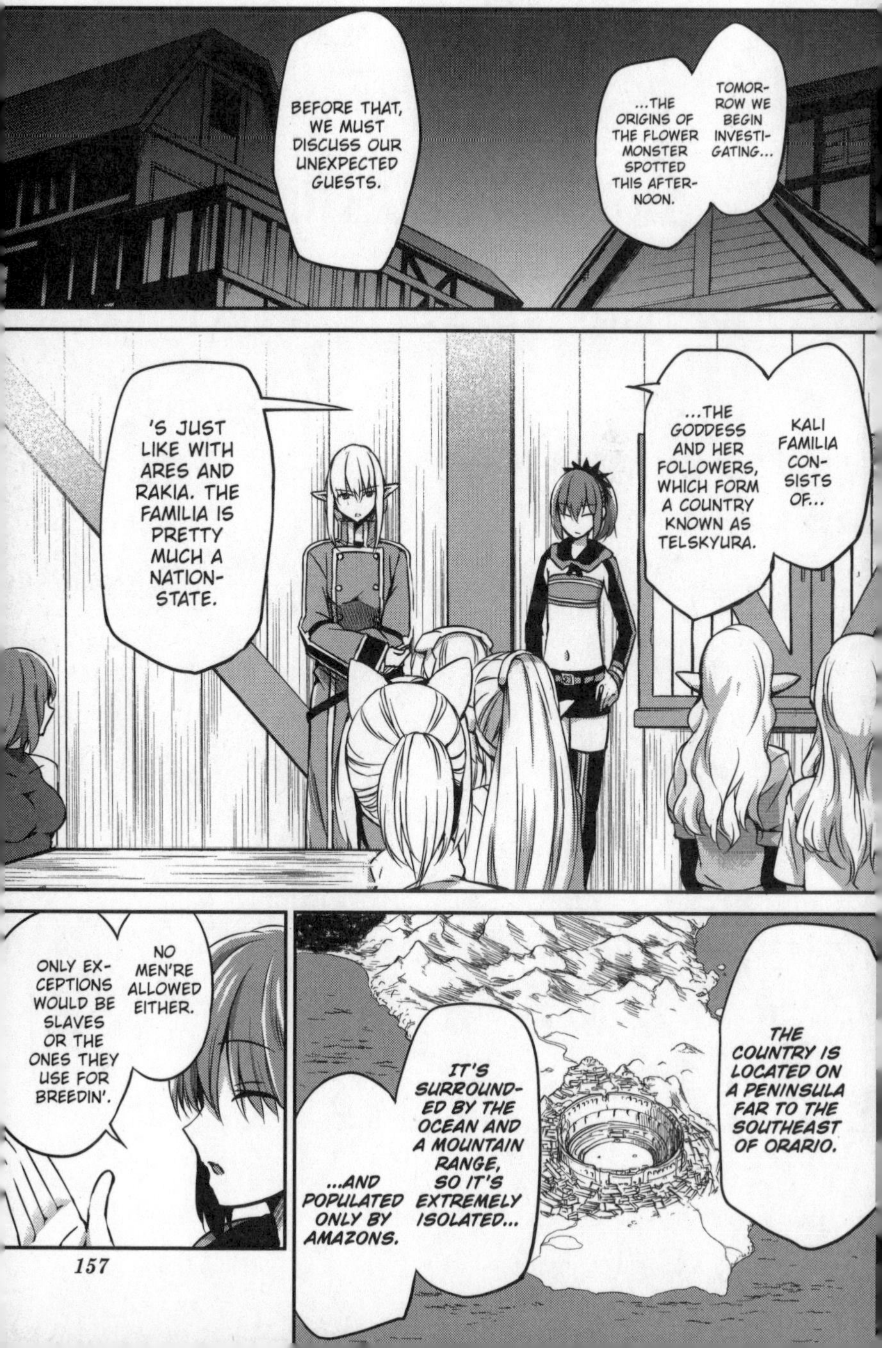
TOMORROW WE BEGIN INVESTIGATING...
...THE ORIGINS OF THE FLOWER MONSTER SPOTTED THIS AFTERNOON.
BEFORE THAT, WE MUST DISCUSS OUR UNEXPECTED GUESTS.
KALI FAMILIA CONSISTS OF...
...THE GODDESS AND HER FOLLOWERS, WHICH FORM A COUNTRY KNOWN AS TELSKYURA.
'S JUST LIKE WITH ARES AND RAKIA. THE FAMILIA IS PRETTY MUCH A NATION-STATE.
THE COUNTRY IS LOCATED ON A PENINSULA FAR TO THE SOUTHEAST OF ORARIO.
IT'S SURROUNDED BY THE OCEAN AND A MOUNTAIN RANGE, SO IT'S EXTREMELY ISOLATED...
...AND POPULATED ONLY BY AMAZONS.
NO MEN'RE ALLOWED EITHER.
ONLY EXCEPTIONS WOULD BE SLAVES OR THE ONES THEY USE FOR BREEDIN'.

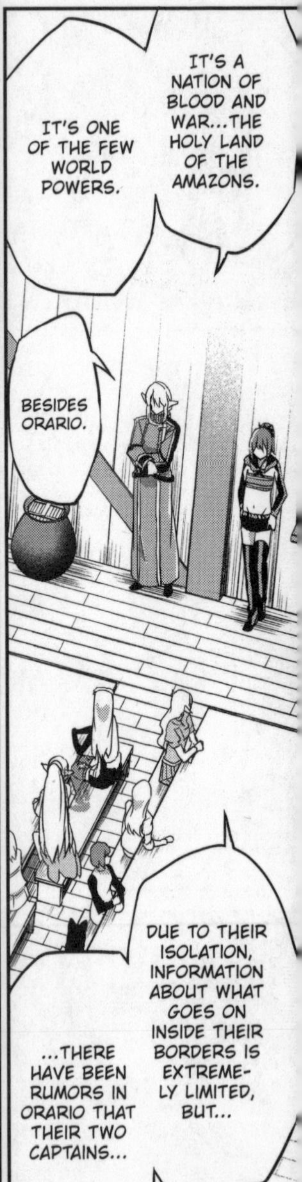
IT'S A NATION OF BLOOD AND WAR...THE HOLY LAND OF THE AMAZONS.
IT'S ONE OF THE FEW WORLD POWERS.
BESIDES ORARIO.
DUE TO THEIR ISOLATION, INFORMATION ABOUT WHAT GOES ON INSIDE THEIR BORDERS IS EXTREME-LY LIMITED, BUT...
...THERE HAVE BEEN RUMORS IN ORARIO THAT THEIR TWO CAPTAINS...
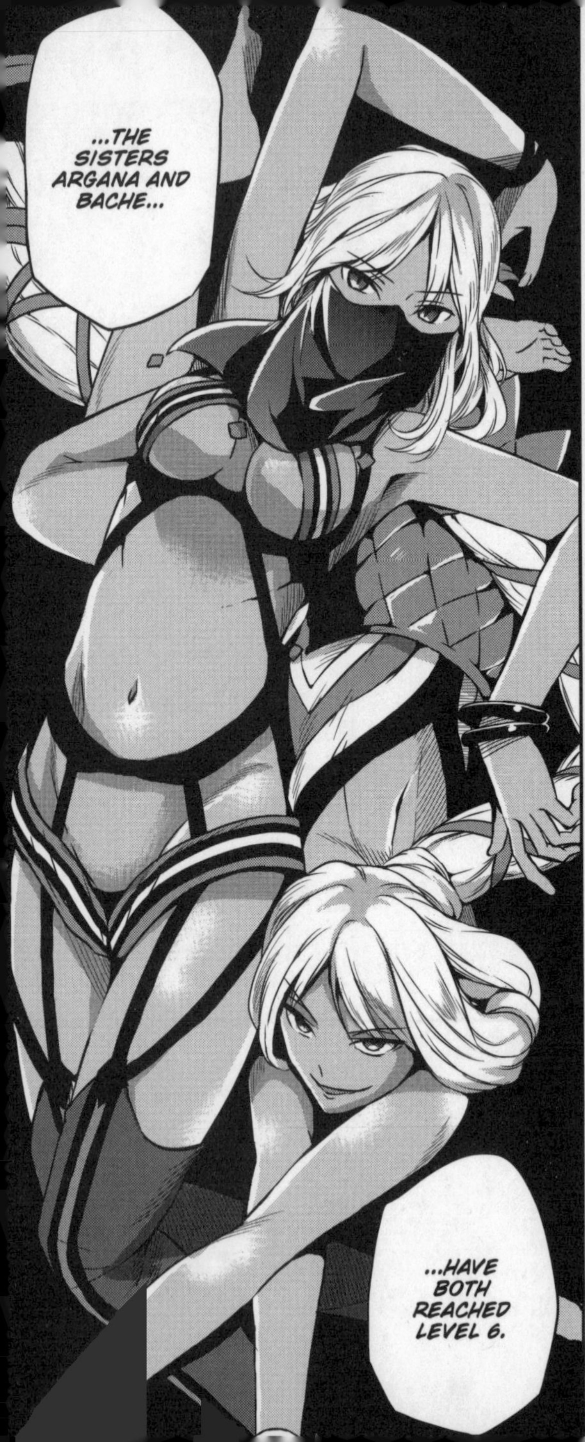
...THE SISTERS ARGANA AND BACHE...
...HAVE BOTH REACHED LEVEL 6.

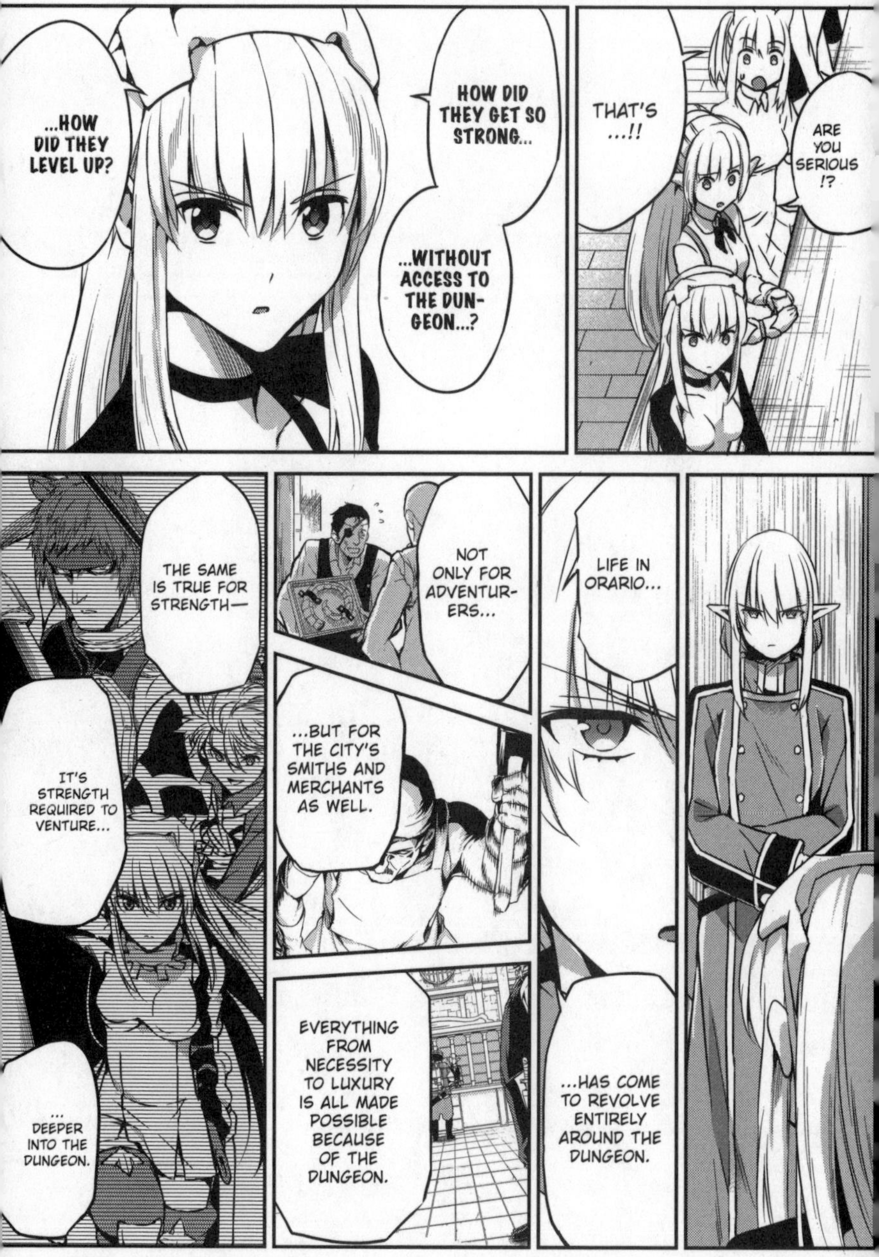
ARE YOU SERIOUS !?
THAT'S ...!!
HOW DID THEY GET SO STRONG...
...WITHOUT ACCESS TO THE DUN-GEON...?
...HOW DID THEY LEVEL UP?
LIFE IN ORARIO...
...HAS COME TO REVOLVE ENTIRELY AROUND THE DUNGEON.
NOT ONLY FOR ADVENTUR-ERS...
...BUT FOR THE CITY'S SMITHS AND MERCHANTS AS WELL.
EVERYTHING FROM NECESSITY TO LUXURY IS ALL MADE POSSIBLE BECAUSE OF THE DUNGEON.
THE SAME IS TRUE FOR STRENGTH—
IT'S STRENGTH REQUIRED TO VENTURE...
... DEEPER INTO THE DUNGEON.

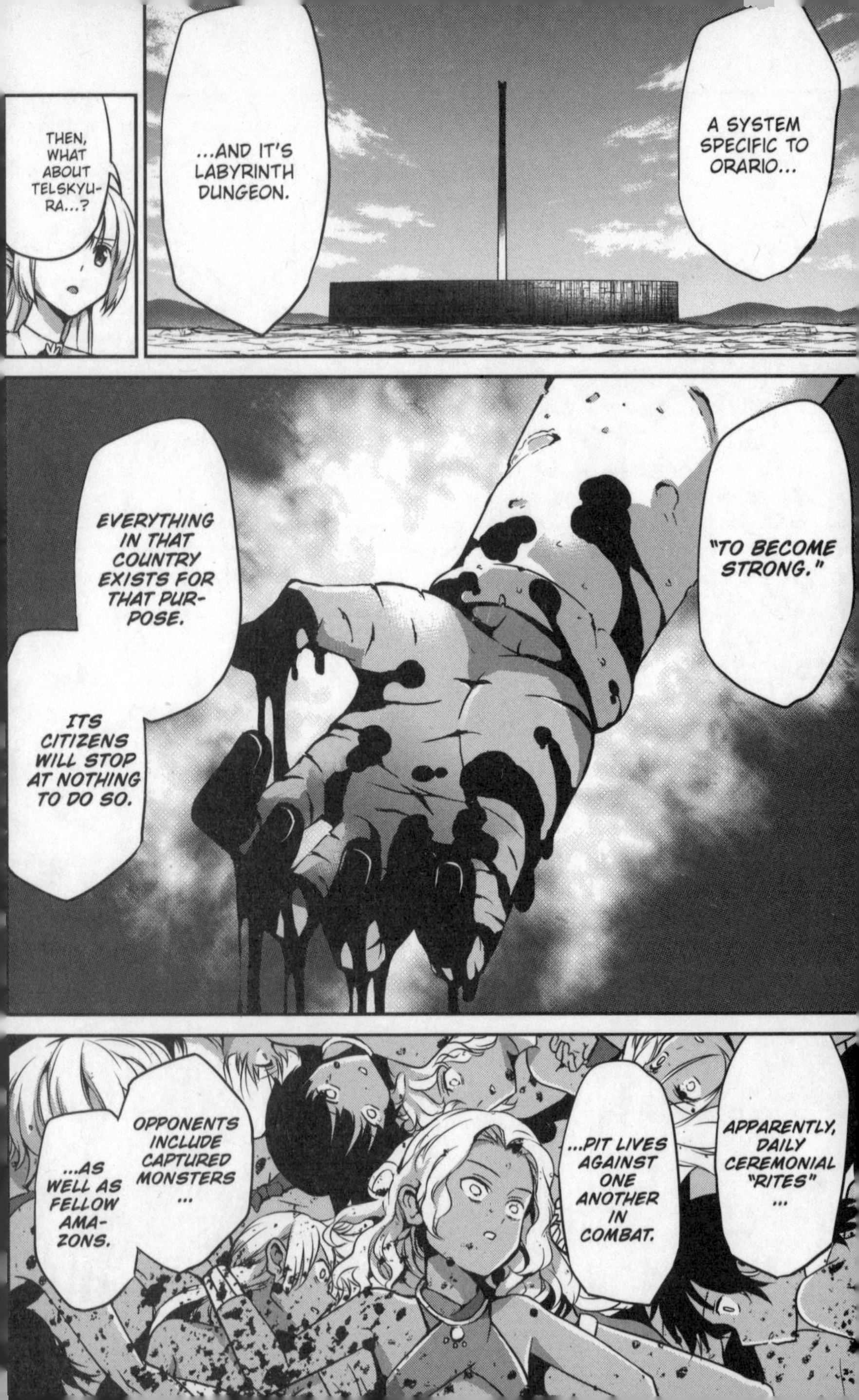
A SYSTEM SPECIFIC TO ORARIO...
...AND IT'S LABYRINTH DUNGEON.
THEN, WHAT ABOUT TELSKYURA...?
"TO BECOME STRONG."
EVERYTHING IN THAT COUNTRY EXISTS FOR THAT PURPOSE.
ITS CITIZENS WILL STOP AT NOTHING TO DO SO.
APPARENTLY, DAILY CEREMONIAL "RITES"...
...PIT LIVES AGAINST ONE ANOTHER IN COMBAT.
OPPONENTS INCLUDE CAPTURED MONSTERS...
...AS WELL AS FELLOW AMAZONS.

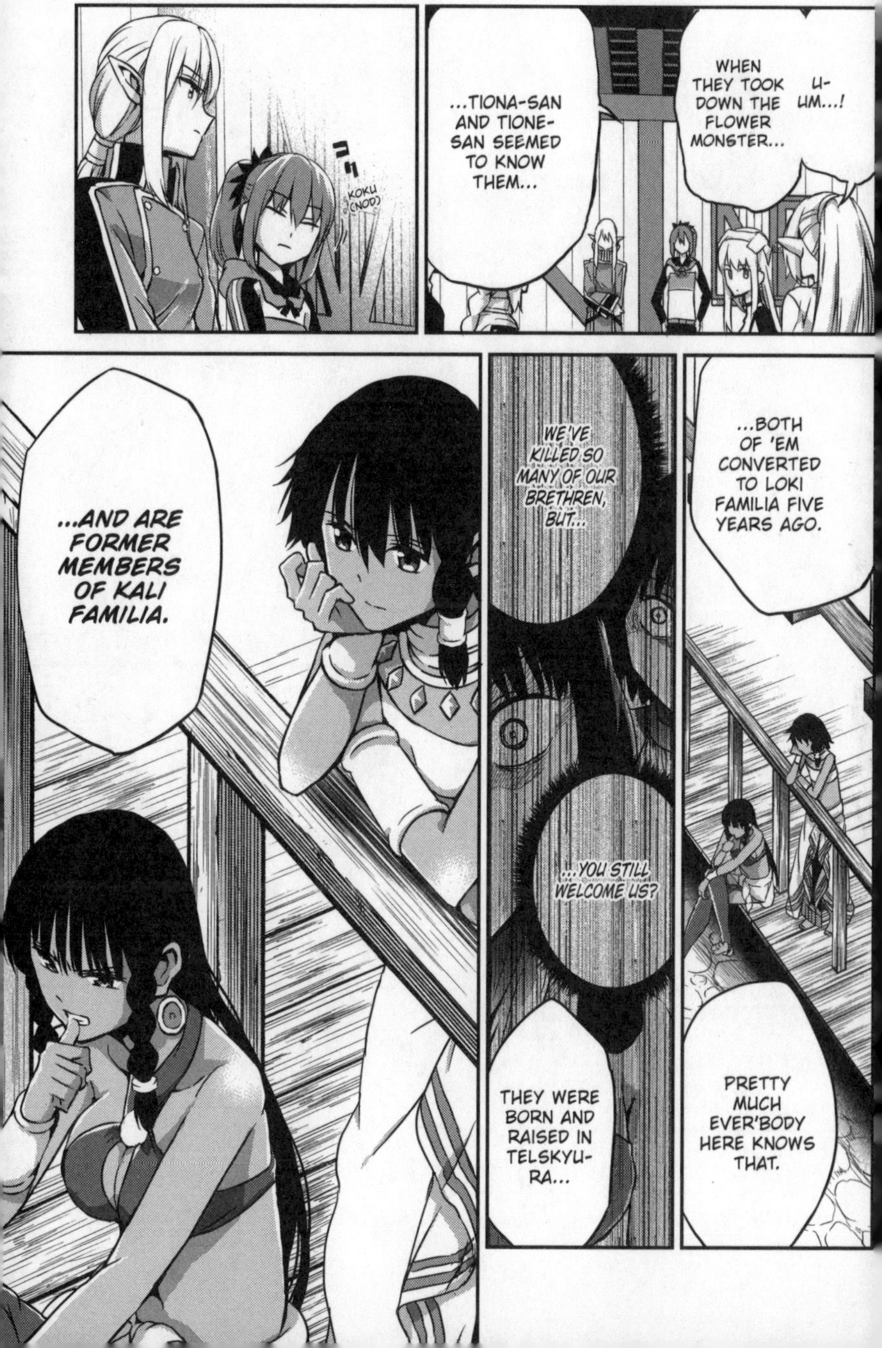
U-UM...!
WHEN THEY TOOK DOWN THE FLOWER MONSTER...
...TIONA-SAN AND TIONE-SAN SEEMED TO KNOW THEM...
コク
KOKU (NOD)
...BOTH OF 'EM CONVERTED TO LOKI FAMILIA FIVE YEARS AGO.
PRETTY MUCH EVER'BODY HERE KNOWS THAT.
WE'VE KILLED SO MANY OF OUR BRETHREN, BUT...
...YOU STILL WELCOME US?
THEY WERE BORN AND RAISED IN TELSKYU-RA...
...AND ARE FORMER MEMBERS OF KALI FAMILIA.

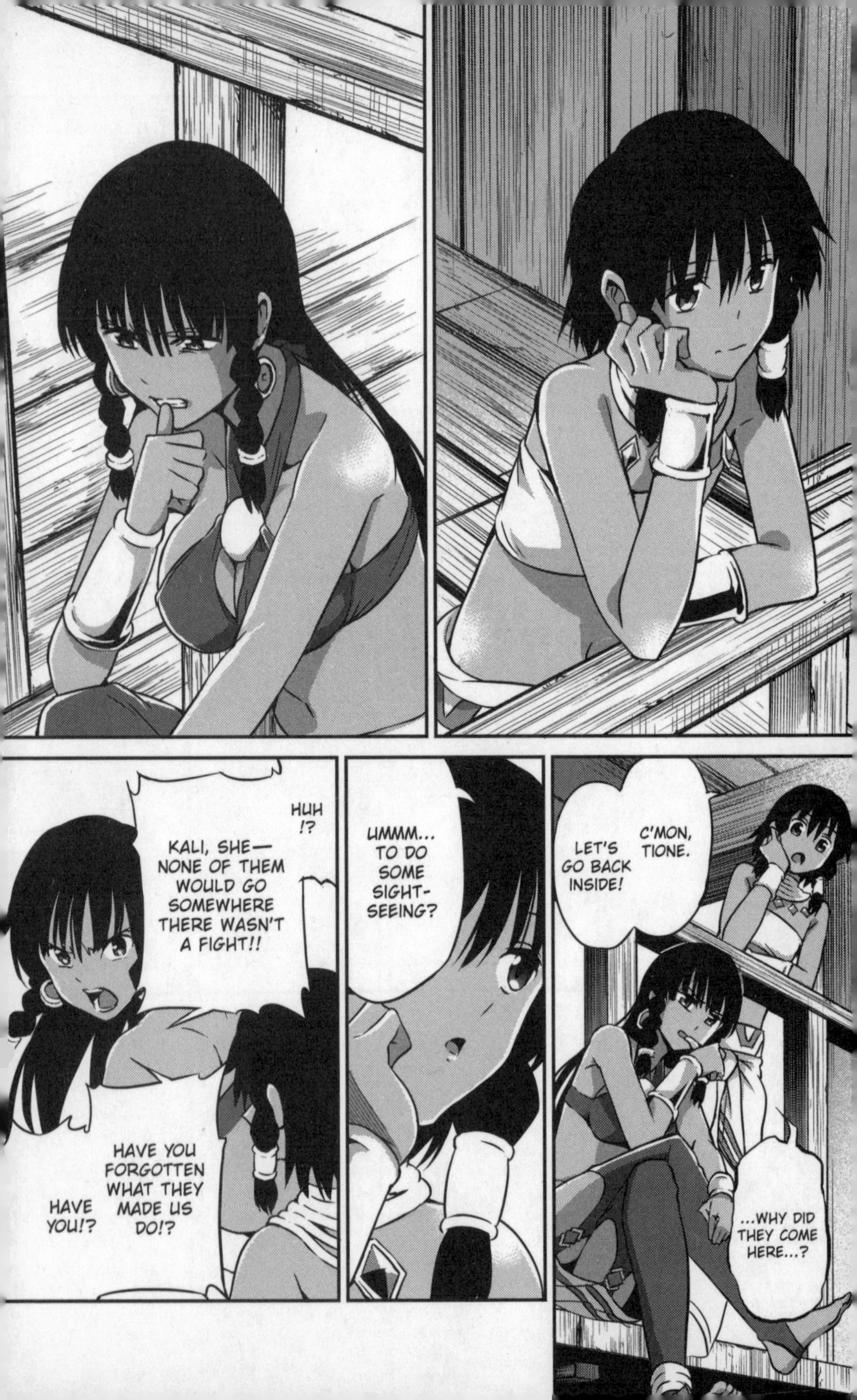
C'MON, TIONE.
LET'S GO BACK INSIDE!
...WHY DID THEY COME HERE...?
UMMM... TO DO SOME SIGHT-SEEING?
HUH!?
KALI, SHE— NONE OF THEM WOULD GO SOMEWHERE THERE WASN'T A FIGHT!!
HAVE YOU FORGOTTEN WHAT THEY MADE US DO!?
HAVE YOU!?

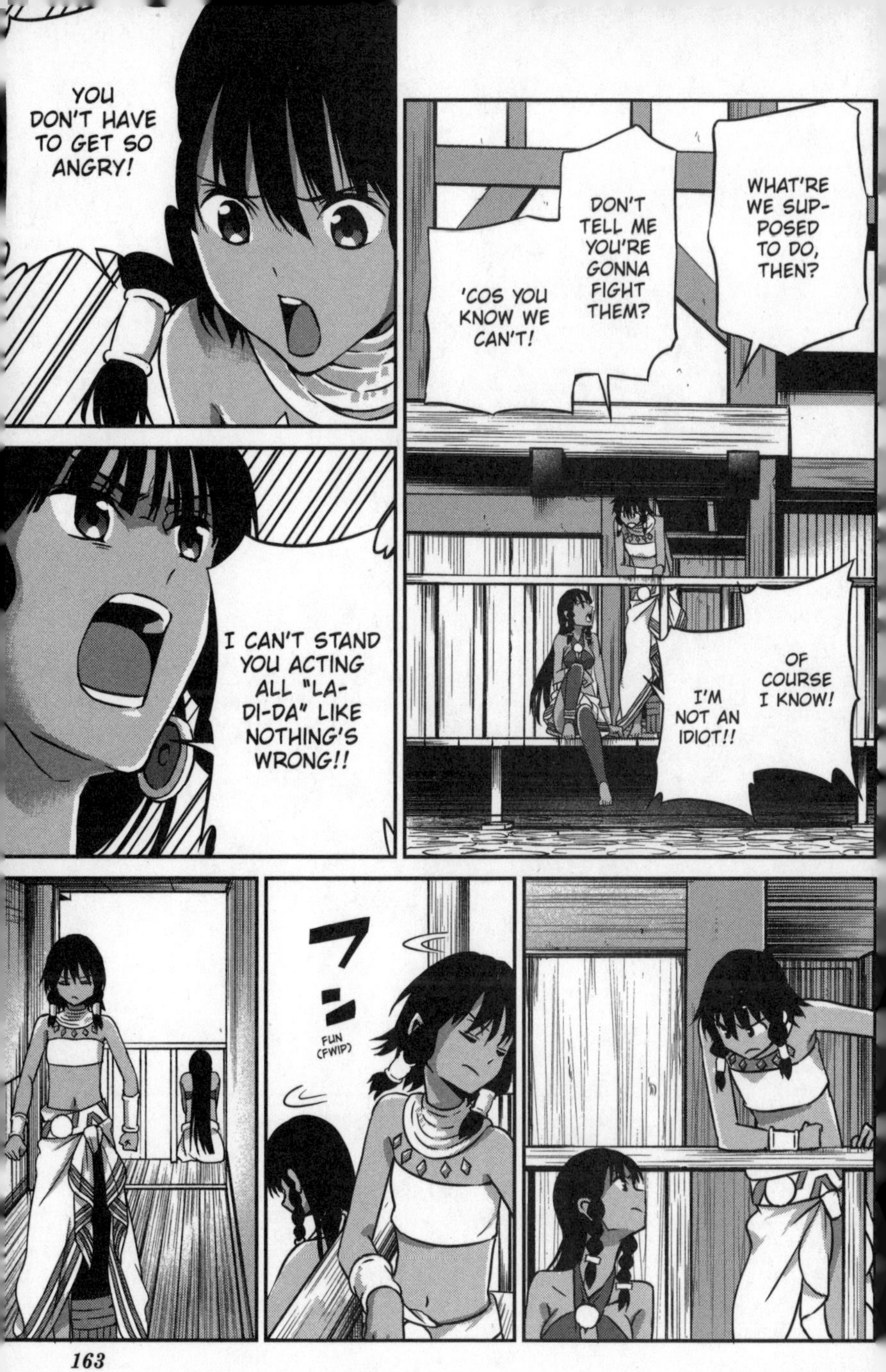
WHAT'RE WE SUP-POSED TO DO, THEN?
DON'T TELL ME YOU'RE GONNA FIGHT THEM?
'COS YOU KNOW WE CAN'T!
OF COURSE I KNOW!
I'M NOT AN IDIOT!!
YOU DON'T HAVE TO GET SO ANGRY!
I CAN'T STAND YOU ACTING ALL "LA-DI-DA" LIKE NOTHING'S WRONG!!
フン
FUN (FWIP)

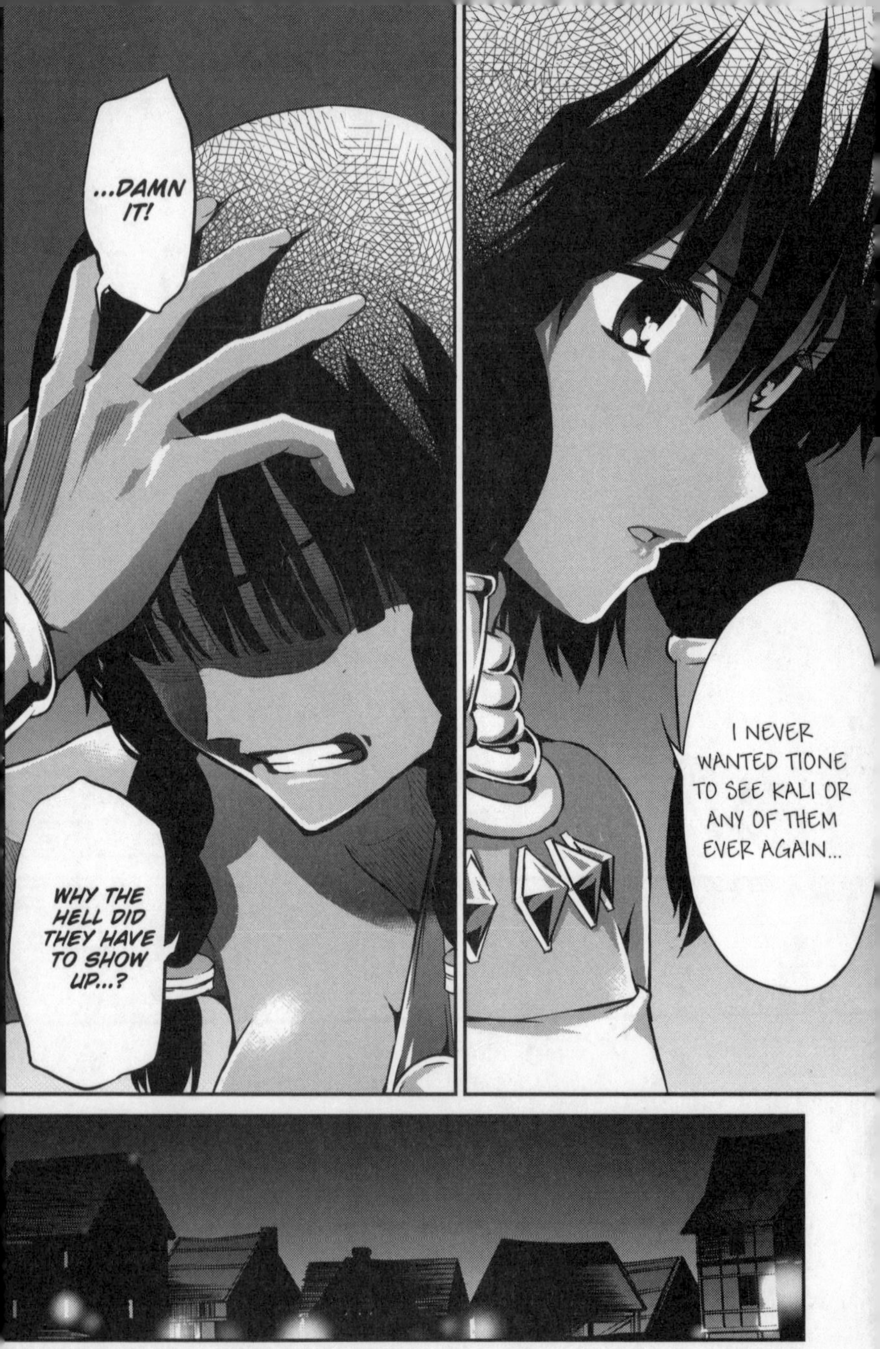
I NEVER WANTED TIONE TO SEE KALI OR ANY OF THEM EVER AGAIN...
...DAMN IT!
WHY THE HELL DID THEY HAVE TO SHOW UP...?

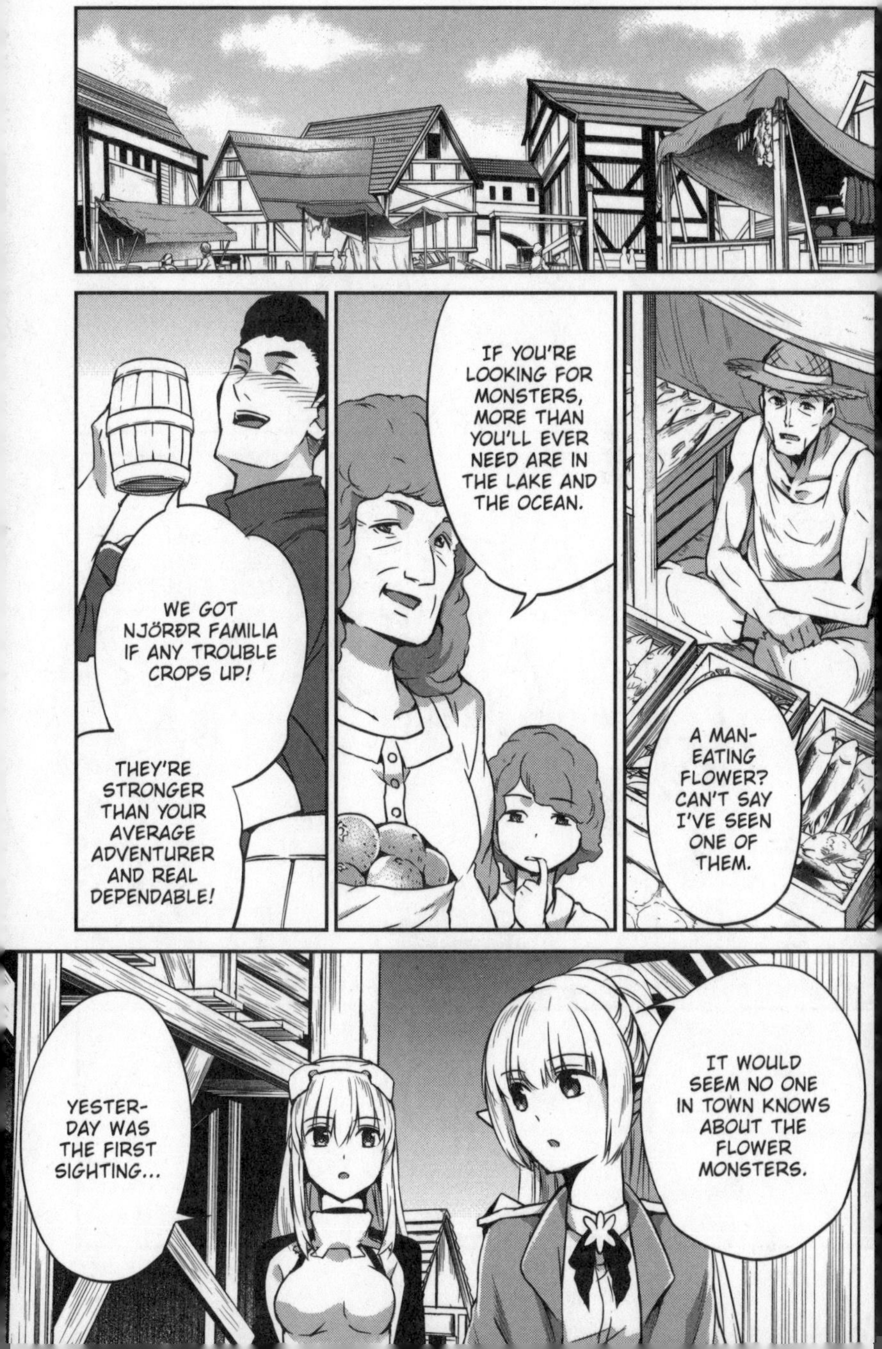
A MAN-EATING FLOWER? CAN'T SAY I'VE SEEN ONE OF THEM.
IF YOU'RE LOOKING FOR MONSTERS, MORE THAN YOU'LL EVER NEED ARE IN THE LAKE AND THE OCEAN.
WE GOT NJÖRÐR FAMILIA IF ANY TROUBLE CROPS UP!
THEY'RE STRONGER THAN YOUR AVERAGE ADVENTURER AND REAL DEPENDABLE!
IT WOULD SEEM NO ONE IN TOWN KNOWS ABOUT THE FLOWER MONSTERS.
YESTER-DAY WAS THE FIRST SIGHTING...

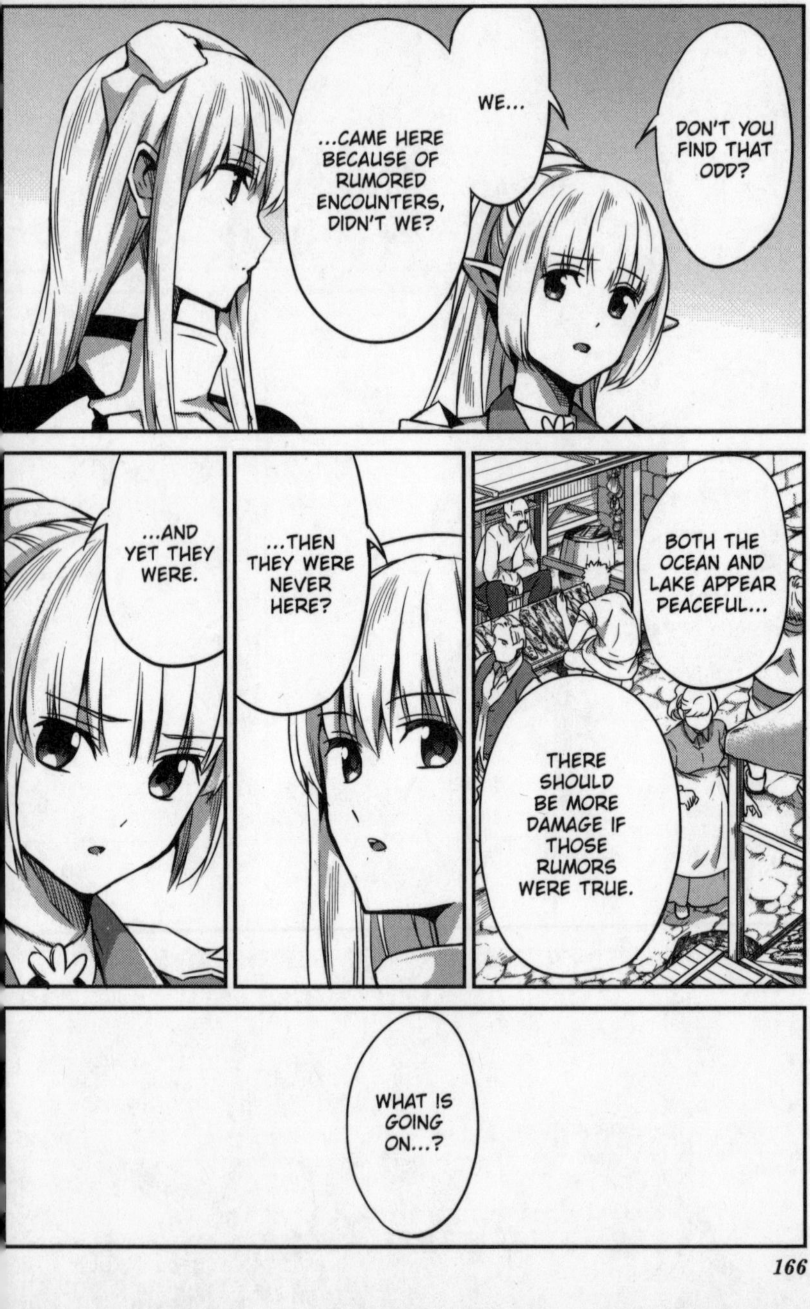
DON'T YOU FIND THAT ODD?
WE...
...CAME HERE BECAUSE OF RUMORED ENCOUNTERS, DIDN'T WE?
BOTH THE OCEAN AND LAKE APPEAR PEACEFUL...
THERE SHOULD BE MORE DAMAGE IF THOSE RUMORS WERE TRUE.
...THEN THEY WERE NEVER HERE?
...AND YET THEY WERE.
WHAT IS GOING ON...?

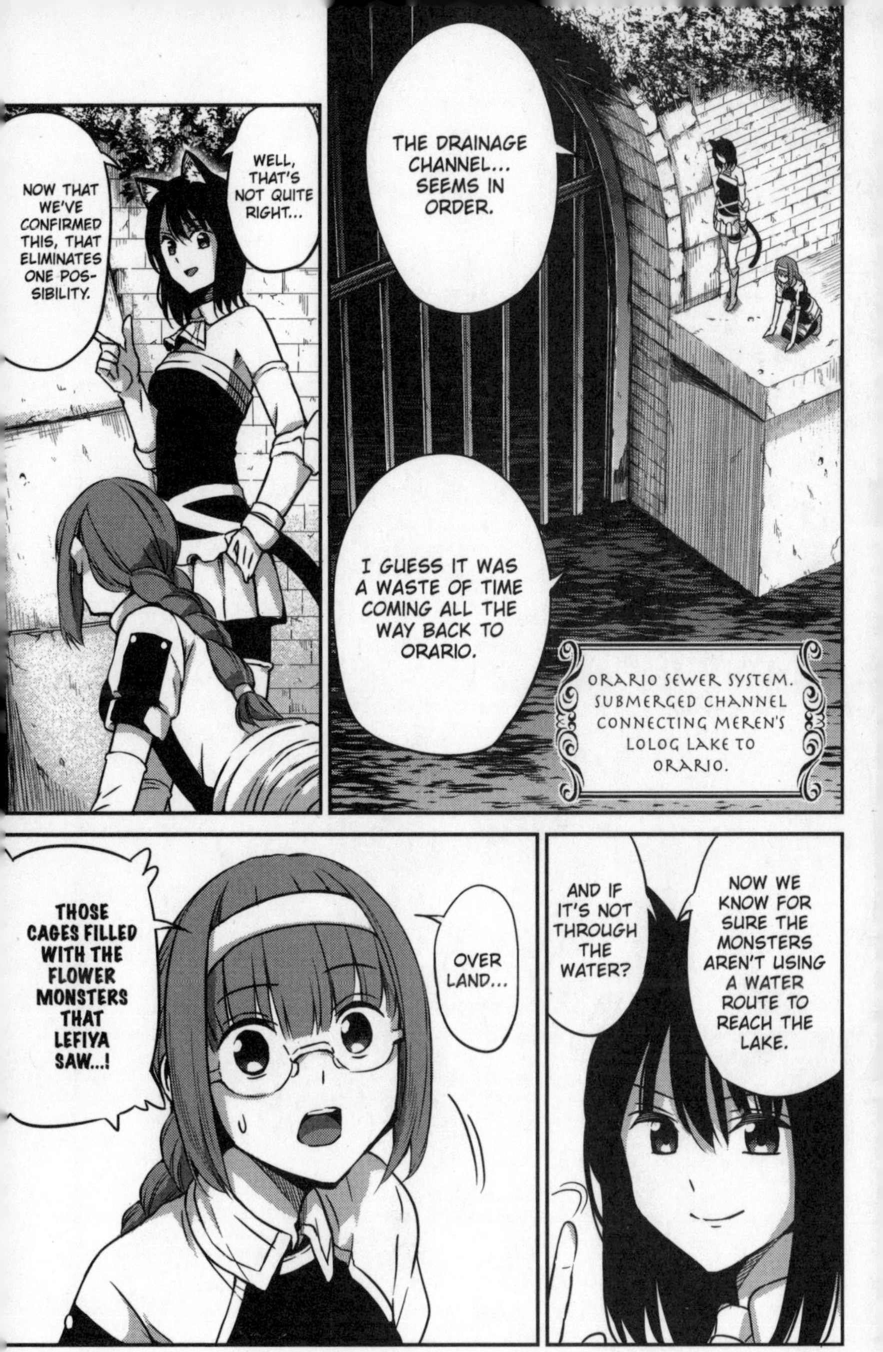
THE DRAINAGE CHANNEL... SEEMS IN ORDER.
I GUESS IT WAS A WASTE OF TIME COMING ALL THE WAY BACK TO ORARIO.
ORARIO SEWER SYSTEM. SUBMERGED CHANNEL CONNECTING MEREN'S LOLOG LAKE TO ORARIO.
WELL, THAT'S NOT QUITE RIGHT...
NOW THAT WE'VE CONFIRMED THIS, THAT ELIMINATES ONE POSSIBILITY.
NOW WE KNOW FOR SURE THE MONSTERS AREN'T USING A WATER ROUTE TO REACH THE LAKE.
AND IF IT'S NOT THROUGH THE WATER?
OVER LAND...
THOSE CAGES FILLED WITH THE FLOWER MONSTERS THAT LEFIYA SAW...!

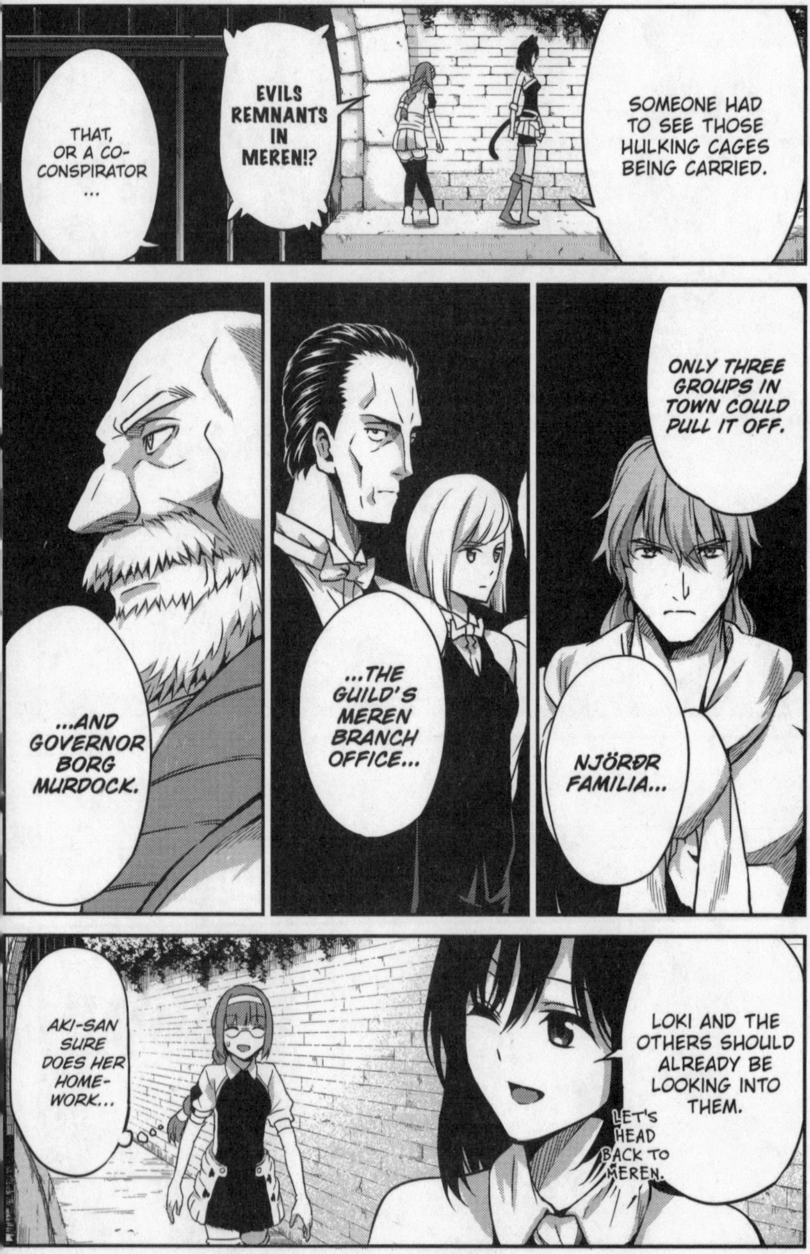
SOMEONE HAD TO SEE THOSE HULKING CAGES BEING CARRIED.
EVILS REMNANTS IN MEREN!?
THAT, OR A CO-CONSPIRATOR ...
ONLY THREE GROUPS IN TOWN COULD PULL IT OFF.
NJÖRÐR FAMILIA...
...THE GUILD'S MEREN BRANCH OFFICE...
...AND GOVERNOR BORG MURDOCK.
LOKI AND THE OTHERS SHOULD ALREADY BE LOOKING INTO THEM.
LET'S HEAD BACK TO MEREN.
AKI-SAN SURE DOES HER HOME-WORK...

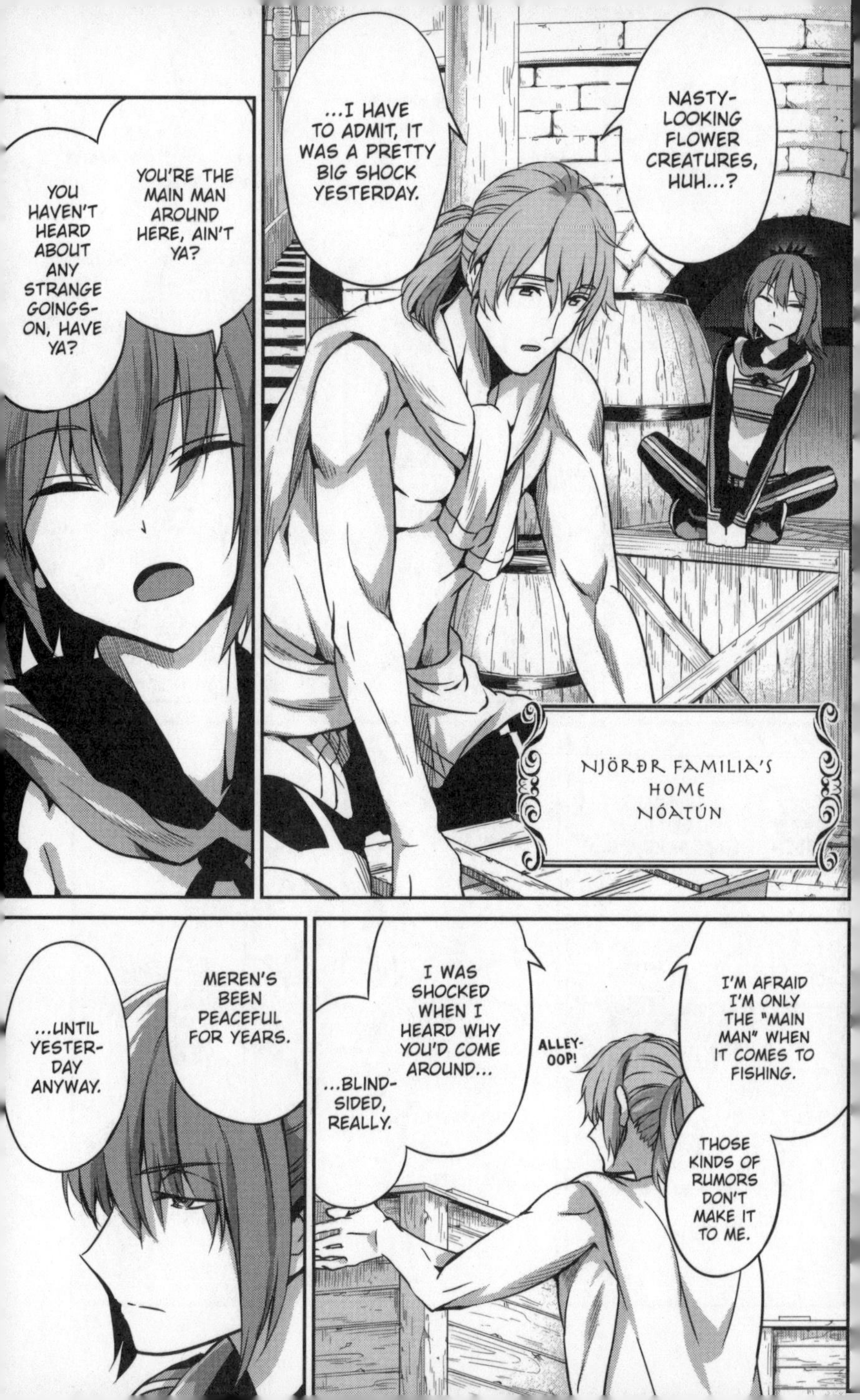
NASTY-LOOKING FLOWER CREATURES, HUH...?
...I HAVE TO ADMIT, IT WAS A PRETTY BIG SHOCK YESTERDAY.
NJÖRÐR FAMILIA'S HOME NÓATÚN
YOU'RE THE MAIN MAN AROUND HERE, AIN'T YA?
YOU HAVEN'T HEARD ABOUT ANY STRANGE GOINGS-ON, HAVE YA?
I'M AFRAID I'M ONLY THE "MAIN MAN" WHEN IT COMES TO FISHING.
THOSE KINDS OF RUMORS DON'T MAKE IT TO ME.
ALLEY-OOP!
I WAS SHOCKED WHEN I HEARD WHY YOU'D COME AROUND...
...BLIND-SIDED, REALLY.
MEREN'S BEEN PEACEFUL FOR YEARS.
...UNTIL YESTER-DAY ANYWAY.

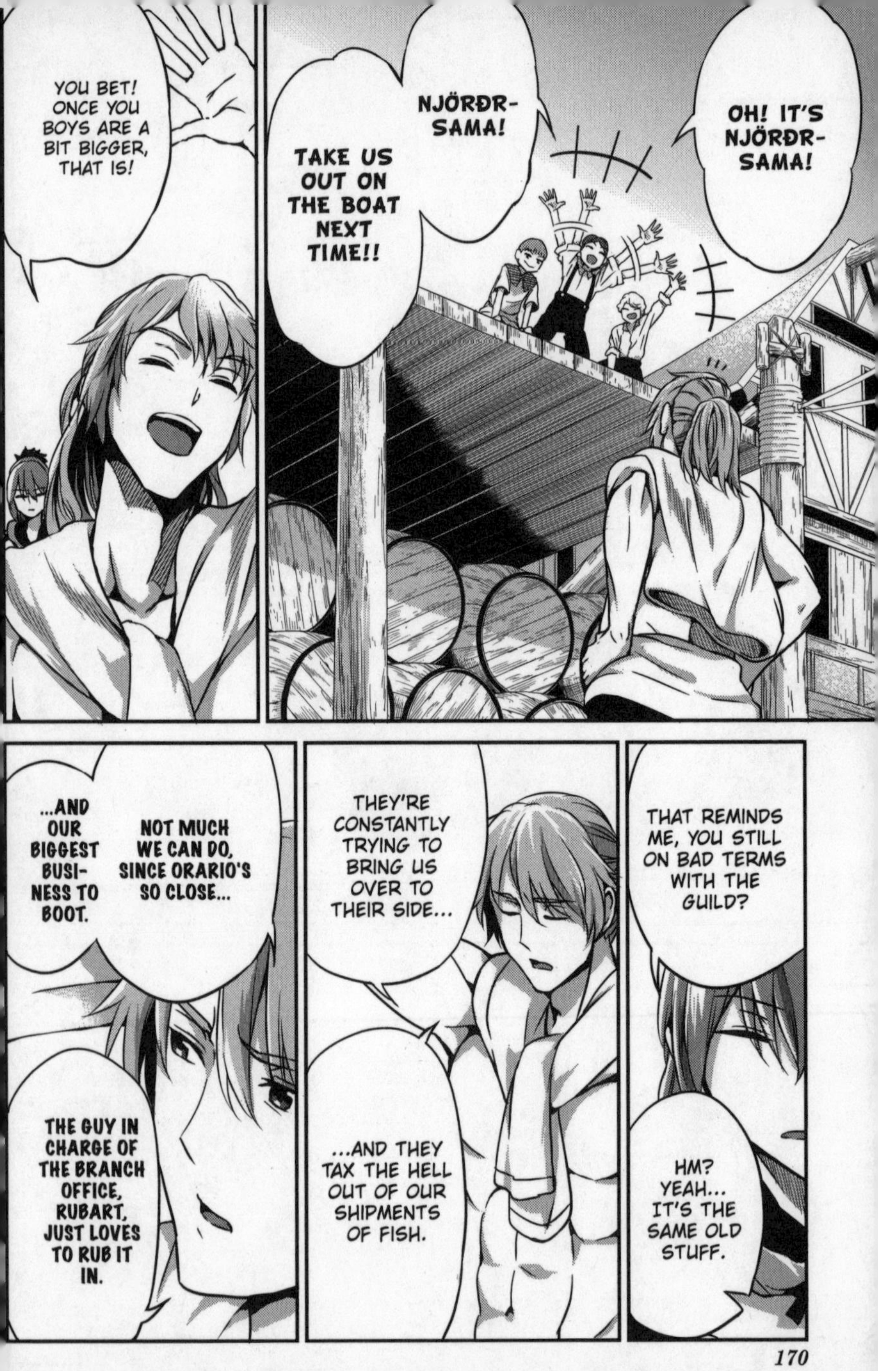
OH! IT'S NJÖRÐR-SAMA!
NJÖRÐR-SAMA!
TAKE US OUT ON THE BOAT NEXT TIME!!
YOU BET! ONCE YOU BOYS ARE A BIT BIGGER, THAT IS!
THAT REMINDS ME, YOU STILL ON BAD TERMS WITH THE GUILD?
HM? YEAH... IT'S THE SAME OLD STUFF.
THEY'RE CONSTANTLY TRYING TO BRING US OVER TO THEIR SIDE...
...AND THEY TAX THE HELL OUT OF OUR SHIPMENTS OF FISH.
NOT MUCH WE CAN DO, SINCE ORARIO'S SO CLOSE...
...AND OUR BIGGEST BUSI-NESS TO BOOT.
THE GUY IN CHARGE OF THE BRANCH OFFICE, RUBART, JUST LOVES TO RUB IT IN.

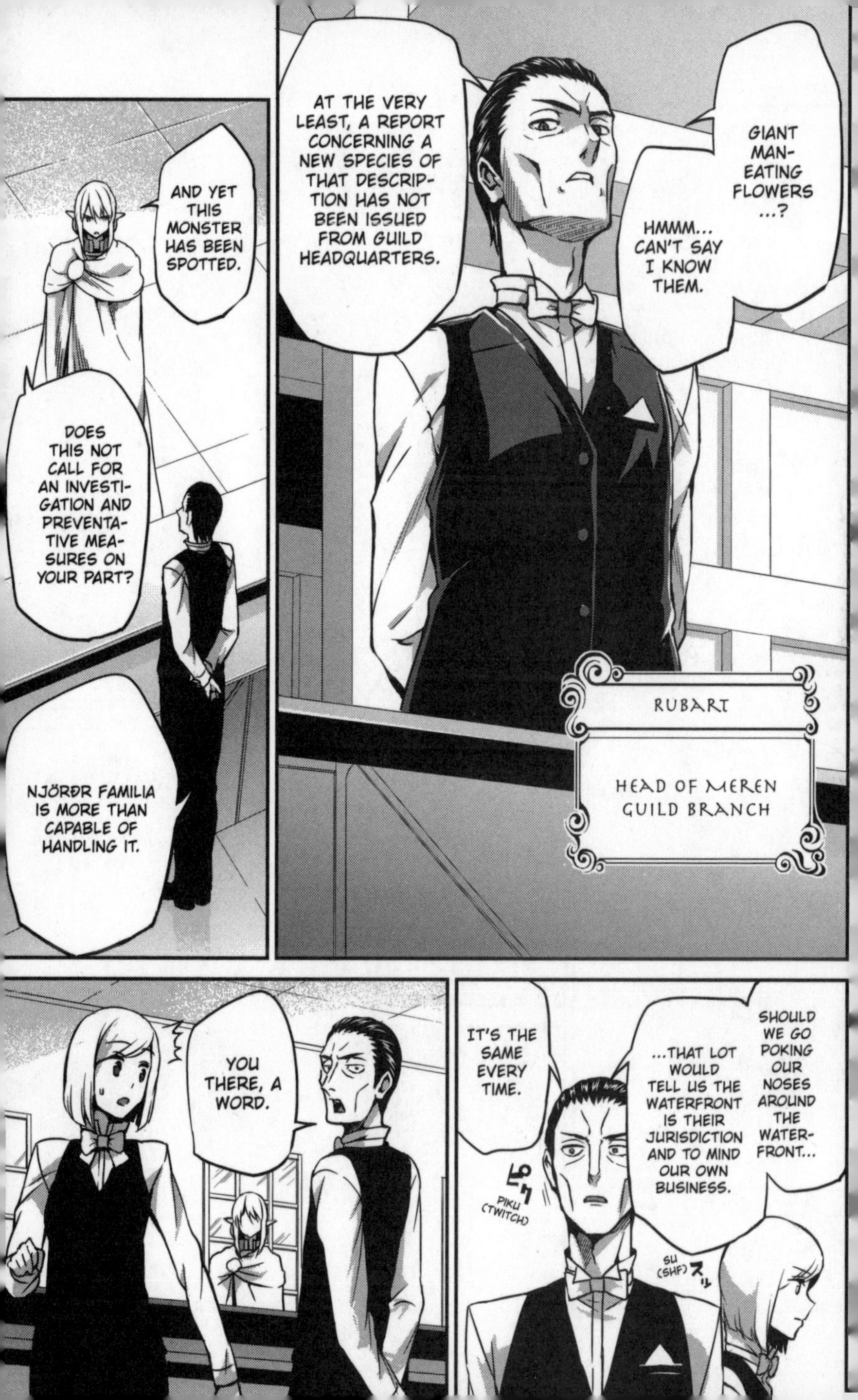
GIANT MAN-EATING FLOWERS ...?
HMMM... CAN'T SAY I KNOW THEM.
AT THE VERY LEAST, A REPORT CONCERNING A NEW SPECIES OF THAT DESCRIPTION HAS NOT BEEN ISSUED FROM GUILD HEADQUARTERS.
RUBART
HEAD OF MEREN GUILD BRANCH
AND YET THIS MONSTER HAS BEEN SPOTTED.
DOES THIS NOT CALL FOR AN INVESTIGATION AND PREVENTATIVE MEASURES ON YOUR PART?
NJÖRÐR FAMILIA IS MORE THAN CAPABLE OF HANDLING IT.
SHOULD WE GO POKING OUR NOSES AROUND THE WATERFRONT...
...THAT LOT WOULD TELL US THE WATERFRONT IS THEIR JURISDICTION AND TO MIND OUR OWN BUSINESS.
IT'S THE SAME EVERY TIME.
SU (SHF) スッ
ピク PIKU (TWITCH)
YOU THERE, A WORD.

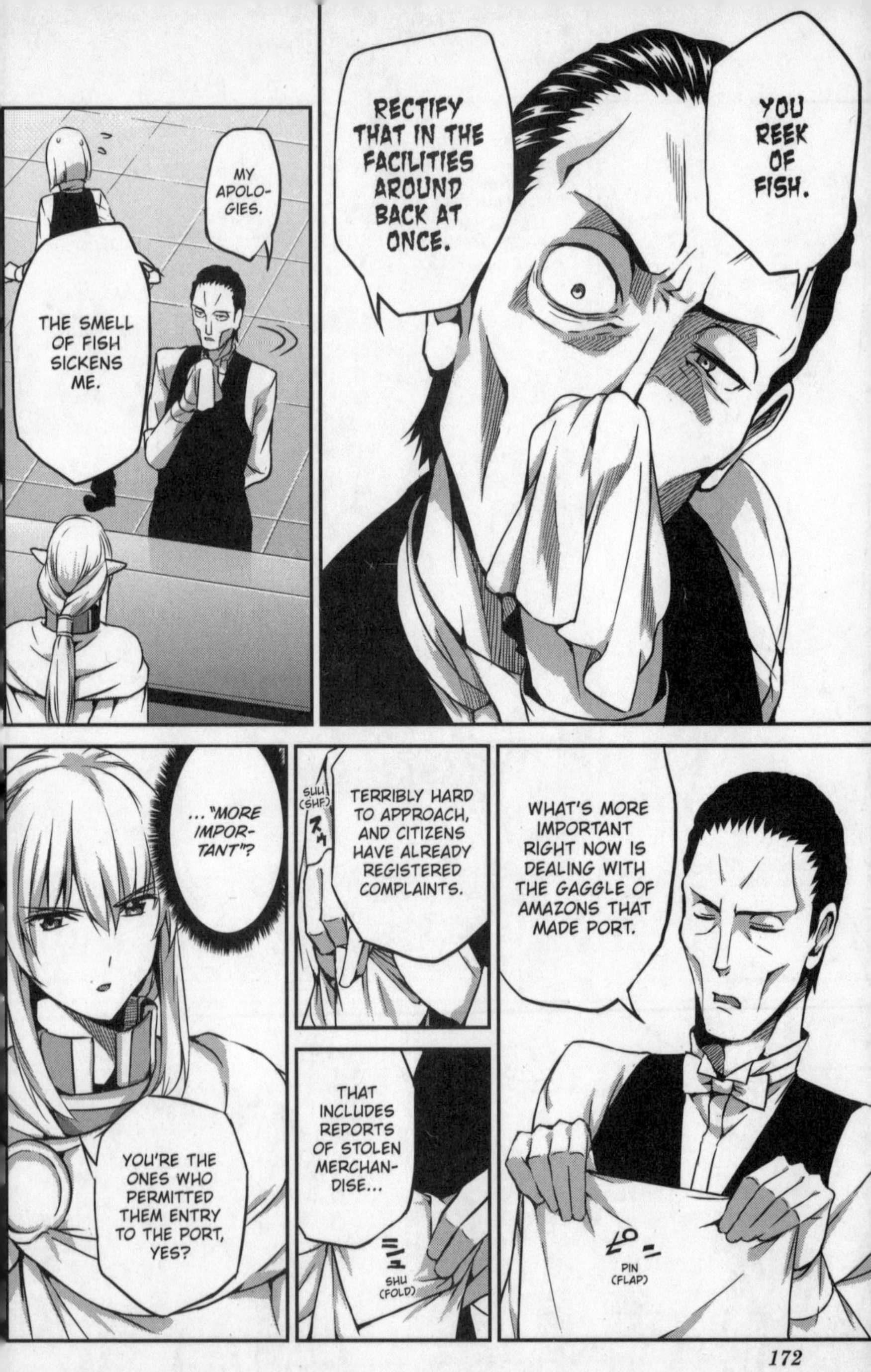
YOU REEK OF FISH.
RECTIFY THAT IN THE FACILITIES AROUND BACK AT ONCE.
MY APOLOGIES.
THE SMELL OF FISH SICKENS ME.
WHAT'S MORE IMPORTANT RIGHT NOW IS DEALING WITH THE GAGGLE OF AMAZONS THAT MADE PORT.
PIN (FLAP)
SHU (SHF)
TERRIBLY HARD TO APPROACH, AND CITIZENS HAVE ALREADY REGISTERED COMPLAINTS.
THAT INCLUDES REPORTS OF STOLEN MERCHANDISE...
SHU (FOLD)
..."MORE IMPORTANT"?
YOU'RE THE ONES WHO PERMITTED THEM ENTRY TO THE PORT, YES?

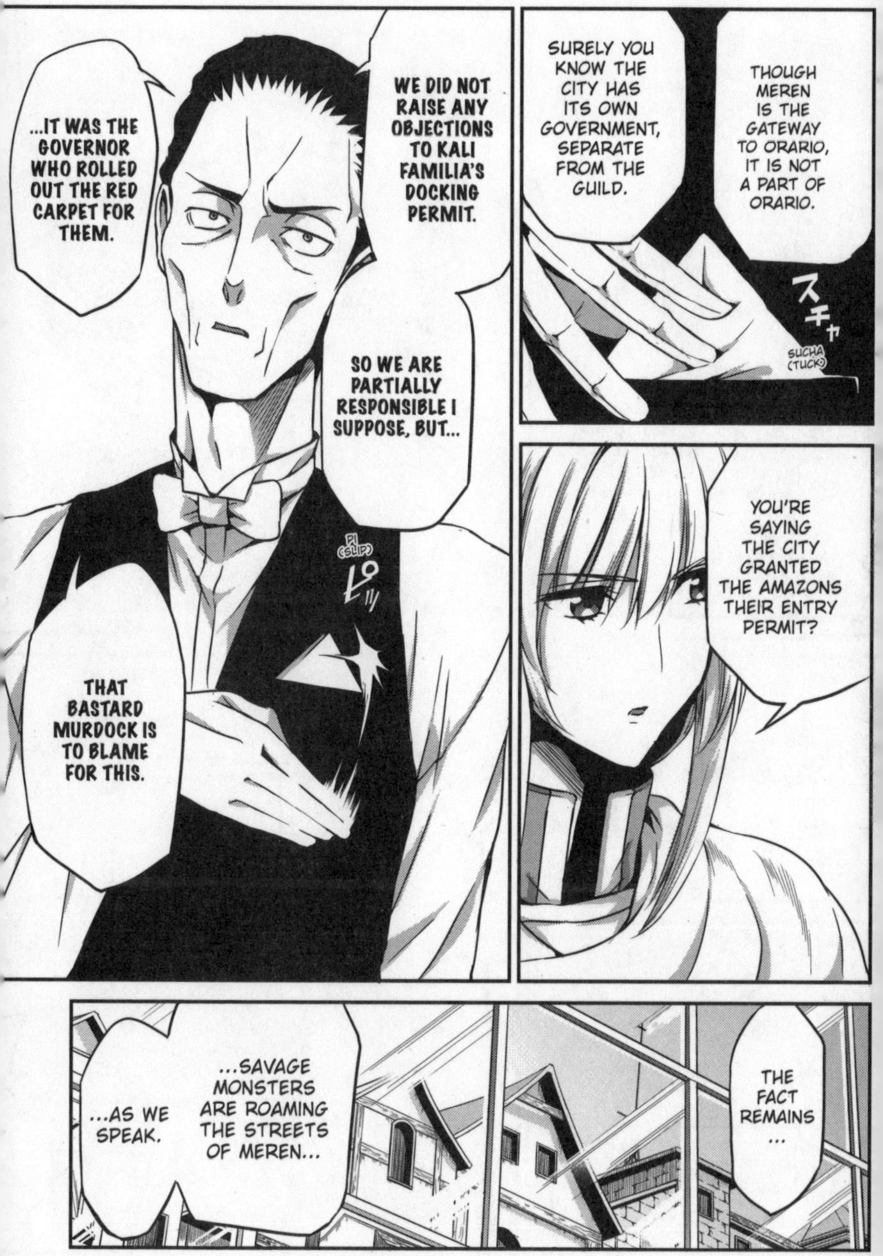
THOUGH MEREN IS THE GATEWAY TO ORARIO, IT IS NOT A PART OF ORARIO.
SURELY YOU KNOW THE CITY HAS ITS OWN GOVERNMENT, SEPARATE FROM THE GUILD.
スチャ
SUCHA (TUCK)
YOU'RE SAYING THE CITY GRANTED THE AMAZONS THEIR ENTRY PERMIT?
WE DID NOT RAISE ANY OBJECTIONS TO KALI FAMILIA'S DOCKING PERMIT.
...IT WAS THE GOVERNOR WHO ROLLED OUT THE RED CARPET FOR THEM.
SO WE ARE PARTIALLY RESPONSIBLE I SUPPOSE, BUT...
PI (SLIP)
ピッ
THAT BASTARD MURDOCK IS TO BLAME FOR THIS.
THE FACT REMAINS...
...SAVAGE MONSTERS ARE ROAMING THE STREETS OF MEREN...
...AS WE SPEAK.

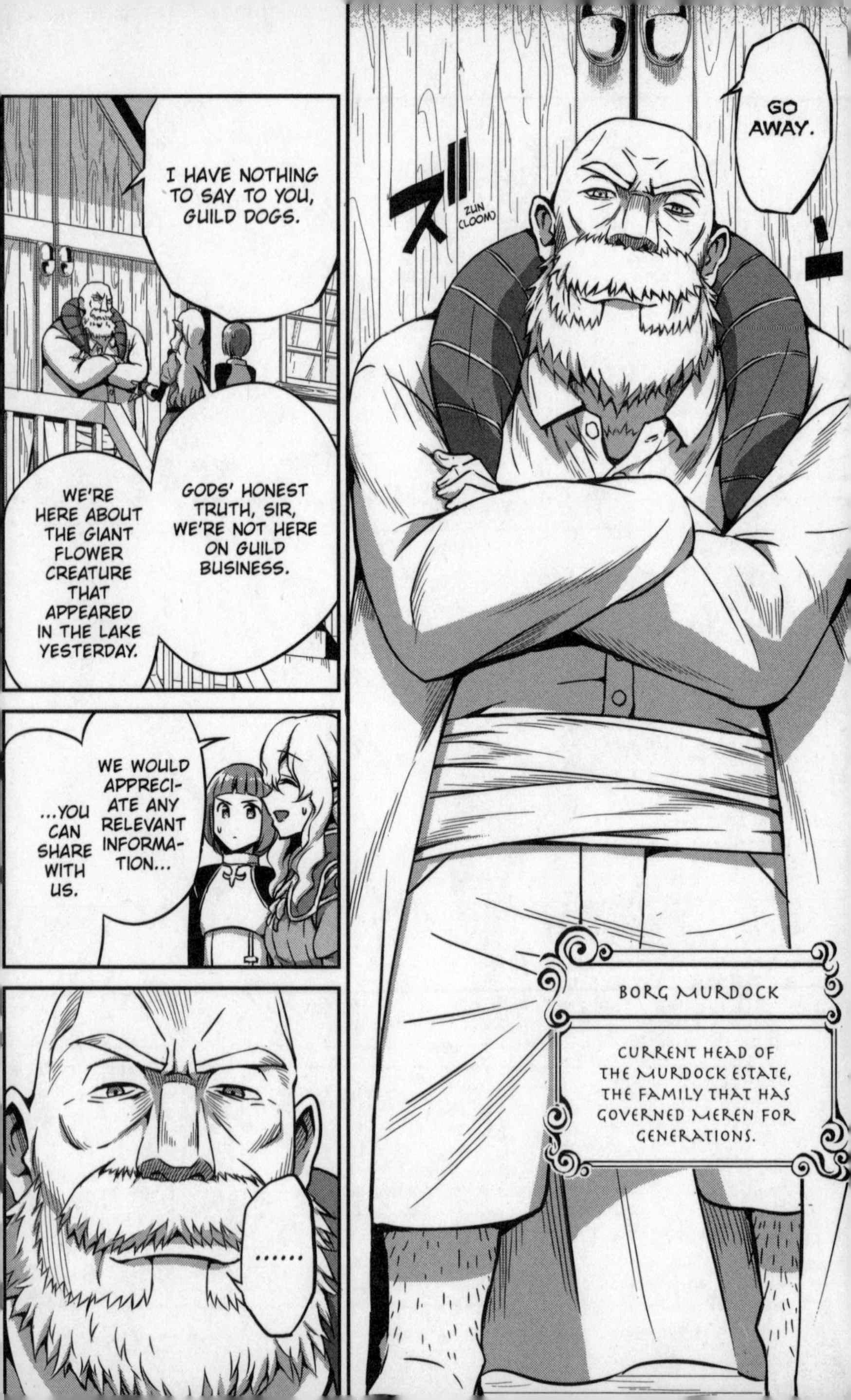
GO AWAY.
ズ
ZUN (LOOM)
BORG MURDOCK
CURRENT HEAD OF THE MURDOCK ESTATE, THE FAMILY THAT HAS GOVERNED MEREN FOR GENERATIONS.
I HAVE NOTHING TO SAY TO YOU, GUILD DOGS.
GODS' HONEST TRUTH, SIR, WE'RE NOT HERE ON GUILD BUSINESS.
WE'RE HERE ABOUT THE GIANT FLOWER CREATURE THAT APPEARED IN THE LAKE YESTERDAY.
WE WOULD APPRECIATE ANY RELEVANT INFORMATION...
...YOU CAN SHARE WITH US.
......

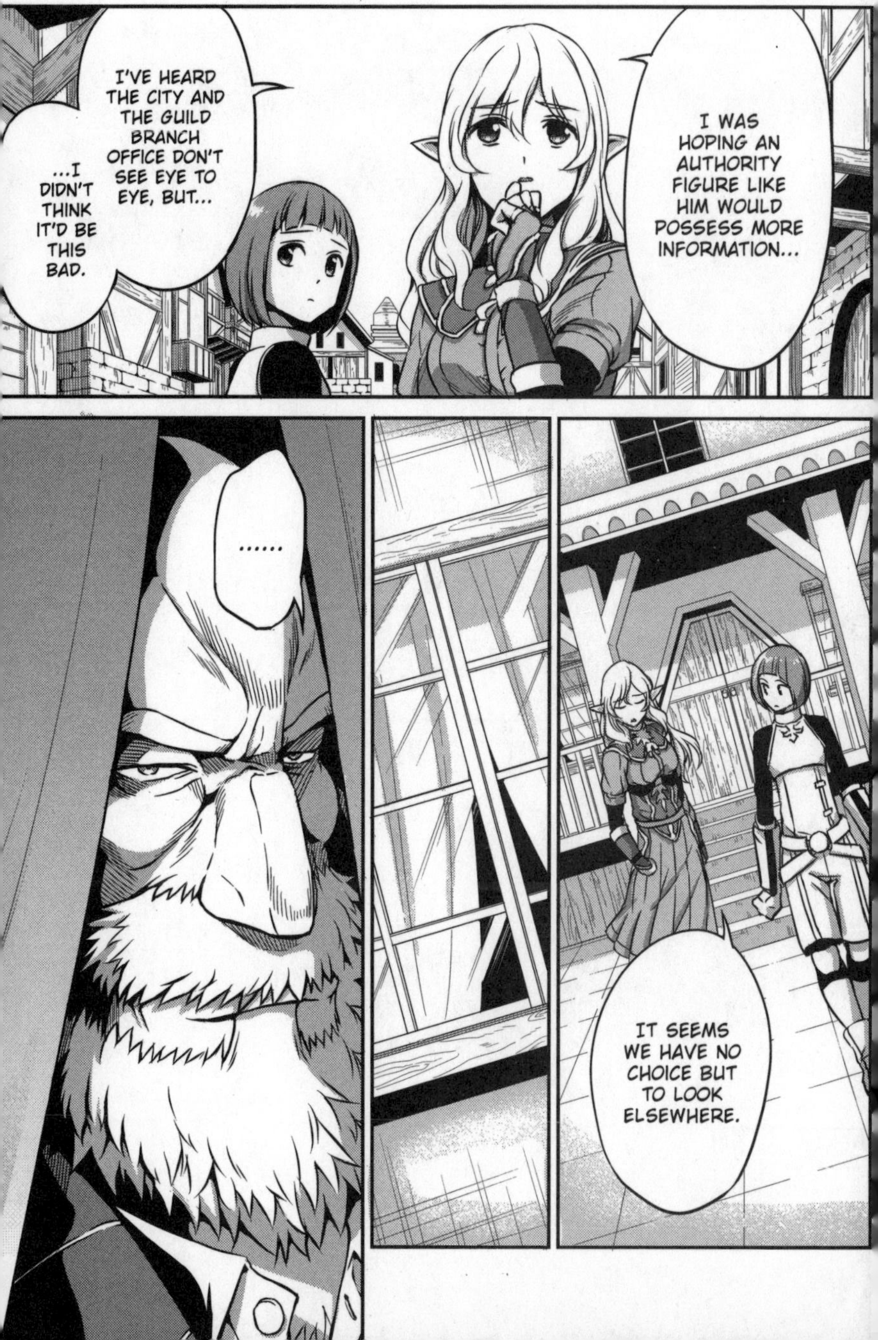
I WAS HOPING AN AUTHORITY FIGURE LIKE HIM WOULD POSSESS MORE INFORMATION...
I'VE HEARD THE CITY AND THE GUILD BRANCH OFFICE DON'T SEE EYE TO EYE, BUT...
...I DIDN'T THINK IT'D BE THIS BAD.
IT SEEMS WE HAVE NO CHOICE BUT TO LOOK ELSEWHERE.
......

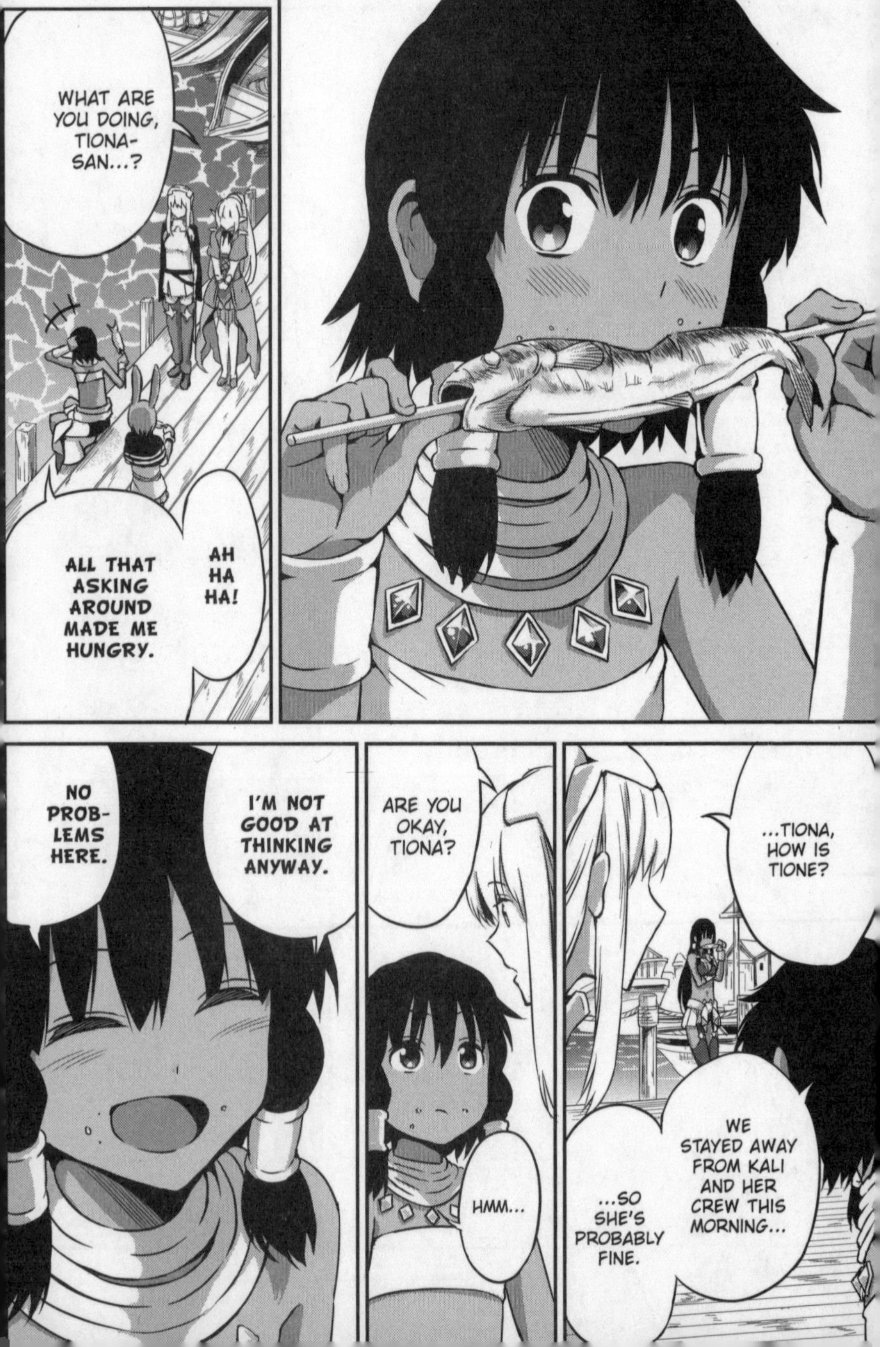
WHAT ARE YOU DOING, TIONA-SAN...?
AH HA HA!
ALL THAT ASKING AROUND MADE ME HUNGRY.
...TIONA, HOW IS TIONE?
WE STAYED AWAY FROM KALI AND HER CREW THIS MORNING...
...SO SHE'S PROBABLY FINE.
ARE YOU OKAY, TIONA?
HMM...
I'M NOT GOOD AT THINKING ANYWAY.
NO PROB-LEMS HERE.

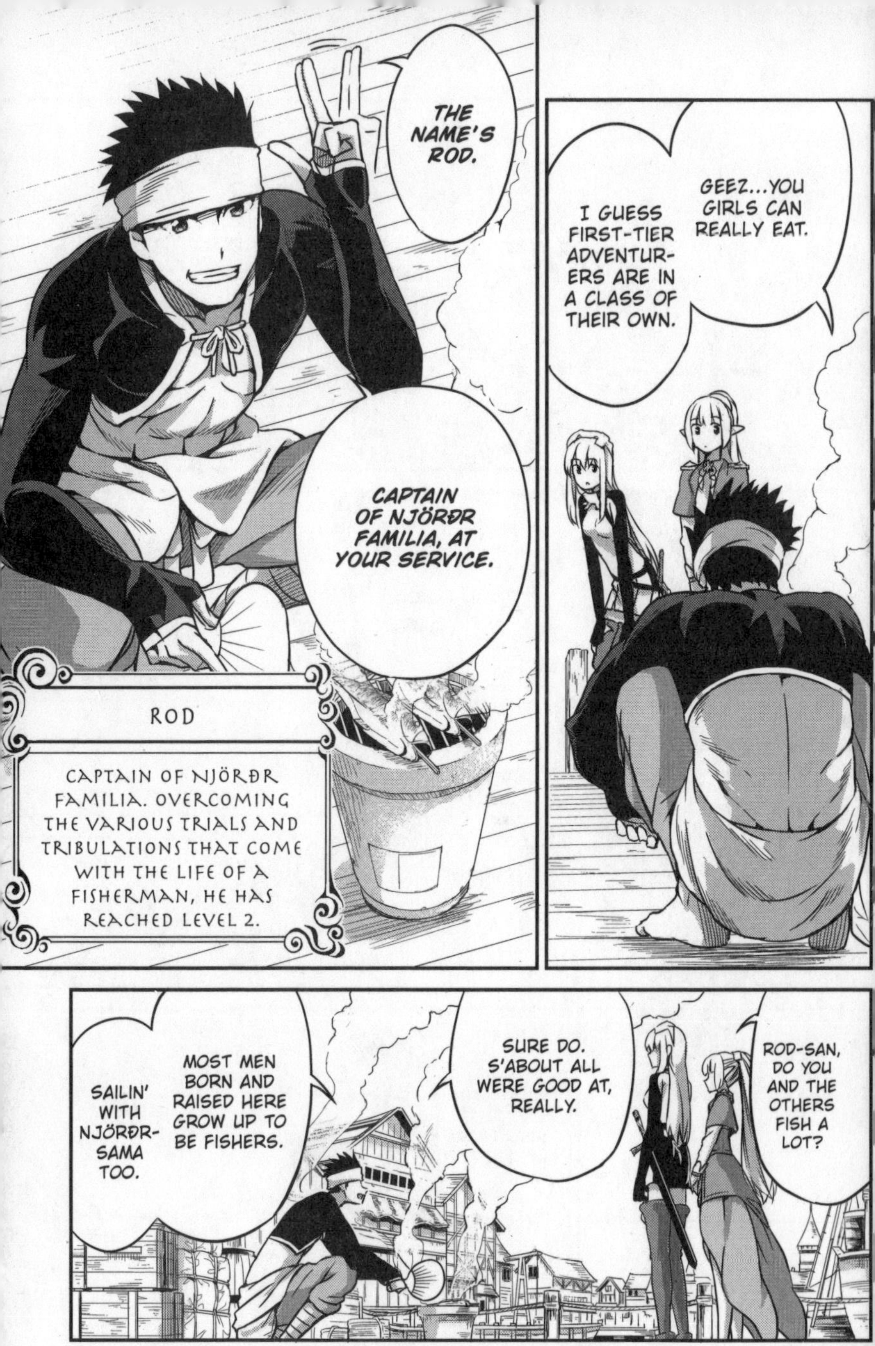
GEEZ...YOU GIRLS CAN REALLY EAT.
I GUESS FIRST-TIER ADVENTURERS ARE IN A CLASS OF THEIR OWN.
THE NAME'S ROD.
CAPTAIN OF NJÖRÐR FAMILIA, AT YOUR SERVICE.
ROD
CAPTAIN OF NJÖRÐR FAMILIA. OVERCOMING THE VARIOUS TRIALS AND TRIBULATIONS THAT COME WITH THE LIFE OF A FISHERMAN, HE HAS REACHED LEVEL 2.
ROD-SAN, DO YOU AND THE OTHERS FISH A LOT?
SURE DO. S'ABOUT ALL WERE GOOD AT, REALLY.
MOST MEN BORN AND RAISED HERE GROW UP TO BE FISHERS.
SAILIN' WITH NJÖRÐR-SAMA TOO.

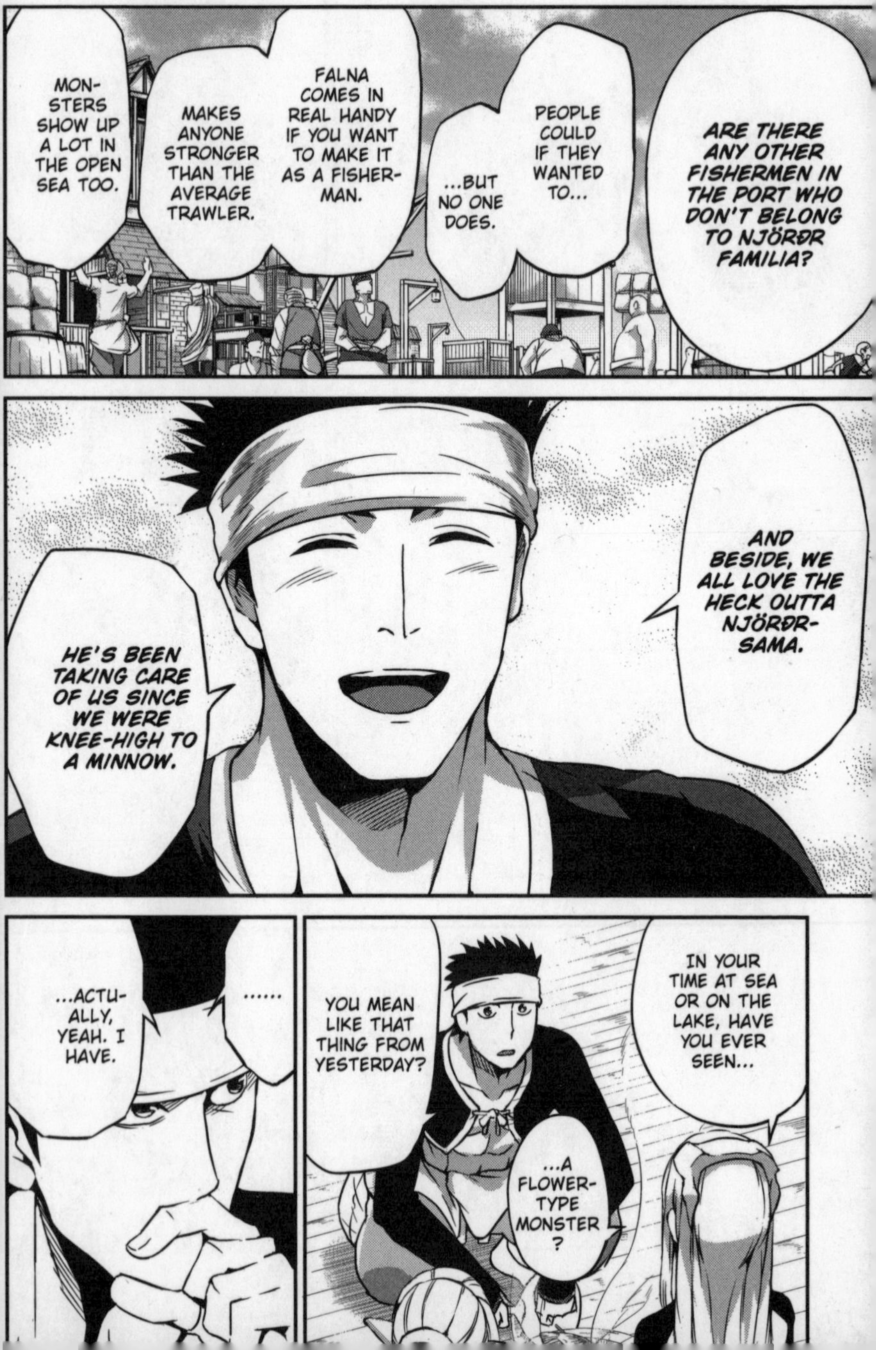
ARE THERE ANY OTHER FISHERMEN IN THE PORT WHO DON'T BELONG TO NJÖRÐR FAMILIA?
PEOPLE COULD IF THEY WANTED TO...
...BUT NO ONE DOES.
FALNA COMES IN REAL HANDY IF YOU WANT TO MAKE IT AS A FISHERMAN.
MAKES ANYONE STRONGER THAN THE AVERAGE TRAWLER.
MONSTERS SHOW UP A LOT IN THE OPEN SEA TOO.
AND BESIDE, WE ALL LOVE THE HECK OUTTA NJÖRÐR-SAMA.
HE'S BEEN TAKING CARE OF US SINCE WE WERE KNEE-HIGH TO A MINNOW.
IN YOUR TIME AT SEA OR ON THE LAKE, HAVE YOU EVER SEEN...
...A FLOWER-TYPE MONSTER?
YOU MEAN LIKE THAT THING FROM YESTERDAY?
......
...ACTUALLY, YEAH. I HAVE.

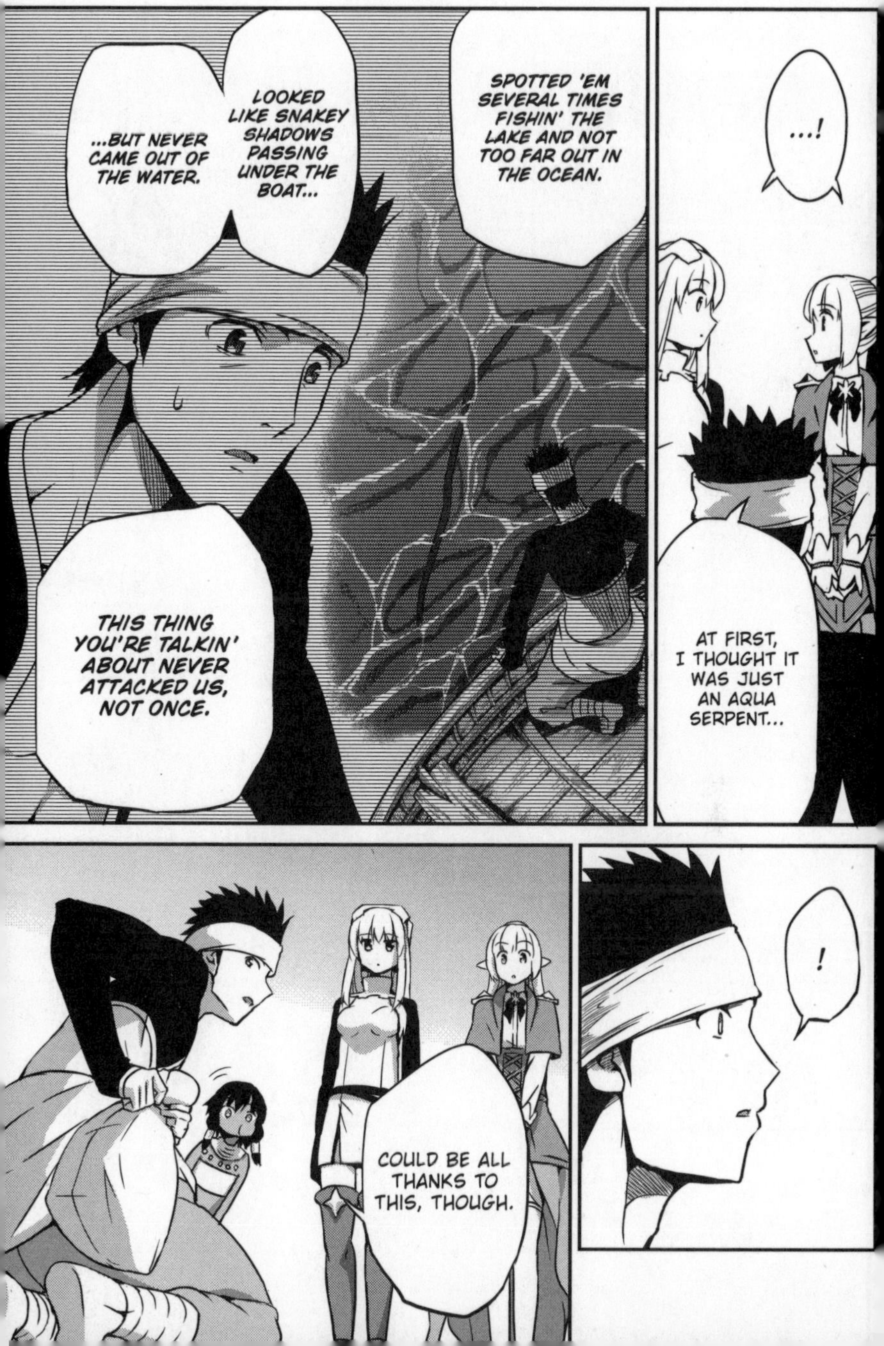
...!
AT FIRST, I THOUGHT IT WAS JUST AN AQUA SERPENT...
SPOTTED 'EM SEVERAL TIMES FISHIN' THE LAKE AND NOT TOO FAR OUT IN THE OCEAN.
LOOKED LIKE SNAKEY SHADOWS PASSING UNDER THE BOAT...
...BUT NEVER CAME OUT OF THE WATER.
THIS THING YOU'RE TALKIN' ABOUT NEVER ATTACKED US, NOT ONCE.
!
COULD BE ALL THANKS TO THIS, THOUGH.

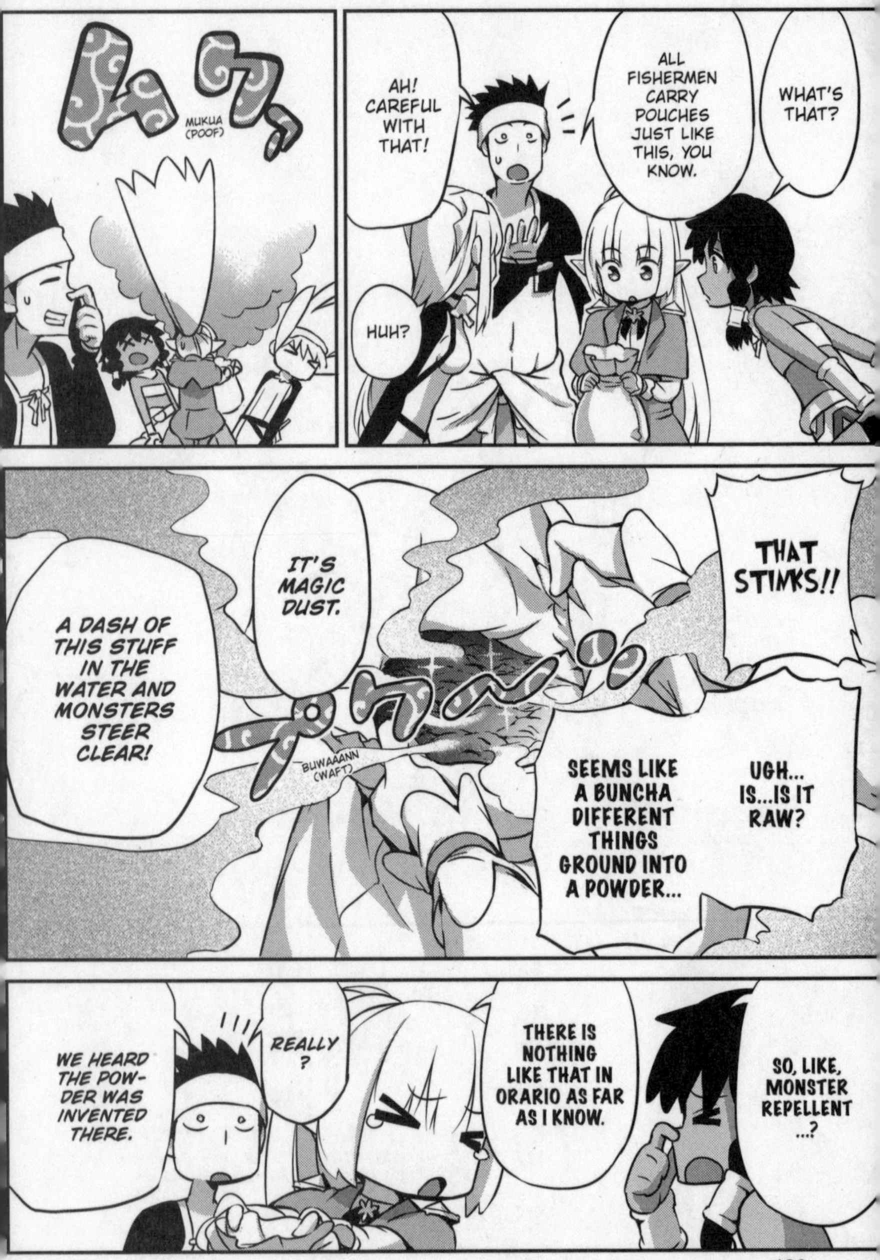
WHAT'S THAT?
ALL FISHERMEN CARRY POUCHES JUST LIKE THIS, YOU KNOW.
AH! CAREFUL WITH THAT!
HUH?
MUKUA (POOF)
THAT STINKS!!
UGH... IS...IS IT RAW?
SEEMS LIKE A BUNCHA DIFFERENT THINGS GROUND INTO A POWDER...
IT'S MAGIC DUST.
BUWAAANN (WAFT)
A DASH OF THIS STUFF IN THE WATER AND MONSTERS STEER CLEAR!
SO, LIKE, MONSTER REPELLENT ...?
THERE IS NOTHING LIKE THAT IN ORARIO AS FAR AS I KNOW.
REALLY ?
WE HEARD THE POW- DER WAS INVENTED THERE.

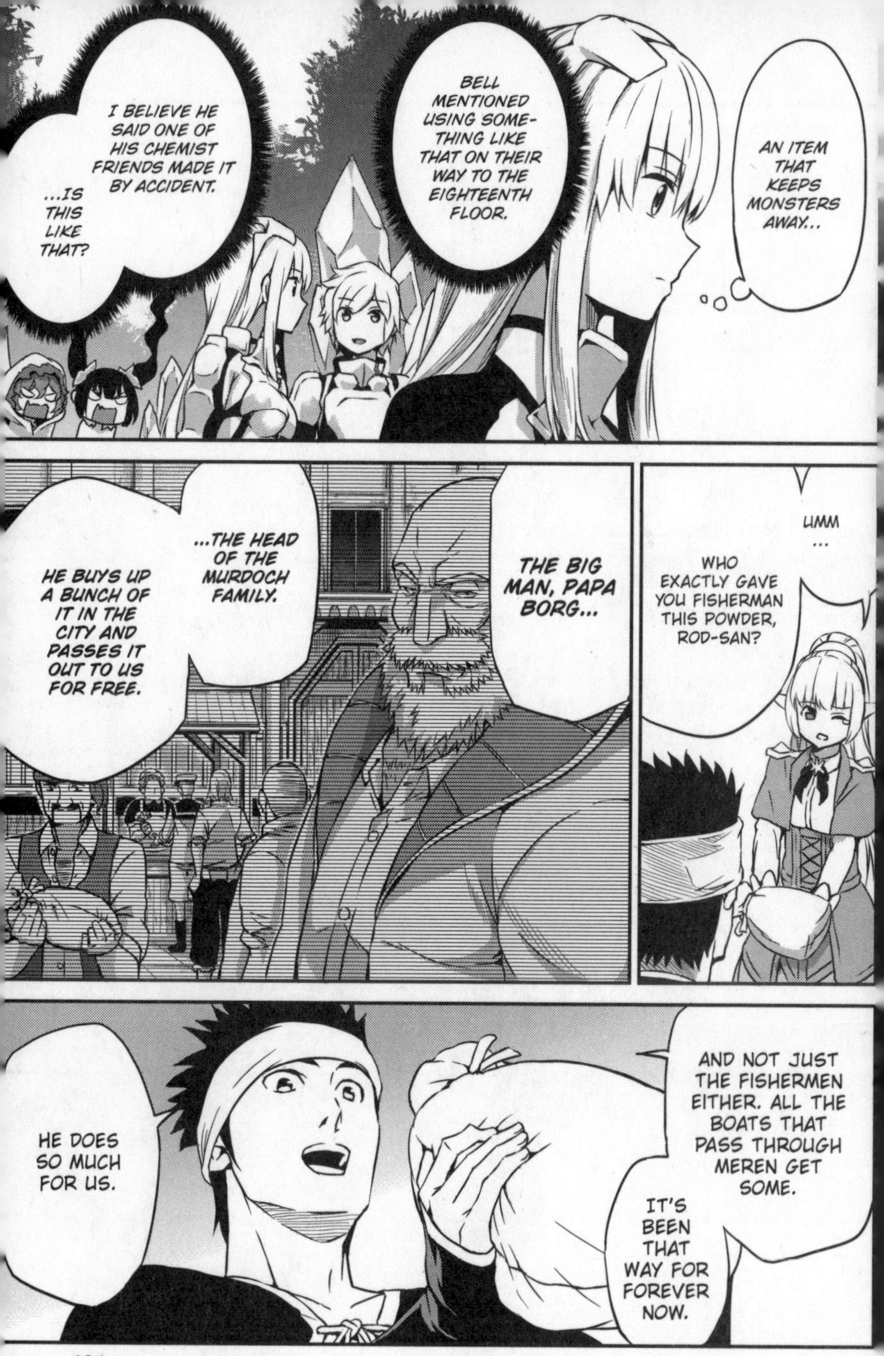
AN ITEM THAT KEEPS MONSTERS AWAY...
BELL MENTIONED USING SOME-THING LIKE THAT ON THEIR WAY TO THE EIGHTEENTH FLOOR.
I BELIEVE HE SAID ONE OF HIS CHEMIST FRIENDS MADE IT BY ACCIDENT.
...IS THIS LIKE THAT?
UMM...
WHO EXACTLY GAVE YOU FISHERMAN THIS POWDER, ROD-SAN?
THE BIG MAN, PAPA BORG...
...THE HEAD OF THE MURDOCH FAMILY.
HE BUYS UP A BUNCH OF IT IN THE CITY AND PASSES IT OUT TO US FOR FREE.
AND NOT JUST THE FISHERMEN EITHER. ALL THE BOATS THAT PASS THROUGH MEREN GET SOME.
IT'S BEEN THAT WAY FOR FOREVER NOW.
HE DOES SO MUCH FOR US.

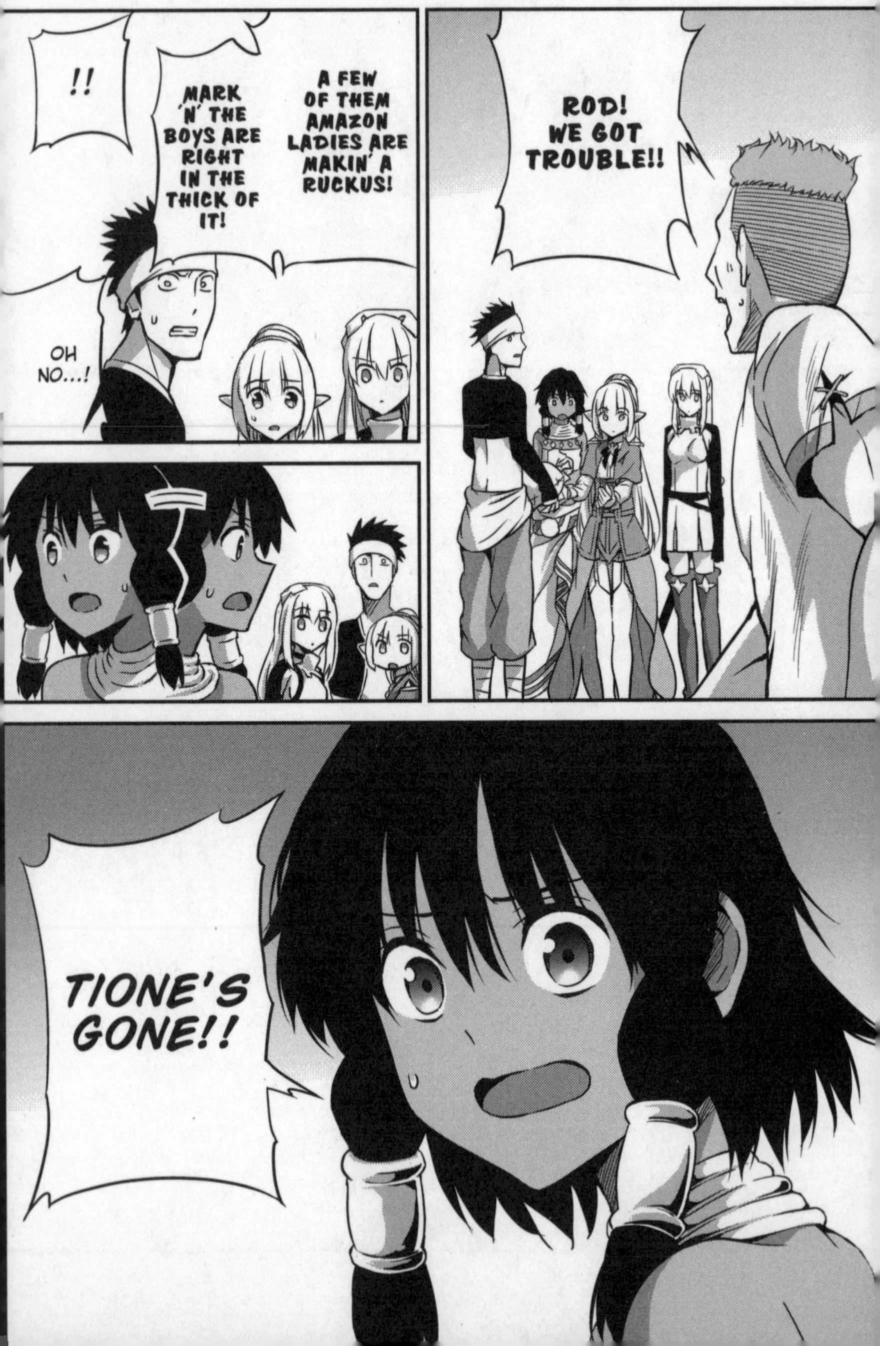
ROD! WE GOT TROUBLE!!
A FEW OF THEM AMAZON LADIES ARE MAKIN' A RUCKUS!
MARK 'N' THE BOYS ARE RIGHT IN THE THICK OF IT!
!!
OH NO...!
TIONE'S GONE!!

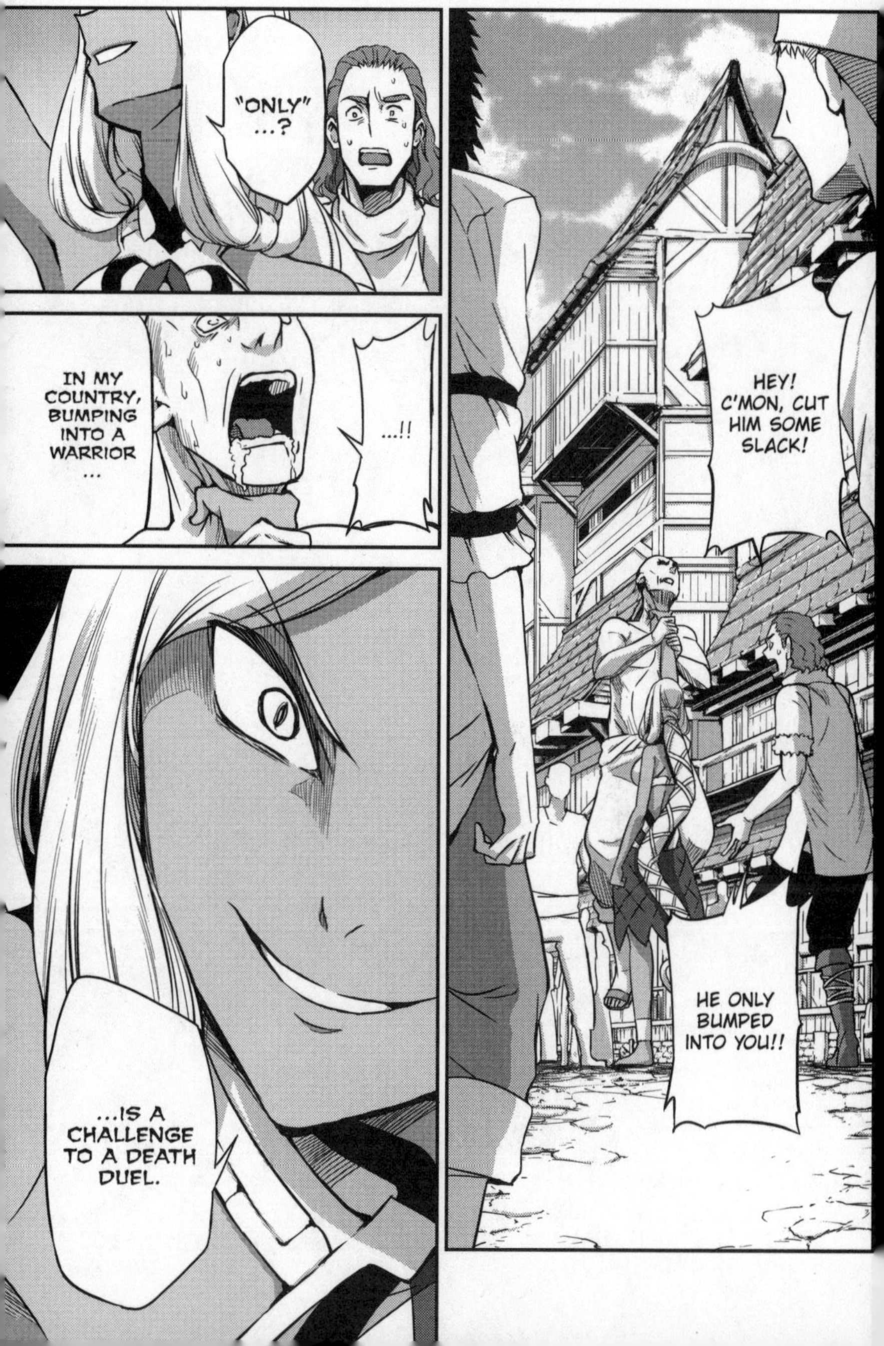
HEY! C'MON, CUT HIM SOME SLACK!
HE ONLY BUMPED INTO YOU!!
"ONLY" ...?
...!!
IN MY COUNTRY, BUMPING INTO A WARRIOR ...
...IS A CHALLENGE TO A DEATH DUEL.

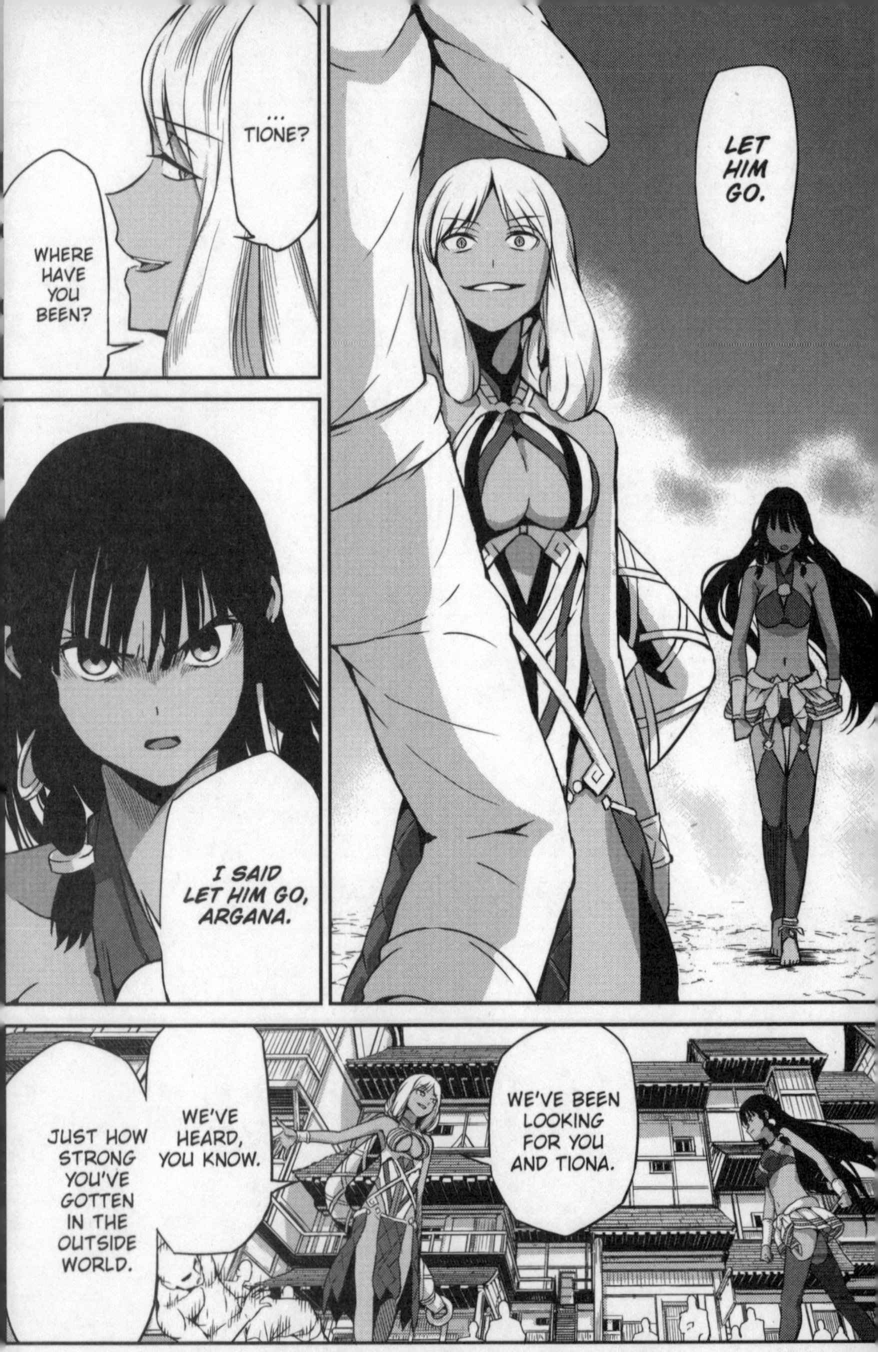
LET HIM GO.
... TIONE?
WHERE HAVE YOU BEEN?
I SAID LET HIM GO, ARGANA.
WE'VE BEEN LOOKING FOR YOU AND TIONA.
WE'VE HEARD, YOU KNOW.
JUST HOW STRONG YOU'VE GOTTEN IN THE OUTSIDE WORLD.

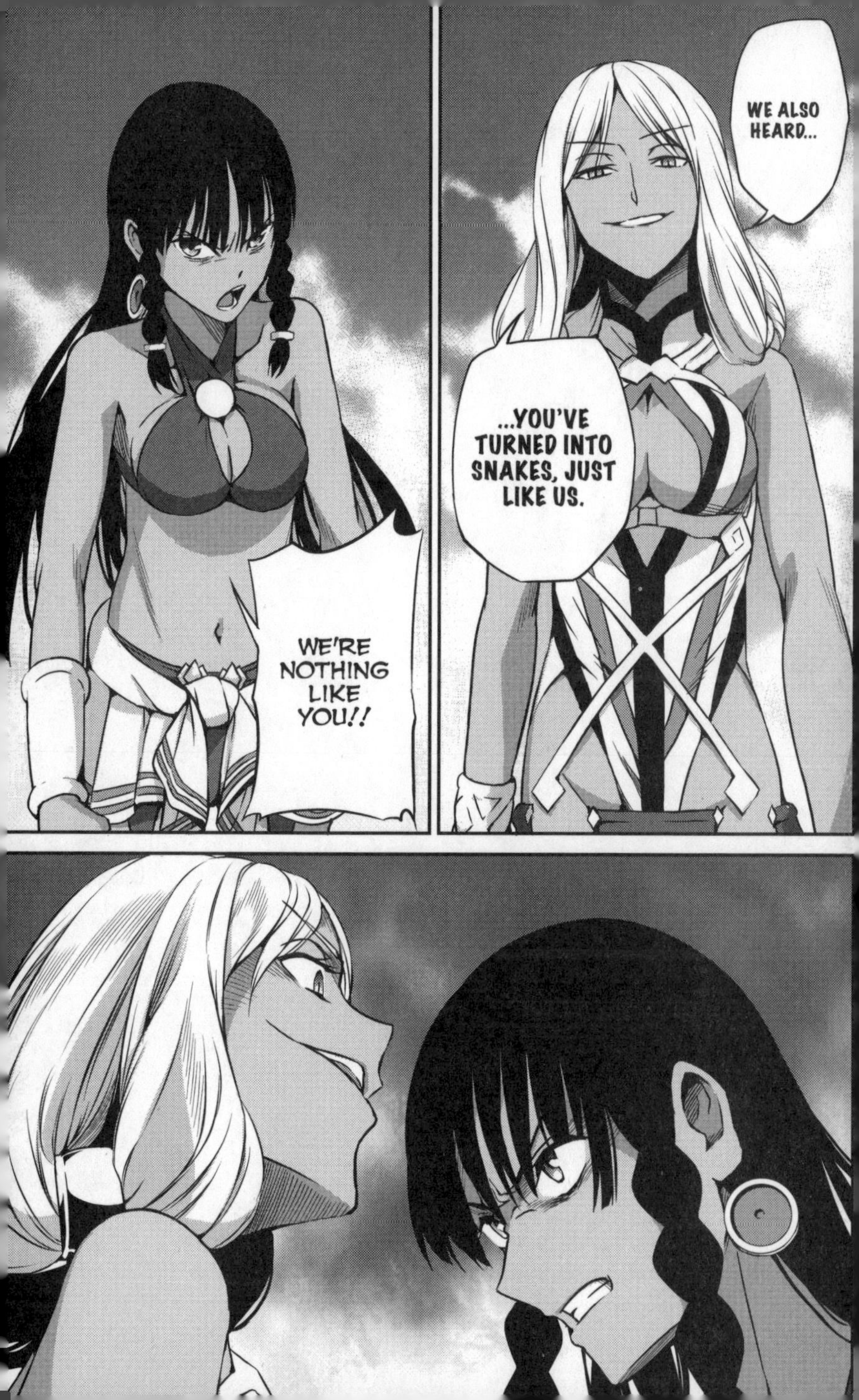
WE ALSO HEARD...
...YOU'VE TURNED INTO SNAKES, JUST LIKE US.
WE'RE NOTHING LIKE YOU!!

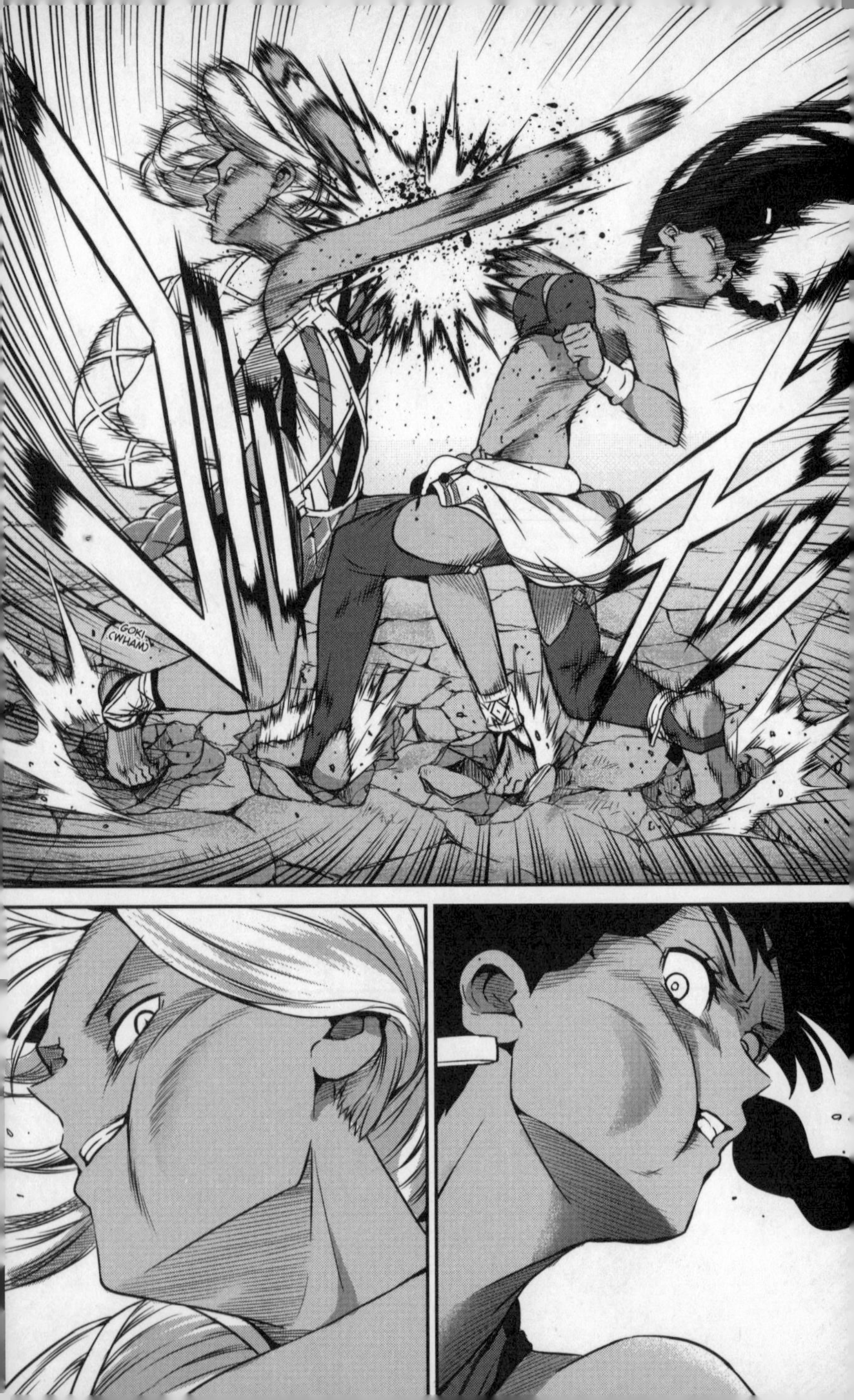
GOKI
(WHAM)

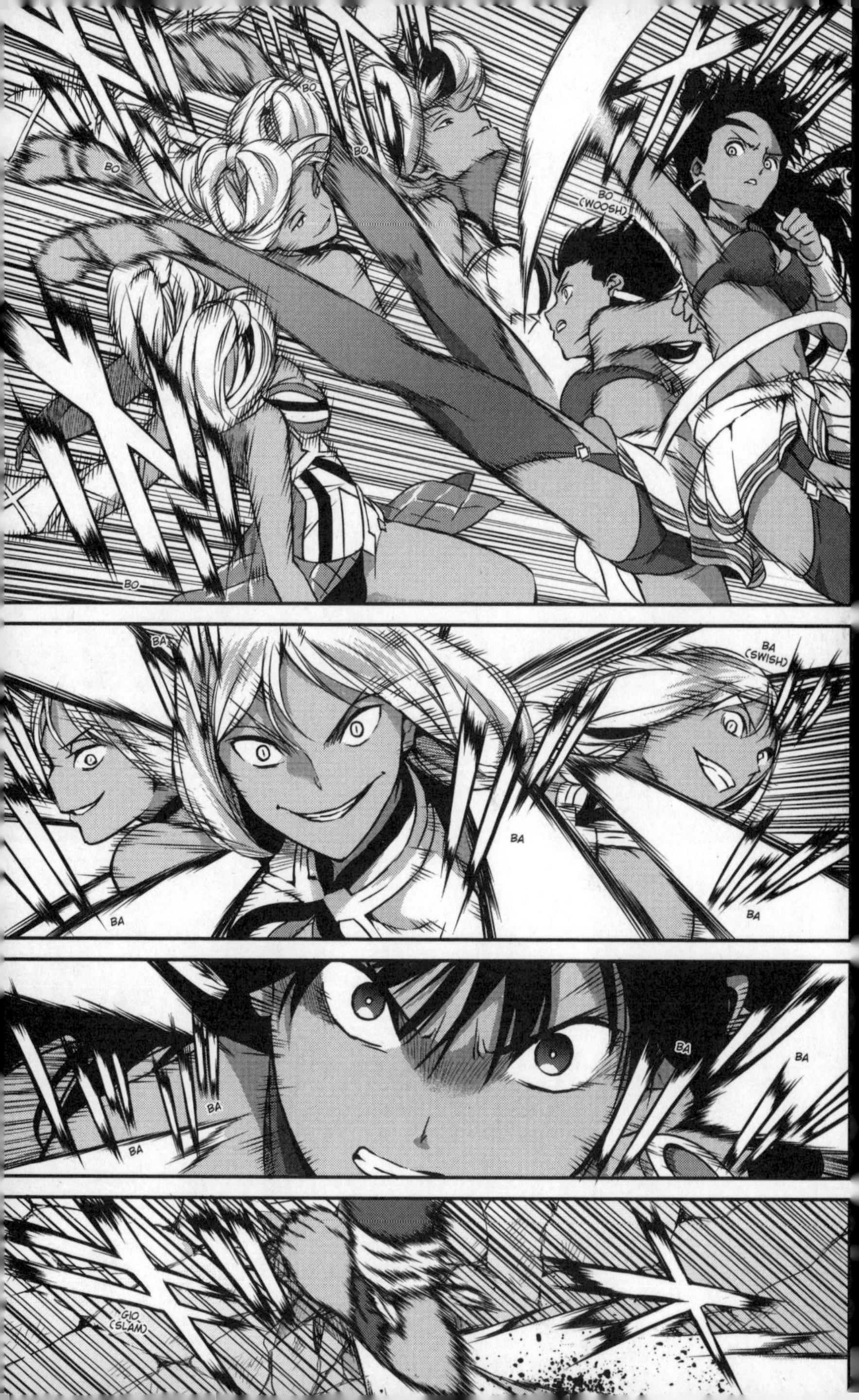
BO
(WOOSH)
BO
BO
BO
BO
BA
(SWISH)
BA
BA
BA
BA
BA
BA
BA
BA
GIO
(SLAM)

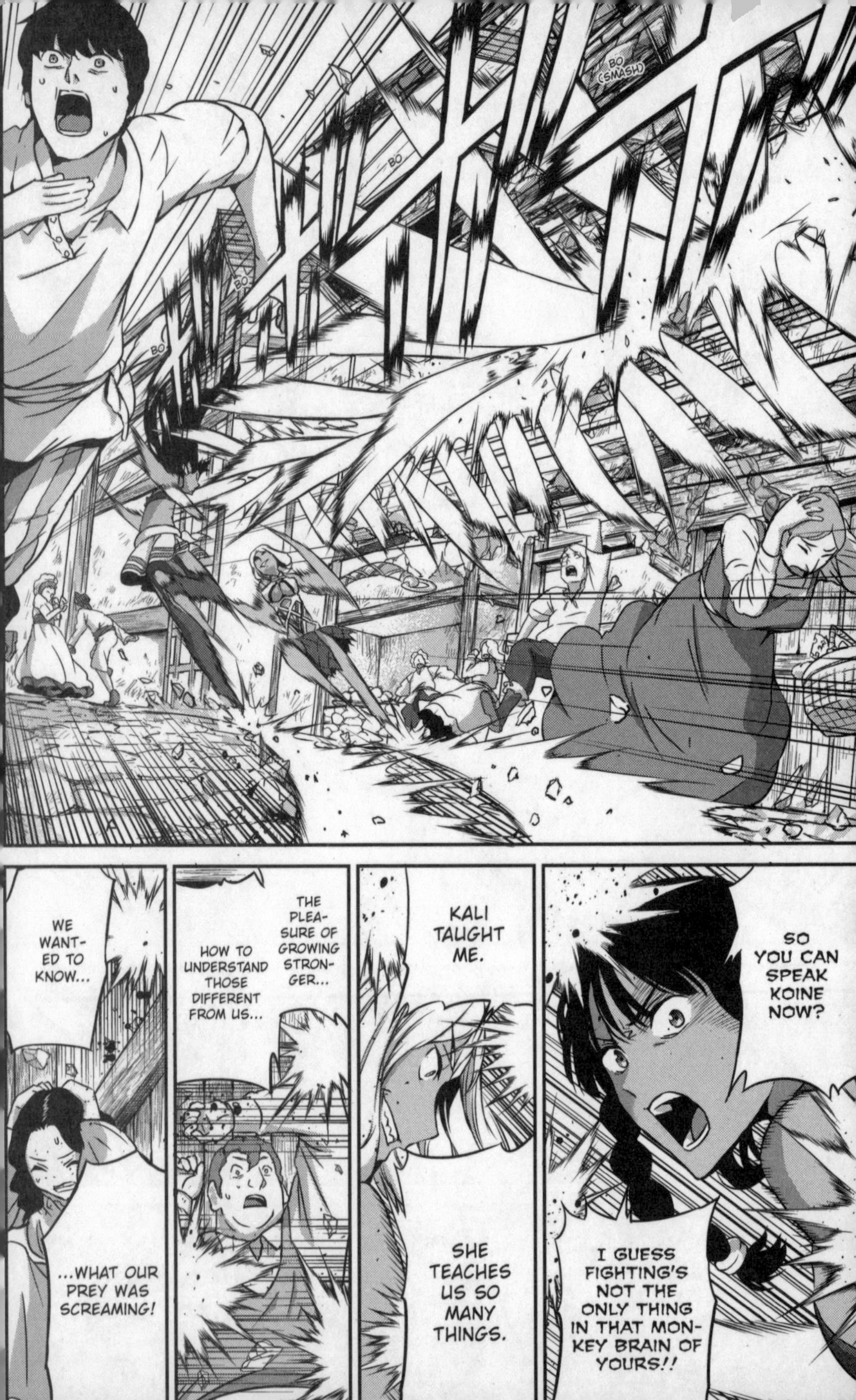
BO (SMASH)
BO
BO
BO
SO YOU CAN SPEAK KOINE NOW?
I GUESS FIGHTING'S NOT THE ONLY THING IN THAT MONKEY BRAIN OF YOURS!!
KALI TAUGHT ME.
SHE TEACHES US SO MANY THINGS.
THE PLEASURE OF GROWING STRONGER...
HOW TO UNDERSTAND THOSE DIFFERENT FROM US...
WE WANTED TO KNOW...
...WHAT OUR PREY WAS SCREAMING!

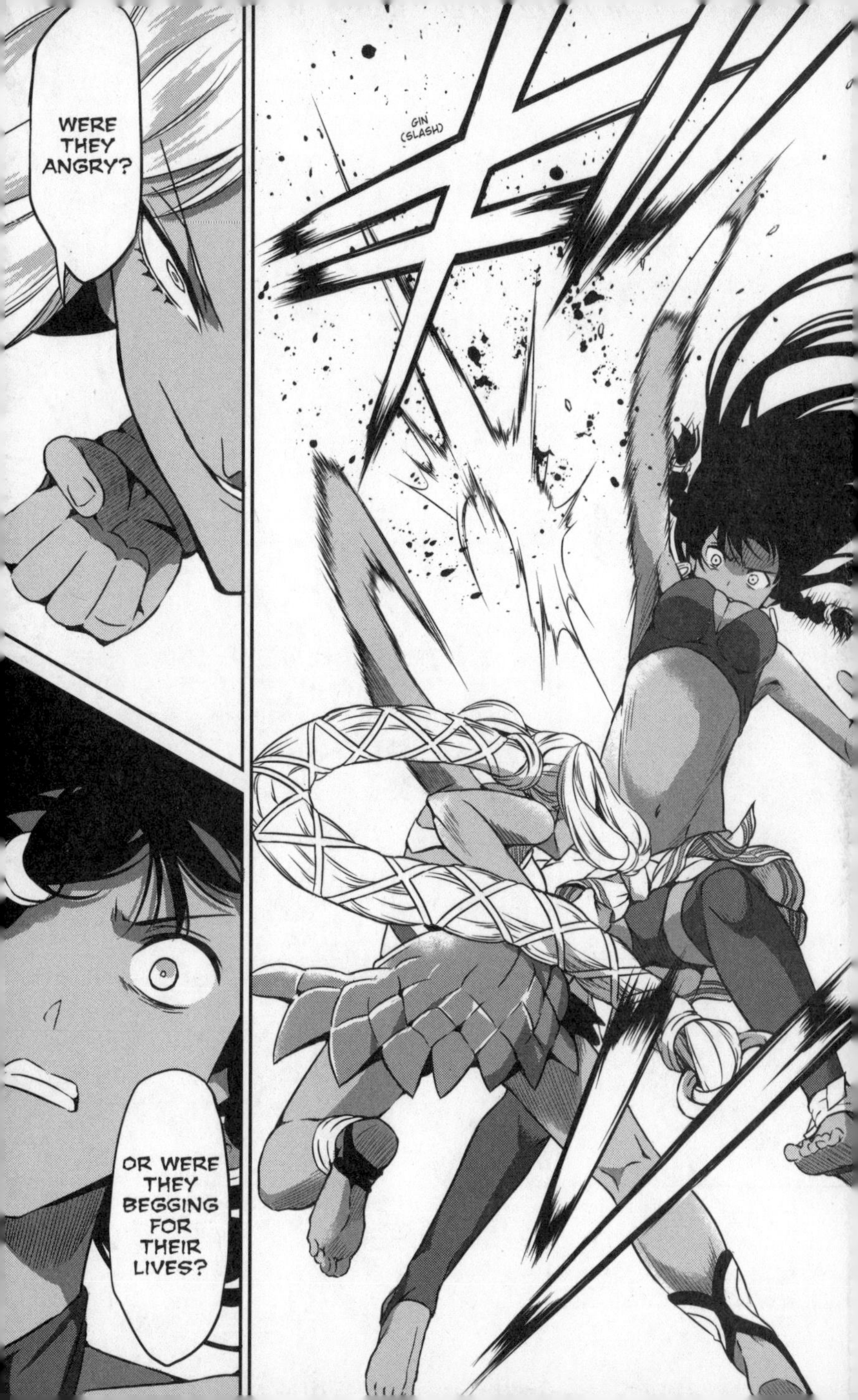
GIN (SLASH)
WERE THEY ANGRY?
OR WERE THEY BEGGING FOR THEIR LIVES?

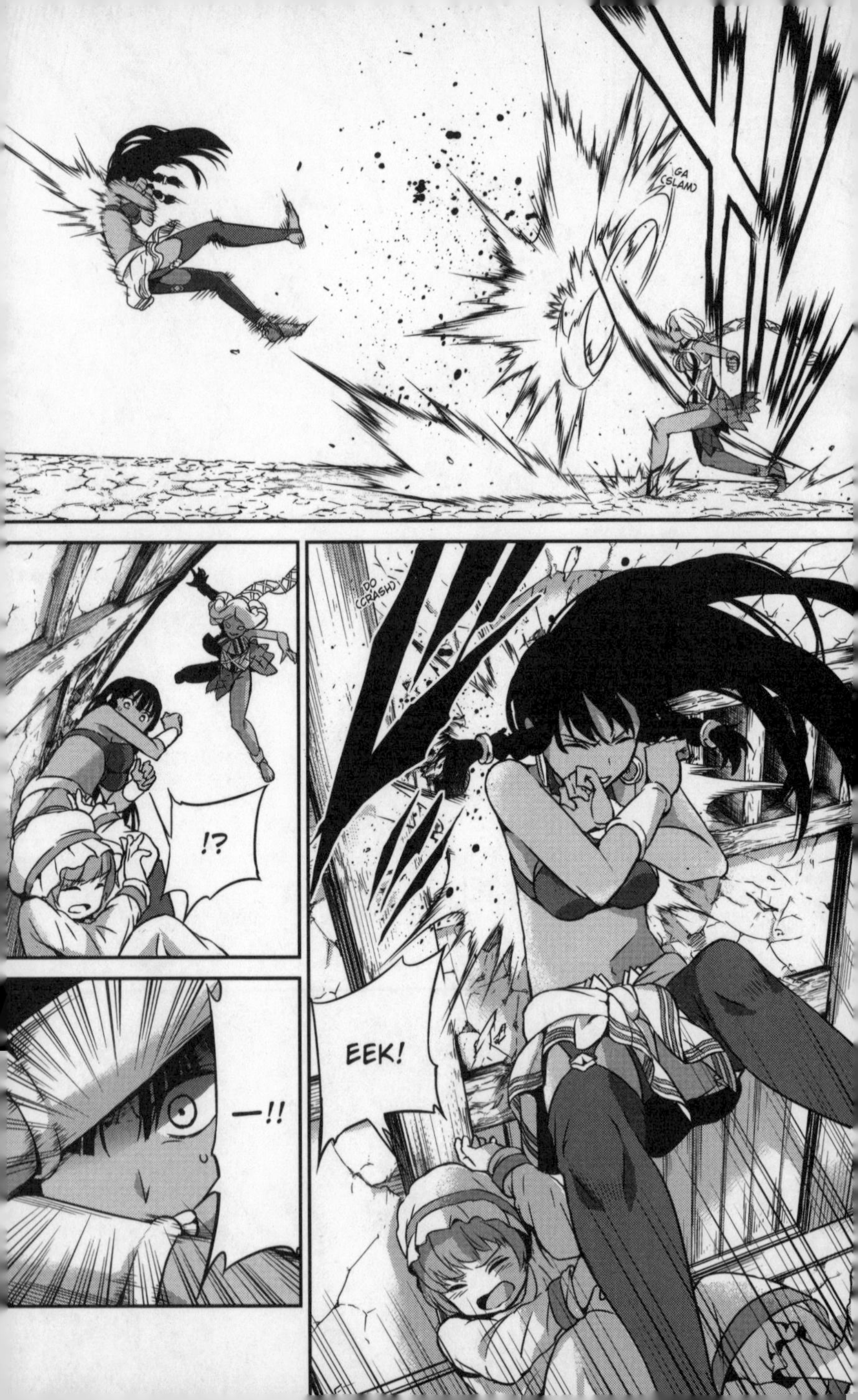
GA (SLAM)
DO (CRASH)
EEK!
!?
—!!

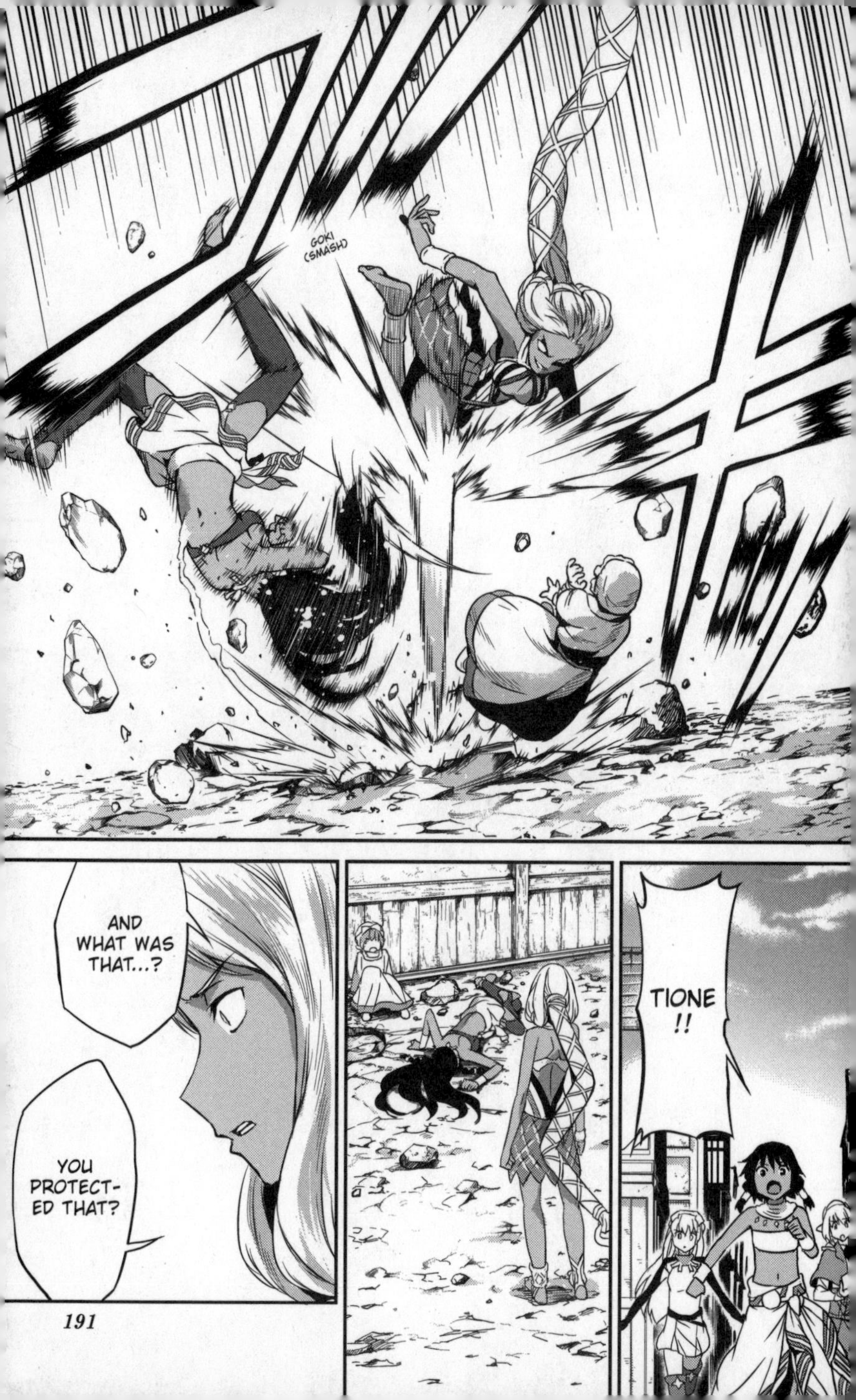
GOKI (SMASH)
TIONE !!
AND WHAT WAS THAT...?
YOU PROTECTED THAT?

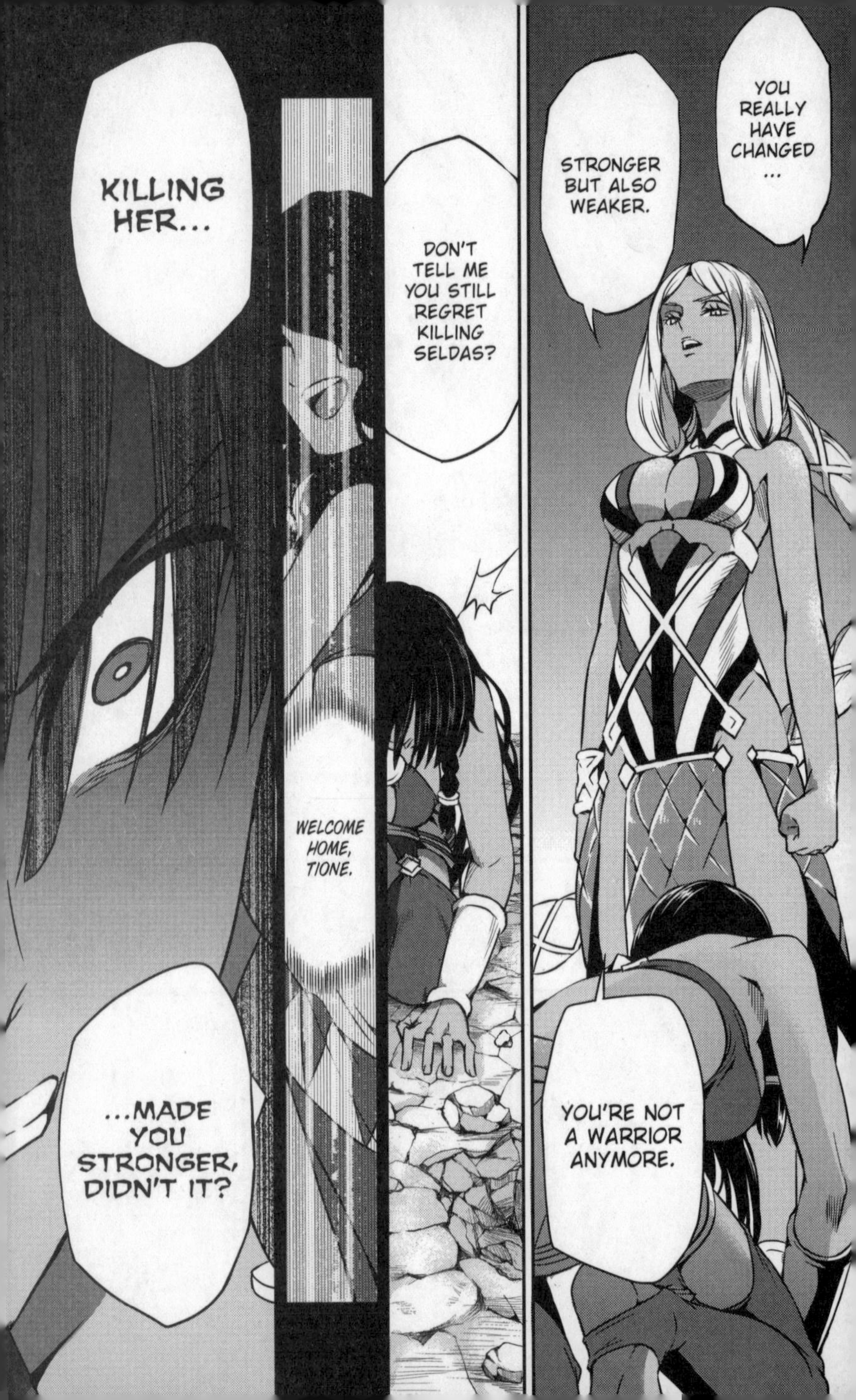
YOU REALLY HAVE CHANGED...
STRONGER BUT ALSO WEAKER.
YOU'RE NOT A WARRIOR ANYMORE.
DON'T TELL ME YOU STILL REGRET KILLING SELDAS?
WELCOME HOME, TIONE.
KILLING HER...
...MADE YOU STRONGER, DIDN'T IT?

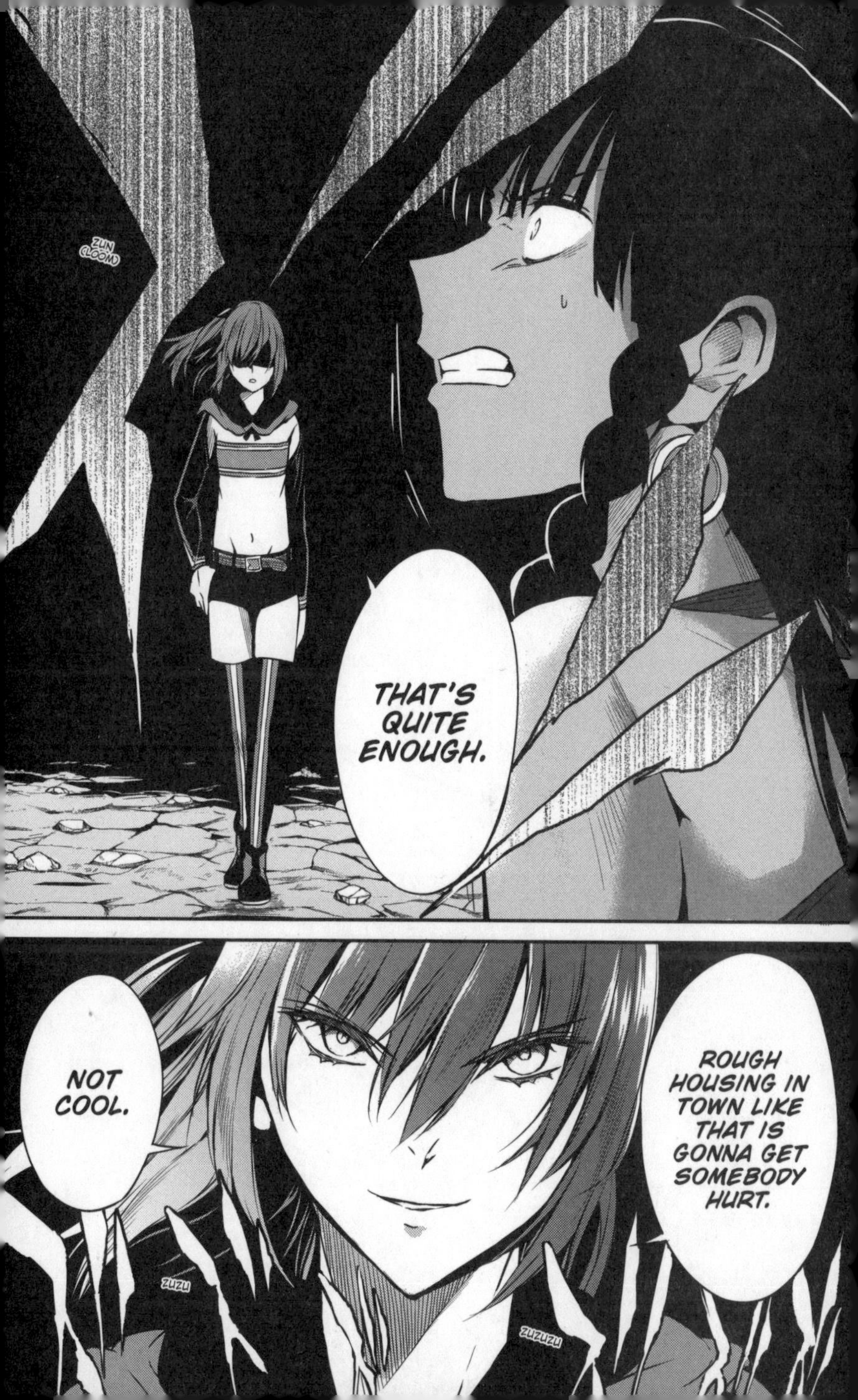
ZUN (LOOM)
THAT'S QUITE ENOUGH.
ROUGH HOUSING IN TOWN LIKE THAT IS GONNA GET SOMEBODY HURT.
NOT COOL.
ZUZUZU
ZUZU

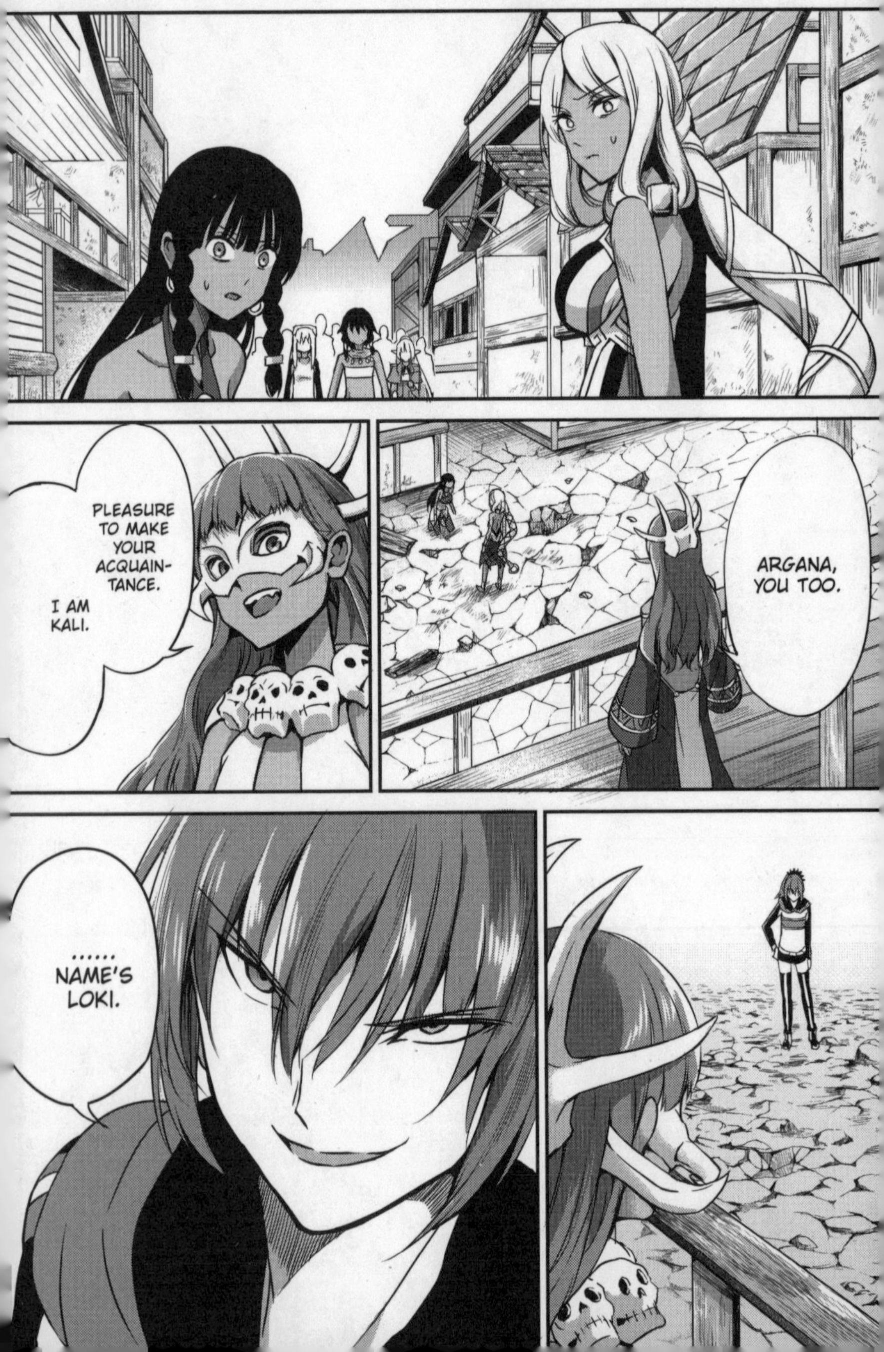
ARGANA, YOU TOO.
PLEASURE TO MAKE YOUR ACQUAIN-TANCE.
I AM KALI.
...... NAME'S LOKI.

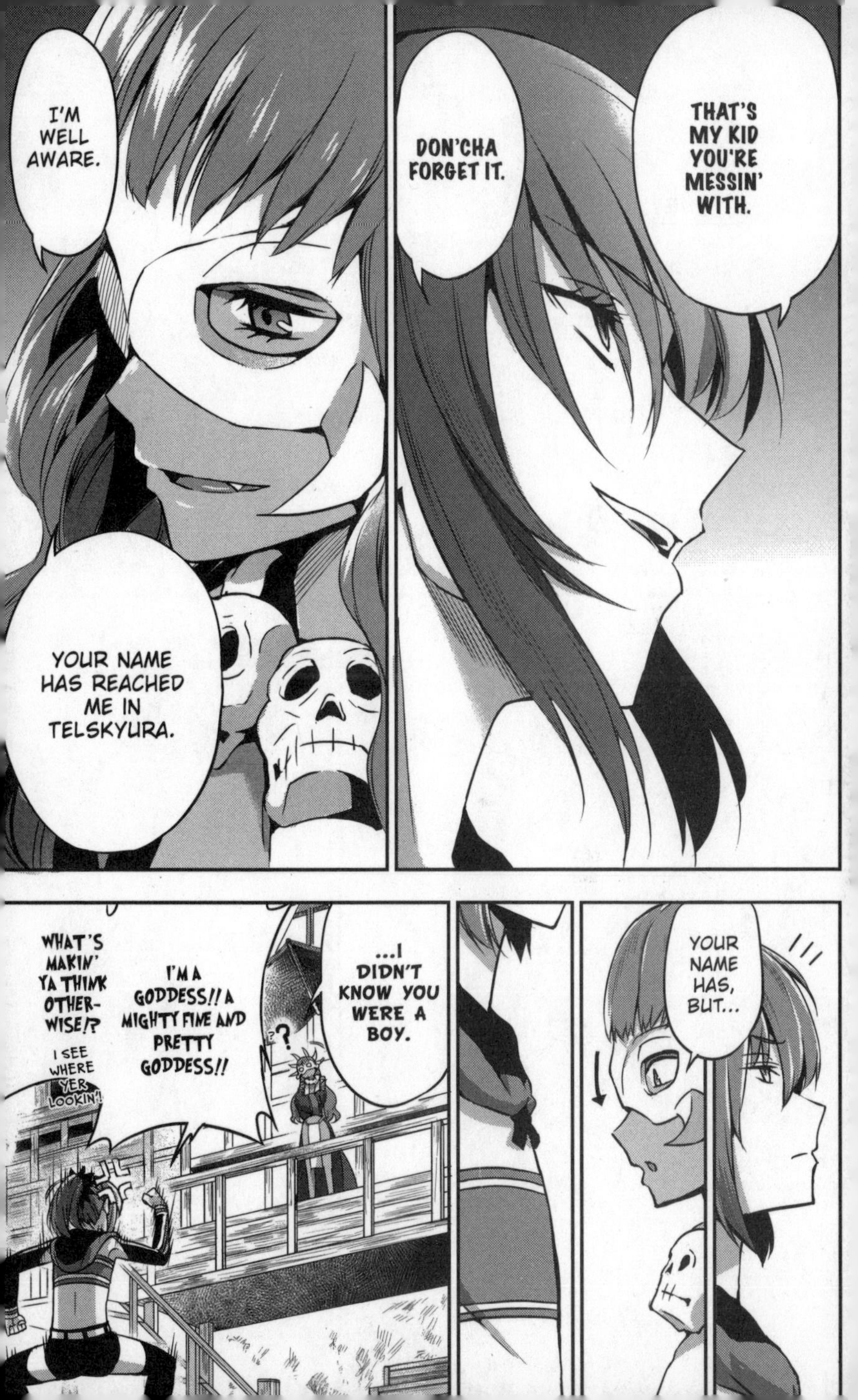
THAT'S MY KID YOU'RE MESSIN' WITH.
DON'CHA FORGET IT.
I'M WELL AWARE.
YOUR NAME HAS REACHED ME IN TELSKYURA.
YOUR NAME HAS, BUT...
...I DIDN'T KNOW YOU WERE A BOY.
I'M A GODDESS!! A MIGHTY FINE AND PRETTY GODDESS!!
WHAT'S MAKIN' YA THINK OTHERWISE!?
I SEE WHERE YER LOOKIN'!

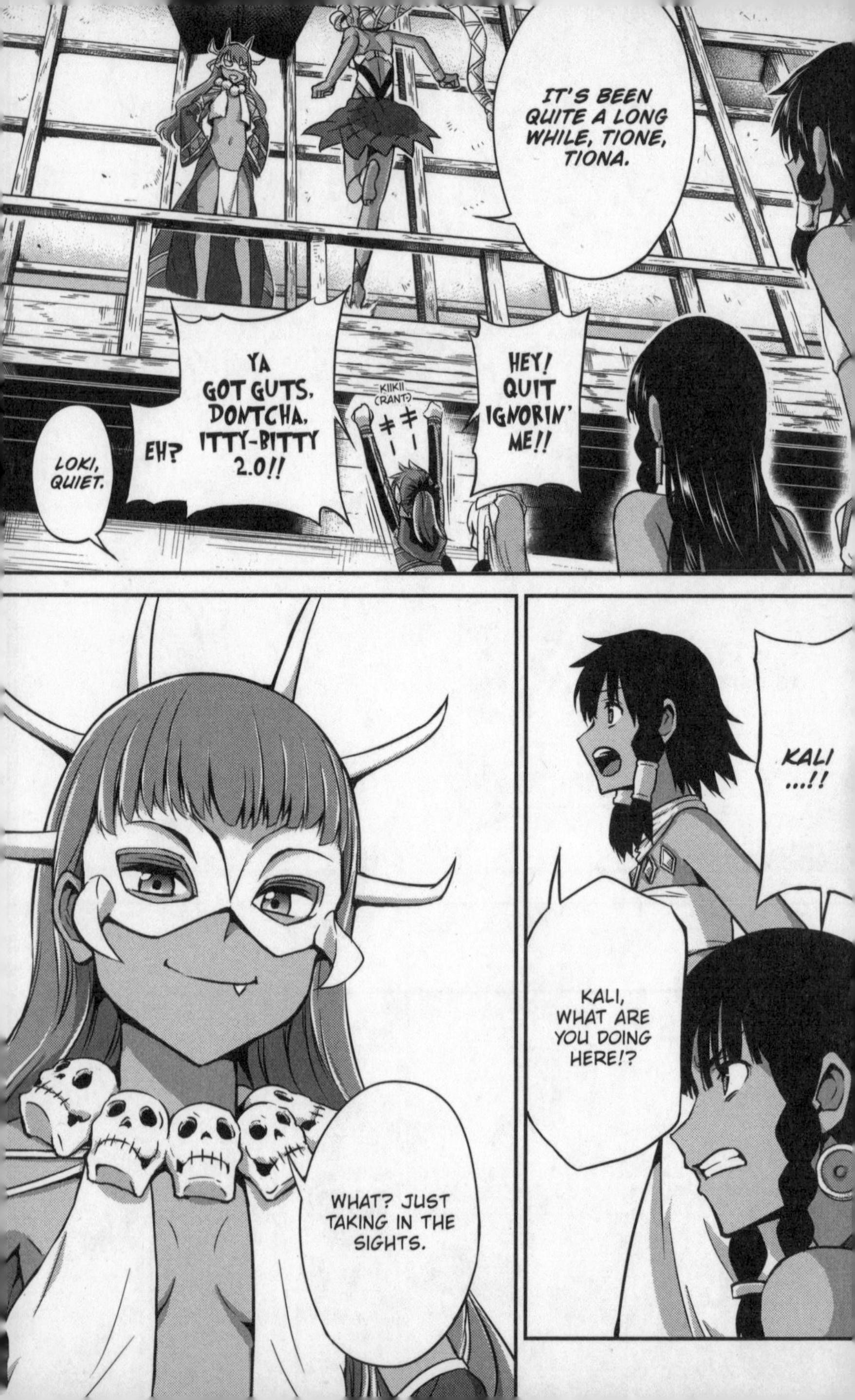
IT'S BEEN QUITE A LONG WHILE, TIONE, TIONA.
HEY! QUIT IGNORIN' ME!!
KIIKII (RANT)
EH? YA GOT GUTS, DONTCHA, ITTY-BITTY 2.0!!
LOKI, QUIET.
KALI ...!!
KALI, WHAT ARE YOU DOING HERE!?
WHAT? JUST TAKING IN THE SIGHTS.

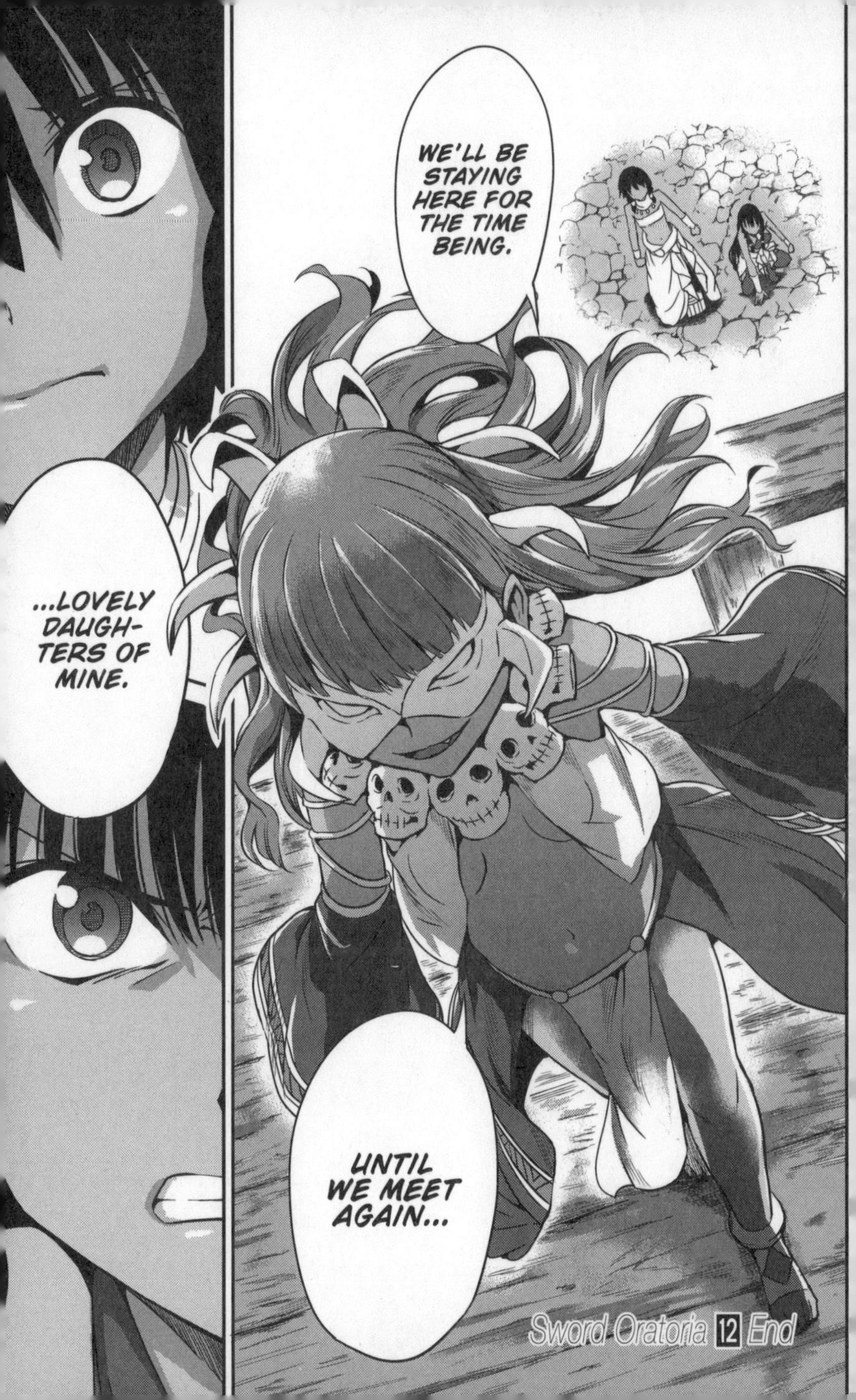
WE'LL BE STAYING HERE FOR THE TIME BEING.
UNTIL WE MEET AGAIN...
...LOVELY DAUGH-TERS OF MINE.
Sword Oratoria 12 End

AFTERWORD

THANK YOU SO MUCH FOR PURCHASING THIS BOOK!
I'VE BEEN ABLE TO COMPLETE TWELVE VOLUMES,
THANKS TO ALL OF YOU OUT THERE. WITH TWO
MANGA COMING OUT AT THE SAME TIME AND THE
MOVIE ALSO BEING RELEASED, IT'S A VERY EXCITING
TIME FOR DANMACHI! THOUGH, I FEAR FOR YOUR
WALLETS...AT ANY RATE, SWORD ORATORIA IS STILL
GOING STRONG, SO KEEP COMING BACK FOR MORE!!

TAKASHI YAGI

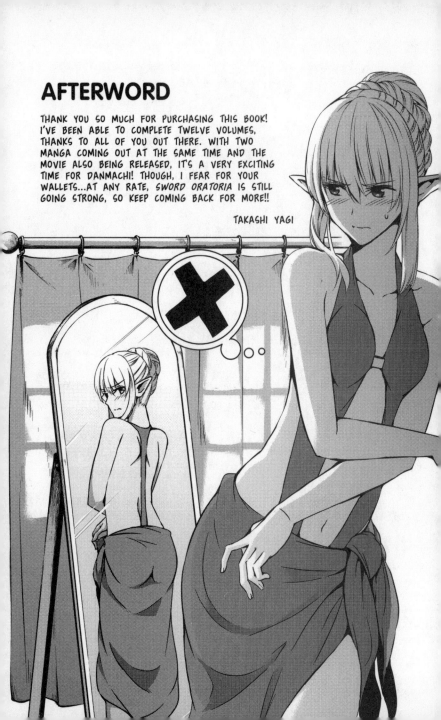

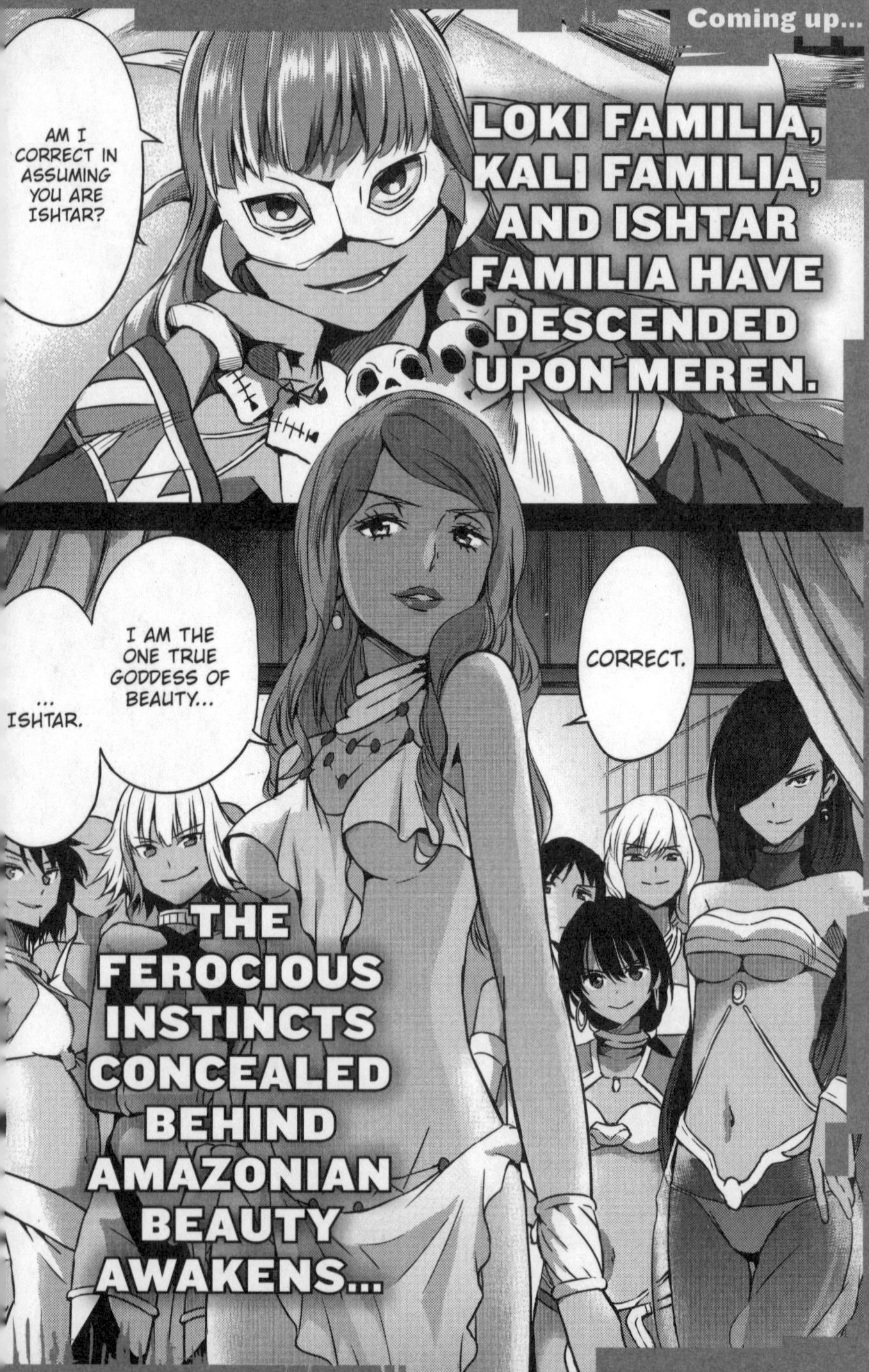
Coming up...
LOKI FAMILIA, KALI FAMILIA, AND ISHTAR FAMILIA HAVE DESCENDED UPON MEREN.
AM I CORRECT IN ASSUMING YOU ARE ISHTAR?
CORRECT.
I AM THE ONE TRUE GODDESS OF BEAUTY... ...ISHTAR.
THE FEROCIOUS INSTINCTS CONCEALED BEHIND AMAZONIAN BEAUTY AWAKENS...

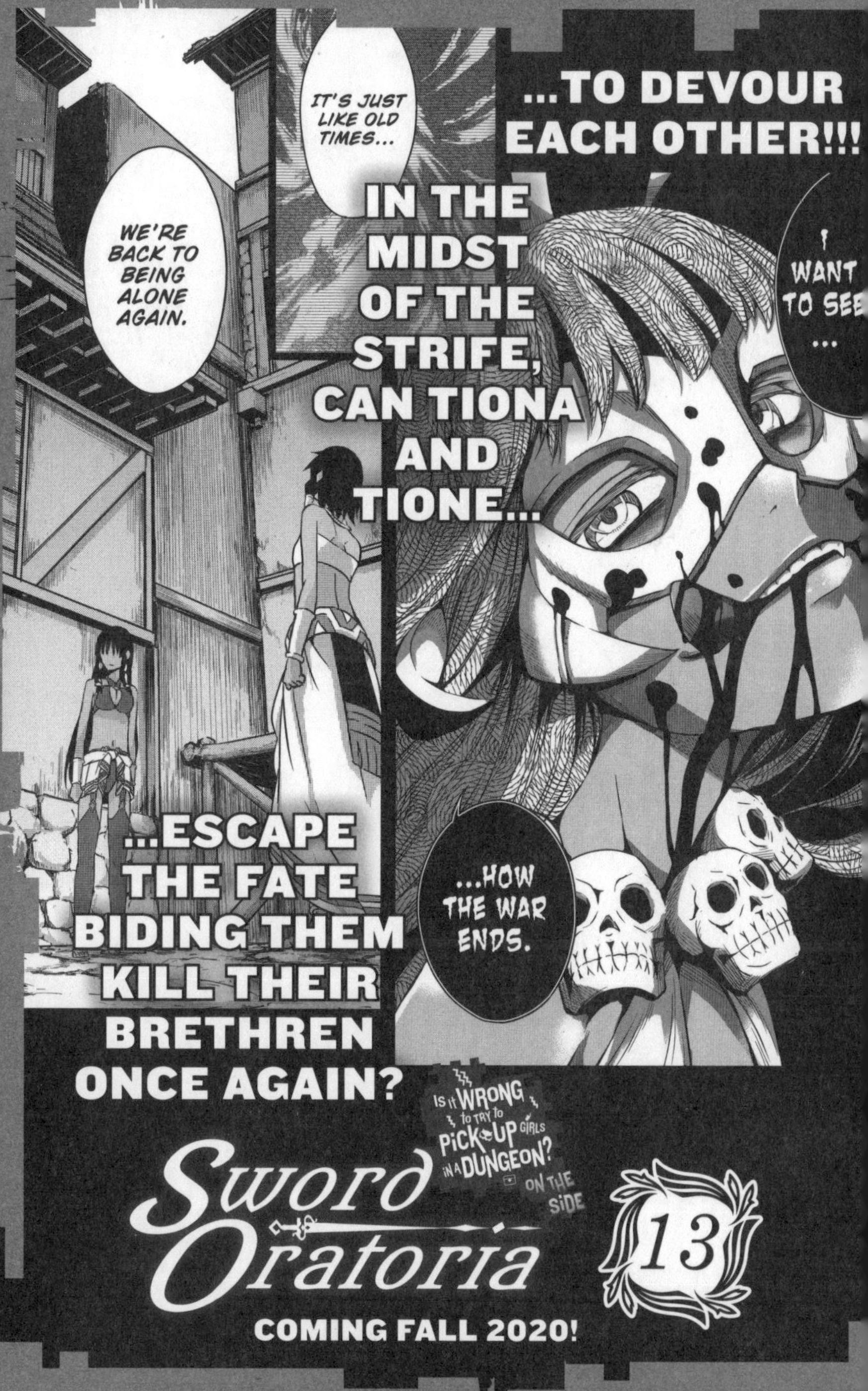
...TO DEVOUR EACH OTHER!!!
I WANT TO SEE...
...HOW THE WAR ENDS.
IT'S JUST LIKE OLD TIMES...
IN THE MIDST OF THE STRIFE, CAN TIONA AND TIONE...
WE'RE BACK TO BEING ALONE AGAIN.
...ESCAPE THE FATE BIDING THEM KILL THEIR BRETHREN ONCE AGAIN?
IS IT WRONG TO TRY TO PICK UP GIRLS IN A DUNGEON? ON THE SIDE
Sword Oratoria
13
COMING FALL 2020!

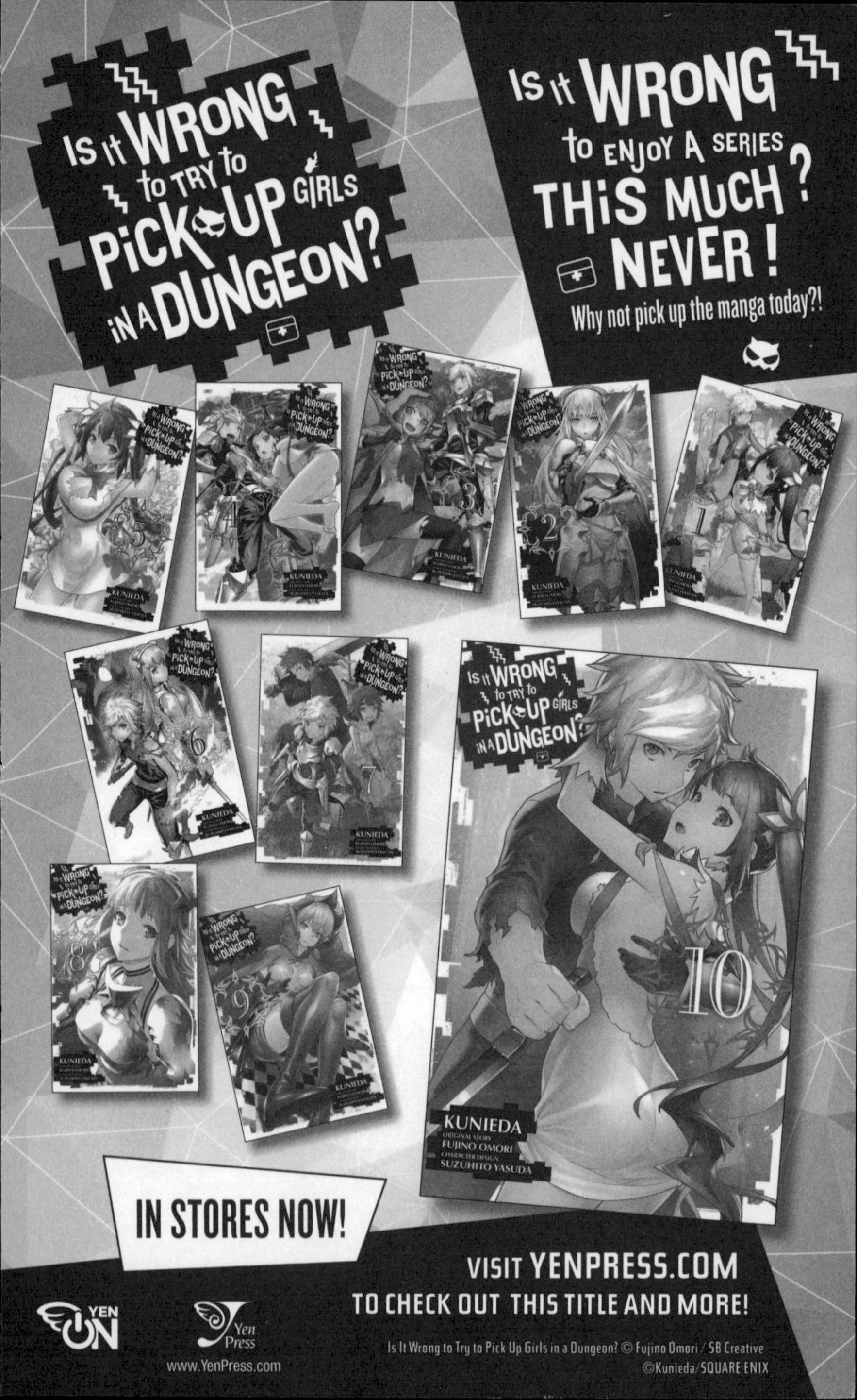
Is it WRONG to Try to Pick-Up Girls in a DUNGEON?
Is it WRONG to ENJOY A SERIES THIS MUCH? NEVER!
Why not pick up the manga today?!
KUNIEDA
ORIGINAL STORY FUJINO OMORI
CHARACTER DESIGN: SUZUHITO YASUDA
IN STORES NOW!
VISIT YENPRESS.COM
TO CHECK OUT THIS TITLE AND MORE!
YEN ON
Yen Press
www.YenPress.com
Is It Wrong to Try to Pick Up Girls in a Dungeon? © Fujino Omori / SB Creative
©Kunieda/SQUARE ENIX

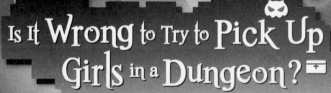

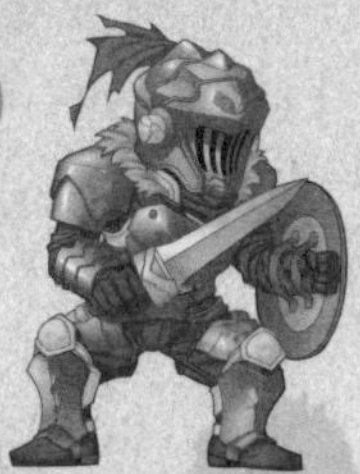

HE DOES NOT LET ANYONE ROLL THE DICE.

A young Priestess joins her first adventuring party, but blind to the dangers, they almost immediately find themselves in trouble. It's Goblin Slayer who comes to their rescue—a man who has dedicated his life to the extermination of all goblins by any means necessary. A dangerous, dirty, and thankless job, but he does it better than anyone. And when rumors of his feats begin to circulate, there's no telling who might come calling next...

Light Novel
V.1-9
Available
Now!

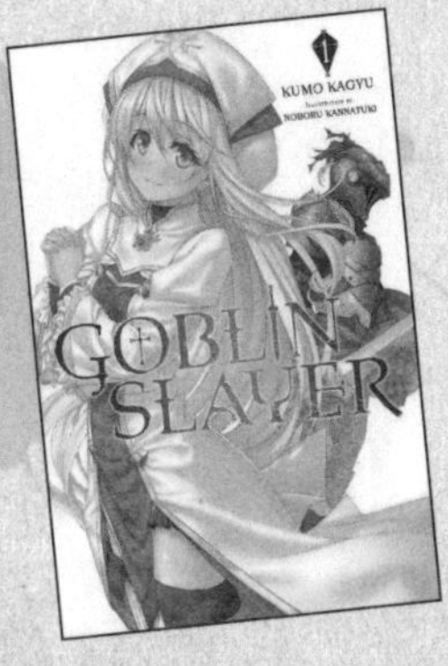
1
KUMO KAGYU
NOBORU KANNATUKI
GOBLIN SLAYER

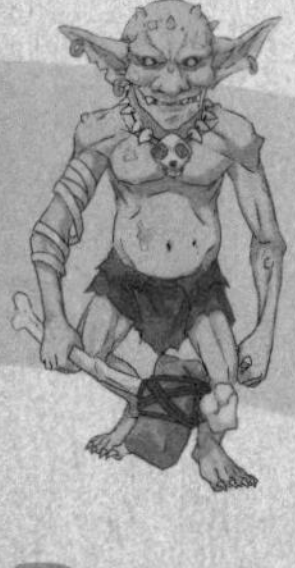

Check out the
simul-pub manga chapters
every month!

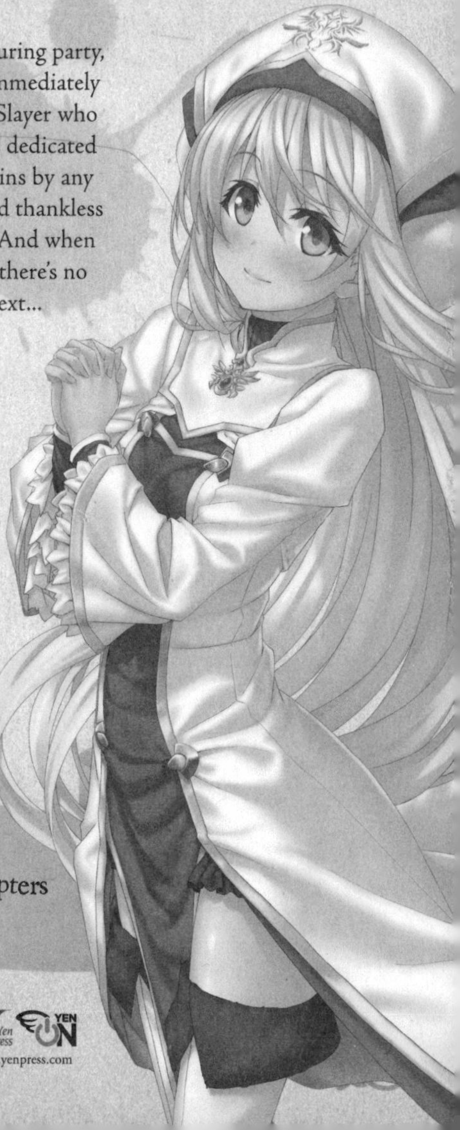

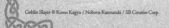

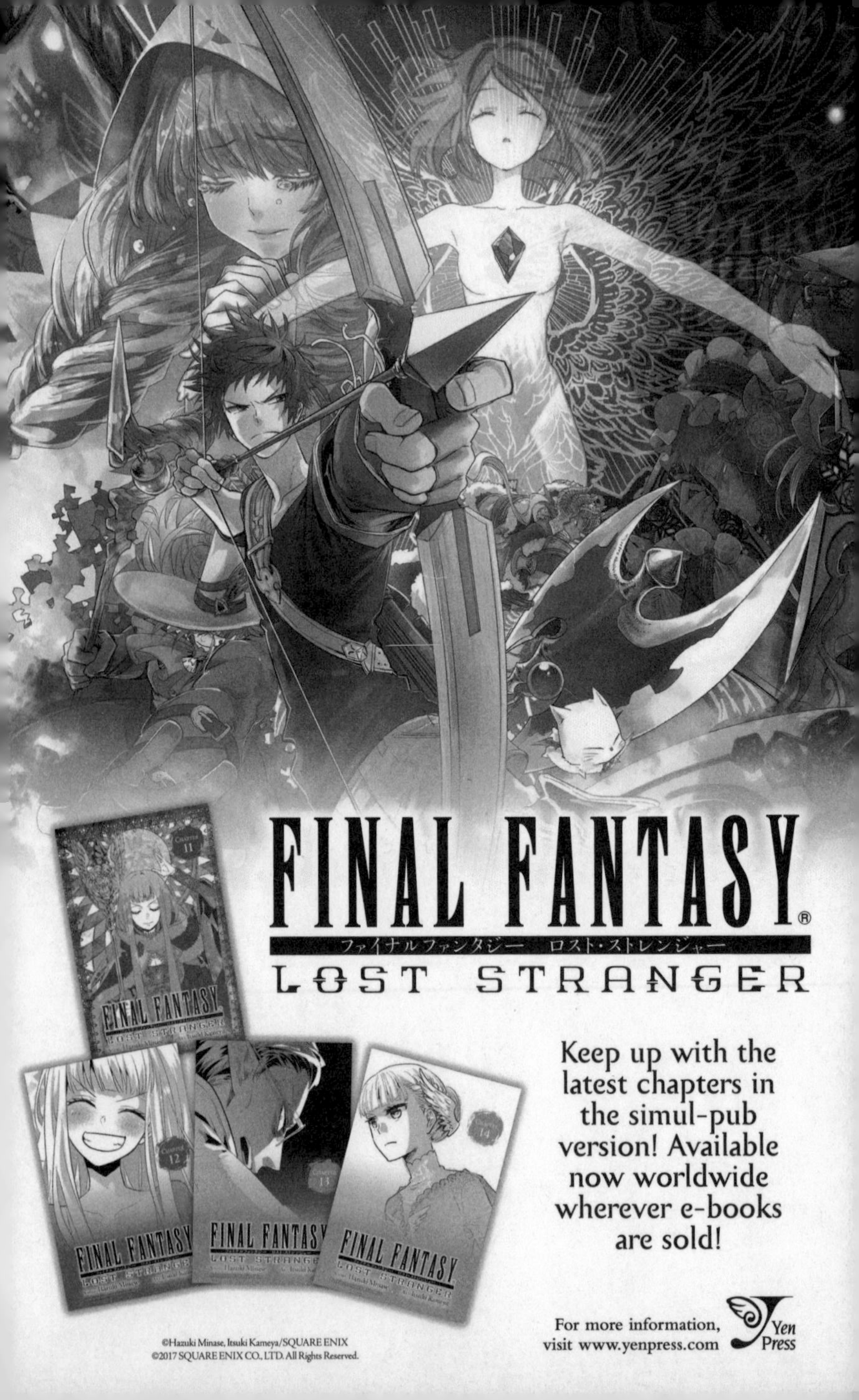
FINAL FANTASY®
ファイナルファンタジー　ロスト・ストレンジャー
LOST STRANGER
Keep up with the latest chapters in the simul-pub version! Available now worldwide wherever e-books are sold!
For more information, visit www.yenpress.com
Yen Press
©Hazuki Minase, Itsuki Kameya/SQUARE ENIX
©2017 SQUARE ENIX CO., LTD. All Rights Reserved.

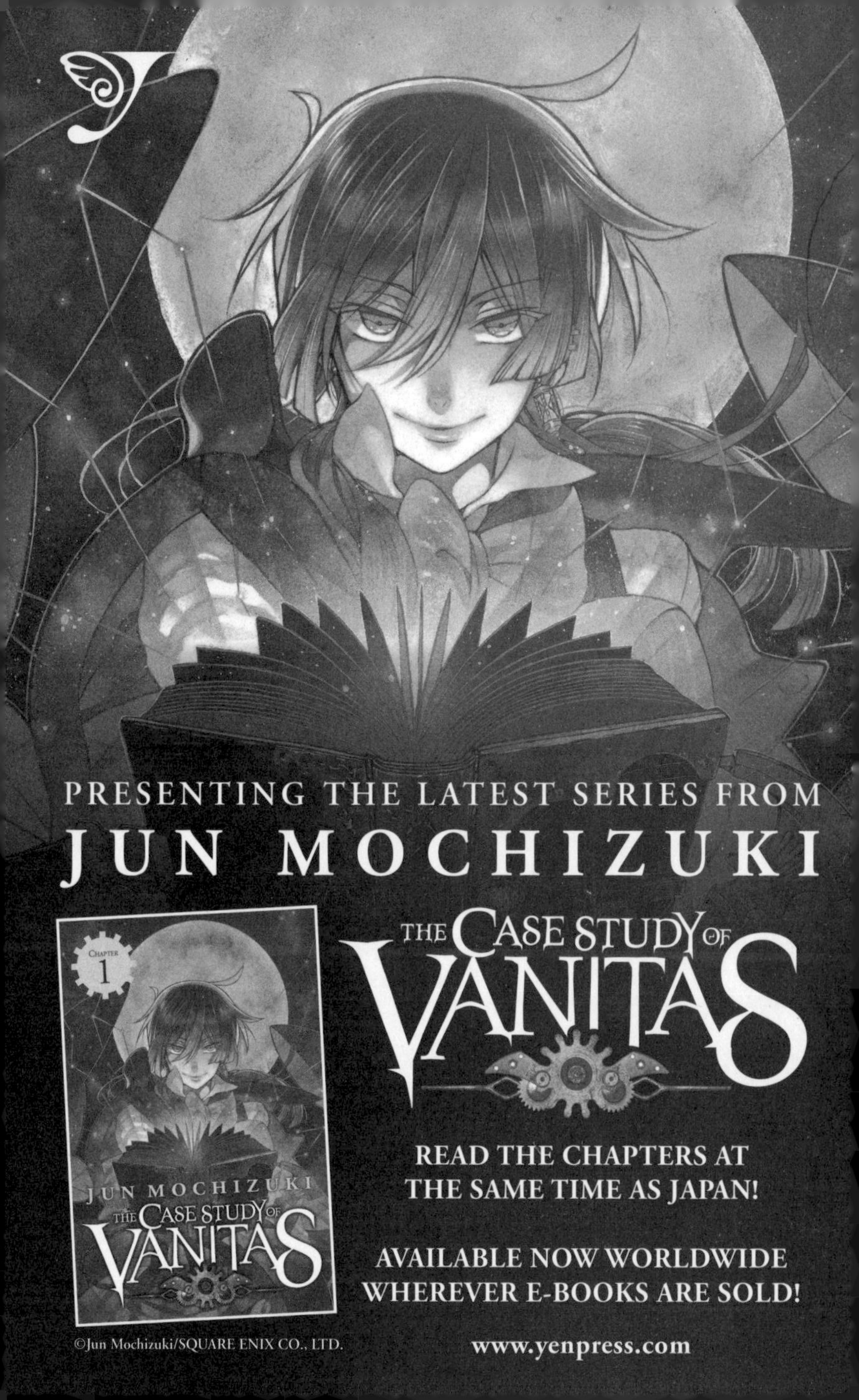
PRESENTING THE LATEST SERIES FROM
JUN MOCHIZUKI
THE CASE STUDY OF VANITAS
CHAPTER 1
JUN MOCHIZUKI
THE CASE STUDY OF VANITAS
READ THE CHAPTERS AT THE SAME TIME AS JAPAN!
AVAILABLE NOW WORLDWIDE WHEREVER E-BOOKS ARE SOLD!
©Jun Mochizuki/SQUARE ENIX CO., LTD.
www.yenpress.com

RED IS THE NEW BLACK IN THIS BLOODY, ACTION-PACKED SERIES ABOUT A GROUP OF RIGHTEOUS ASSASSINS!

Teenage country bumpkin Tatsumi dreams of earning enough money for his impoverished village by working in the Capital—but his short-lived plans go awry when he's robbed by a buxom beauty upon arrival! Penniless, Tatsumi is taken in by the lovely Miss Aria, but just when his Capital dreams seem in reach yet again, Miss Aria's mansion is besieged by Night Raid—a team of ruthless assassins who targets high-ranking members of the upper class! As Tatsumi is quick to learn, appearances can be deceiving in the Capital, and this team of assassins just might be... the good guys?!

Akame ga KILL!

FULL SERIES AVAILABLE NOW!

ceya

IS IT WRONG TO TRY TO PICK UP GIRLS IN A DUNGEON? ON THE SIDE: SWORD ORATORIA ⑫

Fujino Omori
Takashi Yagi
Haimura Kiyotaka, Yasuda Suzuhito

Translation: Andrew Gaippe • Lettering: Barri Shrager

DUNGEON NI DEAI WO MOTOMERU NO WA MACHIGATTEIRUDAROUKA GAIDEN SWORD ORATORIA vol. 12
© Fujino Omori/SB Creative Corp.
Original Character Designs: © Haimura Kiyotaka, Yasuda Suzuhito/SB Creative Corp.
© 2019 Takashi Yagi/SQUARE ENIX CO., LTD.
First published in Japan in 2019 by SQUARE ENIX CO., LTD.
English translation rights arranged with SQUARE ENIX CO., LTD. and Yen Press, LLC through Tuttle-Mori Agency, Inc.

English translation © 2020 by SQUARE ENIX CO., LTD.

Yen Press
150 West 30th Street, 19th Floor
New York, NY 10001

Visit us at yenpress.com
facebook.com/yenpress
twitter.com/yenpress
yenpress.tumblr.com
instagram.com/yenpress

First Yen Press Edition: August 2020

Yen Press is an imprint of Yen Press, LLC.
The Yen Press name and logo are trademarks of Yen Press, LLC.

The publisher is not responsible for websites (or their content) that are not owned by the publisher.

Library of Congress Control Number: 2016946068

ISBNs: 978-1-9753-1307-4 (paperback)
       978-1-9753-1306-7 (ebook)

10 9 8 7 6 5 4 3 2 1

WOR

Printed in the United States of America